CW00673270

RELIGION AND TRADE

Religion and Trade

CROSS-CULTURAL EXCHANGES
IN WORLD HISTORY, 1000–1900

Edited by

Francesca Trivellato, Leor Halevi, and Cátia Antunes

OXFORD
UNIVERSITY PRESS

Oxford University Press is a department of the University of Oxford.
It furthers the University's objective of excellence in research, scholarship,
and education by publishing worldwide.

Oxford   New York
Auckland   Cape Town   Dar es Salaam   Hong Kong   Karachi
Kuala Lumpur   Madrid   Melbourne   Mexico City   Nairobi
New Delhi   Shanghai   Taipei   Toronto

With offices in
Argentina   Austria   Brazil   Chile   Czech Republic   France   Greece
Guatemala   Hungary   Italy   Japan   Poland   Portugal   Singapore
South Korea   Switzerland   Thailand   Turkey   Ukraine   Vietnam

Oxford is a registered trademark of Oxford University Press
in the UK and certain other countries.

Published in the United States of America by
Oxford University Press
198 Madison Avenue, New York, NY 10016

© Oxford University Press 2014

Chapter 10, African Meanings and European-African Discourse: Iconography and Semantics in
Seventeenth-Century Salt Cellars from Sierra Leone © 2014 Peter Mark

All rights reserved. No part of this publication may be reproduced, stored in a
retrieval system, or transmitted, in any form or by any means, without the prior
permission in writing of Oxford University Press, or as expressly permitted by law,
by license, or under terms agreed with the appropriate reproduction rights organization.
Inquiries concerning reproduction outside the scope of the above should be sent to the
Rights Department, Oxford University Press, at the address above.

You must not circulate this work in any other form
and you must impose this same condition on any acquirer.

Library of Congress Cataloging-in-Publication Data

Religion and trade : cross-cultural exchanges in world history, 1000–1900 /
edited by Francesca Trivellato, Cátia Antunes, and Leor Halevi.
pages cm
Includes bibliographical references and index.
ISBN 978–0–19–937919–4 (paperback) — ISBN 978–0–19–937918–7 (hardcover)   1. Commerce—
History.   2. International economic relations—Religious aspects—History.   3. Religion—Economic
aspects—History.   I. Antunes, Cátia, 1976–   II. Halevi, Leor.   III. Trivellato, Francesca, 1970–
HF352.R45 2014
382—dc23
2013046456

Contents

Acknowledgments

Most chapters in this volume are substantially revised versions of papers presented at four interlocking sessions on "Commerce and Religion in Medieval and Early Modern Times" at the European Social Science History Conference held in Ghent, Belgium, in April 2010. We wish to thank the conference organizers, who—unwittingly, perhaps—permitted us to hold a mini-conference within that larger conference, as well as all the speakers and panel chairs who contributed to the lively debate that took place on that occasion. The latter include Leonard Blussé, Ivana Elbl, Yvonne Friedman, Juan E. Gelabert Gonzáles, Ghislaine Lydon, Viorel Panaite, Amélia Polónia, Tijl Vanneste, and Peer Vries. As a genuinely international gathering, the biannual European Social Science History Conference brings together participants who know the pleasures and perils of cross-cultural intellectual exchanges firsthand. We are also grateful to Eric Tagliacozzo and Peter Mark for joining the project at a later stage. Along the way, two anonymous readers, as well as Jennifer Lofkrantz and especially Paul E. Lovejoy, provided candid and helpful critiques. The usual caveat applies more than ever: our gratitude does not imply their agreement with what follows. The faith that Tim Bent at Oxford University Press has had in this project has made all the difference.

After Ghent, some of us had the good fortune of discussing the idea of this book with Jerry H. Bentley, who was characteristically generous until his untimely death in July 2012. The volume is dedicated to his memory.

Introduction

THE HISTORICAL AND COMPARATIVE STUDY OF
CROSS-CULTURAL TRADE

Francesca Trivellato

COMMERCIAL EXCHANGES ACROSS religious, geographical, and political boundaries have always been risky propositions. E-commerce, Bitcom, the World Trade Organization, and other recent technologies and institutions have solved some problems, and created others. Risks were greatest in the pre-industrial period, when in order to engage in cross-cultural trade, seafaring vessels and overland convoys often had to overcome tremendous physical obstacles. Marco Polo is only the better-known name among a small and audacious group of merchants from Venice and Genoa who made their way to India and China at a time when traveling such distances came with hardships and dangers defying the modern imagination.[1] Once they reached distant markets, merchants had to grapple with strange customs and manners. Little wonder that specialized intermediaries emerged in most towns and ports to facilitate dealings between strangers. Foreign merchants, however, had to exercise necessary caution when relying on intermediaries who possessed insiders' knowledge and may have wished to take advantage of newcomers and passersby. Defying all odds, merchants across the globe, along with ordinary people, travelers, pilgrims, missionaries, and interlopers, nonetheless concocted ways of bartering,

---

[1] Robert Sabatino Lopez, "European Merchants in the Medieval Indies: The Evidence of Commercial Documents," *Journal of Economic History*, 3 (1943): 164–184.

securing credit, and establishing durable commercial relations with persons who did not speak their language, wore different garb, and worshipped other gods.

Along docks and caravan routes, in bazaars and city squares, they exchanged precious and bulky merchandise. Some of these goods acquired new value when they entered a new environment; hugely desirable and popular, they could also be seen as menacing. Religious and secular leaders from around the world thus sought to curb tobacco consumption when the use of this new drug spread rapidly in the early seventeenth century, while rulers as different as the Safavid Shah and the English Crown soon adopted more lenient attitudes.[2] Cross-cultural trade, in other words, was both a boon and a threat to the status quo. For every institution and group that sought to promote it, there were others that wished to quell it. Guardians of religious orthodoxy were often among those who differentiated between legitimate and illegitimate exchanges, between stigmatized and upright groups of traders, between pure and corrupting commodities.

This volume seeks to advance the historical understanding of cross-cultural trade by focusing on commercial exchanges between groups of different religious backgrounds and by examining both day-to-day operations and the broader cultural meanings and political underpinnings of these exchanges. To this effect, the ten chapters that follow investigate the infrastructures (political, legal, technological, and social) that expedited or hindered cross-cultural economic transactions and the meanings associated with the goods involved in these transactions. They explore examples from across the world, spanning the course of the second millennium C.E. Taken together, they pursue two aims: to offer a fine-grained analysis of individual cases and to provide a roadmap for the historical and comparative study of cross-cultural trade.

Thirty years ago, Philip Curtin's groundbreaking *Cross-Cultural Trade in World History* inaugurated an exciting new field of inquiry.[3] The chapters gathered in this volume take stock of Curtin's milestone contribution, as well as others that appeared before and after, and seek to advance their scholarly agenda. The insights of *Cross-Cultural Trade in World History* remain challenging and wide-ranging, and will be discussed again both below and in several chapters. Thematically, they include geographical and chronological breadth that is simply stunning and which, for example, helped to integrate Africa and Southeast Asia into world historical analysis. Curtin also highlighted Islam's friendliness to trade. In so doing, he brought that theme, too, to the attention of a wider audience. His analytical

---

[2] Rudi Matthee, *The Pursuit of Pleasure: Drugs and Stimulants in Iranian History, 1500–1900* (Princeton, NJ: Princeton University Press, 2005), 137–140.

[3] Philip D. Curtin, *Cross-Cultural Trade in World History* (Cambridge: Cambridge University Press, 1984).

contributions were no less provocative and focused on identifying patterns that cut across time and space, such as the function of foreign resident brokers and the role of trade diasporas. By his own admission, and by the very nature of the project that he undertook, Curtin did not aim to provide a detailed treatment of cross-cultural trade in each corner of the world. Rather, the categories that he deployed to make sense of an arresting heterogeneity of cases have defined his legacy across fields and special-izations—as well as generated heated debates. None of them has enjoyed greater for-tune or ignited more controversies than that of trade diasporas. Curtin's definition is intentionally broad and aims to group together a variety of communities that were scattered across distant regions and that performed important functions as com-mercial and cultural mediators. Borrowing from the anthropologist and Africanist Abner Cohen, Curtin conceives of a trade diaspora as a group of merchants "linked to one another by several kinds of mutual solidarity: common profession, religion, language, and so on."[4] These diasporas generally lacked sovereign authority and the monopoly of violence. But in some instances Curtin adopts the same terminology for enterprises that operated as the commercial and military arm of European states. Later in this introduction I will return to the implications of this ambiguity in the definition of trade diasporas for the study of cross-cultural trade.

In the opening chapter, Leor Halevi expands on Curtin's study as part of a critical appraisal of landmark contributions to the literature on cross-cultural trade pro-duced over the last century by a diverse array of sociologists, anthropologists, econo-mists, and scholars of religion. A historian of religion and a specialist of Islamic law and material culture, Halevi treats the concept of "religion" with a higher degree of sophistication and precision than in most of the existing scholarship on cross-cultural trade. He thus sets the tone for the rest of the volume. He also invites us to pursue the material-culture angle, that is, to examine the very objects that crossed religious boundaries rather than, as is more frequently done, only the agents and modalities of those material exchanges. The focus on materiality provides an important, and so far under-explored, comparative framework. For example, both the papacy and Islamic law prohibited trade in goods that could aid "infidels" in waging holy wars (notably weapons, but also certain types of metals and wood), but only Islamic law included the notion of "impure" or defiling goods, which jurists associated in many cases with commodities manufactured by non-Muslims.

---

[4] Curtin, *Cross-Cultural Trade*, 46. See also Abner Cohen, "Cultural Strategies in the Organization of Trading Diasporas," in *The Development of Indigenous Trade and Markets in West Africa*, ed. Claude Meillassoux (London: Oxford University Press for the International African Seminar, 1971), 266–281. Via Curtin, Cohen's article has become a staple citation among historians. For its usage, see also Chapters 1 and 8 in this volume.

Other parallels cut across the Christian-Muslim divide. On both sides of what is sometimes described as a civilizational cleavage, we find not only that merchants regularly infringed rules about prohibited goods, but also that the elites charged with preserving religious orthodoxy defined those proscriptions with an awareness of their political implications. In other words, when both Muslim clerics and Catholic theologians granted exceptions to stringent norms about the conduct of foreign trade, they did so knowing the impact these exceptions could have on the political economy of their states.

UBIQUITOUS AND ELUSIVE: CROSS-CULTURAL TRADE AS
A PUZZLE IN HISTORICAL WRITING

It would be only slightly hyperbolic to maintain that cross-cultural trade has existed everywhere and at all times. Some populations lived in greater isolation than others. Now that older views about the immobility of pre-modern societies have faded away, however, most places and epochs have become good candidates for the study of circulation, connectivity, transculturalism (if not cosmopolitanism of assorted varieties), and associated phenomena. Ongoing interest in cross-cultural trade reflects this broader trend. Yet precisely because cross-cultural trade is ubiquitous and impinges on so many aspects of life, it can be approached from multiple perspectives. Differences in scales of analysis and defining criteria account for some of the imprecision that continues to surround the topic, as well as the polarization between different approaches to it.

Before it became fashionable to speak of "cross-cultural trade," Shelomo Dov Goitein was engaged in a lifelong project that in many respects we can group under that rubric. Goitein was, in Isaiah Berlin's famous metaphor, a fox—someone who "knows many things" and "pursues many ends," as opposed to a hedgehog, who "knows one thing" and "relate[s] everything to a single central vision, one system, less or more coherent or articulate."[5] Goitein devoted his career to deciphering and interpreting the records of an exceptional trove of documents known as the Cairo Geniza; he sought to unearth details with which to draw larger pictures. His monumental, five-volume *A Mediterranean Society*, published between 1967 and 1993, is an epic portrayal of a segment of the Jewish diaspora living under Muslim rule in North Africa and trading as far as Iberia and South Asia between the tenth and thirteenth centuries.[6] Underneath this seemingly inductive project lies a concerted

---

[5] Isaiah Berlin, *The Hedgehog and the Fox: An Essay on Tolstoy's View of History* (Chicago: Ivan R. Dee, 1993 [1953]), 3.

[6] S. D. Goitein, *A Mediterranean Society: The Jewish Communities of the Arab World as Portrayed in the Documents of the Cairo Geniza*, 5 vols. (Berkeley: University of California Press, 1967–1993).

attempt to single out "interfaith relations," especially business relations, between the Jewish minority and the Muslim majority.[7]

An idealized view of affluent, upwardly mobile postwar America as a melting pot colored Goitein's meticulous close readings of Geniza documents. The result is a rosy tableau of a medieval Mediterranean in which "free trade" and harmonious religious coexistence were the norm. The sources for this tableau are fragments of records written in a language, Judeo-Arabic, that few Muslims were able to read. This selection bias makes references to Jewish-Muslim business transactions all the more telling. But it also explains why these references are rare—so rare that in one recent and influential re-interpretation of the same body of documents, the commercial organization mirrored in the Cairo Geniza becomes the antithesis of cross-cultural trade. Instead, it is a commercial organization that revolves around a closed "coalition," a sub-group of Jewish merchants who, deprived of recourse to state legal institutions, oversaw the degree of compliance of its own members via reputational control and social ostracism but was unable to build durable commercial alliances with outsiders, whether non-Jews or other groups of Jews.[8]

The scholar who introduced the twin notions of "cross-cultural trade" and "trade diaspora" into the mainstream of the historiographical vocabulary was Philip Curtin, who, in contrast to Goitein, was a hedgehog and built on his extensive historical knowledge of Africa and the Atlantic slave trade to pioneer the field of world history.[9] Before and after Curtin, other quintessential hedgehogs were drawn to the study of cross-cultural trade, most notably Fernand Braudel, who never explicitly adopted the expression, but whose magna opera on the Mediterranean and on pre-modern capitalism focus on commerce as a vehicle for interaction between

---

[7] For a concise statement of this intellectual pursuit, see the talk that Goitein delivered at Columbia University on October 22, 1973, published as *Interfaith Relations in Medieval Islam* (Jerusalem: Jerusalem Post Press, 1973). The position of Jews in medieval Muslim societies and, specifically, Goitein's reading of Jewish-Muslim economic relations remain highly contested subjects. Pertinent reflections can be found in Leor Halevi, "Christian Impurity versus Economic Necessity: A Fifteenth-Century Fatwa on European Paper," *Speculum*, 83 (2008): 917–945, 921, and Jessica L. Goldberg, "On Reading Goitein's *A Mediterranean Society*: A View from Economic History," *Mediterranean Historical Review*, 26.2 (2011): 171–186.

[8] Avner Greif, *Institutions and the Path to the Modern Economy: Lessons from Medieval Trade* (Cambridge: Cambridge University Press, 2006). Margariti in Chapter 8 expands on Goitein's lessons to demonstrate the richness of Geniza records for the study of cross-cultural trade when they are used alongside other sources, including non-textual records.

[9] In assessing the disputed position of world historians amidst the larger group of professional historians, Philip Pomper emphasized that "the task of grand synthesis requires hedgehogs, Isaiah Berlin's great system-builders or holists, whereas the history profession attracts foxes, Berlin's thinkers who relish detail and particularity." Pomper, "World History and Its Critics," *History and Theory*, 34.2 (1995): 1–7, 1–2. Among Curtin's many earlier publications on African and Atlantic history, see in particular his *The Atlantic Slave Trade: A Census* (Madison: University of Wisconsin Press, 1969) and *Economic Change in Precolonial Africa: Senegambia in the Era of the Slave Trade*, 2nd ed. (Madison: University of Wisconsin Press, 1975).

distant peoples and distant regions and as the preeminent agent of change.[10] Midway in his career, the late Jerry H. Bentley also chose the optic of a hedge-hog, putting his earlier interest in Renaissance Italy aside and turning to found-ing, in 1991, *The Journal of World History* and to publishing, in 1993, *Old World Encounters: Cross-Cultural Contacts and Exchanges in Pre-Modern Times*. The lat-ter covers the millennia leading up to 1492: it paints in broad strokes processes of migration, conversion, economic expansion, and state formation that transformed the geopolitical and cultural landscape of the planet before the rise of the West. For the purpose of his wide-ranging analysis, Bentley takes "civilization" (one of Braudel's most controversial terms) to be synonymous with "culture" and charts the existence of vast cultural spheres separated by wide gaps that trade, missionary work, and military expansion helped bring closer together.[11]

Goitein, Curtin, Braudel, and Bentley are only the most illustrious names among a galaxy of scholars who, whether foxes or hedgehogs, have delved into the mul-tifaceted relation between commerce, politics, and religion. Landmark studies by Immanuel Wallerstein and Janet L. Abu-Lughod mapped the geography of inter-regional and intercontinental trade to advance opposing theses about the timing and structural patterns of an integrated world system and of Europe's com-mercial domination of it.[12] From a radically different perspective, one that is more actor-centered, studies of diasporic merchant communities active from the South China Sea to the Atlantic and from the Mediterranean to Central Asia have pro-liferated, all aiming to flesh out the impact of trading networks operating in the interstices of multiple states and empires.[13] Scholarship on merchant networks and

---

[10] Fernand Braudel, *The Mediterranean and the Mediterranean World in the Age of Philip II*, trans. Siân Reynolds, 2 vols. (New York: Harper and Row, 1972–1973) and *Civilization and Capitalism, 15th–18th Century*, trans. Siân Reynolds, 3 vols. (New York: Harper and Row, 1981–1984). Braudel has been recog-nized as an early proponent of what became the study of trade diasporas, specifically regarding his inter-est in the Armenian merchants of the seventeenth century. Ina Baghdiantz McCabe, *The Shah's Silk for Europe's Silver: The Eurasian Trade of the Julfa Armenians in Safavid Iran and India (1530–1750)* (Atlanta, GA: Scholars Press, 1999), xxi–xxii, 27.

[11] Jerry H. Bentley, *Old World Encounters: Cross-Cultural Contacts and Exchanges in Pre-Modern Times* (New York: Oxford University Press, 1993).

[12] Immanuel Wallerstein, *The Modern World-System*, 3 vols. (New York: Academic Press, 1973–1989); Janet L. Abu-Lughod, *Before European Hegemony: The World System, A.D. 1250–1350* (New York and Oxford: Oxford University Press, 1989).

[13] A few titles will suffice, listed here in chronological order. Ng Chin-Keong, *Trade and Society: The Amoy Network on the China Coast, 1683–1735* (Singapore: Singapore University Press, National University of Singapore, 1983); Stephen Frederic Dale, *Indian Merchants and Eurasian Trade, 1600–1750* (Cambridge: Cambridge University Press, 1994); Claude Markovits, *The Global World of Indian Merchants, 1750–1947: Traders of Sind from Bukhara to Panama* (Cambridge: Cambridge University Press, 2000); Scott C. Levi, *The Indian Diaspora in Central Asia and its Trade, 1550–1900* (Leiden: Brill, 2001); Ina Baghdiantz McCabe, Gelina Harlaftis, and Ioanna Pepelassis Minoglou, eds., *Diaspora: Entrepreneurial Networks* (Oxford and New York: Berg, 2005); Francesca Trivellato, *The Familiarity of Strangers: The Sephardic Diaspora, Livorno, and Cross-Cultural Trade*

diasporas often exalts the figure of cross-cultural brokers, those called to bridge linguistic, legal, economic, and diplomatic divides.[14] It also collectively makes a decisive contribution to advancing a less Eurocentric, less hierarchical notion of what we may call "globalization before globalization."[15] Far from being the exclusive province of historians, the study of cross-cultural trade has been pioneered by anthropologists and has gained currency among economists and sociologists, particularly in relation to the concept of trust. It is thus not surprising that, as we will see, several contributions in this volume engage with ideas and models developed in the social sciences.

Across this vast if amorphous literature, *Cross-Cultural Trade in World History* stands out as the field-defining work.[16] In the mid-1980s, Curtin located his contribution in "the small but growing field of comparative world history."[17] The present volume takes up many of the challenges that he put before us with renewed focus. However, it departs from Curtin's ambition to synthesize by means of a unified theory of cross-cultural trade. It zooms in on specific episodes to inject analytical precision while preserving the diversity that comes with a plurality of approaches and primary sources. In this respect, it remains mindful of Clifford Geertz's urging, in his justly famous 1973 essay "Thick Description," that "the essential task of theory building…is not to codify abstract regularities but to make thick description possible, not to generalize across cases but to generalize within them."[18]

Therefore, the volume as a whole endeavors to develop a comparative framework from the ground up. The questions elaborated in the last section of this introduction capture this twin effort at thick description and comparative analysis. Since they are rooted in the examples discussed in various chapters, a brief overview of the chapters' content is in order.

---

in the Early Modern Period (New Haven, CT: Yale University Press, 2012 [2009]); David Hancock, *Oceans of Wine: Madeira and the Emergence of American Trade and Taste* (New Haven, CT: Yale University Press, 2009); Sebouh David Aslanian, *From the Indian Ocean to the Mediterranean: The Global Trade Networks of Armenian Merchants from New Julfa* (Berkeley: University of California Press, 2010).

[14] Among a larger literature, see Alida C. Metcalf, *Go-Betweens and the Colonization of Brazil, 1500–1600* (Austin: University of Texas Press, 2005), and Simon Schaffer, Lissa Roberts, Kapil Raj, and James Delbourgo, eds., *The Brokered World: Go-Betweens and Global Intelligence, 1770–1820* (Sagamore Beach, MA: Science History Publications, 2009), which includes critical remarks on the concept of "go-between" by Sanjay Subrahmanyam (429–440).

[15] For a highly readable yet sophisticated account, see Kenneth Pomeranz and Steven Topik, *The World That Trade Created: Society, Culture, and the World Economy, 1400–the Present* (Armonk, NY: M. E. Sharpe, 2006 [1999]).

[16] An Ngram search in the English-language collections of Google Books shows that, with some ups and downs, the expressions "trade diasporas" and "cross-cultural trade" have become more and more frequent since the 1970s.

[17] Curtin, *Cross-Cultural Trade*, ix.

[18] Clifford Geertz, "Thick Description: Toward and Interpretive Theory of Culture," in his *The Interpretation of Culture: Selected Essays* (New York: Basic Books, 1973), 3–30, 26.

OVERVIEW

Each of the chapters presents an in-depth analysis of relevant episodes of cross-cultural trade on the basis of original, often little-known primary sources. Whereas world history is often written on the basis of secondary sources to provide grand, synthetic narratives, here authors roam across the globe scouting for and parsing new evidence.

And they roam far: the volume spans multiple regions of the globe, from roughly 1000 C.E. to 1900 C.E. By choice and by necessity, it does not cover every corner of the world. The chapters concentrate on three maritime spaces—the Mediterranean, the Atlantic, and the Indian Ocean—and the vast regions that surrounded them, because there, encounters and clashes between religious groups have sparked the most controversy, both historically and historiographically. There, members of the three so-called religions of the book lived side by side and, in certain areas, also interacted with non-monotheistic religious groups. Religious conflicts and coexistence shaped, and in turn were shaped by, commercial exchanges of both commodities and human beings. If other regions, such as East and Central Asia or Latin America, fall outside the purview of this volume, it is not because they were unaffected by the trends described here, and the volume aspires to offer insights that might extend to those contexts as well.

After Halevi's primarily historiographical piece, the empirically grounded chapters begin with the early phase of Europe's expansion into the Atlantic, and thus with the meeting of people with no previous knowledge of each other. David Harris Sacks (Chapter 2) detects references to "silent trade" in English traders' accounts of exchanges with native inhabitants of Newfoundland, where the English first landed in 1612. Many scholars hold silent trade to be a myth. Sacks shows that an implicit understanding of gift-giving rituals shared by the two sides allowed complete strangers to barter goods in terms regarded equitable by all, at least for the brief period before colonialists turned to violence and expropriation. Giuseppe Marcocci (Chapter 3) reads Latin disquisitions that today economic historians normally neglect in order to appreciate the political and theological arguments underpinning the first century of Portuguese overseas expansion. Rather than a conflict between church and state, he finds that the Portuguese Crown marshaled subtle theological justifications in order to grant leeway to its subjects in their trade with certain groups of "infidels" but not others, depending on the perceived political threat and commercial utility of those groups and the interests of various factions at court.

Wolfgang Kaiser and Guillaume Calafat (Chapter 4), as well as Kathryn Miller (Chapter 5), bring new evidence and concepts to bear on a well-known feature of the medieval and early modern Mediterranean: the ransoming of captives taken by Christians, Muslims, and Jews. Unlike a multitude of studies that give preference to the symbolic dimension of this singular branch of trade, both chapters focus on the day-to-day aspects of the exchange of human booty. Predicated upon violence and religious war, the "economy of ransoming" only worked if "infidels" cooperated with one another. Cooperation, in turn, built upon the services of middlemen and legal institutions that, on both the Muslim and the Christian sides, created regularities of behavior and managed expectations across the religious divide. In the following two chapters, Cátia Antunes (Chapter 6) and Silvia Marzagalli (Chapter 7) dissect the many ways in which legal contracts facilitated some (and yet not other) joint economic ventures between members of different religious groups, whether in the post-Reformation United Provinces (the most tolerant of all European countries at the time) or in eighteenth-century France (traditionally described as a country in which religious obscurantism stifled capitalism). Roxani Eleni Margariti (Chapter 8) and Eric Tagliacozzo (Chapter 9) examine cross-cultural trade along the shores of the Indian Ocean at the beginning and the end of the period under consideration here. Margariti identifies minted coins as tools that facilitated commercial transactions between Jews and Muslims in a context of highly fragmented political authority. Tagliacozzo explores the economic determinants of the pilgrimage to Mecca (the Hajj) undertaken by men and women from Southeast Asia and thus documents the relationship of mutual interdependence between religious worship and profit-making activities.

Finally, Peter Mark (Chapter 10) brings us back to the early modern Atlantic in a probing analysis of artwork produced by West African artists for an affluent European clientele in the late sixteenth and early seventeenth centuries. A historian of art and culture, Mark follows Curtin in insisting on the role of middleman groups who acted as brokers across vast cultural divides—in his case, Portuguese known as *lançados*, including some of Jewish descent, who settled in coastal West Africa, where they mixed with local populations and provided essential services to both African and European traders. By focusing squarely on the artifacts that emerged from the meeting of foreign merchants with local artists, Mark also adds to Curtin's agenda the importance of integrating the study of material culture in relation to cross-cultural trade.

Chronologically, then, the volume spans nearly an entire millennium. By embracing such a capacious time frame, it does not provide a new periodization for the writing of world history. That has been one of the pursuits of Jerry Bentley, for example, for whom the intensity and scale of cross-cultural interactions led by mass migrations, large-scale conversion movements, imperial expansion, and the growth of long-distance trade offer alternative yardsticks to periodize the history of humanity.[19] Nor does any chapter delve at length into the usefulness and drawbacks of

---

[19] Jerry H. Bentley, "Cross-Cultural Interaction and Periodization in World History," *American Historical Review*, 101.3 (1996): 749–770. The chapters in this volume would fall across two of the six eras in which

categories such as "medieval" and "early modern" for the purpose of comparisons on a planetary scale.[20] A different thread weaves the chronological span of the chapters together. In keeping with two of their main foci—the relationship between commerce and religion, and the infrastructures of long-distance trade—the examples collected here turn to times and places in which cross-cultural trade occurred between actors who saw themselves as belonging to distinct, if not also antagonistic, religious groups and to times and places in which trade occurred with the help of only fragile transportation technology.

With respect to both religion and technology, the period from 1000 C.E. to 1900 C.E. does not represent a coherent unit. But it does allow us to observe continuities and discontinuities. After circa 1000, and at an increasing pace after the sixteenth century, ever more distant regions of the globe came into closer relation with one another. With these increased connections came more opportunities for cross-cultural trade. It was the "Westernization of the world commerce between about 1740 and 1860," Curtin writes, that decreased the importance of trade diasporas.[21] As sociologists of "middleman minorities" before him had shown, and as he recognizes, religious and ethnic networks continued to occupy important economic niches well beyond the mid-nineteenth century, and still do to this day.[22] But industrialization, the rise of nation-states, and the consolidation of European colonial rule altered significantly the conditions under which these networks operated. In addition to new transportation technology—steam power, as an instance, and steel-hulled ships—European nations and territorial empires engaged in systematic reclassifications of individual and collective identities, in ways that also affected cross-cultural trade. Citizenship as inscribed in passports, for example, became at

---

Bentley divides the history of the world: the "age of transregional nomadic empires (1000–1500 C.E.)" and the "modern age (1500 C.E. to the present" (756).

[20] The expression "early modern," in particular, has for some time now been used in the writing of world and global history. The *Journal of Early Modern History: Contacts, Comparisons, Contrasts* is one prominent example of this tendency. As "the first scholarly journal dedicated to the study of early modernity from this world-historical perspective," it characterizes the period between 1300 and 1800 as one "marked by a rapidly increasing level of global interaction" http://www.brill.com/journal-early-modern-history (accessed on December 1, 2012). For recent reappraisals of a now long-standing historiographical debate on the potential and limits of "early modern" as a periodization in world history, see Jack A. Goldstone, "Divergence in Cultural Trajectories: The Power of the Traditional within the Early Modern," R. Bin Wong, "Did China's Late Empire Have an Early Modern Era?," and Kenneth Pomeranz, "Areas, Networks, and the Search for 'Early Modern' East Asia," all in *Comparative Early Modernities, 1100–1800*, ed. David Porter (New York: Palgrave Macmillan, 2012), 165–193, 195–216, 245–269, respectively. For the use of the term "medieval" in relation to the history of the Indian Ocean, see Chapter 8 by Roxani Eleni Margariti in this volume.

[21] Curtin, *Cross-Cultural Trade*, 230, 253.

[22] Edna Bonacich, "A Theory of Middleman Minorities," *American Sociological Review*, 38.5 (1973): 583–594; James E. Rauch, "Business and Social Networks in International Trade," *Journal of Economic Literature*, 39.4 (2001): 1177–1203.

least as important as religious affiliation in defining group membership and in allowing recourse to political, financial, and legal institutions.

The chapters that follow show that discontinuities occurred at different times in different regions of the world and that these discontinuities stemmed from different causes, both internal and external. Before the sixteenth century, when no large polity in the Indian Ocean controlled vast regional territories, the circulation of silver and gold coins, more than far-reaching legal jurisdictions, simplified transactions between discrete religious groups. The early modern Mediterranean also remained a politically fragmented space. The conditions for the ransoming of captives there were not radically altered by the appearance of northern European creations, such as the stock market and the joint-stock company. It was the cumulative effect of centuries of diplomatic and commercial exchanges between Christian and Muslim powers that oiled the mechanisms of ransoming. In Southeast Asia, the impact of colonialism on cross-cultural trade was not felt until the late nineteenth century, and even then, colonial power did not alter all extant trade patterns. Eric Tagliacozzo explains in his contribution that Dutch and British colonial governments found aspects of the Hajj, along with other pan-Islamic networks, threatening, but by making more secure steam lines and cheaper loans available to those who wished to embark on the pilgrimage to Mecca, they also fueled the Hajj's expansion while profiting from it.

In unraveling the multiple dimensions of cross-cultural trade, historians are sometimes confined by a dearth of sources and at other times overwhelmed by an overabundance of documents. Whether scarce or plentiful, textual or non-textual, records are never transparent. In some cases, evidence of economic transactions between religious groups that eyed each other with suspicion was purposefully suppressed, though a careful inquiry can turn up fragments of those transactions.[23] Even when the absence of records is accidental rather than intentional, the search for indirect clues leaves us with highly mediated accounts. Legal compendia compensate only in part for the lack of surviving business records from medieval Muslim Spain (Kathryn Miller). European travel narratives and engravings are all we have left to reconstruct the commercial logic of Native Amerindians (David Harris Sacks). Portuguese travel accounts omit any references to kola, an important commodity in West African trade, which nonetheless turns up in the artwork the Portuguese imported from West Africa (Peter Mark).

---

[23] For another example of how to read against the grain sources that document cross-cultural economic transactions in a context in which those very transactions were prohibited, see Teofilo F. Ruiz, "Trading with the 'Other': Economic Exchanges between Muslims, Jews, and Christians in Late Medieval Northern Castile," in *Medieval Spain: Culture, Conflict, and Coexistence: Studies in Honour of Angus MacKay*, ed. Roger Collins and Anthony Goodman (New York: Palgrave Macmillan, 2002), 63–78.

As the last example suggests, written records documenting cross-cultural trade are often missing entirely or are less abundant than material artifacts. To supplement the paucity of local archives, Roxani Margariti creatively combines numismatics and hard-to-decipher fragments written in Judeo-Arabic in order to uncover the forms of Jewish-Muslim commercial cooperation across the Indian Ocean in the first three centuries of the second millennium. Mark juxtaposes textual descriptions of West African coastal societies written by Portuguese traders and missionaries to other ethnographic sources in order to interpret the iconography of ivory carvings sculpted by West African artists for European consumption. In so doing, he seeks to recover the meanings of figural and natural representations as they traveled across groups that, even when they shared a linguistic understanding, continued to maintain radically different (though not necessarily incommensurable) symbolic frames of reference.

In some cases, then, mentions of cross-cultural trade are far and wide, but historians have been blinded by their own assumptions and have failed to notice them, as Silvia Marzagalli argues in relation to Old Regime France. In other cases, the paper trail is so rich that only statistical sampling can yield meaningful trends (Cátia Antunes). In yet other instances, the religious affiliation of the parties involved is purposefully distorted or at least needs to be contextualized accurately. Thus, Jews expelled or forced to convert to Catholicism in Iberia during the 1490s, and their descendants who fled to France and the United Provinces, had different contractual rights depending on whether documents identified them as Jews, as Catholics, or as so-called "New Christians."

FIVE QUESTIONS

Earlier in this introduction I contrasted influential studies of cross-cultural trade authored by two ideal-types of scholars—foxes and hedgehogs. Although they are too reductive to encapsulate the contributions of historians like Goitein, Braudel, Curtin, and Bentley in their entirety, these metaphors capture a real contrast in approaches. This volume strives to bring together the strengths of both foxes and hedgehogs by addressing a set of five questions that tie the chapters together. The same questions will also, I hope, offer springboards for further research and comparisons.[24]

---

[24] For the complementarity of fox- and hedgehog-like approaches to historical inquiry, see David Harris Sacks's review essay on Robert W. Fogel and Geoffrey R. Elton, *Which Road to the Past?: Two Views of History* (New Haven, CT: Yale University Press, 1983): "The Hedgehog and the Fox Revisited," *Journal of Interdisciplinary History*, 16.2 (1985): 267–280.

I. Did Religion Affect Cross-Cultural Trade?

The word "culture" in "cross-cultural trade" operates on two levels: it denotes the boundaries (whether religious, ethnic, or linguistic) across which trade occurred, but it can also signal the existence of a shared understanding of the terms of the exchanges (notions of value and contractual obligations, for example) that allowed for the crossing of those very boundaries. To disentangle these two dimensions is a crucial first step in pursuing any further analysis. To simplify, we can distinguish between cultural identities, including religious affiliations, that predated a durable commercial interaction and those that emerged in the process.

This analytical distinction may appear artificial, since in many instances it is difficult to isolate the commercial norms that were specific to one group but not the others or the cultural transformations that were the direct result of trading relations. The distinction, however, is worth preserving in order to make an important point: a mutual understanding of economic transactions between strangers would not necessarily blur all preexisting cultural boundaries. This was a key conclusion reached by the Norwegian anthropologist Fredrik Barth.[25] Curtin's contribution to this line of thought was to insist on the mediating role that trade diasporas fulfilled in those situations and to conclude that "cross-cultural brokerage was often best performed by a foreign merchant of long residence."[26] Questions II and III below probe these insights further by asking what other mechanisms eased trade across groups that remained fundamentally separate.

Special consideration is given here to the role that religion played in the definition of group boundaries, as well as in the mechanics and the political economy of cross-cultural trade. The chapters of this volume do not claim that religious affiliations or religious institutions were invariably determining factors in cross-cultural trade. Rather, they ask when and how these factors mattered and how they were understood in whatever context. Therefore, they begin by clarifying when and how religion constituted a primary marker of group identity, since religious boundaries were not always contiguous with linguistic and political identities. Sometimes they were not even unequivocal. Marzagalli wrestles with the implications of the period in French history when segments of the merchant community hid their religious beliefs: Jews in southwestern France before 1723 and Calvinists from the revocation of the Edict of Nantes (1685) to the promulgation of the Toleration Act (1787).

---

[25] Fredrik Barth, "Ecological Relationship of Ethnic Groups in Swat, North Pakistan," *American Anthropologist*, 58.6 (1956): 1079–1089; Barth, ed., *Ethnic Group and Boundaries: The Social Organization of Cultural Difference* (Bergen/Oslo and London: Universitets Forlaget; George Allen and Unwin, 1969).

[26] Curtin, *Cross-Cultural Trade*, 174.

Catholic in earnest or nominally, these people all operated within the same legal and linguistic realm. Marzagalli asks whether religious affiliations made a difference in determining merchants' choices of entering into contractual obligations with one another and whether "cross-religious trade" (that between Christians and Jews) and "trans-confessional trade" (that between Catholics and Protestants) followed the same patterns.

The politics and the mechanics of cross-cultural trade often defined the categories of religious ascription for the individuals and groups involved in those exchanges. When examining papal bans against commerce with "infidels," Marcocci argues, it would be anachronistic to conclude that the omnipresence of contraband rendered those bans dead letters. In sixteenth-century Portugal, papal proscriptions were taken seriously, but were also adapted to political circumstances. In the course of Portugal's commercial and military expansion along the African coast and in the Indian Ocean, secular and ecclesiastical authorities debated the definition of "prohibited goods" and the classification of Muslim and pagan societies as "infidels" in relation to strategic needs. That is, they asked whether different goods, and the societies that traded them, were dangerous or economically useful. In redesigning the map of legitimate trade and contraband, Portuguese authorities thus also redefined religious taxonomies. "Infidel" turned out to be a flexible term.

In short, a renewed focus on the role of religion in cross-cultural trade permits us to revisit long-standing historical questions about how religious norms affected the everyday conduct of trade and how, in turn, religious beliefs and institutions were themselves affected by commercial relations with members of other religions. In many cases, moreover, commercial networks were intertwined with military and missionary expeditions. Ultimately, we are thus confronted with the question of when trade between religious groups gave way to more tolerant views of "the other" and when, by contrast, it coexisted with hostile images of commercial partners that were decried as "infidels."

The focus on religion also presents specific challenges for historians of cross-cultural trade, for religious boundaries were done and undone in the process of establishing economic ties with non-coreligionists. Socioeconomic historians often take for granted that a common religious affiliation sealed the boundaries of merchant communities and thus aided these communities' commercial success by reducing the risk of opportunism among coreligionists. In this view, religious affiliations create more stable market exchanges. Meanwhile, cultural historians have progressively challenged characterizations of religious groups as monolithic blocks and have turned instead to concepts of fluidity, hybridity, cross-fertilization, and border-crossing to describe them. How to square these two approaches is an important and challenging task, which brings us to our next question.

II. Did Trust Work across Religious Groups?

The word "trust" peppers historical accounts of long-distance commerce, and of trade diasporas in particular. In spite of protracted scholarly debates—across the humanities, social sciences, and behavioral sciences—about the definition and usefulness of the concept of trust, there remains among historians a tendency to invoke the word as if it were self-evident, that is, to assume that relatives and coreligionists trusted one another and that their bonds gave them an advantage over merchants operating without the support of extended kin or other social ties. This basic assumption holds more than a grain of truth: personal allegiances can compensate for the lack of effective means of coordination, such as rapid transportation or reliable and fair tribunals. But it also stems from the projections of modern scholars looking at past societies as traditional, as dominated by family and religious solidarities. In fact, relatives and coreligionists were not always the most competent or best equipped to open new market opportunities; from time to time, they also willfully undermined one another. Even among the Quaker community that traversed the eighteenth-century Atlantic, brotherly love could give way to bitter disputes.[27] As if these issues weren't sufficiently complicated, a diaspora's internal cohesion—whatever its sources—does not automatically explain how economic alliances were sustained with outsiders. That is, what made long-lasting intergroup economic ties possible?

For Curtin, as mentioned, the answer lies in trade diasporas' distinctive ability to mediate across groups. The means through which different diasporas fulfilled this function, however, varied greatly, not only because different environments called for different solutions to problems of commitment, but also because Curtin offers different definitions of what a trade diaspora was. He oscillates between a more specific definition, which identifies trade diasporas with stateless groups living in dispersal while linked by kinship, religion, language, profession, or place of origin, and a looser definition that conceives of them simply as "trade communities of merchants living among aliens in associated networks."[28] This looser definition is at the same time the strength and the weakness of Curtin's analysis. It allows for more capacious comparisons, but it also groups together organizations that had recourse to radically different means of contract enforcement. It can thus apply to stateless minorities, such as Greek, Armenian, or Jewish traders, or to entities, such as the Dutch and English East India companies or the Hudson's Bay Company, which were granted the monopoly right to deploy military force overseas on behalf of their respective

---

[27] Hancock, *Oceans of Wine*, 148.
[28] Curtin, *Cross-Cultural Trade*, 3.

states. This looser definition, in other words, has the virtue of deflecting the prevailing Eurocentrism that singles out chartered companies as forerunners of modern corporations and agents of radical change in the conduct of transoceanic commerce.[29] Curtin, however, did not elaborate on the analogy between trade diasporas as "moral communities" and as state-chartered companies by means of a sustained comparison of their respective business organization, and specifically their respective methods of contract enforcement within and across group boundaries. This vagueness may explain why one critic deemed *Cross-Cultural Trade in World History* "in many ways inconclusive."[30]

It is the more conventional definition of trade diasporas as stateless and geographically scattered merchant communities that has become preponderant. The preference for this notion of trade diaspora is another measure of the widespread and commonsensical definition of "trust," mentioned above, which has continued to obfuscate our understanding of cross-cultural trade. Even those historians who do not take the internal solidarity of stateless diasporas for granted, for the most part scrutinize the sources of intragroup cooperation more than they do the mechanisms allowing for economic transaction across (rather than within) groups. In so doing, they implicitly regard a trade diaspora's geographical dispersion as indication of that group's engagement in cross-cultural trade more than they analyze how a diaspora actually conducted business relations with outsiders.[31]

A distinction between intra- and cross-group economic cooperation hardly preoccupies those economists who avoid the notion of trust altogether on the grounds that it can be replaced—and improved upon—by the standard tools of economic theory.[32] This proposition echoes Adam Smith's credo that "the propensity to truck, barter, and exchange one thing for another...[is] common to all men."[33]

---

[29] For a conventional articulation of this argument, see Douglass C. North, "Institutions, Transactions Costs, and the Rise of Merchant Empires," in *The Political Economy of Merchant Empires*, ed. James D. Tracy (Cambridge: Cambridge University Press, 1991), 22–40.

[30] David Abulafia, "The Role of Trade in Muslim-Christian Contact during the Middle Ages," in his *Mediterranean Encounters: Economic, Religious, Political, 1100–1550* (Aldershot, UK, and Burlington, VT: Ashgate, 2000), I: 3.

[31] This tendency is visible, for example, in Levi, *The Indian Diaspora* and Aslanian, *From the Indian Ocean to the Mediterranean*. A sophisticated and well-documented account of the early modern Armenian trading diaspora (to which Curtin had devoted an innovative chapter at a time when the secondary literature on the subject was negligible [*Cross-Cultural Trade*, 179–206]), Aslanian's study nonetheless illuminates the sources of intra-Armenian solidarity more than the way in which Armenian merchants sealed economic contracts with non-Armenians.

[32] See Oliver Williamson, "Calculativeness, Trust, and Economic Organization," *Journal of Law and Economics* 36.1 (1993): 453–486, and the exchange that ensued between the author and Richard Craswell in the same issue of the journal (487–502).

[33] Adam Smith, *An Inquiry into the Nature and Causes of the Wealth of Nations* [1776], ed. Edwin Cannan; with a new preface by George J. Stigler (Chicago: University of Chicago Press, 1976), 17 (Book 1, Chapter 2).

Following this line of argument, K. N. Chaudhuri has challenged Curtin's interpretation of merchant communities active across the Indian Ocean, including Parsees, Armenians, and Jews, and has attributed their vitality not to their social organization and spatial dispersion, but to "the general characteristics of human behaviour," by which he means a universally shared economic rationality.[34] Contrary to Curtin, Chaudhuri regards these merchant communities as less effective in curbing the risks of long-distance trade than "the bureaucratic operations of the Dutch and English East India Companies," which he views as having imposed not only the use of force, but also more rational forms of economic organization in the Indian Ocean.[35]

The gulf that separates scholars whom Curtin would have labeled either as "substantivists" or "formalists" has, on the one hand, widened over the last half century, because of the formalists' increased use of mathematics, and, on the other, contracted, thanks to the adoption by historians of tools from the new institutional economics and network analysis, for example. Paul E. Lovejoy and David Richardson borrowed insights from transaction cost economics to interpret the use of human pawns in contractual obligations between British and African dealers in the Atlantic slave trade.[36] My study of the Western Sephardic diaspora adopts the idea of selective trust to examine how credit relations worked within different circles of coreligionists and with non-Jews.[37] Several chapters in this volume pursue these lines of inquiry by examining what specific threats, incentives, and guarantees facilitated economic transactions across religious groups. In using the words "trust" and "trade diasporas" sparingly and judiciously, these contributions inspire others to clarify the meaning they may wish to attribute to these expressions.

Wolfgang Kaiser and Guillaume Calafat borrow the concept of "credibility without trust" from sociologist Erving Goffman in order to explore the economy of ransoming and to illustrate the bases on which credibility was built, even among sworn religious enemies. Kathryn Miller turns to a related concept, that of "diffused reciprocity," articulated by political scientists of modern international relations, in order to interpret the legal opinion of a Muslim jurist from fifteenth-century Malaga, who advised against reneging on a commitment to release a Christian captive on the ground that future

---

[34] K. N. Chaudhuri, *Trade and Civilization in the Indian Ocean: An Economic History from the Rise of Islam to 1750* (Cambridge: Cambridge University Press, 1985), 226.

[35] Chaudhuri, *Trade and Civilization*, 5.

[36] Paul E. Lovejoy and David Richardson, "Trust, Pawnship, and Atlantic History: The Institutional Foundations of the Old Calabar Slave Trade," *American Historical Review*, 104.2 (1999): 333–355. Lovejoy has expanded on some of Curtin's interests in both African history and the study of trade disaporas and cross-cultural trade in several studies, beginning with his *Caravans of Kola: The Hausa Kola Trade 1700–1900* (Zaria, Nigeria: Ahmadu Bello University Press, 1980).

[37] Trivellato, *The Familiarity of Strangers*.

treatments of Muslim captives, and future exchanges in general, depended on honoring binding agreements, since merchants based their decisions on past experience.

A persistent challenge lurks even in these sophisticated approaches: the issue of group identification. In order for moral suasion and common values or for certain institutions, ranging from marriage to corporate tribunals, to sustain a high degree of conformity within a trade diaspora, middleman groups at least in theory need to possess finite and homogeneous boundaries.[38] That in reality the identification of such boundaries is not always uncontroversial should warn us against assuming that merchant communities could deploy informal mechanisms such as ostracism in order to enforce compliance among their members and thus reduce the risks of long-distance trade.

Roxani Margariti applies the notion of trade diaspora to the Jewish merchants documented in the records of the Cairo Geniza. Yet she highlights the lack of consistency in the religious taxonomies that appear in those records. More than one label could indicate the religious identity—Jewish or Muslim—of those involved in a contract. In certain cases, it is not even possible to pinpoint religious status beyond a doubt; in others, that religious status is accompanied by other markers of identity, such as geographical origin. A similar set of problems emerges in relation to the Sephardic merchants of France and the United Provinces. Until 1723, everyone of Jewish descent living in southwestern France was qualified as a "Portuguese merchant." Generations of intermarriage with local Catholic families interfere with the assumption that all Iberian refugees were crypto-Jews and formed a tight community. In the Protestant countries of northern Europe, by contrast, Jews were allowed to congregate, but some wealthy New Christians did not join community life or attend services in synagogue in order to better their chances of integrating into the dominant society. Such examples, and more could be cited, demand that we dig deeper into the empirical evidence to determine a trade diaspora's composition and the effectiveness of informal mechanisms of internal self-policing, not to mention the means that made a diaspora able to enforce contracts with outsiders.

---

[38] On the importance of group identification in transaction costs economics, see Janet Tai Landa, *Trust, Ethnicity, and Identity: Beyond the New Institutional Economics of Ethnic Trading Networks, Contract Law, and Gift Exchange* (Ann Arbor: University of Michigan Press, 1994), esp. 101–113. For the same author, only groups of small size can solve coordination problems informally: Robert Cooter and Janet T. Landa, "Personal versus Impersonal Trade: Size of Trading Groups and Contract Law," *International Review of Law and Economics*, 4 (1984): 15–22.

III. What Role Did Legal Institutions Play in Building Cross-Cultural Trade?

If not trust, what governed cross-cultural economic exchanges? Economists who are skeptical of the notion of trust tend for the most part to emphasize the importance of reliable legal institutions that protected property rights and enabled economic transactions between strangers. Several chapters engage with this hypothesis by asking what difference the law made for trade across religious groups, particularly when we examine not simultaneous transactions, but deferred payments and long-lasting partnerships. Legal forums were not always available and were not always the most effective deterrents of devious behavior. It is also unclear whether merchants from disparate backgrounds shared a common set of rules, as proponents of the existence of a universal *lex mercatoria* in the medieval Mediterranean would have it. More commonly, merchants had to navigate among a multitude of foreign legislation and courts. When that happened, local merchants belonging to the dominant or resident population could realistically count on more favorable treatment than merchants in transit, or at least on better knowledge of the intricacies of the system and the men who staffed it. The central issue, then, is to determine when efficient legal regimes and reputational oversight reinforced and when they replaced one another.

Those contributions to this volume that concern the infrastructure of cross-cultural trade do not posit an opposition between the enforcing mechanisms assured by state-sponsored enterprises and those mobilized by family and religious ties. They start from a different perspective: they ask what range of resources—written contracts, intermediaries, social pressure, minted coins—helped merchants from different religious groups arrive at a common understanding of the terms of exchange and how these different resources enhanced the chances that all counterparts would abide by their promises.

The ransoming of Christian, Muslim, and Jewish captives in the medieval and early modern Mediterranean existed because the region was religiously and politically divided. Its persistence over the centuries did not lead to the creation of a unified legal system. Rather, what made possible the enforcement of obligations between Christian, Muslim, and Jewish agents was a mixture of diplomatic agreements, specialized brokers, and widely shared customary norms and routines about the exchange of war prisoners and commodities. Particularly important was the mutual recognition of written agreements stipulated on either side of the Christian-Muslim political and legal divide. A fifteenth-century Malaga Muslim jurist favored standing by contractual obligations toward Christian dealers (Miller), and in the seventeenth and eighteenth centuries civil and commercial courts of Mediterranean Europe accepted as binding contracts signed before a Muslim judge in North Africa (Kaiser and Calafat).

Early modern France and the United Provinces represent an example unlike the Mediterranean. In those states, merchants belonging to multiple religious groups had easy access to a common legal and jurisdictional system, at least insofar as their business contracts were concerned. The challenge there is to recognize when this legal homogeneity made merchants indifferent to the religious identities of their contractual parties and when, by contrast, extralegal elements affected decisions about whom to enter into a contract with and on what terms. Antunes and Marzagalli develop a typology of contractual agreements that allows us to move beyond the question of whether cross-cultural business cooperation existed or not, and to determine instead for what purposes and under what circumstances parties were willing and able to cooperate with members of other religious and confessional groups. Across most of seventeenth- and eighteenth-century Europe, certain types of credit contracts, such as marine insurance or freight contracts, entailed less risk than general partnerships, because their stipulations were specific and could thus be more easily monitored via the courts. In those types of contracts, we should not be surprised to find a high degree of opportunistic alliances between merchants of different religions and confessions. General partnerships, by contrast, were normally formed by relatives or at least coreligionists because their members were fully liable to one another and thus needed to count on robust social incentives, rather than on the threat of the law, in order to behave honestly.

IV. When and How Did Violence Coexist With Cross-Cultural Trade?

The word "trade" conjures images of willing parties coming together to bridge all other differences in the name of the pursuit of profit. As Sacks reminds us, the European discourse that depicts the international division of labor as an instrument of peace and prosperity harks back to Aristotle. In spite of the legacy left by colonial exploitation and the vast economic inequalities that exist between nations, irenic views of international trade die hard. In the period considered in this volume, military conquest, piracy, contraband, slavery, and pillage accompanied most overseas trading ventures. Defensive reactions against foreign goods and foreign traders can be documented more frequently than not. And it is often impossible to draw a clear line between private and state violence or between institutions devised to deploy violence and those promoting commercial enterprise. One need only think of the Portuguese *Estado da Índia* and English East India Company to know how intertwined these functions were.

The captive trade in the Mediterranean offers striking evidence of the interdependence of commercial cooperation and religious antagonism. It flourished precisely because Christian and Muslim powers were in a state of open and permanent conflict. Yet it operated on the basis of rules established not only for the exchange of prisoners but also for commodity trade, and it even promoted commodity trade. Spanish authorities, for example, issued licenses to trade in forbidden goods to those merchants willing to invest in the ransoming of Christian captives in North Africa. The Muslim jurist from Malaga who urged respect for contractual obligations with Christian traders did not argue in favor of a peaceful embrace of the "infidels." He worried about the possible interruption of trade flows. The medieval and early modern Mediterranean was not a "middle ground," in the sense in which Richard White has defined it, because, although neither side had the ability to subjugate the other by force, elaborate legal and diplomatic systems determined the modalities of legitimate trade.[39] By contrast, the first encounter between English and native traders in Newfoundland can indeed be described according to the "middle ground" model, not only because the parties involved stood on equal footing, at least until violence ensued, but also because they lacked formalized rules of contracting and dispute resolution.

V. Do Material Artifacts Bear the Imprint of Cross-Cultural Trade?

Variations of this question have interested older generations of art historians and today animate broader debates in the humanities. Halevi and Mark in this volume make a strong case for why we should pay more attention to the material traces left by cross-cultural trade. Artifacts are sometimes all that remain of ancient trade routes; other times, they are as numerous as written records. Even natural goods—a colorant or some spices—changed meanings and functions as they changed hands. Halevi reflects on those objects that divided symbolically one culture from another and, specifically, on the problems that cross-religious trade in books, candles, meat, clothes, slaves, and weapons of war posed to Islamic scholars. He insists, however, that many other goods traversed religious boundaries without causing hostile reactions.

Different interpretive challenges emerge when that was the case. Mark takes up some of those challenges. To interpret the semantics of elaborate creative objects in the absence of direct evidence of artistic patronage is particularly arduous when the objects traversed vast cultural frontiers. Orders had to be communicated across wide linguistic and cultural divides. Forged in one semantic field, religious symbols were absorbed into a new one. Mark's study of West African ivory carvings highlights how trade was more than an infrastructure for cultural exchange. The artwork

---

[39] Richard White, *The Middle Ground: Indians, Empires, and Republics in the Great Lakes Region, 1650–1815*, Twentieth Anniversary Edition (Cambridge: Cambridge University Press, 2011), esp. 50–93. See also Chapters 2 and 4 in this volume.

produced by local artists for European consumers includes representations of the very objects that were exchanged with those consumers and with others. It thus offers a commentary—sometimes tragic, sometimes ironic—of the very trade networks to which artistic objects belonged. The spiritual and ritualistic meanings embodied in certain figures can be very hard to decipher but point to a double hermeneutics in which religious constructs both crossed boundaries and remained estranged—that is, one that fits neither a model of incommensurability (in which producers and consumers passed like ships in the night), nor one of hybridity and *métissage* (in which multiple symbolic references converged and influenced one another in a seemingly fluid process).

* * *

By means of these five interlocking questions, this volume pursues an alternative approach to what Curtin called "comparative world history." Certain phenomena and institutions, such as port cities or middlemen, can be found in many corners of the world. For this reason alone, it is important to tease out meaningful comparisons and to challenge Europe's conceptual and empirical function as the standard against which comparisons are drawn—two principal goals of world history writing. At the same time, this book registers some dissatisfaction with the degree of generality that is required to write a synthetic history of the world, or even the history of one phenomenon on a planetary scale. Prompted by Geertz and some microhistorians, my questions chart a different route: one that generalizes the questions we ask more than the conclusions we can reach on the basis of individual case-study.[40] It is a route that forces us to delve into salient details while also developing a grammar for comparisons. Naturally, other questions could be added to those I proposed.

If a broad canvas is not part of this research agenda, out of the great diversity of cases and approaches that the ten chapters discuss, we can nonetheless emphasize two larger points. First, a creative combination of contract enforcement mechanisms, including the entire spectrum ranging from social coercion to legal means, characterizes the majority of cases analyzed here. More specifically, legal specialists and institutions were central to the commercial organization of both Christian and Muslim traders. This creative combination calls for a more refined analysis of the governance of both intra- and intergroup economic transactions.

Second, protracted commercial relations between members of different religious groups did not invariably generate more benevolent attitudes toward those viewed as enemies of one's faith. In other words, accommodation and utilitarian pragmatism in the face of cross-cultural trade were widespread, but did not necessarily

---

[40] Francesca Trivellato, "Is There a Future for Italian Microhistory in the Age of Global History?" *California Italian Studies*, 2.1 (2011). Permalink: http://escholarship.org/uc/item/0z94n9hq.

express an incipient form of secularism. Sustained economic exchanges between traders of different religious backgrounds existed where (and sometimes because) religious boundaries were clearly demarcated. Political rulers, religious leaders, and legal scholars could adjust to the imperatives of commerce while they also injected religious concerns into their economic pursuits and military strategies.

These two points should, of course, be subjected to further specification and scrutiny. Even when stated in such general terms, though, they demonstrate why cross-cultural trade has become a linchpin of world, transnational, and comparative history, and can offer a new impetus to test these hypotheses the world over.

1

Religion and Cross-Cultural Trade

A FRAMEWORK FOR INTERDISCIPLINARY INQUIRY

Leor Halevi

ᴄ᠎——————————————————————————————

"RELIGION AND CROSS-CULTURAL trade" is a phrase that makes me think in the first place of the problem of buying a Christian's sandals in a market governed in theory by Islamic law. A Christian had sold a pair of sandals to a Muslim. Could the Muslim now lawfully wear the shoes? Malik ibn Anas, a famous jurist from Medina, ruled that he could not. This was a forbidden good.[1]

Why this founder of a school of law thought this way is a bit of a mystery. After all, Malik deemed it lawful for a Muslim to wear clothes that had previously belonged to a Christian, after laundering them. An Egyptian jurist brought the case to Malik's attention, and it was eventually recorded in a ninth-century collection of legal opinions assembled in Córdoba. Its social relevance in al-Andalus or Egypt is obvious, for in these Mediterranean lands Christians and Muslims frequently exchanged with each other in the *suq* or the *zoco*. But it is more difficult to relate the case of the Christian sandals to historical reality in early Islamic Medina. By no account was the city teeming with non-Muslims. Some Christians had made it their home in pre-Islamic times. Jewish tribes had lived there, too, during the lifetime of the Prophet Muḥammad. Yet they had been expelled, according to oral traditions narrated by Malik himself, so that only one religion would remain in "the land of the

---

[1] Leor Halevi, "Christian Impurity versus Economic Necessity: A Fifteenth-Century Fatwa on European Paper," *Speculum*, 83 (2008): 917–945, 931.

Arabs."[2] Presumably, there were very few, if any, Christians residing in the Hijaz when Malik was asked the question. If goods made by Christians reached his city, they arrived by means of long-distance trade—more than likely conveyed by Muslim merchants, though possibly by Christians authorized to sojourn briefly in Arabia's sacred towns in order to trade.[3]

As he reflected on sandals sold by Christians, as well as on clothes made and worn by Christians, Malik did not think in general terms about pre-industrial production and cross-cultural consumption. Although his proscription may have derived from a preoccupation with ritual purity and bodily pollution, or from a desire to maintain a symbolic boundary between Muslims and Christians, he did not express any interest in segregation along confessional lines. To restrict social exchanges between Muslims and Christians in the markets of Cairo or Córdoba was simply not part of his juridical agenda. There is, furthermore, no sign that he worried broadly about Muslim-Christian trade. Instead of formulating general principles about all things that Christians themselves produced and sold to Muslims, he addressed only select articles, new and worn, that a Muslim might purchase and then use to dress his body. Yet within this circumscribed purview, Malik's reflections give us some idea of how sharply a religious scholar in the remote past dealt, from a juridical-theological perspective, with an aspect of the problem of cross-religious commerce.

Modern perspectives on this problem are, of course, entirely different. Rather than dwell on sandals and tunics—rather than ponder goods casuistically so as to distinguish, like Malik, between the lawful and the forbidden—modern scholars have addressed cross-cultural trade on a more abstract level. They have endeavored to explain, for example, how different cultural institutions or economic systems made it more or less efficient for goods to flow across long distances. In the following pages, I will present and analyze selectively some twentieth-century approaches to the problem that Malik confronted long ago. I will explain why Max Weber and Bronislaw Malinowski paid little or no attention to cross-cultural trade. I will then show that, after World War II, Clifford Geertz and other scholars began to reflect on the subject more seriously and systematically—in a process that culminated in the 1980s, with Philip Curtin's ambitious synthesis, *Cross-Cultural Trade in World History*. The field of research that Geertz and Curtin heralded promised to yield the crops of interdisciplinary labor. Social and environmental historians, as well as

[2] Mālik ibn Anas, *Al-Muwaṭṭa'*, recension by Yaḥyā ibn Yaḥyā al-Laythī al-Andalusī, ed. Bashshār 'Awwād Ma'rūf, vol. 2 (Beirut: Dār al-Gharb al-Islāmī, 1996–1997), 470–471.

[3] Al-Shāfi'ī, *Kitāb al-umm: mawsū'at al-Imām*, 2nd ed. (Damascus: Dār Qutayba, 2003), 9: 136, no. 13482–3. See also Antoine Fattal, *Le statut légal des non-musulmans en pays d'islam* (Beirut: Imprimerie Catholique, 1958), 86–87.

cultural and economic anthropologists, have found some common ground in this field, while, disappointingly, institutional economists and international business psychologists have remained worlds apart. Still, to establish a framework for inquiry, I will feature here the diverse contributions of Jacob Katz, Karl Polanyi, Fernand Braudel, Avner Greif, Geert Hofstede, Richard White, Nicholas Thomas, Marshall Sahlins, Francesca Trivellato, and Olivia Constable, among other scholars.

In the course of the chapter, I will develop three arguments. First, rather than representing cross-cultural trade as a mechanism for the creation of peaceful or exploitative relations among nations, I will juxtapose violent conjunctures and trusted conjunctions: adventurous, risky trading ventures in strange new lands against fairly normalized, predictable commercial exchanges within merchants' networks. Second, I will argue for the need to pay greater attention to spatial context, given the goal of understanding the cultural dynamics at play in economic exchange between members of different religions in particular locales. Finally, in the last section, I will argue against economic historians' tendency to aggregate goods into broad categories or sectors so as to detect patterns of trade across religious boundaries. Instead, I will insist on the need to disentangle commodities by paying close attention to theological or legal views about foreign material objects. Economic historians, even more so than scholars in other disciplines, have used religion loosely as a category of analysis; this lack of reflection on what constitutes a "religious" matter has led to ill-founded generalizations about the relationship between religion and cross-cultural trade. This is where Islamic law, like Jewish law and other theological-legal systems, can help us to determine, with far greater precision, what precisely religion has to do with cross-cultural commerce.

KEYWORDS

Before we analyze various disciplinary and methodological approaches to the topic at hand, we should pause to think about the phrase "religion and cross-cultural trade." What exactly does it mean? The word "religion" itself is used in various senses. It can refer to a system of faith in salvation from a world of death and suffering; to belief in a transcendent power; or to ritual action that indicates reverence for a god or obeisance to an ancestral spirit. In the seventeenth century, Jesuit missionaries were not altogether sure whether to describe Confucian rites and ceremonies as the elementary forms of a religion.[4] Scholars in religious studies departments today consider, by contrast, such a bewildering array of beliefs, values, and institutions as

---

[4] Paul A. Rule, *K'ung-Tzu or Confucius: The Jesuit Interpretation of Confucianism* (Sydney: Allen & Unwin, 1986), xiii, 88–111.

formal objects of investigation that it has become harder and harder to determine what "religion" might possibly refer to. One critic of "religion" as an analytical concept contends that scholars in the field study totems, Christmas cakes, witchcraft, tea ceremonies, vegetarianism, ghosts, gift exchanges, and Marxism, among other things. "Religion," consequently, has become "meaningless as an analytical concept."[5] Another critic, a Christian theologian, would concur, pointing out the confusion that reigns among experts in religious studies when they try to justify the use of a key category, "world religion." According to his narrow definition, "religion" should properly "denote human action that springs from desire for closer union...with the God of Abraham, Isaac, Jacob, and Jesus." As for "world religion," it is, from his point of view, a term that "developed and is still often deployed for the properly theoretical purpose of depicting alien practice as a consumable good."[6] This evocation of a boundary between native religion and foreign practice deserves some attention. Western scholars often envision religions metaphorically as entities, and even personify them as military actors on the world stage. Arguably, as suggested by an expert on the "very idea of religions," such reification arises when human beings cross "cultural boundaries," encountering "multiple, rival, or new traditions."[7]

Traveling long distances, traders encountered new religious systems that forced them to think about the very meaning of religion. We see this in the East, for example, where Muslim caravans in Central Asia encountered Kazakhs, whom they described as "neither infidels, nor Muslims" because they identified with Islam but worshipped idols.[8] And we see this in the West, across the Atlantic in the period of first contacts, where, as Jonathan Smith has revealed, "religion" came to mean that which the natives lacked. Indeed, in the middle of the sixteenth century, Richard Eden, the English translator of geographic works that promoted overseas trade, wrote that Columbus found in the Canary Islands inhabitants that "went naked, without shame, religion or knowledge of God."[9] From this perspective, cross-cultural

---

[5] Timothy Fitzgerald, "A Critique of 'Religion' as a Cross-Cultural Category," *Method and Theory in the Study of Religion*, 9.2 (1997): 91–110.

[6] Paul J. Griffiths, "On the Future of the Study of Religion in the Academy," *Journal of the American Academy of Religion*, 74.1 (2006): 66–74.

[7] Robert Ford Campany, "On the Very Idea of Religions (in the Modern West and in Early Medieval China)," *History of Religions*, 42.4 (2003): 287–319, 312.

[8] Richard C. Foltz, *Religions of the Silk Road: Overland Trade and Cultural Exchange from Antiquity to the Fifteenth Century* (New York: St. Martin's Press, 1999), 141.

[9] Jonathan Z. Smith, "Religion, Religions, Religious," in *Critical Terms for Religious Studies*, ed. Mark C. Taylor (Chicago: University of Chicago Press, 1998), 269–284, 269. Reading Smith, it becomes clear that the formula for religious tolerance that Stuart B. Schwartz refers to in *All Can Be Saved: Religious Tolerance and Salvation in the Iberian Atlantic World* (New Haven, CT: Yale University Press, 2008), 138–139, may not necessarily apply to Native Americans.

barter in the New World involved those who possessed religion and those who still needed to find it.

"Trade" may appear to be the simplest keyword to define, but it also has its complexities. It typically means a passage for the purpose of exchanging goods or services for profit—voluntarily and by mutual agreement. Such a definition implies that both parties share an understanding of the terms of commerce and that they engage in the transaction freely, without coercion. It is easy to envision such an exchange between equal partners—two powerful and independent nations, for example, bound by treaties or conventions. It is also easy to envision such an exchange between two merchants who live in different countries yet find reasons to trust each other, even to trade on credit, because they belong to the same religion or kinship group. But a "cross-cultural" transaction can involve people who have had little or no contact historically. If they do not speak the same language and communicate only by gestures and signs, how can they reach a mutual agreement about the terms of exchange? What one party may see as barter, pure and simple, the other party may see as a gift-giving ceremony. Moreover, if one party arrives with overwhelming military force, the other party, feeling threatened, might find itself compelled to buy and sell at whatever cost. Equally perplexing are transactions between local and diasporic merchants that involve credit, rather than an immediate exchange of goods, in countries where governmental institutions are so weak or corrupt that nobody can count on the effective enforcement of contracts.

Economic historians often relate to trade as an engine of historical change with great enthusiasm. Thus, to take one example, Robert Lopez argued that by the late medieval period long-distance trade became "the driving force of economic progress, and in the end affected every aspect of human activity almost as decisively as the Industrial Revolution changed the modern world."[10] Yet from a world-historical perspective, the economic significance of peaceful commerce in pre-modern times is, in fact, debatable.[11] If the goal is to understand how the flow of material objects affected the development of societies and therefore, in the broadest sense, the course of history, it would be better to focus capaciously on the multiplicity of mechanisms that led to the transfer of goods across cultures. Thereby, alongside trade, barter, and gift-giving, we should consider plunder, pillaging, piracy, tribute, and a variety of

---

[10] Robert Lopez, *The Birth of Europe*, trans. J. M. Dent & Sons (New York: M. Evans, 1967), 126.

[11] Near the end of the eighteenth century, only about 4 percent of Europe's "gross national product was exported across national frontiers," with perhaps just 1 percent shipped to Africa, Asia, and the Americas. See Patrick O'Brien, "European Economic Development: The Contribution of the Periphery," *Economic History Review*, 35.1 (1982): 1–18, 4.

other depredations and extortions; and we should recognize the fact that before the modern era, trade itself frequently depended on coercion and violence.[12]

The expression "cross-cultural trade" entered scholarly discourse largely through the publication in 1984 of Philip Curtin's famous book.[13] But it appeared occasionally in books and articles before that date. An essay on "The Bazaar Merchant," published in the 1950s, argues that "the conservative" Middle Eastern merchant believes that Western goods, "such as plumbing fixtures, however valuable for conspicuous consumption or as status-increasing accouterments, are overpriced in comparison with serviceable and familiar products indigenous to the culture." This impression represents one of the "awkward characteristics of cross-cultural trade."[14] Similar use of the term appears in an article published in the 1970s on an initiative by the Peace Corps to establish a cooperative society for an aboriginal tribe in northeastern Panama. "Although the Cuna have been in contact with Europeans and African blacks since the sixteenth century," writes the author, "they have maintained an extraordinarily low level of intermarriage and cross-cultural trade, exhibiting a strong sense of pride in their racial identity."[15] These scholars understood trade as a path that crosses over a high cultural barrier—a barrier that has divided Western culture, with its "civilized" conveniences (faucets, toilets, bathtubs), from an indigenous culture characterized, above all, by commitment to tradition, allegiance to tribe, and resistance to foreign things. There is no guarantee in such circumstances of a trading venture's success; peacefully inducing natives to consume imported commodities will not always yield the desired results. But if trade does take place successfully, it will happen between unequal partners on colonial or postcolonial soil.

"Culture" is a very complex word that has, as Raymond Williams and Terry Eagleton have shown, a long history and multiple meanings.[16] The adjective "cross-cultural" suggests a pluralistic frame of reference. There is no suggestion here that one party has culture, in a refined artistic and literary sense, while the other

---

[12] Frederic C. Lane, *Venice and History: The Collected Papers* (Baltimore, MD: Johns Hopkins Press, 1966), 399–428; Kenneth Pomeranz and Steven Topik, *The World That Trade Created: Society, Culture, and the World Economy*, 2nd ed. (London: M. E. Sharpe, 2006), 141–174.

[13] Philip D. Curtin, *Cross-Cultural Trade in World History* (Cambridge: Cambridge University Press, 1984). Curtin also used the term "cross-cultural" earlier to refer to "misunderstanding" between Europeans and others; see Philip D. Curtin, *Economic Change in Precolonial Africa: Senegambia in the Era of the Slave Trade* (Madison: University of Wisconsin Press, 1975), 94.

[14] Dalton Potter, "The Bazaar Merchant," in *Social Forces in the Middle East*, ed. Sydney Nettleton Fisher (Ithaca, NY: Cornell University Press, 1955), 99–115, 108.

[15] Nancy Brennan Hatley, "Cooperativism and Enculturation among the Cuna Indians of San Blas," in *Enculturation in Latin America: An Anthology*, ed. Johannes Wilbert (Los Angeles: UCLA Latin American Center Publications, University of California, 1976), 67–94, 68.

[16] Raymond Williams, *Keywords: A Vocabulary of Culture and Society* (New York: Oxford University Press, 1976), 76–82; Terry Eagleton, *The Idea of Culture* (Malden, MA: Publishing House, 2000), 1–31.

either lacks it altogether or possesses it only in small measure. Every tribe, every nation, possesses its own culture. In this romantic sensibility, the values, behavior, and customs that give meaning to a way of life and coherence to a social group are worth celebrating and preserving. The desire to acquire foreign objects drives the putative representatives of one and another culture to interact. First encounters produce discord and harmony, a preliminary understanding of differences and similarities. But cross-cultural trade presents, in the course of time, a threat to the romantic ideal of cultural diversity. As merchants introduce novel commodities into the bazaar and establish contact with remote tribes, they alter local ways in some respects. Although indigenous people are perfectly capable, as Nicholas Thomas has shown, of "appropriating" Western goods according to their own cultural values, political systems, and economic calculations, there is no denying the fact that the exchange profoundly alters their material culture.[17] Moreover, despite all that is lost in translation, trade can also produce some degree of cultural affinity, without leading to convergence, when the artifacts that move across frontiers effectively script social behavior.

Derived from the Latin *cultus*, which refers to worship, the word "culture" can describe a system of religious devotion. Even if one does not define religion as a "cultural system," following Clifford Geertz, the phrase "religion and cross-cultural trade" appears mildly tautological.[18] What purpose does it serve, then? It signals a focus on religion and trade, of course, as well as a commitment to pluralistic cultural analysis. But, more important, it implies a different understanding of exchange than the expression "interfaith commerce." This alternative conveys a narrow, restrictive definition of religion, revolving around spiritual belief in the truth of a divine revelation. It privileges faith, rather than works, as the essential orientation in religious life. It adopts a Lutheran perspective on traders who might well see their religion as consisting primarily not of faith, but of rites, customs, and traditions. Furthermore, the expression suggests that members of different "faiths" have reached some sort of mutual agreement, tacit or explicit, to conduct a business transaction. If commerce between "faiths" follows rules and conventions established to minimize violence and maximize profit, trade across cultures unfolds as a risky proposition, an awkward flirtation, with unpredictable consequences.

---

[17] Nicholas Thomas, *Entangled Objects: Exchange, Material Culture and Colonialism in the Pacific* (Cambridge, MA: Harvard University Press, 1991), 83–124.

[18] Clifford Geertz, "Religion as a Cultural System," in his *The Interpretation of Cultures: Selected Essays* (New York: Basic Books, 1973), 87–125.

DISCIPLINES AT A CROSSROADS

"Religion and cross-cultural trade" may appear as an ideal crossroads for interdisciplinary research. Imagine theologians arriving at the junction with an interest in the gifts of interfaith communication or the morality of unequal exchanges. Economists eager to analyze the institutions that blocked or facilitated long-distance trade would join them. Anthropologists intrigued by the power of objects to symbolize cultural identities would come from another direction. The last group to reach the intersection would be historians, fascinated by encounters between diverse peoples in an era of arduous travel and infrequent communications. Yet relatively little research on the topic exists, and most of it does not qualify as interdisciplinary. When we search for books or articles on religion and cross-cultural trade in the first half of the twentieth century, what is most notable is a lack of scholarship. This absence is nowhere more obvious than in the work of Max Weber and Bronislaw Malinowski.

More than any other intellectual, Max Weber reflected deeply on "the economic ethics of the world religions." That is, in fact, the title that he gave to a massive, unfinished set of volumes. As any reader of *The Protestant Ethic and the Spirit of Capitalism* knows, Weber was centrally concerned with the economic consequences of different religious orientations. How do ethical principles or religious interests affect economic behavior, the organization of labor, or the spirit by which human beings pursue material wealth? This was the essential question. To answer it, Weber delved into each religious tradition as if it existed more or less independently. He acknowledged that historical circumstances shaped the economic ethic of certain minorities, most notably the Jews. In pre-modern Europe, the Jews were restricted to certain occupations, including money lending. As members of a persecuted or despised minority with a tradition of social and ritual segregation, they developed "pariah capitalism," a distinct, though hardly unique, perspective on commerce with others. According to a principle stated already in Deuteronomy 23:20, which permitted lending with interest to strangers, but not to brothers, they elaborated a double ethic that allowed them to make moral distinctions between trading with Jews and trading with Gentiles.[19] In general, however, Weber paid no attention to commerce between members of different religions. A discussion on Muslim-Hindu trade or Calvinist-Catholic exchange might have clarified differences and similarities in religious approaches to the economy. But it would have engendered some confusion, making the boundaries between religious groups less discrete. Weber had a classificatory mind. He aimed at producing typologies, powerful abstractions to

---

[19] On Weber, religion, and economy, see Richard Swedberg, *Max Weber and the Idea of Economic Sociology* (Princeton, NJ: Princeton University Press, 1998), 108–145.

divide people by religion. The very problem of cross-cultural trade would have perturbed and indeed undermined this sociological mode of analysis.

To describe and understand alternative systems of trade was an essential goal for the founders of anthropology. In *Argonauts of the Western Pacific*, Bronislaw Malinowski provided a detailed account of a ceremonial exchange system that existed around the Trobriand Islands, coral atolls located in Papua New Guinea. The inhabitants of these island communities made red necklaces and white bracelets out of shells, which then traveled by canoe, clockwise or counterclockwise, around a ring of islands. Commercially speaking, the articles appeared useless: they did not form objects or currency that could be used to purchase useful things. Recipients of the artifacts could not possess them permanently—rather quickly they had to place them back into circulation in the Kula ring. But the exchange involved complex rituals and deep emotions; and it served to establish a hierarchy, for the extent to which an individual participated in the Kula trade corresponded to his prestige and social standing in the community. Describing this system allowed the Polish ethnographer to show that human beings were not everywhere materialistic, an argument that he advanced against the capitalistic conception of man as someone who will pursue "nothing but his material advantage" with a "purely utilitarian heart."[20] More familiar and therefore less revealing to Malinowski was the system of external trade that ran parallel to the Kula. Known as *gimwali*, this form of naked bartering dispensed with elaborate ceremonies. It showed a more utilitarian and less exotic side to Trobriand islanders, who simply sought, like the "economic man" that Malinowski deplored, a good bargain. Malinowski paid relatively little attention to this trade, which ran against his nostalgic romanticism.[21] More significant, he edited European traders and goods altogether out of his ethnography, despite their presence in the region. At the time, objects made in Europe circulated within one and the other system of exchange; and Europeans had already changed the local economy in some respects. In the words of one critic, as he yearned "for a period untouched by European contact," Malinowski turned a blind eye to historical reality.[22]

Scholars began to devote greater attention to "interfaith" commerce after World War II, propelled either by a desire to find the roots of religious tolerance or by an interest in economic development. A pioneer in this area was the Hungarian Zionist

[20] Bronislaw Malinowski, *Argonauts of the Western Pacific: An Account of Native Enterprise and Adventure in the Archipelagoes of Melanesian New Guinea* (New York: S. P. Dutton, 1950 [1922]), 516.

[21] Malinowski, *Argonauts*, 83, 96, 99–100, 189–191, 362–364.

[22] Stuart Berde, "The Impact of Colonialism on the Economy of Panaeati," in *The Kula: New Perspectives on Massim Exchange*, ed. Jerry W. Leach and Edmund Leach (Cambridge: Cambridge University Press, 1983), 431–444, 436. Also see, in the same book, Giancarlo M. G. Scoditti, with Jerry W. Leach, "Kula on Kitava," 249–276, 259.

Jacob Katz. Having completed in the 1930s a doctoral dissertation on Jewish assimilation in Germany, Katz immigrated to Palestine under the British Mandate. After the war, he entered academia, where he devoted himself to the historical-sociological analysis of the Jewish tradition, with a concentration on Jewish law. Around 1960 he completed a book, funded in part by the Conference of Jewish Material Claims Against Germany, entitled *Exclusiveness and Tolerance: Studies in Jewish-Gentile Relations in Medieval and Modern Times*. This book included a chapter on "Economic Intercourse and the Religious Factor" that showed how straitened economic circumstances led rabbinical scholars in medieval times to make all sorts of doctrinal concessions to render it lawful for Jews in the Diaspora to deal commercially, as a minority, with non-Jews. Such concessions led eventually to an enlightened ethic—to the formulation of the principle of tolerance for other faiths.[23]

While Katz's work has been entirely neglected by specialists on cross-cultural trade, the postwar contributions of another migrating Hungarian scholar, Karl Polanyi, had a tremendous impact on economic historians and economic anthropologists who developed the field in the late twentieth century. Polanyi famously opposed "formalist" endeavors to analyze pre-modern economic systems on the basis of neoclassical economic models, which he considered applicable only to a capitalistic market economy. Stimulated by Malinowski, he sought instead to explain how, before the rise of industrial capitalism, economic systems depended entirely on social configurations. To illustrate this perspective he advanced, among other ideas, the concept of the "port of trade." In pre-modern times, he argued, "ports of trade, not market places, were the growing points of the world economy."[24] He defined the port of trade as a neutral zone, typically located outside a riparian village or a coastal city, where foreign merchants met native ones. Local authorities had an interest in administering such trade—through commercial treaties, for example—partly for pragmatic reasons, in order to keep track of transactions so as to assess customs and taxes, and partly out of a paternalistic concern. They worried that the foreigners, who arrived with the whiff of social disruption, would outrage and scandalize the natives in their charge. These foreign merchants did not necessarily belong to a different religious group. They symbolized a different culture above all because they arrived overseas as professional traders to tread on the outskirts of a non-market society.[25]

---

[23] Jacob Katz, *Exclusiveness and Tolerance: Studies in Jewish-Gentile Relations in Medieval and Modern Times* (West Orange, NJ: Behrman House, 1961), 24–36.

[24] Karl Polanyi, "Ports of Trade in Early Societies," *The Journal of Economic History*, 23.1 (1963): 30–45, 36.

[25] Also see S. C. Humphreys, "History, Economics, and Anthropology: The Work of Karl Polanyi," *History and Theory*, 8.2 (1969), 165–212, 191–196; Abraham Rotstein, "Karl Polanyi's Concept of Non-Market Trade," *The Journal of Economic History*, 30.1 (1970): 117–126; and the articles on ports of trade by Robert B. Revere, Anne C. Chapman, and Rosemary Arnold in *Trade and Market in the Early Empires: Economies*

Several aspects of Polanyi's theories have provoked criticism and debate. His arguments against the formal application of modern economic theory to the study of archaic economies gave rise to the deepest academic disagreements.[26] The contrast that he formulated between socially embedded and disembedded exchanges is far too stark to be convincing. But all that matters for our purposes is the attention he drew to the fact that, in pre-colonial times, long-distance trade frequently took place in a buffer zone. This basic insight underlies Philip Curtin's framework, with one critical difference: overseas traders became, in Curtin's work, embedded in diasporic communities; and they would play a key role, as "cross-cultural brokers," in communicating with the host society.[27] Polanyi's perspective also inspired Kirti N. Chaudhuri, who would describe Indian Ocean "emporia" as politically neutral markets "before the age of Portuguese sea-power."[28] Polanyi influenced a generation of historians and anthropologists as well by insisting on the importance of paying close attention to the spatial context where social exchanges and economic transactions actually took place.

Among Polanyi's fiercest critics was a historian who reflected deeply and systematically on the relationship between human societies, economic exchange, and geographic space. Fernand Braudel criticized Polanyi's use of "heterogeneous samples" to construct a general theory about the great historical transformation of the nineteenth century, when capitalism "burst fully on the world" and impersonal markets supposedly replaced socially embedded ports of trade. Braudel reacted against Polanyi's theory in part because he appreciated social diversity and historical continuity but, more important, because he aimed in his history to grasp the "topology" of capitalism *before* the rise of industrial capitalism. Unlike Polanyi, Braudel wanted to understand how capitalism operated as a "foreign" system in societies and economies whose main structures were not yet capitalistic.[29]

In Braudel's *The Wheels of Commerce*, no person embodies the "foreignness" of capitalism in early modern Europe better than the foreign merchant. Unable to enforce contracts abroad, merchants wanting to engage in overseas trade needed reputable, trustworthy agents to carry out their transactions. Trading networks, bound together by kinship and religion, helped to solve the problem. Braudel sketches the

in History and Theory, ed. Karl Polanyi, Conrad M. Arensberg, and Harry W. Pearson (Glencoe, IL: Free Press, 1957).

[26] For an assessment of Polanyi's role in the formalist/substantivist debate, see Barry L. Isaac, "Karl Polanyi," in *A Handbook of Economic Anthropology*, ed. James G. Carrier (Cheltenham, UK: Edward Elgar, 2005) 14–25.

[27] Curtin, *Cross-Cultural Trade*, 13–14.

[28] K. N. Chaudhuri, *Trade and Civilisation in the Indian Ocean: An Economic History from the Rise of Islam to 1750* (Cambridge: Cambridge University Press, 1985), 224.

[29] Fernand Braudel, *Civilization and Capitalism, 15th–18th Century*, trans. Siân Reynolds, 3 vols. (New York: Harper & Row, 1983), 2: 226–227, 238–239.

stories of several of these networks. He tells of Hindus in Moscow, Florentines in Lyon, and Huguenots in London, but focuses in particular on the far-flung networks of Jews and Armenians. He accounts for their success as traders by explaining that minorities tend to form close ties, defending each other from the majority. He makes the intriguing suggestion that minorities, feeling the weight of discrimination and oppression, might readily find dispensation from being "over-scrupulous" in dealing with the majority. This very point brought Braudel to consider the German economist Werner Sombart's thesis that the origins of the capitalist spirit lie in the Jews' double ethic, which justifies dealing with outsiders by a different moral compass. Disagreeing with Sombart, Braudel approached the question from a sociological perspective. He argued that Jewish as well as Armenian trading networks emerged because minorities established a "natural" association with coreligionaries and fellow countrymen in exile.[30] Minorities flourished commercially because they cooperated effectively at a time when relatively few institutions existed to reduce uncertainty in foreign exchanges.

BREAKTHROUGHS IN ECONOMIC ANTRHOPOLOGY AND WORLD HISTORY

It was in the postwar period as well, a few years before Polanyi and his disciples published *Trade and Market in the Early Empires*, that Clifford Geertz began, as a graduate student, to reflect in a direction that would eventually lead him to make a significant contribution to the study of cross-cultural trade. A decade after serving in the US navy near the end of World War II, he published an article on "Religious Belief and Economic Behavior in a Central Javanese Town" in a new journal, *Economic Development and Cultural Change*, in 1956. Highly influenced by Weber's sociology of religions and eager to contribute to the postwar commentary on the problem of "economic development in the so-called 'underdeveloped' countries," Geertz described how—after the departure of the Dutch colonists—the inhabitants of a small town in Java, "shaken by the depression and shattered by the war and revolution," approached various economic fields according to their religious orientations. Most of the population identified as Muslim, but they approached Islam in radically different ways, depending on whether they belonged to the reformist camp, intent on establishing orthodoxy, or the traditional Javanese side, where Brahman-Buddhist elements mixed with Muslim ones. Their differing religious outlooks had an effect, according to Geertz, on their professional occupations and

---

[30] Braudel, *Civilization and Capitalism*, 2: 160, 165–167.

on their attitude toward commerce and industrialization. It may also have affected in some ways their relationship with the local Chinese shopkeepers, who imported foreign commodities and dominated, despite their small number, the town's commercial connection to the outside world. Yet in this article, as in the book that would present the subject in a more conclusive form, Geertz showed relatively little interest in the intricacies of Muslim-Chinese or, for that matter, Muslim-Hindu trade.[31]

In *Peddlers and Princes*, published in 1963, we do hear about tense negotiations over profit margin between a Chinese shopkeeper and the Muslim owners of a hat-making factory—merchants who were no less pious than entrepreneurial. However, instead of emphasizing the economic institutions that brought together members of different religious groups, Geertz focused in this book on religious and cultural divisions. He described the Muslim reformers as possessing a piety that placed them in "moral tension with society." Like Weber's Calvinists, they had a particular way of approaching religion and economy. Bent on "purifying" Indonesian Islam, they also displayed "the typically 'Protestant' virtues of industry, frugality, independence and determination in almost excessive abundance." They lived in relative isolation when they moved to a new location. To illustrate, Geertz tells us about the entry of a "piously Islamic, market-born-and-bred group of adroit traders" into a Balinese town dominated by an entrenched Hindu hierarchy. These Muslims, who saw the Hindus as "pork-eating infidels," settled down "segregated in a mosque-centered" neighborhood, behind the Chinese shops, where they "became the butchers, furniture-makers, tailors, shoemakers, restaurant-keepers, cloth merchants, tobacco-traders and vegetable-sellers."[32]

Like Weber, Geertz endeavored to place each social group in a separate compartment, with its own religious ethic and economic spirit. He knew, of course, that in practice there existed an abundance of compromises—exceptions to every rule. But it is, he wrote, "as Max Weber once remarked, only because things are so very confused in practice that we must make our distinctions clear in theory."[33] Geertz also worked, like Katz, with the legacy of the Holocaust on his mind. This event led him to emphasize the potential tension between religious minorities and host societies. Reflecting on the obstacles toward economic development faced by a Javanese town populated mostly by Muslims, the anthropologist referred to the "Chinese question." The Chinese, many of them born in foreign lands, were loyal to Peking, and

---

[31] Clifford Geertz, "Religious Belief and Economic Behavior in a Central Javanese Town: Some Preliminary Observations," *Economic Development and Cultural Change*, 2 (1956): 134–158.

[32] Clifford Geertz, *Peddlers and Princes: Social Development and Economic Change in Two Indonesian Towns* (Chicago: University of Chicago Press, 1963), 26, 28, 49, 65, 127.

[33] Geertz, "Religious Belief and Economic Behavior," 157.

were relatively successful economically. As a result, the Javanese suspected, resented, and even hated them. "But short of a total solution through voluntary emigration, which seems rather unlikely, or some variant of Hitler's treatment of Germany's Jews, which would totally corrupt the moral foundations of Indonesian culture," a rapprochement between Muslim and Chinese was necessary, if not inevitable.[34] What is remarkable about this passage is the fact that Geertz himself raised the specter of the Holocaust, despite the fact that he viewed the event as extraneous and irrelevant.

In the late 1970s, Geertz returned to the intersection of religion and economy in a long essay titled "Suq: The Bazaar Economy in Sefrou." A small city in Morocco, Sefrou resembled Modjokuto (the pseudonymous name that Geertz gave to his Javanese town) in many respects. Instead of Dutch, it had remnants of French colonialism: "machine-driven olive-oil" factories, stores with glass fronts displaying "plumbing fixtures" and bicycles, a bank, a pharmacy—all of them "poor fragments of European capitalism" that constituted "commercial modernity" as it existed in Sefrou.[35] And this predominantly Muslim town had—instead of a Chinese minority—a Jewish minority actively engaged in trade. Geertz focused on the bazaar as an economic institution where "information is poor, scarce, maldistributed, inefficiently communicated, and intensely valued." Bargaining in this space, where a buyer has little or no knowledge of production costs and a seller has a limited grasp of market prices, rests "on a personal confrontation between intimate antagonists."[36] In the haggling over prices, did tensions between Jews and Muslims, who occasionally regretted "one another's existence," flare up? They did not, Geertz argued. Here he adopted a very different perspective on cross-cultural trade from the one he had advanced in the 1950s and early 1960s. Jewish institutions in the bazaar were in "sharp contrast" to Muslim ones, but Jews and Muslims mixed in this space "under uniform ground rules," for a "cash nexus" made them "indifferent to religious status." For the Muslim customer, the Jew in the bazaar was, first and foremost, a "cloth seller, peddler, shopkeeper, shoemaker, and porter," and he was dealt with accordingly.[37]

Why did Jews in Sefrou fare so much better than the Chinese in Modjokuto? Geertz does not pose this question himself. But he explains that the Jews did not play a "privileged role" in this Moroccan bazaar. (The Chinese in Java, by contrast, had an enviable commercial advantage.) At the same time, despite or because

---

[34] Geertz, *Peddlers and Princes*, 76–78.

[35] Clifford Geertz, "Suq: The Bazaar Economy in Sefrou," in Clifford Geertz, Hildred Geertz, and Lawrence Rosen, with a photographic essay by Paul Hyman, *Meaning and Order in Moroccan Society: Three Essays in Cultural Analysis* (Cambridge: Cambridge University Press, 1979), 123–313, 128–129.

[36] Clifford Geertz, "The Bazaar Economy: Information and Search in Peasant Marketing," *American Economic Review*, 68.2 (1978): 28–32.

[37] Geertz, "Suq," 143, 165.

of their marginal status, the Jews of Sefrou occupied a key niche as middlemen in a rural trading network that linked competing Arab and Berber zones.[38] Also missing from Sefrou is the kind of fundamentalist zealotry that could translate into social segregation in the marketplace. Moroccan society, Geertz remarks tellingly, "copes with diversity by distinguishing with elaborate precision the contexts (marriage, diet, worship, education) within which men are separated by their dissimilitudes and those (work, friendship, politics, trade) where, however warily and however conditionally, men are connected by their differences."[39] The critical issue here is not any contrast between Modjokuto and Sefrou or, more broadly, between Indonesia and the Middle East. What we sense, rather, is a significant change in Geertz's own treatment of religious and ethnic diversity in the context of economic exchange.

This change reflects broader trends in academia. Sustained scholarly interest in cross-cultural trade dates from the last few decades of the twentieth century, stimulated by a confluence of factors: first, the heightened pace of global trade, with an increase in the movement of goods and peoples across national borders; second, a deepening political commitment to multiculturalism—that is, a growing recognition by public intellectuals of the need to deal with sensitivity, abroad and at home, with people who identify as belonging to different cultures; third, the growing influence of evangelical, revivalist, and fundamentalist movements.

Philip Curtin's comparative work on cross-cultural commerce, published in the 1980s but based largely on secondary sources from the 1970s, reflects this rising interest in researching religion, as well as trade, on a global scale. Religion indeed appears prominently in this book—usually as a barrier that divides cultures. It forms one of several barriers; language, kinship, economic niche or lifestyle, tribe, and nation also work to separate communities—often in a physical sense, for the trade diasporas on which the book concentrates typically operated, as politically disengaged communities, at a distance from their host societies. Yet religion affected trade on a number of levels. It had an impact in the first place on attitudes toward commerce and the acquisition of property. Thus, for example, Curtin refers to the Ibāḍī Muslims who settled down in the Mzab valley of Algeria as a community that "was governed by a puritanical code of conduct that proscribed not only drinking, but also smoking, music, dancing, levity in general, and any kind of conspicuous consumption." This puritanism—an austere approach to consumption, coupled with a powerful sense of "internal solidarity" that led to the exclusion of strangers from the

---

[38] Geertz, "Suq," 169–170.
[39] Geertz, "Suq," 141.

community—helped Ibāḍī trade diasporas to succeed commercially outside their homeland in southern Algeria.[40]

Exclusivist tendencies by religious communities had a profound effect on long-distance commerce as well. As an example, Curtin refers to Portugal's role in maritime trade. The Portuguese began the voyages of navigation along the coast of Africa in the fifteenth century. The crusading Order of Christ under the administration of Prince Henry of Portugal financed "all kinds of commercial ventures, including privateering, surely one of the most coercive forms of private enterprise." Portuguese merchants continued exploring eastward, and by the sixteenth century they began playing a key role in the Indian Ocean spice trade. Many different communities lived and traded in this region. Muslim ones, who had dominated before the Portuguese incursions, "rarely tried to interfere with trade by other religious communities." Had they chosen to follow this pattern, the Portuguese might "have joined in free competition with existing traders." Instead, they approached religion and trade in a more combative way. Their management of the pepper trade serves as a good example. Hindus produced the spice, and typically sold it to Nestorian traders, who transported it to the coast. But the Portuguese refused to buy the pepper directly from Christians who would not profess Catholicism; they preferred to engage Muslim traders instead, as middlemen. By the seventeenth century, the Portuguese approach to trading was so militarized that it provoked "an ideological shift in local Muslim thought," with the result that in some regions Muslims began to call for a holy struggle against the infidels from Europe.[41]

But divisions along confessional lines did not remain static. The lines between religions shifted as a consequence of long-distance trade, for some merchants sought not merely "to protect their cultural integrity" but also to "convert their hosts." Curtin attributes to "commercial missionaries" large-scale conversions in Southeast Asia first to Hinduism and then to Islam. Such agents operated as "cross-cultural

---

[40] Curtin, *Cross-Cultural Trade*, 49–51. On trade diasporas, see also the influential article by Abner Cohen, "Cultural Strategies in the Organization of Trading Diasporas," in *The Development of Indigenous Trade and Markets in West Africa*, ed. Claude Meillassoux (London: Oxford University Press for the International African Seminar, 1971), 266–281. For a criticism of Curtin's view that trade "diasporas" were politically disengaged from their host societies, see Sanjay Subrahmanyam, "Iranians Abroad: Intra-Asian Elite Migration and Early Modern State Formation," *Journal of Asian Studies*, 51.2 (1992): 240–363. On South Asian and Indian Ocean trade diasporas, see also André Wink, *Al-Hind: The Making of the Indo-Islamic World, vol. 1: Early Medieval India and the Expansion of Islam, 7th–11th Centuries* (Leiden: E. J. Brill, 2002), chap. 3; and Claude Markovits, "Ethnicity, Locality and Circulation in Two Diasporic Merchant Networks from South Asia," in *The South Asian Diaspora: Transnational Networks and Changing Identities*, ed. Rajesh Rai and Peter Reeves (New York: Routledge, 2009), 15–27. For a critique of the "unitary notion" of a trade diaspora, see Claude Markovits, *The Global World of Indian Merchants, 1750–1947: Traders of Sind from Bukhara to Panama* (Cambridge: Cambridge University Press, 2000), 4–5 and 20–24.

[41] Curtin, *Cross-Cultural Trade*, 137–139, 147.

brokers."[42] The religious conversions that they brought about did not make all cultural divisions vanish, but they significantly lowered cultural barriers, and facilitated trade. Their story is, of course, part of a grand historical narrative about the spread of "world religions" through long-distance trade.[43]

When William McNeill reviewed *Cross-Cultural Trade in World History*, he remarked that Curtin made "far too little of China's pre-eminence in commerce between about 1000 and 1450 A.D." A couple of years before the appearance of Curtin's book, McNeill himself published a book, *The Pursuit of Power*, that highlighted China's significant influence on the Old World's economy before the emergence of Europe as the predominant power. Under the Song and Yuan dynasties, he argued, vigorous markets and trading networks served to diffuse technological innovations throughout Eurasia, stimulating economic growth.[44] In the 1990s, Janet Abu-Lughod's *Before European Hegemony* and Stephen Dale's *Indian Merchants and the Eurasian Trade* would make seminal contributions to the field by highlighting the commercial dynamism of a "world system" or "world economy" that did not center on Europe's expansion.[45] Along these lines, too, Kenneth Pomeranz in *The Great Divergence* and Andre Gunder Frank in *ReOrient* would argue that Asians— the Chinese in particular—continued to dominate the world economy until around 1800.[46] Influenced by Curtin, these historians developed world-historical narratives that displaced Europe from its pedestal.

Now, Curtin assumed that trade between members of different religions constituted, by definition, a cross-cultural exchange. But religious and cultural boundaries cannot be drawn so neatly on maps, as if they were national borders; they are constructs. Commerce between, say, a Catholic from Venice and a Muslim from

---

[42] Curtin, *Cross-Cultural Trade*, 12, 103.

[43] For a few examples of this process in diverse historical contexts, see Bruce G. Trigger, "The French Presence in Huronia: The Structure of Franco-Huron Relations in the First Half of the Seventeenth Century," *Canadian Historical Review*, 49 (1968): 107–141; Charles Holcombe, "Trade-Buddhism: Maritime Trade, Immigration, and the Buddhist Landfall in Early Japan," *Journal of the American Oriental Society*, 119.2 (1999): 280–292; Stephen F. Dale, "Trade, Conversion and the Growth of the Islamic Community of Kerala, South India," *Studia Islamica*, 71 (1990): 155–175; Michael Brett, "Islam and Trade in the *Bilād al-Sūdān*, Tenth-Eleventh Century A.D.," *Journal of African History*, 24.4 (1983): 431–440.

[44] William McNeill, Review of Curtin's *Cross-Cultural Trade in World History* in *Canadian Journal of History* (1985): 251–253; William H. McNeill, *The Pursuit of Power: Technology, Armed Force, and Society since A.D. 1000* (Chicago: University of Chicago Press, 1982), 24–62.

[45] Janet L. Abu-Lughod, *Before European Hegemony: The World System A.D. 1250–1350* (New York: Oxford University Press, 1989); Stephen Frederic Dale, *Indian Merchants and the Eurasian Trade, 1600–1750* (Cambridge: Cambridge University Press, 1994).

[46] Kenneth Pomeranz, *The Great Divergence: China, Europe, and the Making of the Modern World Economy* (Princeton, NJ: Princeton University Press, 2000); Andre Gunder Frank, *ReOrient: Global Economy in the Asian Age* (Berkeley: University of California Press, 1998), 52–53.

Istanbul arguably takes place within a shared Mediterranean culture. During the act of exchange the two merchants might well dwell on similarities rather than differences, and easily recognize that they jointly form part of a common business culture—with its own conventions, gestures, and jargon. In conducting their commercial transaction, they might not see themselves as representatives of Islam or Christianity, nor as ambassadors for the Republic of Venice or the Ottoman Empire, but simply as merchants acting independently for their own self-interest. Although they may well be aware of the fact that one is a Muslim and the other a Christian, they might well regard religion as impertinent to the exchange.

The key is not to assume that religion always mattered, but rather to investigate its significance in relation to cross-cultural trade. In certain historical circumstances, as Molly Greene has shown in *Catholic Pirates and Greek Merchants*, traders indeed assigned great importance to their religious identity. They did so, as subjects of multi-confessional states or empires, to claim certain legal prerogatives or gain commercial advantages.[47] Yet in other historical circumstances, religious affiliation played a far less critical role. In his history of dispersed networks of merchants from Sind, Claude Markovits showed that Hindus and Muslims in this northwestern province of South Asia did not form homogeneous groups, and he suggested that their religious practices are best characterized as eclectic. As a source of communal solidarity, religious identity mattered far less to Sindi traders than a historical relation to a particular town in the homeland.[48]

Perhaps Curtin dealt with the problem of religious and cultural identity superficially because he focused on making a contribution to comparative and world history—not to religious studies or cultural anthropology. But this distinction does raise a question about disciplinary boundaries in the study of a subject that beckons more than one discipline. It is, in fact, exceedingly rare to find any scholar working on religion and cross-cultural trade adopting a transdisciplinary perspective. Geertz constitutes the notable exception. Coming early to this line of work, he sought to make a contribution, as an anthropologist, to economics. Economists contributing to development studies elaborated theories about a nation as a whole on the basis of aggregate economic data. Anthropologists, by contrast, delved into a particular social context without thinking much about the world economy at large. Geertz endeavored to bridge the two disciplines, by reflecting comparatively on the broader economic effects of distinct religious and social systems.[49] His expansive framework

---

[47] Molly Greene, *Catholic Pirates and Greek Merchants: A Maritime History of the Early Modern Mediterranean* (Princeton, NJ: Princeton University Press, 2010), 18, 157, 178–179, 188, 197.

[48] Markovits, *Global World of Indian Merchants*, 6, 26–27, 49, 250–252.

[49] Geertz, *Peddlers and Princes*, 4–5.

leads us toward some other disciplines that can be summoned to the junction of religion and cross-cultural trade.

ECONOMIC STEREOTYPING, SOCIOLOGICAL PSYCHOLOGIZING

Economists discovered religion three decades ago; and thus far they have written relatively little about religion in relation to foreign exchange. They have focused instead on Weberian concerns about religious approaches to the pursuit of profit. In a survey of the literature published in the late 1990s, Laurence R. Iannaccone remarked, contra Weber: "People's religious affiliation or degree of religiosity seems not to influence their attitudes concerning capitalism, socialism, income redistribution, private property, free trade, and government regulation." In every tradition or denomination "one finds a bewildering variety of economic statements." There exists "enough ambiguity" in the sacred literature, he concludes, "to justify any number of economic positions."[50]

Despite this sensible warning against religious stereotyping, the economics of religion, a booming field, has established as one of its central concerns the comparative analysis of world religions in relation to capitalism.[51] Economists and sociologists have begun to examine statistically the possible effects of religious affiliation and piety (measured by such factors as rate of church attendance and prevalence of a belief in hell) on attitudes toward external commerce and the market economy. Indulging in generalizations, three of these authors conclude: "On average, Christian religions are more positively associated with attitudes that are conducive to economic growth, while Islam is negatively associated."[52] But the statistical analysis undertaken does not really establish any causal connection between religion and economic performance; it merely suggests correlations that confirm, in this case, popular prejudices.

As a fine example of an economist's approach to the nexus of religion and trade, Avner Greif's *Institutions and the Path to the Modern Economy* deserves special attention. Although published in 2006, this book belongs intellectually to the late

---

[50] Laurence R. Iannaccone, "Introduction to the Economics of Religion," *Journal of Economic Literature*, 36 (1998): 1465–1496, 1477–1478.

[51] For a sense of developments in the field, see Rachel M. McCleary, ed., *The Oxford Handbook of the Economics of Religion* (Oxford: Oxford University Press, 2011).

[52] Luigi Guiso, Paola Sapienza, and Luigi Zingales, "People's Opium? Religion and Economic Attitudes," *Journal of Monetary Economics*, 50.1 (2003): 225–282, 280. Also see Joseph P. Daniels and Marc von der Ruhr, "God and the Global Economy: Religion and Attitudes towards Trade and Immigration in the United States," *Socio-Economic Review*, 3 (2005): 467–489; Robert J. Barro and Rachel M. McCleary, "Religion and Economic Growth across Countries," *American Sociological Review*, 68 (2003): 760–781.

1980s and early 1990s, when Greif, a new institutional economist, began to analyze coalitions of medieval traders. The book's complex disquisitions on game theory and institutional change need not detain us. More relevant for our purposes are the empirical case studies, where Greif compares Maghribi and Genoese institutions—that is, systems of "rules, norms and organizations that together generate a regularity of (social) behavior."[53] Agreeing with Robert Lopez's exaggerated view of the historical role of long-distance trade, Greif argues that Europe grew into an economic powerhouse as "the commercial center of gravity" shifted from the southern to the northern shores of the Mediterranean Sea. This shift happened, Greif suggests, thanks to institutions that favored "anonymous exchange" and facilitated economic growth.[54]

Juxtaposing eleventh-century Maghribis and twelfth-century Genoese, Greif analyzes trade in a comparative framework. Critical to the contrast that Greif draws is the notion that Maghribi and Genoese traders belonged to societies with different "cultural beliefs." The Maghribis came from a "collectivist" society, the Genoese from an "individualist" one. As a result, they developed different institutions to enforce contracts, establish commercial agency, and distribute wealth—institutions that had, in turn, profound implications for economic development. On this basis, Greif compares individualistic and collectivist strategies, advancing hypothetical scenarios based on game theory to explain, in the end, the rise of the West.[55] What allows Greif to draw a contrast between individualist and collectivist trajectories is a mode of interpretation that he calls "cultural analysis," though it may be better to characterize it as cultural typologizing.[56]

Works on international business and cross-cultural marketing basically favor the same form of typological analysis, yet as part of a more comprehensive framework. Expanding on four categories originally proposed in 1980 by Geert Hofstede, a comparative organizational sociologist and international business psychologist who analyzed a vast database of surveys of the IBM Corporation's international employees, they rank national cultures according to five or six "dimensions." These are, first, the individualism/collectivism index (IDV), which refers to the capitalistic values and behavior that promote personal as opposed to communal interest; second, a masculinity/femininity index, which measures assertiveness; third, an uncertainty avoidance index, which focuses on the willingness to take risks, trust strangers, and adopt

[53] Avner Greif, *Institutions and the Path to the Modern Economy: Lessons from Medieval Trade* (Cambridge: Cambridge University Press, 2006), 30.

[54] Greif, *Institutions*, 24 and 301.

[55] Greif, *Institutions*, 269–276 and 300–301.

[56] Greif, *Institutions*, 21, 358.

innovations; fourth, a power distance index, which compares hierarchical and egali-
tarian impulses; fifth, a long-term orientation index, which measures the extent to
which the members of a society focus on future goals; and, finally, the indulgence/
self-restraint index, which incorporates analysis based on the World Values Survey
to distinguish national cultures from each other. Although international marketing scholars apply all of these indexes in their research on the diffusion of products across national boundaries, they tend to find the first one particularly useful.
Developed countries, such as Australia, the United States, and Great Britain, earn
a high mark on the IDV; unsurprisingly, developing countries, such as Guatemala,
Indonesia, and Pakistan, attain a low grade on the same test.[57] Hofstede knew, of
course, that many of his international subjects did not themselves identify according to these values: male employees appear "feminine" in their consumer behavior when, for example, they read fiction passionately and find foreign commodities
relatively unappealing. Focusing on "invisible" values that "become evident in
behavior," the social psychologist's main goal was to identify "invisible cultural
differences" that affect international business.[58] Based on coarse generalizations of
questionable validity, the entire scheme comes closer to cultural stereotyping than
to cultural analysis. Despite the abiding popularity of Hofstede's model in certain
circles, his essentialist notions easily come apart under methodological scrutiny.[59]

While making use of the individualism/collectivism framework, Greif does not
cite Hofstede's work directly; he rather refers to the work of other scholars who
drew inspiration from Hofstede.[60] When Greif tries to prove or illustrate the collectivist mentality of the Maghribis (Jewish traders from the eleventh century), he
adduces a Muslim duty to command right and forbid wrong. The Maghribi Jews, he
argues, belonged to the same *umma* (community or nation) as the Muslims; they

---

[57] Thus, for instance, with reference to Geert H. Hofstede's *Culture's Consequences: Comparing Values, Behaviors, Institutions and Organizations across Nations*, 2nd ed. (Thousand Oaks, CA: Sage Publications, 2001), see Philip R. Cateora and John L. Graham, *International Marketing*, 12th ed. (Boston: McGraw-Hill/Irwin, 2005), 104–106. Also see Marieke de Mooij, *Global Marketing and Advertising: Understanding Cultural Paradoxes* (Thousand Oaks, CA: Sage Publications, 1998), 72–88; Sean Dwyer, Hani Mesak, and Maxwell Hsu, "An Exploratory Examination of the Influence of National Culture on Cross-National Product Diffusion," *Journal of International Marketing*, 13.2 (2005): 1–28. In 1980, Hofstede envisioned only four dimensions; he later incorporated into his scheme a fifth dimension, long-term orientation, proposed by Michael H. Bond and his team. Eventually, by 2010, Hofstede incorporated a sixth dimension, on which see Geert Hofstede, Gert Jan Hofstede, and Michael Minkov, *Cultures and Organizations: Software of the Mind; Intercultural Cooperation and Its Importance for Survival* (New York: McGraw-Hill, 2010), 44–45.

[58] Hofstede, *Culture's Consequences*, xv, 10, 312.

[59] See Brendan McSweeney, "Hofstede's Model of National Cultural Differences and Their Consequences: A Triumph of Faith—A Failure of Analysis," *Human Relations*, 55.1 (2002): 89–118.

[60] See Greif, *Institutions*, 269. Among the works influenced by Hofstede and cited by Greif is Harry C. Triandis's *Individualism and Collectivism* (Boulder, CO: Westview Press, 1995).

therefore shared with them the moral value to decry wrongdoing.[61] Unfortunately, nowhere does Greif show that eleventh-century Jews from North Africa actually saw themselves as belonging, together with Muslims, to one *umma*. Nor does he cite any historical evidence to demonstrate that they adopted the duty to prohibit wrong. Muslim jurists actually held that this duty is incumbent on Muslims alone, not on unbelievers. Even if evidence can be located to show that Jews forbade wrong, like Muslims, Greif's proposition that the duty in question reflects collectivism is debatable. One could easily argue that it rather reflects an individualist ethic—contrived by individuals who saw themselves as empowered on account of their knowledge to act, at great personal risk, as a vigilante police force.[62] But the most glaring problem with Greif's abstractions is the failure to show that the duty to command right and forbid wrong affected in even the slightest way the economic behavior of Jewish traders.

Such casual use and abuse of evidence in order to support an economic model points to the tension, which runs through Greif's work, between an empirical and a theoretical approach to the problem at hand. It also points to the wide gap between institutional economics (represented by Greif) and cultural anthropology (represented by Geertz). Anticipating Greif, Geertz had analyzed religious attitudes toward trade in a comparative framework, in *Peddlers and Princes*, and he had approached the bazaar as an economic institution, in "Suq." Moreover, in these publications he focused on the questions at the heart of Greif's work: how religious beliefs relate to trade and how different cultural institutions might lead, or not lead, to economic growth. Given these contributions by Geertz, and given Greif's professed interest in cultural analysis, one would expect Greif's work to build on Geertz's. But nowhere in his long bibliography does Greif cite Geertz. Much less does he show any inclination toward a thick description of cultural beliefs in relation to commercial behavior.

Greif does not tell us what might have happened, around 1100, when a collectivist from North Africa and an individualist from Genoa met each other, somewhere in the Mediterranean, so as to trade. He deals with each group, the Maghribi Jews and the Genoese Christians, as if they existed in separate worlds. But around the

---

[61] Greif, *Institutions*, 279.

[62] Indeed, a major point of debate in Muslim theology and law is the nature of the duty to forbid wrong. Michael Cook's monograph *Commanding Right and Forbidding Wrong in Islamic Thought* (Cambridge: Cambridge University Press, 2000) even includes an entry in the index (672–673) subtitled: "Is the obligation individual or collective?" On pages 570–573, Cook discusses Jewish parallels that Greif might have cited to make a proper case for the existence of an analogous "cultural value" among Jews living in the Muslim world. In *Forbidding Wrong in Islam: An Introduction* (Cambridge: Cambridge University Press, 2003), 13, Cook clarifies that, according to Muslim scholars, "[f]orbidding wrong is a duty of Muslims, not of unbelievers."

time that Greif began working on these subjects, in the late 1980s, anthropologists and historians keen on cultural analysis, informed by Geertz and by Curtin, set out to understand dynamically the very act of exchange. Instead of assuming that cultural differences would determine economic behavior, they showed how trade itself worked as an acculturating force.

However intriguing methodologically, formalist social scientific approaches to cross-cultural trade claim but never really prove that "invisible" cultural orientations affect economic behavior. To label a nation, a religious community, or an organization "individualist" or "collectivist" is simply to indulge in generalizations and abstractions—and for no other reason than to explain, on the basis of a circular logic, why individuals in economically developed countries produced, adopted, and diffused most technological innovations, while collectivities in the remaining countries remained, well, underdeveloped.

New institutional economists have much to learn from cultural historians and economic anthropologists, who have studied how members of different religious communities themselves relate to exchanges with strangers. Instead of beginning analysis with broad, external categories based on such ill-defined and multivalent words as "religion" and "culture" or on qualities such as "collectivist" and "individualist," the challenge is to figure out how religious leaders and critics—the historical actors who tried to define what it meant to belong to an imagined community— construed foreign commerce in accordance with their own cultural systems. With their overly theoretical classifications, economists have not yet contributed much to our understanding of the historical dynamics of cross-cultural or cross-religious trade. Historians and anthropologists therefore have a unique opportunity to elucidate processes that should be of special interest to economists. We can accomplish this by analyzing the historical circumstances, the spatial contexts, and the commercial goods that compelled strangers trading with one another to reflect on cultural or religious differences.

ENTANGLEMENTS IN THE MIDDLE GROUND

Richard White's *The Middle Ground* and Nicholas Thomas's *Entangled Objects* are perhaps the best antidotes to the formalist typological analysis favored by some new institutional economists, cross-cultural psychologists, and international business sociologists. In his classic study of European relations with Native Americans, published in the early 1990s, Richard White calls the place where cross-cultural trade occurred "the middle ground." Here, on account of trade, "the boundaries of the Algonquian and French worlds melted at the edges and merged. Although identifiable Frenchmen and identifiable Indians obviously continued to exist," he continues, "whether a particular practice or way of doing things was French or Indian was, after a time, not so clear."[63] Examining the fur trade around the Great Lakes, White suggests how, in some respects, the Algonquian economic approach differed from the French one. Construing trade as an exchange of gifts, the Algonquian goal "was not necessarily profit" but rather the mutual satisfaction of needs. The ideal transaction would not take place between strangers, by Algonquian standards, but rather would engage buyer and seller in a social relationship, as allies or friends.[64] On this basis, an economist might be tempted to reduce the Algonquian approach to collectivism and the French approach to self-interested individualism. But White warns against such reductionism. When Frenchmen and Algonquians met to trade in the middle ground, they negotiated cultural differences; and they entered into muddy compromises that make economic models of cultural differences seem far too neat.

Nicholas Thomas came to similar conclusions in *Entangled Objects*, an anthropological account of European-native exchange in the Pacific, also published in the early 1990s. "The character of early contact," he writes, "was often such that foreigners were in no position to enforce their demands." Consequently, they often agreed to follow "local terms of trade." Natives, he shows, did not become hopelessly obsessed with the acquisition of European goods. Much like the Europeans, they calculated carefully the benefits and disadvantages of exchange. At times they flatly refused to trade, causing great consternation to the foreigners. When they did purchase European objects, they appropriated them for their own purposes, and they gave these objects symbolic meanings that derived from their experiences with cross-cultural contact. The trade that took place with the advance of colonialist explorations produced a cultural entanglement that affected one as well as the other side.[65]

In scholarship on interfaith commerce or cross-cultural trade from the 1950s to the 1980s, scholars from Katz to Curtin generally assumed that hard and fast boundaries divided confessional groups. Social exchange facilitated by trade might lead to conversions but not to heterodoxy and hybridity. By the 1990s, however, multiculturalism and postmodernism made it appealing for historians to challenge the construction of religious boundaries and, in this spirit, to regard cross-cultural trade as a mechanism for breaking down those boundaries. Religious intolerance, they held, did not reign everywhere in the late medieval and early modern periods. In the East, Mongol emperors asked Christian, Muslim, Buddhist, and Taoist figures to

---

[63] Richard White, *The Middle Ground: Indians, Empires, and Republics in the Great Lakes Region, 1650–1815*, Twentieth Anniversary Edition (Cambridge: Cambridge University Press, 2011), 50.

[64] White, *The Middle Ground*, 97–98.

[65] Thomas, *Entangled Objects*, 83–124; the quotation is from page 84.

pray for them; and they endowed temples ecumenically. They imposed few restrictions on customs and rites, according to Richard Foltz's *Religions of the Silk Road*, allowing much freedom of worship.[66] In the West, as Stuart Schwartz shows in his book *All Can Be Saved*, Portuguese traders in Brazil sometimes crossed to the other side. As sojourners entering "a cultural middle ground" where the Catholic Church had little sway, they developed hybrid practices that signify, more than tolerance for Amerindian culture, a religious wanderlust: a desire to step outside one's own parochial faith.[67]

TRUSTED CONJUNCTIONS, VIOLENT CONJUNCTURES

Whereas White and Thomas reflected on the risks and rewards that natives appreciated when they embarked on commerce with foreigners, Braudel emphasized, as we have seen, the benefits that Jews and Armenians enjoyed by trading with fellow believers in foreign lands. The early modern period is of critical importance, as Braudel and other economic historians have shown, for understanding the rise of new institutions that facilitated the mobility of capital among strangers. The Dutch and English East India Companies, for example, were established as joint-stock companies: individual investors purchased transferable shares to fund multiple overseas ventures. Through such ventures, shareholders were able to divide high protection costs and take calculated risks. The loss of one ship's cargo as a result of piracy or shipwreck would not bring the entire enterprise to bankruptcy. Business would continue as well upon the death of a partner, whose shares could simply be sold to new investors. These companies represent, then, a movement toward a complex system of impersonal exchange, which economists view as critical for modern economic development.[68]

Yet in *The Familiarity of Strangers*, Francesca Trivellato has challenged an aspect of the Braudelian framework. She has called into question the commercial advantages of blood ties and religious or cultural propinquity. She has shown how Sephardic Jews from the Tuscan port of Livorno, Italian Catholics based in Lisbon, and Hindus from Goa established overlapping networks devoted to the trade in coral and diamonds. These "networks of trust," she concludes, "were not amorphous, boundless, and spontaneous, but inscribed in social norms, legal customs, and rules

---

[66] Foltz, *Religions of the Silk Road*, 113.

[67] Schwartz, *All Can Be Saved*, 186–187.

[68] Braudel, *Civilization and Capitalism*, 2: 443–455. See also Larry Neal, *The Rise of Financial Capitalism: International Capital Markets in the Age of Reason* (Cambridge: Cambridge University Press, 1990); Douglass C. North, "Institutions," *Journal of Economic Perspectives*, 5.1 (1991): 97–112.

for communication that gave them stability. Rather than hindering cross-cultural trade, the preservation of group boundaries could ease trade between strangers insofar as it enforced intragroup expectations and gave substance to the language of obligations."[69] State institutions granted foreign minorities protection and access to markets, while internal cohesion gave each community representing a link in the chain of networks the means to censor or punish individual misconduct.

The evidence that Trivellato advances stems from the first half of the eighteenth century; and it is not yet evident whether the cross-cultural trading networks that she describes are anomalous or representative.[70] Yet it is already clear that a vast market could grow by this mechanism, as one network would link to another. Even in situations where a single religious or ethnic group controlled a trading network, it engaged in different places with outside groups. The merchants dealing with external trade would, at the edges, seek stable collaborations with outsiders—not with wanderers and vagrants, at risk of flight, but with well-connected persons who had deep ties to their own communities. Accordingly, if we conceive of long-distance trading networks mathematically as intersecting sets, we can define the cross-cultural trader par excellence as that merchant who, as a member of two or more sets, facilitated foreign exchange.

If Trivellato's history calls attention to trusted conjunctions—to mechanisms that existed to make long-distance trade between strangers more predictable, orderly and efficient—other historians and anthropologists have brought to light violent conjunctures. This era of overseas exploration had its share of first encounters, too. People who had neither language nor religion in common, who had no history of dealing with one another, met for the first time. They communicated, with excitement and suspicion, by physical gestures. Thus Columbus and his crew, pointing to gold ornaments, could signal their desire for precious metals. But they could not easily agree on the terms of trade—much less understand fully each other's economic systems and norms of exchange. In such encounters, the potential for miscommunication and violence was high. The consequences could be tragic, as they were for the Inca warriors who met Pizarro's guns and horses in Cajamarca.

No one has elaborated a more elegant model for this form of trade, involving the crossing of a high cultural barrier, than Marshall Sahlins. First in *Historical Metaphors and Mythical Realities* and then in *Islands of History*, both published in the 1980s, Sahlins analyzed how historical actors, operating within a traditional Hawaiian

---

[69] Francesca Trivellato, *The Familiarity of Strangers: The Sephardic Diaspora, Livorno, and Cross-Cultural Trade in the Early Modern Period* (New Haven, CT: Yale University Press, 2009), 275.

[70] For methodological comparison, in a very different historical context, see Joseph P. Daniels and Marc von der Ruhr, "Trust in Others: Does Religion Matter?" *Review of Social Economy*, 68.2 (2010): 163–186.

cultural system, responded to the crisis of first contact with Europeans.[71] Native and foreigner tended to act each according to his own norms and conventions, but as the encounter itself had no precedent, each party shocked the other with strange actions. Unwittingly, mischievously, or deviously, the Europeans quickly broke Hawaiian taboos. When a chief, before whom the islanders fell prostrate, approached by canoe a European ship, the captain gave the revered native a friendly slap on the shoulder and then offered him the wondrous gift of long iron nails. Many encounters followed this first one. The most sensational involved Hawaiian women offering their bodies to the British seamen and obtaining, in exchange for love, bananas, coconuts, and pork—sacrificial foods that had been prohibited to them, but which they now consumed in the company of strange men. On the islands, ritual laws had barred them, not just from eating forbidden fruit, but also from dining with men. Hawaiian commoners began to disregard prohibitions on trade. At Kealakekua Bay in January 1779, they traded with Captain Cook, at his urging. A ruler from Maui was about to arrive, and local norms dictated a suspension of trading activities for the welcoming ceremony. A chief therefore tried to prevent the exchange from taking place; but the British scattered shot over his canoe, scaring him away, and the commoners resumed trading.

Sahlins shows what stresses cross-cultural trade could place on religion, undermining, in this case, an entire system of taboos. The story that he tells matters, too, because it takes place in the late eighteenth century. It should therefore serve as a warning against any attempt to write a history of cross-cultural trade that focuses on processes by which institutions became more efficient, in a prelude to capitalism. It would be a mistake to focus solely, as is common in the teleological narratives of economic historians, on the few structures, institutions, or networks that facilitated foreign trade in anticipation of capitalism or globalization. Economic and cultural arrangements in early modern times were extremely varied. Despite the fact that, by 1800, we can already speak of capital markets, joint-stock companies, or long-distance networks enabling peaceful commerce in certain parts of the world, trade between strangers—people who had little familiarity with the other's cultural system—remained a dangerous affair.

[71] Marshall David Sahlins, *Historical Metaphors and Mythical Realities: Structure in the Early History of the Sandwich Islands Kingdom* (Ann Arbor: University of Michigan Press, 1981); Sahlins, *Islands of History* (Chicago: University of Chicago Press, 1985).

MOORING OUR SPATIAL IMAGINATION

White's metaphor of the "middle ground," together with Polanyi's concept of the "port of trade," invites us to envision cross-cultural trade occurring in specific locations or meaningful spaces. Indeed, as William Jordan argued in the 1970s, cross-cultural exchange "cannot be understood apart from its spatial context." In a suggestive article, "Jews on Top," Jordan examined the social and psychological dynamics in play when Christians borrowed money from Jews in thirteenth-century France. Analyzing court records statistically, he argued that many of the borrowers were women taking modest loans. To obtain the principal, they needed to visit Jewish micro-financiers in their own homes. (A similar provision existed to regulate the sale of meat, which Christians could buy from Jewish butchers in the Jewish part of town, "but not in Christian markets.") Entering Jewish domestic space meant, for the Christian women as well as for the children they carried in tow, humiliation— a degrading inversion of the ideal hierarchy, which ranked Christians above Jews. The circumstances surrounding these financial transactions colored the image of the Jew as a greedy moneylender.[72]

Eager to envision things on a grand scale, world historians have tended to conceive of the Mediterranean Sea, the Atlantic Ocean, and the Indian Ocean as the settings for exchange, while world system theorists have divided the globe into vast circuits linked by trade.[73] These huge spaces may appear as natural settings for a history of maritime trade. But the exchange of property rarely took place at sea; and we must moor our spatial imagination, lost at sea, so as not to envision commerce where there was none.[74] People and goods did not move freely within these tremendous zones. As Polanyi realized long ago, trade occurred in designated, restricted areas that delimited contact between native and foreigner. At the local level, institutions existed to control social mingling between members of different religious groups. These spatial restrictions are critical to any understanding of the character of cultural contact.

In the era of the Crusades, Christian merchants trading on the southern Mediterranean coast found lodging not in Polanyi's ports of trade but in a residential institution called the *fondaco*. Under the title *Housing the Stranger in the Mediterranean World*, Olivia Remie Constable has devoted a fine book to this institution. She argues that, before the Crusades, the *funduq*, as the institution

---

[72] William Chester Jordan, "Jews on Top: Women and the Availability of Consumption Loans in Northern France in the Mid-Thirteenth Century," *Journal of Jewish Studies*, 29 (1978): 39–56.

[73] For an illustration, see the map in Abu-Lughod, *Before European Hegemony*, 34.

[74] Greene's *Catholic Pirates and Greek Merchants* succeeds precisely because it approaches the vast subject from the particular vantage point of Malta.

was known in Arabic, served as an inn or tavern that sheltered, among others, needy Muslim pilgrims and wayfarers. But in the twelfth century, as the volume of Mediterranean trade increased, *fondaci* became commercial enclaves with the specialized function of housing Christian merchants from Europe. In the bustling port of Alexandria, each foreign "nation" had its own *fondaco*. Traders from Genoa, Venice, Barcelona, and Marseille stayed with fellow citizens at separate sites. Like the port of trade, the *fondaco* imposed restrictions on foreign merchants. A curfew prevented them from carousing at night through the city—openly consuming pork and cavorting with prostitutes—to protect the Muslim city from offensive behavior. But the *fondaci*, which Constable describes as "colonies before colonialism," promoted the interests of foreigners as well. Beyond obtaining the permission to buy and sell goods, each "house" negotiated certain rights and privileges with the government. It procured, for example, the right to make use of public baths, drink wine, and attend church services. In Constable's view, the *fondaci* "represented a new venture in Muslim-Christian economic relations." In an era of war, when religious tensions were high, these institutions productively regulated cross-cultural trade, reducing the risk of violence.[75]

If *fondaci*, like ports of trade, confined external commerce, institutions also existed in pre-modern times to regulate internal commerce between members of different religions. In the Muslim world, the *ḥisba* developed to ensure moral dealings in the marketplace. The *sūq*, or marketplace, typically included a number of establishments: a butcher shop, a pharmacy, a bathhouse, a site for buying slaves and pack animals. The *muḥtasib*, the official in charge of morality in these commercial spaces, did not interfere in all things economic. Yet he served as the official protector of the Muslim community's interests. His duties included preventing foreign men from speaking in seclusion with women; visiting the butcher, to make sure that he turned toward Mecca while slaughtering animals; keeping an eye on the pharmacist, if he lacked religion, lest he deceive Muslims with secret mixtures; verifying whether local Jews and Christians entered the bathhouse wearing an iron or copper necklace that would set them apart, in the absence of clothes, from Muslims; and prohibiting the sale of Muslim slaves to non-Muslim customers. The *ḥisba* did not function like the walls of a *funduq* to segregate physically Muslims from non-Muslims. Jews, Christians, and Muslims rubbed shoulders in the urban marketplace, perhaps even

---

[75] Olivia Remie Constable, "Funduq, Fondaco and Khān in the Wake of Christian Commerce and Crusade," in *The Crusades from the Perspective of Byzantium and the Muslim World*, ed. Angeliki E. Laiou and Roy P. Mottahedeh (Washington, DC: Dumbarton Oaks Research Library and Collection, 2001), 145–156, 150; Constable, *Housing the Stranger in the Mediterranean World: Lodging, Trade, and Travel in Late Antiquity and the Middle Ages* (Cambridge: Cambridge University Press, 2003), 107–157.

in the bathhouse. But the *ḥisba* did reflect cultural norms that dictated a degree of spatial separation between members of different religions. It is a good example of an institution designed to enforce religious boundaries in commercial spaces, where the market inspector's policies depended on the kind of establishment.[76] To appreciate the social dynamics at play in cross-religious trade, we must indeed dock our maritime fantasies: rather than gaze at the sea, we should turn our attention to the taverns and slaughterhouses and other places that gave economic exchanges between members of different religions a heightened cultural significance.

DISENTANGLING COMMODITIES: THE BOUNDARIES OF A SACRED LAW

Just as it is necessary to distinguish between different kinds of spaces in order to understand better the significance of cross-cultural trade in a particular society, so, too, it is essential to discriminate, through cultural analysis, between different kinds of commodities. Economic historians enjoy listing the commercial articles that moved in long-distance commerce. They evoke images of camels or ships laden with frankincense and myrrh; flax, wool, silk, coral, glass, copper, and silver; or wine, olives, cumin, pepper, and, of course, salt. When they categorize these goods, they think about exotic luxuries and basic necessities; they contemplate which items were easy to ship, due to their light weight and small volume, and which ones served as ballast. While they consider price and utility, too, they rarely, if ever, think about the cultural or religious significance of the objects in question.

When we seek "native" responses to foreign things, we discover that many commercial articles provoked no major cultural or religious reactions. Moralists did *not* preach against them. Consumers adopted them without encountering resistance. Why should such goods be considered the objects of cross-cultural or cross-religious trade? Devoid of any profound cultural or religious significance, these goods should simply be categorized as foreign commodities. Certainly, to reach native shores, they crossed political or geographical borders, but not, in any meaningful way, cultural or religious borders.

By contrast, certain goods either caused an immediate religious reaction, or they came eventually to bear what Thomas has called, in reference to European guns in Polynesian hands, "a heavy cultural burden."[77] When moralists decried the consumption of foreign things that for one or another reason they deemed forbidden,

---

[76] Al-Shayzarī, *Nihāyat al-rutba fī ṭalab al-ḥisba (Book of the Muḥtassib)*, ed. Al-Sayyid al-ʿArīnī (Cairo: Lajnat al-Taʾlīf wa-al-Tarjama wa-al-Nashr, 1946), 12, 14, 23, 47, 84, 106.

[77] Thomas, *Entangled Objects*, 103.

offensive, or impure, we witness a deliberate attempt on their part to imagine a cultural or religious boundary. Similarly, when lawmakers enacted laws to bar coreligionists from selling to the enemy military goods, we witness their effort to protect the political interests of a religious community. In these instances, we can clearly speak of cross-cultural or cross-religious trade from an internal—as opposed to an external academic—perspective. Whether merchants failed or succeeded in selling forbidden goods, they obviously needed to cross a barrier, purposefully or unwittingly, as they faced well-known proscriptions or new, unfamiliar taboos. This barrier might be of ancient provenance; or it might be a relatively novel construction, hastily erected in response to strange goods. It might be formidable or easily trodden upon, depending on what institutions existed to ban effectively the trade in objects of controversy. Yet the key point is that the flow of goods can no longer be taken for granted. We must take into account, in such cases, religious qualms and cultural compunctions.

What commodities acted as boundary markers to divide symbolically one culture from another? There are, of course, no universal taboos. Each culture has its own standards for measuring repugnance and disgust, and these standards change over time. But certain categories of goods have appeared repeatedly in native reactions to foreign things. Nothing has elicited more criticism and revulsion than food and clothes—and they represent, more than local habits and ancestral traditions, the articles most closely associated with the human body. Households spent a large portion of their income on these items. What people wore and what they ate signified powerfully socioeconomic status, as well as personal taste and cultural identity. If flaunting foreign garments might show contempt for local ways, ingesting foreign foods could reflect a manifest disregard of purity laws. As a result, those advocating restrictions on foreign trade in pre-modern times focused extensively on protecting local populations from exposure to "impure" foods and "dangerous" clothes. In at least one curious case, these separate concerns about food and clothes converged: when Muslim jurists discussed the problem of purchasing used garments from Christians, they specifically mentioned the risk of wearing to the mosque garments potentially contaminated with pork fat.[78]

Because relatively little scholarly research exists on the traffic of goods across religious frontiers, I will draw on my expertise in the history of Islamic law to elucidate the problem. For several decades, anthropologists and historians have, of course, paid close attention to material culture and the consumption of things; and several scholars have devoted articles and books to the subject of goods crossing cultural

---

[78] Halevi, "Christian Impurity versus Economic Necessity," 928ff.

boundaries.[79] But I examine this topic through the prism of Islamic law, where the passage of goods has given rise to theological and legal questions. I should emphasize, however, that Muslim juridical impediments to cross-cultural trade were not unique. When Muslim jurists focused on the problem of ritual purity, they reasoned much like the rabbinical experts on *halakhah*, Jewish law; and when they focused on the trade in arms, they reasoned much like Christian theologians and canon lawyers.

Salvation goods represent another key category of things that could become, through commodification, objects of cross-religious trade. Now, in Max Weber's and in Pierre Bourdieu's sociological models, religions attract customers in the world market with salvation goods (*heilsgüter* or *biens de salut*), which can range from the distinction of membership in a select social club to the promise of a blessed afterlife.[80] Religious actors seldom think of religion itself as a commodity that can be purchased in the market-place. They do, however, frequently ponder the problem of buying and selling religious things; and no object stands better as an emblem for the concept of salvation goods than a holy book.

The Qur'an, at 2:79 and elsewhere, disapproves of those who sell "for a small price" the book that they marketed as coming from God although they manufactured it themselves. In evaluating the piety of the People of the Book, who received divine revelations before the Prophet Muḥammad, the Qur'an makes a distinction between those who engaged in such wretched commerce (3:187) and those who refused, out of devotion and humility, to barter with God's revealed verses (3:199). It is not clear whether these passages refer to the selling of scriptural texts in reality or metaphorically. Yet early Islamic scholars would abhor the selling of the Qur'an in its written form (*muṣḥaf*). Clever jurists, it is true, found an ingenious way to work around this pious barrier by permitting Muslims to charge fellow Muslims not for the Qur'an itself, but for the pages of the book and for the labor of the scribe. During the Arab conquests, a Christian from Al-Ḥīra, a Persian city erected on the west bank of the Euphrates, apparently copied the Qur'an for a Muslim. Charging 70 dirhams for his work, he provides us with an exquisite example of cross-religious business.[81]

---

[79] See, for example, Marcy Norton's *Sacred Gifts, Profane Pleasures: A History of Tobacco and Chocolate in the Atlantic World* (Ithaca, NY: Cornell University Press, 2008), Paul Freedman's *Out of the East: Spices and the Medieval Imagination* (New Haven, CT: Yale University Press, 2008), and Finbar B. Flood's *Objects of Translation: Material Culture and Medieval "Hindu-Muslim" Encounter* (Princeton, NJ: Princeton University Press, 2009). In a modern context, see David Howes, ed., *Cross-Cultural Consumption: Global Markets, Local Realities* (London: Routledge, 1996) and James L. Watson, ed., *Golden Arches East: McDonald's in East Asia* (Stanford, CA: Stanford University Press, 1997).

[80] See Terry Rey, "Marketing the Goods of Salvation: Bourdieu on Religion," *Religion*, 34 (2004): 331–343; and the essays in Jörg Stolz, ed., *Salvation Goods and Religious Markets: Theory and Applications* (Bern: Peter Lang, 2008).

[81] 'Abdallāh ibn Muḥammad ibn Abī Abī Shaybah, *Muṣannaf Ibn Abī Shaybah fī al-aḥādīth wa-al-āthār*,

Despite these dispensations, trading in Muslim scripture remained controversial. The jurist Ibn Ḥanbal found problematic the sale of an amulet containing Qur'anic verses to a non-Muslim.[82] Although some jurists, reasoning like missionaries, perceived a potential benefit to allowing non-Muslims to read a copy of the Qur'an, Ibn Ḥanbal worried about the possible defilement and desecration of Muslim scripture. Muslim scholars generally held that only those who have entered a state of ritual purity should be permitted to handle the holy book.[83] Beyond merely outlawing the sale of the Qur'an to non-Muslims, jurists forbade Muslims from carrying a copy of the book to enemy territory, lest it fall into "the hands of the infidel, who would treat it in a humiliating manner."[84] Evidently, then, it is a mistake to construe salvation goods as wares in a missionary peddler's cart. Believers guarded these goods with a hedge.

If Muslims made an effort to keep their own salvation goods out of the market, they also distinguished the salvation goods of others from profane commodities. According to Islamic law, Muslim troops are entitled to take all sorts of things, as booty, from the house of war. They must exercise great caution, however, when they encounter Christian books. Jurists recommended that warriors either burn these books or sell their pages individually—after blotting out the text so as to eliminate doctrinal distortions.[85] They designed this restriction to prevent the spread, by means of material objects, of divergent theological beliefs among Muslims. What also bothered them, when they reflected on Christian goods, was the prospect that Muslims might contribute materially to the worship of other gods. Associating candles with Christian devotions, including the rite of Communion, they banned the seller of spices and perfumes from manufacturing candles for Christians and in general from selling wax directly to Christians because this trade would help them to worship their own gods.[86] Jurists similarly considered reprehensible the sale of meat, spices, or clothes to Christians during their festivals, as this trade would exalt their idolatry

---

ed. Saʿīd al-Laḥḥām, 9 vols. (Beirut: Dār al-Fikr, 1989), 5: 30–32; ʿAbd al-Razzāq ibn Hammām al-Ṣanʿānī, *Al-Muṣannaf*, 2nd ed., 11 vols. (Johannesburg: Al-Majlis al-ʿIlmī, 1983), 8: 110–114.

[82] Christopher Melchert, "Aḥmad Ibn Ḥanbal and the Qur'an," *Journal of Qur'anic Studies*, 6.2 (2004): 22–34, 24.

[83] M. J. Kister, "*Lā Yamassuhu illā 'l-muṭahharūn*…Notes on the Interpretations of a Qur'ānic Phrase," *Jerusalem Studies in Arabic and Islam*, 34 (2008): 309–334.

[84] Aḥmad al-Wansharīsī, *Al-Miʿyār al-muʿrib wa-al-jāmiʿ al-mughrib ʿan fatāwā ʿulamāʾ Ifrīqiyā wa-al-Andalus wa-al-Maghrib*, 13 vols. (Rabat: Wizārat al-Awqāf wa-al-Shuʾūn al-Islāmiyya lil-Mamlaka al-Maghribiyya, 1981–1983), 2: 114–115.

[85] Halevi, "Christian Impurity versus Economic Necessity," 934.

[86] Al-Wansharīsī, *Miʿyār*, 5: 213–214. The case of a Muslim convert suspected of following a crypto-Christian cult can also serve to document this association between candles and Christian devotions. See Al-Wansharīsī, *Miʿyār*, 2: 349–350.

(*shirk*) and abet their infidelity (*kufr*).[87] These theological restrictions on economic exchange resemble the Talmudic prohibition on selling wine to idol worshippers.[88]

Like holy books and votive candles, human commodities also possessed a religious identity. When jurists considered the slave trade, they paid close attention to religion. Religious affiliation played a key role in the conditions for enslavement, the laws of possession, and the rules for ransoming captives; and it was a complex and shifting role because slaves could alter their religious, as well as in some cases their social, status through conversion. According to Islamic law, Muslims could enslave infidels captured in war; and they had the right to retain possession of these slaves even if they converted to Islam. Yet they were strictly prohibited from enslaving free Muslims as well as non-Muslims who had the right to remain free because they were either residents of a Muslim state (*dhimmis*) or protected foreign visitors (*musta'mins*). *Dhimmis* were also entitled to own slaves, but if these slaves converted to Islam, then their non-Muslim masters were obliged either to emancipate them or to transfer their ownership to Muslim masters.[89] Intriguingly, when jurists pondered the sale of copies of the Qur'an to infidels, they reflected analogically on the sale of Muslim slaves to Jewish or Christian masters. In this regard, they debated whether to revoke the sale of the books or force non-Muslim owners to sell the books—as if they were Muslim slaves—back to Muslims.[90]

The basic religious principle that non-Muslims cannot own Muslim slaves gave rise to a curious legal case. Islamic law in general protects the property of foreigners. Yet what is the legal status of Muslim runaway slaves? According to the chief justice of Granada, Ibn Sirāj (d. 1444), if Muslim captives escape from the galley of Christian merchants or corsairs, anchored at a Muslim port, there is no need "from the juridical point of view" to pay their ransom or to return them to their captors. These ships, he explains, have the same standing as Christian lands or strongholds. They cannot obtain any legal protection (*amān*) for Muslim captives, as for other goods, because it is illegal to turn free Muslims into commodities. According to most Maliki jurists, Muslims have the right to compel a ship laden with Muslim captives to release its human cargo, in exchange for its value. So when Muslims captives run away, there is no justification for returning them to the slave ship.[91]

[87] Al-Wansharīsī, *Mi'yār*, 2: 489.
[88] Haym Soloveitchik, *Yenam: Saḥar be-yenam shel goyim 'al gilgulah shel halakhah be-'olam ha-ma'aśeh* (Tel Aviv: 'Alma, 2003).
[89] Muḥammad b. Aḥmad al-Sarakhsī, *Sharḥ Kitāb al-siyar al-kabīr li-Muḥammad ibn Ḥasan al-Shaybānī*, ed. Ṣāliḥ al-Dīn al-Munajjid, 5 vols. (Cairo: Ma'had al-Makhṭūṭāt bi-Jāmi'at al-Duwal al-'Arabiyya, 1971–1972), 5: chap. 216, 2281, no. 4550.
[90] Al-Wansharīsī, *Mi'yār*, 2: 114–115.
[91] Al-Wansharīsī, *Mi'yār*, 2: 118.

Commerce and violence became intertwined in the slave trade, as in no other trade, because this form of exchange depended on raids and military campaigns. Given the fact that merchants conducted trade while soldiers waged war, medieval Muslim jurists elaborated the rules of foreign commerce not in books dedicated to the subject of sales (*al-buyū*ʿ), which by and large concerned commerce among Muslims, but in books dedicated to the laws of war.[92] In these books, they prohibited merchants from selling to the enemy certain goods: slaves, beasts of war, and weapons.[93] Viewing these trades as detrimental to the political and military interests of their own religious community, they advanced more or less the same rationale espoused by Christian canon lawyers, who similarly barred the sale of weapons to infidels.[94]

The juridical Muslim prohibition on instruments of war extended to raw materials used in the manufacture of military equipment. Accordingly, jurists placed restrictions on the export of iron, because it might well be used to make swords, and of raw silk, because it might be used to make long tunics worn by soldiers under their coats of mail. Under the category of beasts of war (*kurāʿ*), jurists included various quadrupeds (horses, mules, donkeys, camels, elephants) that soldiers could either ride to battle or use to transport military provisions.[95] They also forbade merchants from entering enemy territory with slaves, young or old, male or female, because, as the jurist al-Sarakhsī reasoned, these slaves might end up killing Muslims themselves or generate new enemies, through reproduction. If these potential warriors would reinforce the ranks of the enemy, they would contribute more to the war effort than mere weapons of war.[96]

An Islamic legal regime forbade Muslim merchants conducting business in a Muslim country from dealing in pork and wine, goods whose consumption was strictly prohibited to Muslims. Islamic law barred the sale of these goods to fellow Muslims, of course, but also to non-Muslim subjects (*dhimmis*), though they had the

---

[92] Cf. David Abulafia, "The Role of Trade in Muslim-Christian Contact during the Middle Ages," in *The Arab Influence in Medieval Europe: Folia Scholastica Mediterranea*, ed. Dionisius A. Agius and Richard Hitchcock (Reading, UK: Ithaca Press, 1994), 1–24. Abulafia focuses on "what it meant to a western merchant...to penetrate the Christian-Muslim frontier not as a soldier but as a merchant" (10). Even so, merchants participated in the economy of war; Abulafia himself refers to the controversy over European merchants exporting arms to Egypt.

[93] Al-Sarakhsī, *Sharḥ*, 1: 323, no. 459.

[94] James Muldoon, *Popes, Lawyers, and Infidels: The Church and the Non-Christian World, 1250–1550* (Philadelphia: University of Pennsylvania Press, 1979), 34 and 53–54; Henri Gilles, "Législation et doctrine canoniques sur les Sarrasins," in *Islam et chrétiens du Midi (XIIe–XIVe s.)*, Cahiers de Fanjeaux 18 (Toulouse: Éd. Privat, 1983), 195–213. Also see Chapter 3, by Giuseppe Marcocci, in this volume.

[95] Al-Sarakhsī, *Sharḥ*, 4: 1567–1568.

[96] Al-Sarakhsī, *Sharḥ*, 4: 1409, no. 2731.

legal right to consume wine or pork. This moral economic prohibition was designed to ensure that Muslims would neither profit personally from the consumption of forbidden things, nor encourage others to indulge in them. The vast majority of Muslim jurists held that this prohibition also applied to merchants conducting business in a non-Muslim country. Yet a disagreement arose within the Ḥanafi school of law over the relevance and applicability of this prohibition in states whose laws did not derive from the Shariʿa. A series of Ḥanafi jurists argued that Muslim merchants in the House of War are entitled to trade in pork and wine, sell the carcasses of dead animals, and even engage in usury, following the law of the land.[97] They warned Muslim traders conducting business abroad not to commit treachery, fraud, or deceit, counseling them to abide by universal norms and foreign codes, rather than by exclusively Islamic laws pertaining to commercial exchange under Muslim rule.[98]

The Ḥanafi argument in favor of freer trade is based in part on the recognition that no institutions existed in non-Muslim states to interpret or execute the Shariʿa. Within Muslim states, the market inspector, the port authority, or the judge ruling in a court case had the power to enforce Islamic laws. Whether they exercised this power strictly or leniently, regularly or sporadically, effectively or ineffectively, the point is that they could, in theory, restrict the trade in forbidden goods.[99] In foreign countries, however, the Shariʿa had no real institutional power. It functioned as a persuasive moral force that produced an economic effect only insofar as Muslim merchants refused to entangle themselves in commercial exchanges that they considered repugnant as a result of their cultural and religious background. Yet these merchants were relatively free, of course, to make compromises under pressure or to disregard the law of their country of origin.

Broadly speaking, Muslim jurists categorized foreign goods as lawful or forbidden. But they also made a critical distinction, when assessing goods whose consumption was permitted to Muslims, between goods acquired through trade and goods acquired through war. Elaborate rules governed the division of spoils of war. What Muslims were entitled to do with the goods of enemy infidels depended in large part on the mode of acquisition. Their political and social status—as merchants possessing a safe-conduct, as mercenaries, as infantry soldiers, as cavalrymen, or as military

---

[97] Al-Sarakhsī, *Sharḥ*, 4: 1410, no. 2734, and 1492, no. 2914. Compare to al-Sarakhsī, *Sharḥ*, 4: 1303–1305, nos. 2476–2477, a discussion on the problem of Christian wine, which in theory has no value for a Muslim.

[98] Al-Sarakhsī, *Sharḥ*, 4: 1486, no. 2898.

[99] Cf. Cemal Kafadar, "A Death in Venice (1575): Anatolian Muslim Merchants Trading in the Serenissima," *Journal of Turkish Studies*, 10 (1986): 191–218, 209–212. Kafadar argues that the Ottoman *ʿulemā* favored long-distance, cross-cultural trade. He also shows that religious-political bans were not necessarily enforced, recording an intriguing transaction involving the sale of weapons (199).

commanders—also played a key role in determining whether and if so, how they could gain ownership of foreign things, in whole or in part.

A juridical discussion on "the gift of the enemy" (*hadiyya ahl al-ḥarb*) should serve to highlight this feature of Islamic law. According to a Ḥanafī jurist, the commander of a Muslim army may accept a gift from the king of the enemies. But this property is then categorized as chattel belonging to the Muslim community in general (*fay' lil-muslimīn*), rather than as the personal property of the recipient. The commander has the prerogative to reject disdainfully certain things, such as disbelievers' butter. If he chooses to accept the gift, however, then he should feel obliged to reciprocate by offering the king a gift in exchange. This gesture helps to establish goodwill, and it may lead to the conversion of the enemy to Islam. (At work here was the moral mechanism, analyzed long ago by Marcel Mauss, that compels a gift's recipient to offer a gift in return. Yet this counter-gift, imbued with a missionary spirit, does not occur in a gift economy, where goods and services flowed with ease, but within the constraints of wartime.) An expert on legal opinions or a preacher receiving a gift from the king of the infidels might also feel the compulsion to reciprocate in his own modest way. Unlike the military commander, however, the religious authority does not act in this exchange as the Muslims' official representative. As a result, the foreign gift becomes, in this case, part of his personal property, as opposed to a good that needs to be shared with other Muslims.[100]

These juridical-theological deliberations on the transfer of objects from Muslim to non-Muslim hands bring us back to our opening case, on the Muslim consumption of the goods of Christians. As an expert on law and religion, the jurist Malik distinguished between sandals and used clothes, considering one but not the other a forbidden good. So, too, we must apply a differentiated logic to the problem of religion and cross-cultural trade. Instead of thinking of all trade between members of different religions as constituting a "cross-cultural" or "interfaith" phenomenon, we should discriminate carefully between trades that mattered culturally or religiously and those that did not. In certain places at certain times, objects passed relatively freely from one polity to another—without encountering a powerful symbolic or institutional barrier. There is no good reason to describe such trades as happening across a cultural or religious barrier. Doing so distorts the past, making culture and religion seem more divisive and more significant than they really were. Rather than conceiving of cultural or religious boundaries as somehow fixed, we must envision dynamic barriers, manipulated by historical actors whose outlook and rationale it is our task to discover. To contemplate the big questions—what effect commerce

---

[100] Al-Sarakhsī, *Sharḥ*, 4: 1237–1240, nos. 2319–2324.

had on religion and what effect religion had on commerce—we need first to delve into particulars. Thus we might begin by wondering, with Malik, about Christian sandals.

ACKNOWLEDGMENT

I am grateful to The National Endowment for the Humanities and the American Council of Learned Societies for granting me the fellowships that enabled me to undertake this research.

2

The Blessings of Exchange in the Making of the Early English Atlantic

David Harris Sacks

INTRODUCTION: CROSS-CULTURAL TRADE

How do peoples coming from different cultures and having little or no previous knowledge of one another initiate trade relations? This chapter, which focuses on experiences of exchange in the emerging Atlantic world, concentrates on some first encounters between Europeans, especially the English, and the native peoples of North America in the sixteenth century and the ideas and practices that made them possible. It is, therefore, a chapter about the early modern foundations of the phenomenon we now know as cross-cultural trade. Focusing especially on an episode that took place in Trinity Bay, Newfoundland, in 1612 between a group of English colonists and some Beothuk Indians, it examines several of the concepts and practices that made possible the transfer of "things" from one set of hands to another in the long-distance trade that emerged in the culturally diverse Atlantic world in the sixteenth and early seventeenth centuries.[1]

Long-distance trade, as Philip Curtin has argued, has been a crucial feature of human history going back to the ancient past.[2] Such trade almost always involves transactions

---

[1] For commentary on the importance of "things" and their meanings in shaping the particular ways of life of particular peoples, see Mary Douglas and Baron Isherwood, *The World of Goods: Towards an Anthropology of Consumption*, 2nd ed. (London: Routledge, 1996); Arjun Appadurai, ed., *The Social Life of Things: Commodities in Cultural Perspective* (Cambridge: Cambridge University Press, 1986); Bill Brown, "Thing Theory," *Critical Inquiry*, 28.1 (2001): 1–22.

[2] Philip D. Curtin, *Cross-Cultural Trade in World History* (Cambridge: Cambridge University Press, 1984), 1–2. See also E. E. Kuz'mina, *The Prehistory of the Silk Road*, ed. Victor H. Mair (Philadelphia: University

between peoples who speak different languages and have little or no direct knowledge of each other's cultural practices and beliefs. In discussing such cases, Curtin referred to a wide range of examples from ancient to modern times and from Africa and the Mediterranean to China, concluding his analysis with a study of the fur trade between North American native peoples and Europeans starting in the period of first encounter in the Gulf of St. Lawrence.[3]

Although furs certainly were prestige items for Europeans, early modern traders, whether they looked to Russian or North American sources, were interested in the furs chiefly for their marketability and the profit that could be gained from selling them. The primary purpose of trade for them was the acquisition of commodities, even though forging alliances of mutual support with the natives might also have been a welcome byproduct of the exchanges. For North American natives, however, the significance of the exchanges was somewhat different. Although many of the European items they acquired—especially metal tools and implements—had practical utility to them, in most instances their importance lay as much, or even more, in their prestige value as signs of the social worth of their owners or in their utility as gifts to be used in binding followers and allies to those providing them. In addition, the natives traditionally had hunted beaver for their own purposes and bartered their skins among themselves.[4] From this perspective, commodity exchange often was also a means to display or assert the status of the trader. Among the indigenous peoples of North America, therefore, the boundary between trade and gift-giving was quite porous.[5] These differences meant that the fur trade in North America was conducted between persons with dissimilar cultural outlooks and aims, with the consequent potential for misunderstanding, conflict, or violence. Despite the potential

---

of Pennsylvania Press, 2008), esp. 88–107; Richard C. Foltz, *Religions of the Silk Road: Overland Trade and Cultural Exchange from Antiquity to the Fifteenth Century* (New York: St. Martin's Press, 1999).

[3] Curtin, *Cross-Cultural Trade*, 207–209.

[4] Shepard Krech, III, *The Ecological Indian: Myth and History* (New York and London: W. W. Norton, 1999), 179–180.

[5] See Melville J. Herskovits, *Economic Anthropology: The Economic Life of Primitive Peoples* (New York: W. W. Norton, 1965; first publ. 1940), 180–181, 155–203, and *passim*; C. A. Gregory, *Gifts and Commodities* (London and New York: Academic Press, 1982), esp. 10–24; Nicholas Thomas, *Entangled Objects: Exchange, Material Culture, and Colonialism in the Pacific* (Cambridge, MA, and London: Harvard University Press, 1991), 1–34, 75–100, 103–110, 118–151, 200–208; James G. Carrier, *Gifts and Commodities: Exchange and Western Capitalism since 1700* (London and New York: Routledge, 1995), viii–ix, 18–38; Avner Offer, "Between the Gift and the Market: The Economy of Regard," *Economic History Review*, 50.3 (1997): 450–476; Karen Ordahl Kupperman, *Indians and English: Facing Off in Early America* (Ithaca, NY, and London: Cornell University Press, 2000), 174–211; Daniel K. Richter, *Facing East from Indian Country: A Native History of Early America* (Cambridge, MA: Harvard University Press, 2003), 14–18, 26–27, 35–53; Karen Ordahl Kupperman, *The Jamestown Project* (Cambridge, MA, and London: Harvard University Press, 2007), 77–108; Daniel K. Richter, *Before the Revolution: America's Ancient Pasts* (Cambridge, MA, and London: Harvard University Press, 2011), 121–142.

obstacles, however, the parties found enough advantages in their exchanges for them to go forward, and it proved possible for relations of trust to form between the parties, at least for a time, sufficient for peaceable trade to proceed.[6]

Almost from the first moments of contact, an intensive commerce in furs, especially beaver, was one of the fruits of this *modus vivendi*.[7] Standing on what Richard White has called "the middle ground," the Europeans adapted their own practices to accommodate those of the natives, while the natives quickly became familiar with the Europeans' desire for furs and as adept as their counterparts in signaling their own willingness to trade.[8] In thus finding ways to communicate, both sides knew that "like diplomacy," trade "was a game of bluff, stratagem, and maneuver," the object of which was to gain as much as possible of what you wanted while giving away as little as possible.[9] What underpinned the establishment of these practices in "middle ground," was, to quote White, "the inability of both sides to gain their ends through force."[10] Engaging in trade on the middle ground, therefore, required

---

[6] According to an early account of the history of the Virginia Company's Jamestown settlement, after some initial clashes and conflicts with the Indians of the region, the English not only swore a "sure and vnuioable" peace with them in 1616, but also lived in "amitie" alongside them for some years, even opening their houses to their indigenous neighbors, "who were always friendly entertained at the tables of the English, and commonly lodged in their bed-chambers." This period of accommodation lasted until March 1622, when 347 of the settlers were killed in attacks on the Jamestown colony, a "great massacre," as it was called, that set off a decade-long war.; [Edward Waterhouse], *A Declaration of the State of the Colony and Affaires in Virginia. With a Relation of the Barbarous Massacre in the time of peace and League treacherously executed by the Natiue Infidels vpon the English, the 22 of March last* (London, 1622), 12–15; Robert Beverley, *The History of and Present State of Virginia*, ed. Louis B. Wright (Chapel Hill: University of North Carolina Press, 1947), 34, 50–55, 60–62. Beverley's book was first published in 1705. See also Karen Ordahl Kupperman, *Settling with the Indians: The Meeting of English and Indian Cultures in America, 1580–1640* (London, Toronto, and Melbourne: J. M. Dent & Sons, Ltd., 1980), 169–198; Kupperman, *Indians and English*, 212–240; James Horn, *A Land as God Made It: Jamestown and the Birth of America* (New York: Basic Books, 2005), 157–191, 249–278; Kupperman, *The Jamestown Project*, 225–230, 304–318.

[7] Harold A. Innis, *The Fur Trade in Canada*, rev ed. (Toronto, Buffalo, London: University of Toronto Press, 1970; first ed. 1930; rev. ed. 1956), 9–42; Krech, *The Ecological Indian*, 173–209. See also Richard White, *The Middle Ground: Indians, Empires, and Republics in the Great Lakes Region, 1650–1815*, Twentieth Anniversary Edition (Cambridge: Cambridge University Press, 2011), 94–141.

[8] White, *The Middle Ground*, xi–xxiv, 50–53, 93; Richard White, "Creative Misunderstandings and New Understandings," *William and Mary Quarterly*, 63.1 (2006): 9–14. Although White's study of relations between the Hurons and the French in the Great Lakes region focuses on different actors in a later period than in this chapter, the relevance of his work to studies of earlier encounters between Europeans and the indigenous peoples living along the Atlantic seaboard of North America is widely recognized; see Susan Sleeper-Smith et al., "Forum: The Middle Ground Revised," *William and Mary Quarterly*, 63.1 (2006): 3–96.

[9] Horn, *A Land as God Made It*, 80. See also Marcel Mauss, *The Gift: The Form and Reason for Exchange in Archaic Societies*, trans. W. D. Halls, forward by Mary Douglas (New York: W. W. Norton, 1990), 1–18, 65–83; Marshall Sahlins, "The Spirit of the Gift" and "Exchange Value and the Diplomacy of Primitive Trade," in his *Stone Age Economics*, new ed. (London and New York: Routledge, 2004; first ed. 1972), 149–184 and 277–314, respectively.

[10] White, *The Middle Ground*, 52.

the employment of common bargaining gestures and rituals and the development of interdependent understandings of exchange. We turn to this subject in the remainder of this chapter.

GIFTS AND COMMODITIES

By the early seventeenth century, fur trading between native peoples and Europeans in and near the Gulf of St. Lawrence already had a long and well-documented history. During the period of their ventures in the region, the Vikings, for example, appear to have traded from time to time for furs with the indigenous peoples of "Vinland," whom they called the *skraelings*.[11] Subsequently, Giovanni da Verrazzano (1485–1528) and Jacques Cartier (1491–1557) also had found the peoples living in the same region very eager to exchange their skins for the things the newcomers brought with them.[12] In this same early period, European fishermen who came to the rich fishing grounds in and around the Gulf of St. Lawrence similarly traded for furs during their seasonal visits.[13]

For present purposes, however, I turn to a later episode, dating from late October and early November in 1612, and involving exchanges between a group of the Beothuk people of Newfoundland and some Englishmen on a voyage of discovery to Trinity Bay conducted on behalf of the Newfoundland Company.[14] According to

[11] "Eirik the Red's Saga," Chapter 11, in *The Vinland Sagas*, trans. Keneva Kunz, ed. Gísli Sigurdsson (London: Penguin Books, 2008), 45. A similar but briefer account is to be found in "The Saga of the Greenlanders," Chapter 6, in *Vinland Sagas*, 16. See also Gísli Sigurdsson's "An Introduction to the Vinland Sagas," Birgitta Linderoth Wallace's "An Archaeologist's Interpretation of the *Vinland Sagas*," and Patricia D. Sutherland's "The Norse and the Native North Americans," all in *Vikings: The North Atlantic Saga*, ed. William W. Fitzhugh and Elizabeth I. Ward (Washington, DC, and London: Smithsonian Institution Press, 2000), 218–237, 238. I thank Dr. Elizabeth Ashman Rowe for these references.

[12] Giovanni da Verrazzano, "Copia di una lettera di Giovanni da Verrazzano al Chiarissimo Re Francesco re di Francia della terra per lui scoperta in nome de Sua Maestà," from the ship *Dauphine*, July 8, 1524, addressed to Bonacorso Ruscellay, business associate of Verrazzano's brother, Gerolamo (Pierpont Morgan Library, *Cèllere Codex*, Morgan Ms 776, fols. 2r, 4v, 5v, 6r–v, 7r, 8v), reprinted in *The Voyages of Giovanni da Verrazzano, 1524–1528*, ed. Lawrence C. Wroth (New Haven, CT: Yale University Press, 1970), 123, 126, 128, 129, 130, English trans. Susan Tarrow, 133, 136, 138, 139, 140–141. [Jacques Cartier], *A shorte and briefe narration of the two nauigations and discoueries to the northweast partes called Newe Fraunce*, trans. John Florio (London, 1580), 1–27. Florio's translation is based on the text initially published in Italian in 1556 in Giovanni Battista Ramusio, *Delle nauigationi et viaggi*, 3 vols. (Venice: Giunti, 1556), 3: 435–440. The first version in French, also translated from Ramusio's edition, appeared in 1598. The manuscript itself, or a fair copy of the original, was discovered in Paris only in 1867. See H. P. Biggar, ed., *The Voyages of Jacques Cartier* (Ottawa: F. A. Acland, 1924), x and xn.3.

[13] Curtin, *Cross-Cultural Trade*, 219.

[14] For the history of the Newfoundland Company, see Gillian T. Cell, "Introduction," in Gillian T. Cell, ed., *Newfoundland Discovered: English Attempts at Colonisation, 1610–1630* (London: Hakluyt Society, 2nd ser. no 160, 1982), 1–59; Gillian T. Cell, *English Enterprise in Newfoundland, 1577–1660* (Toronto and Buffalo: University of Toronto Press, 1969), 53–80.

the journal kept by John Guy of Bristol, the company's first governor, the encounter between the English and the Beothuks began when the Englishmen, sailing in the bay, sighting a fire on shore a mile off, which they understood "could be noe other than the doeing of savages," and took to be a signal that they wished to trade. Afterward we learn that the Beothuks had established a temporary base at this site by making a tent "with a sayle, that they got from some Christian," and by setting up a dozen poles nearby, on "which weare hanged divers furres, & chaines made of shelles." At first, Guy says, the Englishmen "fell not in reckoning to what intent" lay behind the latter, although, as we shall see, they eventually deduced a reason.[15]

Guy and his men, expecting the natives shortly to approach them, repaired aboard their bark, the *Endeavour*, to await their arrival. When they did, the episode unfolded in a series of shared signals and gestures. "Presentlie," Guy says, "two canoaes appeared,

> & one man alone comming towardes vs with a flag in his hand of a wolfe skinne, shaking yt, & making a lowde noice, which we tooke to be for a parlie, whearevpon a white flag was put out & the barke & shallope rowed towardes them: which the savages did not like of, & soe tooke them to theire canoaes againe, & weare goeing away. Whearevpon the barke whearyed onto them & flourished the flag of truce, & came to anker, which pleased them, & then they stayed.[16]

With this George Whittington, one of the colonists aboard the *Endeavour*, went to them carrying the "flag of truce." The natives in turn "landed two men, one of them having the white skinne in his hand." Coming toward Whittington, "the savage made a loude speeche, & shaked the skinne." Whittington answered "in like manner, & as the savage drew neere he threw downe the white skinne onto the grownde." Whittington did the same with his flag. This signaled the two natives to approach Whittington "daunsing leaping, & singing."[17] When they reached him,

---

[15] John Guy, "A Iournall of the voiadge of discoverie made in a barke builte in Newfoundland called the Indeavour, begunne the 7 of October 1612, & ended the 25th of November following," in *Newfoundland Discovered*, 73, 75–77. The original manuscript of this journal is Lambeth Palace MS 250, fols. 406r–12v. Its text is reprinted in *New American World: A Documentary History to 1612*, ed. David Beers Quinn, with Alison M. Quinn and Susan Hillier, 5 vols. (New York: Arno Press, 1979), 4: 152–157 as well as in *Newfoundland Discovered*, 68–78. Henry Crout also provides a similar account in the letter he wrote in April 1613 to Sir Percival Willoughby, *Newfoundland Discovered*, 84–86. A somewhat different version was recorded by Sir David Kirke in 1639; Sir David Kirke to Archbishop William Laud, September 29, 1639, The National Archives (hereinafter TNA), CO 1/10, fols. 112v–113v.

[16] Guy, "Iournall," 73.

[17] Guy, "Iournall," 73

the foremoste of them, presented vnto him a chaine of leather full of small perwincle shelles, [a] spilting [splitting?] knife, & a feather that stucke in his heare. The other gave him ane arrow without a head, & the former was requited with a linen cap, & a hand towell, who put…the linnen cap vpon his head, and to the other he gave a knife. And after hand in hand all three did sing, & daunce.[18]

At this point, Francis Tipton went ashore. One of the natives came running to give him a chain of periwinkle shells, to which Tipton responded by presenting the man with a knife and a small piece of brass.

Then all fower together daunced, laughing & makeing signes of ioy, & gladnes, sometimes strikeing the breastes of our companie & sometymes theyre owne. When signes was made vnto them that they should be winning to suffer two of our company more to come one shoare, for two of theirs more to be landed, & that bread, & drink should be brought ashoare, they made likewise signes that they had in their canoaes meate also to eate.[19]

At about this time, "when signes were made of meate to eate one of the savadges…came to the banke side, & pulled vp a roote, & gave it to master Whittington. Which t'other savage perceiving to be durtie, tooke yt out of his hand, & went to the water to washe yt, & after devided it among the fower." "Yt tasted very well," Guy says.[20] We are fortunate to have a near contemporary engraving by Johann Theodor de Bry (Figure 2.1) representing most of these events by showing its several stages as if they all occurred at the same time. Note, in particular, the natives in the canoe waving the white wolf's skin, which is also seen on the ground near the figure of George Whittington.[21]

After this exchange, Guy himself went ashore, accompanied by another colonist. Guy presented the natives with a shirt, two table napkins, and a hand towel, and gave

---

[18] Guy, "Iournall," 74. It is unclear whether the "spilting" knife was European or North American in origin. In the present day, a "splitting knife" is a large, heavy-duty item of steel kitchen cutlery used in butchering meat. In this instance, however, the kind of knife involved may have been made from bone and used for cleaning fish.

[19] Guy, "Iournall," 74.

[20] Guy, "Iournall," 74.

[21] *Decima Tertia Pars historia Americanae* (Francofurti: Matthaei Meriani, 1634), 5. This image, published by Matthäus Merian, son-in-law of Johann Theodor de Bry, first appeared in 1628 in the German version of the thirteenth part of the de Bry firm's *Historia Americae* series, the volumes of which were published in Frankfurt and Oppenheim between 1590 and 1634; *Dreyzehende Theil Americae* (Frankfurt: Caspar Rötel for Matth. Merian, 1628), 6; Michiel van Groesen, *The Representation of the Overseas World in the De Bry Collection of Voyages (1590–1634)* (Leiden and Boston: Brill, 2008), 481, 485–486. On Merian's relationship to the de Brys see van Groesen, *The Representation of the Overseas World*, 92–102. An account of the exchanges in Trinity

Original in the John Carter Brown Library at Brown University

FIGURE 2.1 Encounter between George Whittington and other members of the Newfoundland Company with the Beothuks at Trinity Bay, Newfoundland, November 6, 1612, engraving by Johann Theodor de Bry, first published in 1618 (here reproduced from the 1628 edition). *Source*: John Carter Brown Library, Providence, RI.

them bread, butter, some raisins, and beer and aquavitae to drink. "And one of them blowing in the aquavitae bottle yt made a sound, which they fell all into a laughture at." Next another two Englishmen landed, who the natives "went to salute giveinge them shell chaines," in return for which they received gloves. Once the group had

Bay, Newfoundland, appears in Samuel Purchas, *Hakluytus Postumus, or Purchas His Pilgrimes; Contayning a History of the World, in Sea voyages, & lande Trauells, by Englishmen and others*, 4 vols. (London, 1625), 4: 10, 1880–1882, the material for which originates from Guy's "Iournall," a copy of which appears to have been made available to Richard Hakluyt before his death in 1616 and then was passed to Samuel Purchas. The engraving itself has often been misidentified as depicting Bartholomew Gosnold's first encounter in 1602 with the Wampanoag Indians on Martha's Vineyard. See, e.g., Kupperman, *Indians and English*, 8; Richter, *Before the Revolution*, plate 28 between 169–170. But as is made clear in the text in chapter three of the thirteenth part of *Historia Americae* series that accompanies the image, there is no doubt that what is depicted is the 1612 voyage in Newfoundland of George Whittington, John Guy, and others from the Newfoundland Company; see William Gilbert, "Guy not Gosnold: A Correction," *Post-Medieval Archaeology*, 41.2 (2007): 264–269. The encounter is discussed in somewhat different terms than mine in Stephen Greenblatt, *Marvelous Possessions: The Wonders of the New World* (Oxford: Clarendon Press, 1991), 99, 101–102, 182n35.

eaten and drunk what the Englishmen had brought, one of the natives went to their canoe and "brought vs deere fleshe dryed in the smoake or wind, and drawing his knife from out of his necke he cut every man a peece." We read that it "savoured very well."[22]

Guy goes on to report that one of the natives who came ashore stood out from the rest of the group. He "came walking," he says,

> with his oare in his hand, & seemed to have some command over the rest, & behaved him selfe civillie. For when meate was offred him he drew of his mitten from his hand, before he would receive yt, & gave ane arrow for a present, without a head, who was requited with a dozen of pointes.[23]

This figure concluded this day's encounter by giving "the white skinne, that they hayled us with...to master Whittington," taking "our white flag" to the natives' canoe. After doing so, he "made signes vnto vs that we should repaire to our barke, & so they put of for yt was almoste nighte."[24]

In consequence, there was no actual bartering or trading on that day. Instead the actions of the parties were framed in terms of the exchange of gifts, in which offerings received are requited with offerings given. From Guy's narrative, as from earlier accounts, it is abundantly clear that the natives were thoroughly familiar with such practices. The fact that the English found a copper or brass kettle and a "fishing reele" in one of the Beothuk dwellings they entered would strongly suggest that the natives already had significant experience of trade with Europeans.[25] Whatever is the

---

[22] Guy, "Iournall," 74.

[23] Guy, "Iournall," 74; the "pointes" mentioned most likely were pieces of ribbon or cord of the kind used in the period to attach hose to a doublet or to lace a garment; cf. Guy, "Iournall," 74.

[24] Guy, "Iournall," 74–75.

[25] Guy, "Iournall," 71, 74. Crout says that what was found along with what he identifies as a brass kettle were "many Fishing hookes" (Crout to Willoughby, *Newfoundland Discovered*, 84). See also Cell, "Introduction," 11 and Guy, "Iournall," 72. Guy describes the hair color of the Beothuks he met as "diverse, some blacke, some browne, & some yellow," which suggests the possibility that by 1612 some of them had descended from European progenitors; Guy, "Iournall," 75. For evidence of earlier trading activities in and around the Gulf of the St. Lawrence frequently by Beothuk Indians, see Edward Hayes, "A reports of the voyage and successe thereof, attempted in the year of our Lord, 1583, by Sir Humfrey Gilbert," in Richard Hakluyt, *The Principall Navigations, Voiages, and Discoveries of the English nation, made by Sea or ouer Land* (London, 1589), 679–697; idem, *The Principal Navigations, Voyages, Traffiqves and Discoveries of the English Nation, made by Sea or ouer-land*, 3 vols. (London, 1598/9–1600), 3: 143–161; George Peckham, "A true Report of the late discoueries, and possession taken in the right of the Crowne of England of the Newfound Lands, By that valiant and worthy Gentleman, Sir Humfrey Gilbert Knight," idem, *Principall navigations* (1589), 701–718; idem, *Principal navigations* (1598/9–1600), 3: 165–181. For similar evidence of trade between the Inuit and Europeans further to the north, see George Best, *A Trve Discovrse of the late voyages if discourie, for the finding of a passage to Cathaya, by the Northvvest, vnder the conduct of Martin Frobisher Generall* (London, 1578), "A true Report of such things as hapned in the second voyage of Captayne Frobysher, pretended for the Discouerie of a new passage

case, the Beothuks seem to have been following well understood conventions and rules in making their signs and gestures, in sharing food with their guests, and engaging in the rhythms of what we can justifiably call a dance of exchange. As we have just seen, Guy not only said that the leader of the Beothuk band they encountered had acted "civillie" toward him, but he also used the word "present" to name the reciprocal offering he received from one of the Beothuks and spoke of the exchanges being "requited." This usage brings the actions Guy reported not only within the spirit, but also the language of the gift, whose practice had come to be understood among Europeans as a mark of civilization.

Guy's usage draws on concepts employed in Seneca's essay *De Beneficiis* and in related texts such as Cicero's *De Officiis* and *De Amicitia*, which were widely known and read in Elizabethan England—in Latin and in English translation.[26] Regrettably, we do not know where Guy, born and apprenticed in Bristol, received his education.[27] But he need not have had special training in the writings of the ancient moralists to adopt their terminology, since the language and ethics of gift exchange they employed to a very large degree provided the grammar and vocabulary for the conduct of social relations throughout Western Europe in his day. It was ubiquitous in popular stories, sermons, plays, historical narratives, and handbooks of proper

---

to Cataya, China, and East India by the Northwest. Anno Do. 1577," 10–12; Dionyse Settle, *A true report of the laste voyage into the West and Northwest regions, &c. 1577 worthily atchieued by Captaine Frobisher of the said voyage the first finder and Generall* (London, 1577), sig. Bv.

[26] The first English translation of Seneca's *De Beneficiis* appeared in 1569: Lucius Annaeus Seneca, *The line of liberalitie dulie directing the wel bestowing of benefites and reprehending the commonly vsed vice of ingratitude*, trans. Nicolas Haward (London, 1569); a second translation appeared in 1587, idem, *The vvoorke of the excellent philosopher Lucius Annaeus Seneca concerning benefyting that is too say the dooing, receyuning, and requyting of good turnes*, trans. Arthur Golding (London, 1578). Cicero's *De Officiis* and *De Amicitia* were often printed together in Latin during the early modern period. The first English translation of *De Officiis* appeared along with the Latin in 1534; Marcus Tullius Cicero, *The thre bokes of Tullius offyce*, trans. Robert Whittington (London, 1534). Another edition appeared in 1540. A new translation first appeared in 1556: idem, *Marcus Tullius Ciceroes thre bokes of duties to Marcus his sonne*, trans. Nicholas Grimald (London, 1556); it was reprinted during Elizabeth I's reign in 1558, 1568, 1574, 1583, 1596, and 1600. There is a modern edition of this translation: idem, *Marcus Tullius Ciceroes thre bokes of duties*, trans. Nicholas Grimalde (1556), ed. Gerald O'Gorman (Washington, DC: Folger Shakespeare Library, 1990). The first English translation of *De Amicitia* appeared in 1481, printed by William Caxton; another edition was published in 1530, idem, *Tullius de amicicia, in Englysh*, trans. John Tiptoft, Earl of Worcester (London, 1530). Another translation appeared in 1562, idem, *The booke of freendeship of Marcus Tullie Cicero*, trans. John Harington (London, 1562); a third appeared in 1577, idem, *Fovvre seuerall treatises of M. Tullius Cicero*, trans. Thomas Newton (London, 1577).

[27] If Guy was formally educated in Bristol, only two schools existed in the city during the years of his youth: the Bristol Grammar School, founded in 1532 by Robert and Nicholas Thorne and the Free Grammar School, later called St. Mary Redcliffe School, founded by royal charter in 1571 in the parish of St. Mary Redcliffe. However, there are no records listing the students attending either of these institutions during Guy's boyhood; see Jean Vanes, *Education and Apprenticeship in Sixteenth-Century Bristol*, Local History Pamphlets, no. 52 (Bristol: Bristol Branch of the Historical Association, 1982); C. P. Hill, *The History of the Bristol Grammar School* (London: Pitman, 1951).

conduct as well as in treatises of moral philosophy. In early modern parliaments, for example, the rhetoric of gift exchange was used not only to describe the granting of taxes, but also to settle disagreements with the monarch. Similar ideas also informed patron-client relations at court and in the country, the rituals and language of diplomatic exchange, the giving and receiving of charity, and, as we shall discuss further, the conduct of merchant business.[28] It is no surprise, therefore, that we often find relations between Europeans and natives initiated by or portrayed as gift exchanges, as Arthur Barlowe did in describing what took place in the Outer Banks, on the coast of what are now the Carolinas, when he and his men first encountered the indigenous peoples of the region in 1584. Similar to the usage adopted by Guy, his narrative of the visit is replete with explicit references to benefits received, to the exchange and requital of gifts and presents, and to expressions of thankfulness for them.[29] Columbus himself did much the same in representing his actions in his own encounters with the native peoples of the Caribbean.[30]

According to Seneca, the giving and receiving of gifts provides the "thing that most of al other knitteth men togither in fellowship," to quote from the Elizabethan translation. A gift "is a frendly goode deede." It is something immaterial, something in our hearts or minds. Accordingly, the money or offices given by a patron to his client are only transitory things—the "badges of benefites," he calls them. "Both misfortune and force may take them from vs. But a good turne endureth still, yea euen when the thyng that was given is gone." The receiving of gifts also calls forth a need for recompense, initially acquitted by our gratitude when we accept what is

---

[28] Garrett Mattingly, *Renaissance Diplomacy* (London: Jonathan Cape, 1955), 34–44, 240–254; Linda Levy Peck, *Court Patronage and Corruption in Early Stuart England* (Boston and London: Unwin Hyman, 1990), David Harris Sacks, "The Countervailing of Benefits: Monopoly, Liberty, and Benevolence in Elizabethan England," in *Tudor Political Culture*, ed. Dale Hoak (Cambridge: Cambridge University Press, 1995), 272–291; Richard Grassby, *Kinship and Capitalism: Marriage, Family, and Business in the English-Speaking World, 1580–1740* (Cambridge: Cambridge University Press, 2001), 244, 12–29; Ilana Krausman Ben-Amos, *The Culture of Giving: Informal Support and Gift Exchange in Early Modern England* (Cambridge: Cambridge University Press, 2008), esp. 5–9, 242–274, 376–389; Keith Thomas, *The Ends of Life: Roads to Fulfillment in Early Modern England* (Oxford: Oxford University Press, 2009), 112, 127, 128, 191, 192, 203, 208.

[29] [Arthur Barlowe], "The first voyage made to the coastes of America, with two barkes, wherein were Captaines Master Philip Amadas and Master Arthur Barlowe, who discouered part of the Countrey now called Virginia, Anno 1584: Written by one of the said Captaines, and sent to Sir Walter Raleigh, knight, at whose charge, and direction, the said voyage was set forth," in Hakluyt, *Principall Navigations* (1589), 728–733; idem, *Principal Navigations* (1598/9–1600), 3: 246–251.

[30] See [Christopher Columbus], *The Diario of Christopher Columbus's First Voyage to America, 1492–1493, Abstracted by Fray Bartolomé de las Casas*, ed. and trans. Oliver Dunn and James E. Kelley, Jr. (Norman, OK, and London: University of Oklahoma Press, 1989), fols. 9r (64–65), 12r (82–83), 16r (106–107); Michael Harbsmeier, "Gifts and Discoveries: Gift Exchange in Early Modern Narratives of Exploration and Discovery," in *Negotiating the Gift: Pre-Modern Figurations of Exchange*, ed. Gadi Algazi, Valentin Groebner, and Bernhard Jussen (Göttingen: Vandenhoeck & Ruprecht, 2003), 381–410.

given "thankfully, by powryng out our affections" and witnessing them everywhere. Through this exchange, gift-giving forms the bonds of human society. "For in what other thing haue wee so muche safetie," Seneca argues, "as in helping one another wt mutuall freendlynes.... Take away this felowship, and yee rend asunder the vnitie of Mankynd, whereby our lyfe is maynteined."[31]

A similar conception grounds Marcel Mauss's discussion in his *Essai sur le don* (*The Gift*), first published in 1924. In that seminal book, Mauss delineates a system of gift exchange which "does not merely carry with it the obligation to reciprocate presents received," but "also supposes two other obligations: on the one hand, to give presents, and on the other, to receive them."[32] Commenting on Mauss's theory, the anthropologist Mary Douglas says that "cycles of obligatory returns of gifts" account for most of the transfer of goods among people "right across the globe and as far back as we can go in the history of human civilization."[33] However, as Mauss made clear, and as Seneca also well understood, gift-giving often is highly competitive and rarely, if ever, entirely disinterested.

Judging by the actions of the Beothuks when they met with Guy and his fellow Englishmen, forms of gift exchange were as well established among them as among the Europeans and, in their own way, had come to serve as constitutive elements of their social life.[34] Viewed in this light, the rituals of exchange in which Guy and the Beothuks engaged in Trinity Bay were recognizable as friendly gestures and provided signs on each side of their peaceful intentions, without which any future buying and selling arguably would have been highly dangerous, and probably impossible. In other words, the ritualized exercise of gift-giving between the Beothuks and the Newfoundland colonists and the acts of sociability and commensality associated with it appear to have been undertaken as preconditions for the conduct of trade between them, with the latter understood to be an extension of the peaceable exchanges that had already occurred.

---

[31] Seneca, *The vvoorke*, fols. 4v, 5v, 22r, 55r; see John M. Wallace, "Timon of Athens and the Three Graces: Shakespeare's Senecan Study," *Modern Philology*, 83.4 (1986): 349–363, esp. 351–353. Cicero also treats the theme in similar terms in his *De Officiis*; see Cicero, *Ciceroes thre bokes of duties*, ed. O'Gorman, 131–136. The classic study of the gift as a social and cultural form is Mauss, *The Gift*; see also Natalie Zemon Davis, *The Gift in Sixteenth-Century France* (Madison, WI, and London: University of Wisconsin Press, 2000), 11–22 and *passim*; Felicity Heal, *Hospitality in Early Modern England* (Oxford: Clarendon Press, 1990), 19–22; Ben-Amos, *Culture of Giving*.

[32] Mauss, *The Gift*, 13.

[33] Mary Douglas, "Forward: *No free gifts*," in Mauss, *The Gift*, viii.

[34] See Barrie Reynolds, "Beothuk," in William C. Sturtevant, ed., *Handbook of North American Indians*, Vol. 15: *Northeast*, ed. Bruce G. Trigger (Washington, DC: Smithsonian Institution, 1978), 101; Ingeborg Marshall, *A History and Ethnography of the Beothuk* (Montréal and Kingston: McGill-Queen's University Press, 1996), 30–41, 72–75.

SILENT TRADE AND THE SPIRIT OF THE GIFT

Although Guy and his men saw no more of the Beothuks on this journey, a form of trade did occur between them as the Englishmen were about to leave Trinity Bay.[35] Having heard "nothing more" of the natives he met, Guy says, he and the others returned to the site of their temporary encampment, near where they had previously encountered them. They "fownde all thinges remaining theare, as yt was when we parted," including "about twelve furres of beavers moste, a foxe skinne, a saple skinne, a bird skinne, & ane old mitten set everye one vpon a severall poule." The Englishmen, now perceiving the significance of this arrangement, were "satisfied fullie" that these items "weare broughte theather of purpose to barter with vs, & that they would stand to our curtesie to leave for yt what we should thinke good." However, because the Englishmen had not brought with them "fit things for to truck," they "tooke onlie, a beaver skinne, a saple skinne, & a bird skinne, leaving for them, a hatchet, a knife, & fower needles threaded." Whittington for his part took "a small beaver skinne," for which he left "a paire of sezers." "All the rest," Guy says, they "lefte theare vntouched."[36] As it turned out, this was the last of the Newfoundland Company colonists' dealings with the Beothuk. When the English returned in the following year, the Beothuks were nowhere to be found.[37]

The practice, as Guy describes it, represents in its essentials an example of what historians and anthropologists call "silent trade." Herodotus says the Carthaginians followed this custom in their dealing with the peoples living in ancient Libya "beyond the Pillars of Hercules." The Carthaginians, he says, believe this mode of trade to be entirely just, since "neither party is ill-used; for the Carthaginians do not take the gold until they have the worth of their merchandise, nor the natives touch the merchandise until the Carthaginians have taken the gold."[38] Numerous travel writers and ethnographers also report similar practices occurring in a variety of places into modern times.[39] Among early modern examples, one of the first is contained in the

---

[35] Guy, "Iournall," 76; Crout to Willoughby, *Newfoundland Discovered*, 85–86.

[36] Guy, "Iournall," 76. The items taken by Guy appear to have been selected as samples to show to the other colonists and perhaps also to the London and Bristol investors the valuable and unusual trading goods that could be acquired in the region. The "bird skin" was probably that of a great auk, now extinct.

[37] Crout to Willoughy, *Newfoundland Discovered*, 84; see also *Newfoundland Discovered*, 86; Cell, "Introduction," 11–12; Cell, *English Enterprise*, 69.

[38] Herodotus, 4:196; *The History*, trans. David Grene (Chicago and London: The University of Chicago Press, 1987), 352–353; Greenblatt, *Marvelous Possessions*, 102.

[39] See P. J. Hamilton Grierson, *The Silent Trade: A Contribution to the Early History of Human Intercourse* (Edinburgh: W. Green & Sons, 1903); idem, "The Silent Trade (1903)," excerpts reprinted in George Dalton, ed., *Research in Economic Anthropology*, Supplement 3: Prehistoric Economies of the Pacific Northwest Coast (1980), 1–74; Elizabeth Ellis Hoyt, *Primitive Trade, Its Psychology and Economics* (London: K. Paul, Trench, Trubner & Co., Ltd., 1926), 115–136; Herskovits, *Economic Anthropology*, 185–187; Lars Sundström, "The

account by David Ingram of his overland journey in 1568 from the shores of the Gulf of Mexico to a region about 50 leagues south of Cape Breton Island. Describing "the maner of trafique and trading" with the people he encountered, he says,

> if you will bargaine for ware with them, leaue the thing you will sell vpon the ground, and go from it a prettie way of[f]: then wil they come and take it, and set downe such wares as they will giue for it in the place: And if you thinke it not sufficient, leaue the wares with signes that you like it not, and they will bring more, vntill either they or you be satisfied, or will giue no more. Otherwise you may hang your wares vpon a long poles end, and so put more or lesse on it, vntill you haue agreed on the bargaine.[40]

Similar accounts are given regarding the trading activities of the Inuit. On Martin Frobisher's voyage to the latter in 1577, for example, he tried to initiate trade with the inhabitants of Baffin Island, only to find that they would not take anything directly from the Englishmen's hands. Instead, they followed a practice of the kind described by Ingram, laying as much of their merchandise as they meant to exchange on the ground, "so looking that the other partie, with whome they trade, shoulde doe the like, they themselues doe departe, and then, if they doe like of their marte, they come againe, and take in exchange the others marchandise, otherwise, if they like not, they take therie owne and departe."[41]

Stephen Greenblatt has called Herodotus's account of the practice "a kind of utopian model," while Philip Curtin treats it as "improbable on the face of it," having interest more for the "inherent fascination" of the story, than for "its accuracy."[42] "To bargain with such elaborate avoidance," Curtin says, "yet to assume that total strangers will act with honesty and good faith, calls for an unusual degree of cross-cultural

---

Trade of Guinea," *Studia Ethnographica Upsaliensia* 24 (1965), 22–31; see also P. F. de Moraes Farias, "Silent Trade: Myth and Historical Evidence," *History in Africa*, 1 (1974): 9–24; John A. Price, "On Silent Trade" and Schinichiro Kurmoto, "Silent Trade in Japan," both in Dalton, ed., *Economic Anthropology*, 75–96 and 97–108, respectively.

[40] David Ingram, "The Relation of Dauid Ingram of Barking, in the Countie of Essex Sayler, of sundry things which he with others did see, in traueiling by land, from the most most Northerly partes of the Baie of Mexico (where he with many others were set to shoare by Master Hawkins) through a great part of America, vntill he came within fiftie leagues or there abouts of Cape Britton," in Hakluyt, *Principall Navigations* (1589), 558.

[41] Best, *A Trve Discovrse*, "A true Reporte," 10; a similar description is provided by Settle, *A true report*, sig. Bv. Joris Carolus, the Dutch navigator and explorer, reports similar trading practices ca. 1614, among the Inuit in the region of the Davis Strait; J. Kupp and Simon Hart, "The Dutch in the Strait of Davis and Labrador during the Seventeenth and Eighteenth Centuries," *Man in the Northeast*, 11.1 (1976): 3–20, 8; Marshall, *A History and Ethnography of the Beothuk*, 30–31.

[42] Greenblatt, *Marvelous Possessions*, 182n34.

understanding from both parties—and to believe it requires unusual credulity from the reader."[43] Nevertheless, Guy was convinced not only that he was correct in seeing the Beothuks as offering a form of silent trade, but also that he was correct in believing that he and his men had acted justly and equitably with them by limiting the items they took to what they believed they could adequately recompense. Indeed, Guy thought the Beothuks "were animated to come vnto" the Newfoundland colonists in the first place because of the pains the latter earlier had taken not to steal from them. Far from being credulous, then, or having any unusual ethnographical or cross-cultural insight, Guy appears to have concluded that if he wished to trade with the Beothuks in the future, as he did, he needed scrupulously to give value for value in the exchange.[44] Frobisher and his men had taken much the same view in their dealings in 1577 with Baffin Island Inuits, who as we have just seen also practiced a form of silent trade.[45] In substance, then, if not in form, Guy reveals the Herodotean mode of silent trade in action.

In the absence of direct evidence, we do not know what beliefs might have made it possible for the Beothuks to engage in the form of equitable exchange that Guy describes. It has been suggested that trading of this kind relates to practices long in use in exchanges between forest peoples like the Beothuks and the Inuit to their north. According to reports by Frobisher's men of the trading practices of the Inuits they encountered on Baffin Island in 1577, the latter initiated their exchanges by waving "a flag…& making great noise," then "skipping, laughing, and daunsing for ioy."[46] Dionyse Settle believed that these practices were first developed by the Inuits in their dealings "with…other people adioyning, or not farre distant from their Countrie."[47] But given that the native peoples of the northern forests lived far from Baffin Island, it is unlikely that Inuits had regular encounters with them for trading purposes. Instead, it seems almost certain that the strangers with whom the Baffin Islanders first engaged in trade by the method described by Ingram and by Frobisher's men were Europeans, probably fishermen who frequented these northern waters.[48] Although the Beothuks organized their dealings with the English according to patterns similar to those observed further to the north, we cannot be

---

[43] Curtin, *Cross-Cultural Trade*, 13.

[44] See Guy, "Iournall," 71, 76; Crout to Willoughby, *Newfoundland Discovered*, 84, 86. Cell, "Introduction," 11–12.

[45] Settle says that when Frobisher, on his second voyage, first observed "some of the people of the countrie neere the shoare" of Baffin Island "leaping and daunsing, with straunge shrikes and cryes," he undertook "to allure them vnto him by faire meanes," and "caused kniues, & other thinges to be proffered vnto them"; Settle, *A true report*, sig. Bv.

[46] Best, *A Trve Discovrse*, "A true Reporte," 10; see also Settle, *A true report*, sig. Bv.

[47] Settle, *A true report*, sig. Bv. Settle's description of Inuit practice is very similar to Best's.

[48] *The Three Voyages of Martin Frobisher in search of a passage to Cathay and India by the North-West, A. D. 1576–8. From the original 1578 text of George Best, together with numerous other versions, Additions, etc.*, ed.

certain, to adapt Ingeborg Marshall's comments, whether "their mode of exchange was an aboriginal…custom," or was learned from outsiders, or was invented by the Beothuks themselves after their first contacts with Europeans, or, as seems most likely, was adapted from existing practices applied to new purposes. Whatever the origins, however, the Beothuks seem clearly to have modeled their dealings with the English on the formation of amicable relations with their prospective trading partners based on the reciprocities of gift-giving and fairness in trade.[49] The English did the same.

Regarding European beliefs about modes of exchange, we are in a somewhat better position, since we have a long record of European discourse on the subject, going back to ancient Greek and Roman commentaries. Herodotus himself supplies one of the key features of this tradition. In giving his account in *The History* of Solon's discussion with Croesus, the historian reports Solon telling the Lydian king that "it is impossible for one who is human to have all the good things together, just as there is no one country that is sufficient of itself to provide all good things for itself, but one has one thing and not another…. So no single person is self-sufficient; he has one thing and lacks another." Solon goes on to say that "the country that has the most is the best" and that the same is true for those persons who can continue to their deaths to possess happiness and the things that make it possible. Solon's— and Herodotus's—point is that human beings, singly and collectively, lack absolute self-sufficiency, which can belong only to the divine. Nevertheless, the passage implies that just as human beings must depend on their families and on social interaction in order to live well, countries, if they are to flourish, must engage in exchange for the essential things they lack.[50] A similar claim is made in the voice of Theseus, King of Athens, in Euripides' *The Suppliant Women*. The gods have provided "commerce over the sea," Theseus says, so "that by exchange / Each country may obtain whatever it lacks."[51]

These ideas, which represent a starting place for what Albert Hirschman called the "doctrine of *doux commerce*" of later centuries, received more systematic attention in the political and ethical writings of Aristotle, particularly the *Politics*, which it was

Vilhjammur Stefansson with the assistance of Eloise McCaskill, 2 vols. (London: The Argonaut Press, 1938), 2:58–59n.

[49] Marshall, *A History and Ethnography of the Beothuk*, 30; on the invention of tradition, see Eric Hobsbawm, "Introduction: Inventing Traditions," in *The Invention of Tradition*, ed. Eric Hobsbawm and Terence Ranger (Cambridge: Cambridge University Press, 1983), 1–14.

[50] Herodotus 1:32, in *The History*, 48; see Thomas F. Scanlon, "Echoes of Herodotus in Thucydides: Self-Sufficiency, Admiration, and the Law," *Historia: Zeitschrift für Alte Geschichte*, 43.2 (1994): 143–176, 145–147.

[51] Euripides, *The Suppliant Women*, trans. Frank Jones, lines 209–210, in *The Complete Greek Tragedies, Euripides IV*, ed. David Grene and Richmond Lattimore (Chicago: University of Chicago Press, 1958), 66

said educated Englishmen "had by rote" in the Elizabethan era.[52] It was, among its other uses, an assigned text on moral philosophy required in university curricula in theology, and so informed the thinking of learned clergy, especially those licensed to preach.[53] In *The Politics*, Aristotle had argued that the skill of exchange, which at first was not necessary for the maintenance of households, began "to be useful when the society increases." "When the family divided into parts," the philosopher says

> the parts shared in many things, and different parts in different things, which they had to give in exchange for what they wanted, a kind of barter which is still practiced among barbarous nations who exchange with one another the necessaries of life and nothing more....[54]

This form of exchange, Aristotle emphasized, is "not contrary to nature, but is needed for the satisfaction of men's natural wants." "For the art of exchange...arises at first from what is natural, from the circumstance that some have too little, others too much."[55] Exchange, then, is based on "demand, which holds all things together," for if people did not need one another's goods at all, he says, "there would either be no exchange, or not the same exchange."[56] In consequence, exchange provides a basis for community, for without the eagerness of each of us for whatever we lack and our willingness voluntarily to give something in return, there would be no association among people. Transactions based on this principle proceed, therefore, to the mutual advantage of those engaged in them. As such, they create or reinforce mutual bonds of community between the parties and result in a unity of mutually interdependent parts.[57]

These ideas took on a new valence in Rome, beginning in the late Republic as the state extended its imperial sway and trade became an ever more important feature

---

[52] Gabriel Harvey to Edmund Spenser (1579) in *Letter-Book of Gabriel Harvey, A. D. 1573-1580*, ed. Edward J. l. Scott, Camden Society, new series, 33 ([Westminster], 1884), 79. See also Charles B. Schmitt, *Aristotle and the Renaissance* (Cambridge, MA, and London: Harvard University Press, 1983), 34–88, Appendix A, 121–133, and *passim*; Albert O. Hirschman, *The Passions and the Interests: Political Arguments for Capitalism before Its Triumph*, Twentieth Anniversary Edition (Princeton, NJ: Princeton University Press, 1977), 59–60.

[53] Anthony Pagden, *The Fall of Natural Man: The American Indian and the Origin of Comparative Ethnology* (Cambridge: Cambridge University Press, 1982), 7.

[54] *Pol.* 1257a20–29, in Aristotle, *The Politics*, trans. Benjamin Jowett, rev. Jonathan Barnes, ed. Stephen Everson (Cambridge: Cambridge University Press, 1988), 12.

[55] *Pol.* 1257a15–17, 30, Aristotle, *The Politics*,, 12.

[56] *Nic. Eth.* V.5.1133a26–29, in Aristotle, *Nicomachean Ethics*, trans. W. D. Ross, revised J. O. Urmson, in *The Complete Works of Aristotle: The Revised Oxford Edition*, ed. Jonathan Barnes (Princeton, NJ: Princeton University Press, 1984), 2: 1788.

[57] See *Nic. Eth.* VIII.8.1159b12–14, V.9.1159b25–32, in Aristotle, *Complete Works*, 2: 1832–1833.

of the civilization it fostered.[58] Seneca, for example, argued that Providence had provided mankind with the winds to make "communication possible between all peoples" and to join "nations which are separated geographically" through commerce and other means. "God, our author," gave them to us, he says, "in order that the advantages of each region might become known to all, and that we would not be untaught animals without experience of affairs."[59]

In the writings of Origen, the third-century Christian theologian, we find an even more explicit reference to the providential basis of exchange. "Lack of the necessities of life," he says, "has…made things, which originate in other places, to be transported to those men who do not possess them by the arts of sailing and navigation; so that for these reasons one might admire the providence."[60] A century later, the rhetorician Libanius gave further emphasis to the role of providence in the economy: "GOD," he says,

> has not bestowed all his Gifts on every Part of the Earth, but has distributed them among different Nations, that Men wanting the Assistance of one another, might maintain and cultivate Society. And to this End has Providence introduced Commerce, that whatsoever is the Produce of any Nation may be equally enjoyed by all.[61]

Although Libanius was a pagan, and a friend and defender of Julian the Apostate, two of his greatest students were St. Basil the Great and St. John Chrysostom. Each held a

---

[58] See, in general, Jacob Viner, *The Role of Providence in the Social Order: An Essay in Intellectual History* (Princeton, NJ: Princeton University Press, 1972), 35–40; Douglas A. Irwin, *Against the Tide: An Intellectual History of Free Trade* (Princeton, NJ: Princeton University Press, 1996), 11–25; Anthony Pagden, "Stocism, Cosmopolitanism, and the Legacy of European Imperialism," *Constellations*, 7.1 (2000): 3–22; idem, "Human Rights, Natural Rights, and Europe's Imperial Legacy," *Political Theory*, 31.2 (2003): 171–199.

[59] Lucius Annaeus Seneca, "De Ventis" [The Winds], *Naturales Quaestiones* V.18.4, 14, in idem, *Seneca in Ten Volumes*, ed. and trans. Thomas H. Corcoran, 10 vols. (Cambridge, MA: Harvard University Press; London: William Heinemann Ltd., 1972), 10: 114–115, 120–123. See also Lucius Annaeus Florus, *Epitomae de Tito Livio Bellorvm Omnivm Annorvm DCC Libri II*, I, xli.6, as paraphrased in Hugo Grotius, *De Jure Belli ac Pacis Libri Tres*, trans. Francis Kelsey, et al., 2 vols. (Oxford: Clarendon Press, 1925), 1: 125 and 2: 199n3; Lucius Annaeus Florus, *The Epitome of Roman History*, ed. and trans. Edward Seymour Forster (Cambridge, MA: Harvard University Press; London: William Heinemann Ltd., 1984), 190–191; Philo, *De Legatione ad Caium* [The Embassy to Gaius], 47–48, as translated from the Latin in Grotius, *De Jure Belli ac Pacis*, II:2.13.5, trans. 2: 199; *Philo with an English Translation*, ed. and trans. F. H. Colson, 10 vols. (Cambridge, MA: Harvard University Press; London: William Heinemann Ltd., 1962), 10: 24–25; Lucius Mestrius Plutarchus, "Aquane an ignis utilior" [Is Water or Fire More Useful?], 7, Plutarch, *Moralia* 957A, in *Plutarch Moralia in Fifteen Volumes*, ed. and trans. Frank Cole Babbitt, 15 vols. (Cambridge, MA: Harvard University Press; London: William Heinemann Ltd., 1957), 12: 299.

[60] Origen, *Contra Celsum*, IV.77, in *Origen: Contra Celsum*, ed. and trans. Henry Chadwick (Cambridge: Cambridge University Press, 1953), 245; Irwin, *Against the Tide*, 16.

[61] The translation used here is from Hugo Grotius, *The Rights of War and Peace*, ed. and trans. into French in 1724 by Jean Barbeyrac, and subsequently into English in 1738, ed. Richard Tuck, 3 vols. (Indianapolis: Liberty

view similar to their teacher on how providence had arranged the distribution of commodities in the world to promote sociability through trade.[62] St. Ambrose, following St. Basil, developed a related image of Creation.[63] With this Early Christian ancestry, it is no surprise that medieval theologians such as Henry of Langenstein and St. Antoninus of Florence repeated the same conception. It was also invoked by priests in blessing the work of the great international trade fairs of the era.[64]

The idea gained further relevance among European thinkers in the new political and economic environment of the late fifteenth and early sixteenth centuries, dominated as the era was by war and by the first stages of the global expansion set in motion by the explorations of Portuguese and Spanish navigators. In response, some commentators came to see trade on Libanius's model as a means to restore peace to the world and bring unity to its diverse peoples. Among the most influential of these figures was Desiderius Erasmus. In his frequently republished *Querela pacis* (*The Complaint of Peace*), which first appeared in 1517, the humanist offers the "reasons Nature has provided for concord."[65] Nature, he argued, was not satisfied

> simply with the attractions of mutual good will; she wanted friendship to be not only enjoyable but essential. So she shared out the gifts of mind and body in a way that would ensure that no one would be provided with everything and not need on occasion the assistance of the lowly; she gave men different and unequal

---

Fund, 2005), 2: 444; Barbeyrac says that "Our Author has given no Hint for guessing out of what Part of LIBANIUS these Words are taken." For an alternative translation, see Grotius, *De Jure Belli ac Pacis*, 1: 119, trans. 2: 199–200. See also Jacob Viner, *Religious Thought and Economic Society: Four Chapters of an Unfinished Work by Jacob Viner*, ed. Jacques Melitz and Donald Winch (Durham, NC: Duke University Press, 1978), 37 and 37n80; Viner, *The Role of Providence*, 36–37. Viner incorrectly states that the passage appears in *Orationes* III; Irwin repeats the same claim in his *Against the Tide*, 16.

[62] St. Basil the Great, "Upon the gathering together of the waters," *The Hexaemeron*, Homily IV.7; *A Select Library of the Nicene and Post-Nicene Fathers of the Christian Church*, 2nd ser., ed. and trans. Philip Schaff and Henry Wace, 14 vols. (Peabody, MA: Hendrickson Publishers, 1994; first publ. 1890–1900), vol. 8: *Basil: Letters and Select Works*, 75; St. John Chrysostom, *To Stelechius* [*On Compunction*, v], in Grotius, *De Jure Belli ac Pacis*, 1: 125, trans. 2: 199n3. For St. Basil's connection with Libanius, see Raffaella Cribiore, *The School of Libanius in Late Antique Antioch* (Princeton, NJ, and Oxford: Princeton University Press, 2007), 2, 100–104; for St. John Chrysostom's connections with the rhetorician, see Cribiore, *School of Libanius*, 2; J. N. D. Kelly, *Golden Mouth: The Story of John Chrysostom—Ascetic, Preacher, Bishop* (Ithaca, NY: Cornell University Press, 1995), 6–7.

[63] See St. Ambrose, *Hexaemeron* III.v.22, St. Ambrose, *Hexameron, Paradise and Cain and Abel*, trans. John J. Savage (New York: Fathers of the Church, Inc., 1961), 83 [*The Fathers of the Church: A New Translation*, ed. Roy Joseph Defferrari et al., vol. 42].

[64] See Viner, *Role of Providence*, 38; Alexander Rüstow, *Das Versagen des Wirstschaftsliberalismus als relgionsgeschichte Problem* (Istanbul, n.p.; Zurich and New York: Europa Verlag, 1945), 121–122.

[65] There were 32 dated and many other undated editions in Latin during the sixteenth century. The work was also quickly translated into French, Spanish, Dutch, Swiss German, and High German, and in 1559 into English; Desiderius Erasmus, *Querela pacis undique gentium ejectae profligataeque* [A Complaint of Peace

capacities, so that their inequality could be evened out by mutual friendships. Different regions provide different products, the very advantage of which taught exchange between them…. Need created cities, need taught the value of alliance between them….[66]

By the mid-sixteenth century, this Libanian-Erasmian model was widely accepted as an intrinsic feature of the world as God had created it. It appears, for example, in the *Discourse of the Commonweal*, written by Sir Thomas Smith in 1549 and published in 1581.[67] In France, Jean Bodin articulated a similar theory in 1568,[68] while in Italy, Giovanni Botero, writing in 1589, did the same in emphasizing the unifying role of seaborne commerce in joining "the West…with the East, and the South with the North."[69] Two decades later, Hugo Grotius in his *Mare Liberum* also put the argument in the context of global trade in stressing that "all men should have free liberty of negotiation among themselves." Paraphrasing Aristotle as saying that "what was wanting to nature was supplied by negotiation that everyone might have enough," he concluded, as had Libanius and the early Church Fathers, that the need for such trade or exchange was providential.[70] "God himself speaketh this in nature," he says,

seeing he will not have all those things, whereof the life of man standeth in need, to be sufficiently ministered by nature in all places and also vouchsafeth some nations to excel others in arts.

Spurned and Rejected by the Whole World], trans. Betty Radice, in *The Collected Works of Erasmus*, ed. A. H. T. Levi, 86 vols. (Toronto, Buffalo, and London: University of Toronto Press, 1974–2012), 27: introduction and 291; Roland Bainton, "The *Querela Pacis* of Erasmus, Classical and Christian Sources," *Archiv für Reformationsgeschichte*, 42 (1951): 32–47, 32.

[66] Erasmus, *Querela pacis*, 295. See also Desiderius Erasmus, *The Complaint of Peace*, trans. Thomas Paynell (London, 1559). Sig. A4[d]r.

[67] [Sir Thomas Smith], *A Discourse of the Commonweal of This Realm of England, Attributed to Sir Thomas Smith*, ed. Mary Dewar (Charlottesville: University of Virginia Press, 1969), 62.

[68] Jean Bodin, *Response to the Paradoxes of Malestroit*, trans. and ed. Henry Tudor and R. W. Dyson, intro. D. P. O'Brien, notes J. C. M. Starkey (Bristol: Thoemmes Press, 1997), 85–86; Jean Bodin, *La Response de Jean Bodin A. M. de Malestroit, 1568*, nouvelle edition, ed. Henri Hauser (Paris: Librairie Arman Colin, 1932), 34; a second revised edition was published in 1578.

[69] Giovanni Botero, *Della Ragion di Stato libri dieci: con tre libri Delle cause della grandezza, e magnificenza delle città* (Venice: Appresso i Gioliti, 1589). An English translation of the second part of this work first appeared in 1606: Giovanni Botero, *A treatise, concerning the causes of the magnificencie and greatnes of cities, deuided into three bookes*, trans. Robert Peterson (London, 1606), 18–19. Another translation into English appeared in 1635: Giovanni Botero, *The cause of the greatnesse of cities. Three bookes. With certaine observations concerning the sea*, trans. Sir T[homas] H[awkins] (London, 1635), 32–33.

[70] Hugo Grotius, *Mare Liberum, sive, De jure quod Batavis competit ad Indicana commercia dissertatio* (Leiden: Ex officina L Elzevirri, 1609); Hugo Grotius, *The Free Sea*, trans. Richard Hakluyt, ed. David Armitage (Indianapolis: Liberty Fund, 2004), 49, quoting *Pol.* 1259a30. The manuscript of Hakluyt's translation is Inner Temple Library, Petyt MS 529.

To what end are these things but that he would maintain human friendship by their mutual wants and plenty, lest everyone think themselves sufficient for themselves [and] for this only thing should be made insociable? Now it cometh to pass that one nation should supply the want of another by the appointment of divine justice, that thereby…that which is brought forth anywhere might seem to be bred with all.[71]

The translation is by Richard Hakluyt, the cosmographer and promoter of English exploration and colonial enterprise, who held very similar views.[72]

By the time Grotius wrote down his version of the theory, its central idea was already a commonplace among the English. Thomas Becon, the religious reformer and commonwealthman, invoked it in "A prayer for Marchaunts," published in 1550. There he called upon "Almightye god maker & disposer of all thynges…to preserue & kepe al such as trauel ether bi land or by sea…& to giue them saf passage both in their going & coming." Merchants, the prayer implied, served the welfare not just of their own communities but humanity more generally, since God had placed the things "necessary for ye vse of men in diuers lands & sundry countries" so that "al kindes of men shuld be knit together in vnity & loue, seinge we al haue need one of a nothers help, one country of another counryes commodity, one realm of a nother realms gifts & frutes."[73]

A similar idea is captured in the epigram—the original is in Latin—that John Wheeler, sometime secretary of the Society of Merchant Adventurers of England, used in 1601 to frame the text of his *Treatise of Commerce*: "By commerce peoples widely separated by sea and mountains are brought together, so that whatever is produced anywhere is distributed to all."[74] As John Wheeler put it: "There is nothing in the world so ordinarie and naturall unto men, as to contract, truck, merchandise,

---

[71] Grotius, *Free Sea*, 10.

[72] David Harris Sacks, "Discourses of Western Planting: Richard Hakluyt and the Making of the Atlantic World," in *The Atlantic World and Virginia, 1550–1624*, ed. Peter Mancall (Chapel Hill: University of North Carolina Press, 2007), 410–453.

[73] [Thomas Becon], *The flour of godly praiers* (London, 1550), fol. 30r–v; for Becon's career, see Derrick Sherwin Bailey, *Thomas Becon and the Reformation of the Church of England* (Edinburgh and London: Oliver and Boyd, 1953); Seymour Baker House, "Becon, Thomas (1512/13–1567)," in *Oxford Dictionary of National Biography*, Oxford University Press, 2004; online ed., Oct 2009, http://www.oxforddnb.com/view/article/1918, accessed January 17, 2011.

[74] "Commercio Gentes mare, montibusque, discretae miscentur, vt quod usqum nascitue, apud omnes affluat"; John Wheeler, *A treatise of commerce vvherin are shevved the commodies* [sic] *arising by a wel ordered, and ruled trade, such as that of the Societie of Merchantes Adventurers is proved to bee, written principallie for the better information of those who doubt of the necessarienes of the said Societie in the state of the realme of Englande* (Middleburgh, 1601), 1.

and traffique with one another" for their respective benefits.[75] This understanding, having first germinated among ancient Greek and Roman thinkers, continued to bear fruit on both sides of the Atlantic well into the early modern era and beyond.[76]

By the ethical traditions and standards in place in medieval and early modern Europe, trade was subject to the principle of justice as it applied to buying and selling. According to the Aristotelian model, in order to be just, mercantile transactions were governed by commutative rather than distributive justice and required equivalence of exchange. It was necessary, therefore, for the parties to find a fair, or just, price for the commodities exchanged, so that the return received by each of them was neither too much nor too little, according to the differing worth of the goods they were trading; each was to give an appropriate share of his surplus to meet the needs of the other.[77] Commerce, in effect, involved the mutual exchange of benefits, running parallel to the exchange of gifts made by individuals to initiate or reinforce friendship in communities.

In ancient and Renaissance moral theory, a gift is taken to be the antithesis of a contract. Theorists agreed that both forms of exchange had the power to bind parties to one another. With gifts, however, what is exchanged is goodwill, symbolized by the material items passing between the parties. On this view, the giving and reciprocating of goodwill induces lasting loyalty between giver and receiver and encourages the creation of long-term bonds of affiliation and affection. Gift exchange, therefore, has the capacity to provide social stability, while contracts, it was believed, cannot, because the mutual obligations they create were considered to dissolve with the completion of the exchange. For trade to hold a society together,

[75] Wheeler, *A treatise of commerce*, 316; Keith Wrightson, *Earthly Necessities: Economic Lives in Early Modern Britain* (New Haven, CT, and London: Yale University Press, 2000), 203–204.

[76] Viner, *Role of Providence*, 40–46; Hirschman, *The Passions and the Interests*, 59–60, 70–81; see Jacques Savary, *Le parfait négociant, ou, Instruction generale pour ce qui regarde le commerce des marchanises de France, & des pays étranger*, 7th ed. (Paris: Chez M, Guignardet et C. Robustel, 1713; first publ. 1675), 1; Charles de Secondat, Baron de Montesquieu, *The Spirit of the Laws*, Part IV, Books 20, 21, trans. and ed. Anne H. Cohler, Basia Carolyn Miller, and Harold Samuel Stone (Cambridge: Cambridge University Press, 1989), 337–397, see esp. 338–339, 387–390; Joseph Addison, *The Spectator*, No. 69, Saturday, May 19 [1711], Joseph Addison, Richard Steele, et al., *The Spectator*, 8 vols. (Dublin: Peter Wilson, 1756), 1: 279; Daniel Defoe, *Review*, February 3, 1713; Benjamin Franklin, "A Modest Enquiry into the Nature and Necessity of Paper-Currency," Philadelphia, April 3, 1729 (Philadelphia: New Printing-Office, 1729) in *Benjamin Franklin: Writings*, ed. J. A. Leo May (New York: The Library of America, 1987), 125; Thomas Hutchinson, *The History of the Colony and Plantation of Massachusetts-Bay*, ed. Lawrence Shaw Mayo, 3 vols. (Cambridge, MA: Harvard University Press, 1936), 2: 343.

[77] *Nic. Eth.* V.5.1132b22–1133b28, in Aristotle, *The Complete Works*, 2:1755–1760; see also Karl Polanyi, "Aristotle Discovers the Economy," in *Trade and Market in the Early Empires: Economies in History and Theory*, ed. Karl Polanyi, Conrad M. Arensberg, and Harry W. Pearson (Glencoe, IL: The Free Press and The Falcon's Wing Press, 1957), 64–94; David Harris Sacks, "The Greed of Judas: Avarice, Monopoly, and the Moral Economy in England, ca. 1350–ca. 1600," *Journal of Medieval and Early Modern Studies*, 28.2 (1998): 263–307, 271–273.

therefore, the community would have to become a perpetual marketplace like early modern London, a "Faire" that "lasts all year," with corruption by greed the expected outcome.[78]

However, as we have just seen, many Western commentators—beginning at least as early at the fifth century B.C.E.—understood commercial dealings to create permanent bonds of mutual dependency of just the kind denied in the analysis of contracts. Hence, it made sense to conceive of exchange—as Erasmus, Grotius, and others had done—in terms of friendship. According to ancient moral theory, friendship "is very necessary" for "living." "[W]ithout friends," Aristotle says, "no one would choose to live." Friendship, therefore, "seems...to hold states together, and lawgivers to care more for it than justice." Accordingly "even rich men and those in possession of office and of dominating power are thought to need friends." "What use" would be their "prosperity" and social rank, Aristotle asks, "without the opportunity of benevolence, which is exercised chiefly and in its most laudable form towards friends?"[79] This understanding treats gift exchange not just as an instrument for making friends, or a consequence of friendships that have already been made, but takes it to be constitutive of friendship itself. For Aristotle and his followers, however, only some friendships were made for virtue's sake, where the friends willed each others' good in the same terms as they willed their own. Others were made for purposes of pleasure.[80] Most were utility friendships, made primarily for advancing self-interest. Nevertheless, as Aristotle had taught, such friendships also were, or could be, socially stabilizing.[81]

Just as the language of the gift permeated the traditions of social interchange among early modern Europeans, so too did the language of friendship. The subject was treated at length in the era's vast outpouring of courtesy books, conduct manuals, and discussions of civility, where what constituted "true friendship" represented a major theme.[82] Most of these commentaries concentrated on the place of friendship

---

[78] John Davies of Hereford, "Vpon English Prouerbes," in *The Scourge of Folly Consisting of satyricall Epigramms and others in honor of many noble and worthy Persons of our Land. Together With a pleasant (though discordant) Descant vpon most English Prouerbes and others* (London, 1611), 42.

[79] *Nic. Eth.* VIII.1.1155a5–25, in Aristotle, *Works*, 2: 1825; A. W. Price, *Love and Friendship in Plato and Aristotle* (Oxford: Oxford University Press, 1989); Lorraine Smith Pangle, *Aristotle and the Philosophy of Friendship* (Cambridge: Cambridge University Press, 2003); Susan Stern-Gillet, *Aristotle's Philosophy of Friendship* (Albany: State University of New York, 1995). Marcus Tullius Cicero, *Laelius de amicitia, in idem, De re publica; De legibus; Cato maior de senectute; Laelius de amicitia*, ed. J. G. F. Powell (Oxford and New York: Oxford University Press, 2006).

[80] See *Nic. Eth.* VIII.2.1155b16–VIII.3.1156b32, in Aristotle, *The Complete Works*, 2: 1826–1828, and Books VIII and IX *passim*; 2:1825–1852.

[81] *Nic. Eth.* VIII.9.1160a9–30, in Aristotle, *The Complete Works*, 2: 1833.

[82] See, e.g., Joseph Hall, *Characters of the Vertvues and Vices: In two Bookes* (London, 1608), 45–50; Ben-Amos, *Culture of Giving*, 255–261; Thomas, *Ends of Life*, 187–197.

in the manners and morals of gentlemen, of course. But friendship and the practices of exchange that went with it also played a critical role in the ethos of civil officials and of merchants like John Guy.[83] The wills of merchants, for example, frequently mention particular individuals as friends, often using the word itself, naming them as beneficiaries, as overseers, as witnesses, and as the guardians of their children.[84] This pattern is hardly surprising given the supreme importance of credit in commercial transactions in this period, and the role of trust between persons of known reputation in sustaining credit relations among business and trading partners.[85]

As a Bristol merchant trained in his calling in the later sixteenth century, John Guy was well aware of this feature in his home city's trading economy. According to his understanding of commercial practices, merchants traded within an interlocking nexus of credit. "Neither the borrower not the lender have any money," he told his fellow MPs in the 1624 Parliament, "for the borrower commonly as he receives with one hand he pays with the other, and for the lender it is ever out of his hands, he will borrow a small sum to make up a greater to put it out."[86] In consequence, merchant activity in Guy's Bristol depended upon mutually supportive relations within a community of merchants whose members not only competed with each other, but also regularly cooperated in trading together. Personally known to one another for their credit-worthiness, these merchants were bound together by trust and multiple ties of association and sociability.[87] In consequence, it was normal practice among them to rely on the services of those they called their friends to handle a host of important transactions for them, as the Bristol merchant John Browne made clear by including two model letters "to a friend" in his widely known handbook for merchant apprentices, his *Marchants Avizo*, first published in 1589. In keeping with the requirements of the form, those letters replicate all the required language of gratitude and "goodwill" and promises of reciprocity that we find discussed in ancient ethical discourse and Renaissance conduct books.[88]

---

[83] See Heal, *Hospitality*, 304–315.

[84] Grassby, *Kinship and Capitalism*, Tables 6.1 and 6.2, 222, 223, 241–247, 309–310. In some circumstances and places, "friend" could also carry the contractual meaning of "agent" in commercial language; see Francesca Trivellato, *The Familiarity of Strangers: The Sephardic Diaspora, Livorno, and Cross-Cultural Trade in the Early Modern Period* (New Haven. CT, and London: Yale University Press, 2009), chap. 7.

[85] Craig Muldrew, *The Economy of Obligation: The Culture of Credit and Social Relations in Early Modern England* (Basingstoke: Macmillan Press Ltd., 1998), 148–195.

[86] Parliamentary Diary of John Holles, 1624, British Library, Harl. MS 6383, fol. 91v; a slightly different version of this speech is to be found in the Parliamentary Diary of John Pym, 1624, Northampton Record Office, Finch-Hatton MS 50, fol. 22. See David Harris Sacks, *The Widening Gate: Bristol and the Atlantic Economy, 1450–1700* (Berkeley and Los Angeles: University of California Press, 1991), 72. For commentary on the culture of credit, see Muldrew, *Economy of Obligation*, 123–147.

[87] Sacks, *Widening Gate*, 65–66, 72–73, 78–79, 81, 83–84, 358.

[88] I[ohn] B[rowne], *The Marchants Avizo very necessarie for their sones and seruants, when they first send them beyond the seas, as to Spaine and Portingale or other countreyes* (London, 1589), 15–16, there were

Most friendships formed in trade were utility friendships in which each party acted for his own advantage. The resulting reciprocities nevertheless created a mutually supporting system of exchange.[89] Drawing on traditions of discourse first developed in the ancient Mediterranean, many early modern theorists saw this blessing of exchange as the steppingstone to universal peace.[90]

THE PARADOXES AND BLESSINGS OF EXCHANGE

We can now return to Newfoundland and John Guy's dealings with its natives. Guy was no philosopher. But his encounter with the Beothuks would have been unthinkable had he not judged them to be human beings possessed with reason, who, for all their cultural differences with the English, were fully capable of seeking their own good, forming beneficial allegiances, and measuring their actions to their ends. As such, he saw them as having the instincts for honest dealing, personal loyalty, and productive commerce, and therefore to be a people subject to the inducements of the gift economy and the arts of persuasion. Hence, Guy took pains to assure that he was scrupulously just in his dealings with them, taking nothing for which he did not leave something he regarded of equal value in return, in order, as he put it, to "winne them by fayre meanes."[91] The fact that these native peoples were not Christians, and that Guy repeatedly referred to them as "savages," did not prevent him from sharing food and engaging sociably with them, and from treating them as naturally free persons in their worldly actions, already possessed of natural reason and a sense of natural justice, and therefore of the capacity to achieve full civility. Writing a few years after Guy had left Newfoundland, Richard Whitbourne called them "an ingenious and tractable people (being well vsed)," albeit they were "something rude and sauage...hauing neither knowledge of God, nor liuing under any kinde of ciuill gouernement."[92]

---

subsequent editions in 1590, 1591, 1607, 1616, and 1640; there is also a modern edition: I[ohn] B[rowne], *The Marchants Avizo...1589*, ed. Patrick McGrath (Boston: Baker Library, Harvard Graduate School of Business Administration, 1957), 17, 18.

[89] See, e.g., Thomas Mun. *England's treasure by forraign trade, or, The ballance of our forraign trade is the rule of our treasure* (London, 166), 84. Muldrew has called this conception the "sociability of credit and commerce"; Muldrew, *Economy of Obligation*, 123–147.

[90] David Harris Sacks, "Rebuilding Solomon's Temple: Richard Hakluyt's Great Instauration," in *New Worlds Reflected: Travel and Utopia in the Early Modern Period*, ed. Chloë Houston (Farnham, Surrey: Ashgate Publishing, 2010), 17–56.

[91] Guy, "Iournall," 71, 76.

[92] Richard Whitbourne, *A Discourse and Discouery of Nevv-found-land* (London, 1620), 2; similar phrasing appears in the conclusion of the pamphlet, sig. P3r; reprinted in *Newfoundland Discovered*, 117, 192; there were earlier editions in 1620 and 1622.

Although in his journal Guy made no mention of a desire to convert the Beothuks, his colonizing company was founded in 1610, quoting its royal charter, "principally to increase the knowledge of the Omnipotent God and the propagation of our Christian faith" among the native peoples of Newfoundland.[93] Many other early documents of the colony also endow the enterprise with a similar proselytizing mission.[94] Although the English in Newfoundland had virtually no success in thus bringing the name of Christ to the Beothuks, it was not possible for them, or for most Europeans, to imagine an enduring imperial enterprise that did not also involve the conversion of indigenous peoples to Christianity.[95] Among other benefits, accomplishing this goal would help them in achieving and maintaining stable relations with their neighbors.

A number of early commentators, including Columbus, Verrazano, Cartier, Hakluyt, and Harriot, thought conversion would be simple and unproblematic.[96] For several of these figures, starting with Columbus, the natives' willingness to trade provided a basis for confidence that their missionary efforts would achieve success without difficulty. The Admiral recorded this belief in recounting his first landing on Guanahani—the island he called San Salvador. Recognizing that its inhabitants "were people who would be better freed [from error] and converted to our Holy Faith by love than by force," he gave them red caps, glass beads, and other small objects "in order that they would be friendly to us." "They took so much pleasure," he says, "and became so much our friends that it was a marvel.... T]hey took everything and gave what they had very willingly.[97] Like Guy afterward, Columbus also stressed the need for fairness as well as reciprocity in his dealings with the natives "in order," he says, that they "would hold us in esteem" and would welcome later visitors sent from Spain.[98] These features—that is, the natives' apparent sense of just dealing and their capacity for goodwill—appear to have suggested to Columbus that they

[93] Pat. Roll. 8 Jac. I, pt.viii: "The Treasurer and Company of Adventurers and Planters of the City of London and Bristol for the Colony of Plantation in Newfound Land, 2 May 1610," in Cecil T. Carr, ed., *Select Charters of the Trading Companies*, [Publications of the Selden Society, vol. 28, 1913] (London: B. Quaritch, 1913), 51–62, 52.

[94] See, e.g., T. C. [possibly Thomas Cary], *A short discourse of the New-found-land Contaynig* [sic] *diverse reasons and inducements, for the planting of that countrey* (Dublin, 1623), sig. A[4]r–v, reprinted in *Newfoundland Discovered*, 228; for references to related religious themes in Newfoundland's early history, see *Newfoundland Discovered*, 102, 110.

[95] Marshall, *History and Ethnography of the Beothuk*, 36–37.

[96] See [Columbus], *Diario*, fols. 9r (64–65), 13v (88–89), 22r (140–141); Verrazzano, "Copia di una lettera," Morgan, Ms. 776, fol. 9r, in *Voyages of Giovanni da Verrazzano*, 130–131, 141; Thomas Harriot, *A briefe and true report of the new found land of Virginia*, ed. Theodor de Bry (Frankfort, 1590), 25; Jacques Cartier, *Relations*, 333n247; Richard Hakluyt, "Discourse of Western Planting," 1584, in *The Original Writings and Correspondence of the Two Richard Hakluyts*, ed. E. G. R. Taylor, 2 vols. (Hakluyt Soc., 2nd ser. Nos. 76–77, 1935), 2: 214–218.

[97] [Columbus], *Diario*, fol. 9r (64–65).

[98] [Columbus], *Diario*, fol. 12r (82–83); see also fol. 12v (84–87).

could be won to Christianity by persuasion and reciprocal acts of kindness, and that making Christians and non-Christians mutually dependent would pave the way for the latter's conversion. He gave orders to his crew, therefore, to prevent the sailors from alienating the natives in separately bartering with them or by taking things from their dwellings.[99] Viewed in this light, fairness and reciprocity are the instrumental means to a practical end, not ends in themselves, but that does not rob them of their moral significance.

However, even in this account of Columbus's first voyage there was more than a hint of potential difficulties arising, not just from the fierce and warlike Caribs, said to be cannibals, but even from the people—the Arawaks—with whom Columbus engaged in amicable exchanges on first landing in the West Indies. "[T]hese people are very gentle," he said, "and because of their desire to have some of our things, and believing that nothing will be given them without their giving something, and not having anything, they take what they can" and rush away.[100] Behavior of this kind was a recurring problem in relations between the Europeans and native peoples not only in the Caribbean but elsewhere in North America.[101] If left unguarded, items that counted for Europeans as private property, whose theft was subject to strict punishment, were sometimes treated by the natives as free for the taking. In some respects, indeed, this conduct followed directly from the systems of signaling and "silent trade" employed in the first encounters between the parties.[102]

The actions of Guy and his men at Trinity Bay in 1612 reveal the common pattern. On observing some fires on shore, they landed at the site to explore. They found several unoccupied tent-like structures containing cooking implements, animal skins, and food items. Guy records that

> order was taken that nothing should be diminished, & because the savages should know that some had bin theare, everything was removed out of his place, & brought into one of the cabines, and laid orderlie one upon he other, & the kettle hanged over them, whearin thear was put some bisket, & three or fower amber beades.[103]

---

99 [Columbus], *Diario*, fols. 10r (72–73), 18r (116–117), 18v (120–121).

100 [Columbus], *Diario*, fol. 10r (70–71); see also Cartier, *Voyages*, 22–23; Cartier, *Relations*, ed. Bideaux, 113.

101 See, e.g., the journal entry for July 16, 1585 made by Sir Richard Grenville, aboard the *Tiger*, on its 1585 voyage to Virginia: "… one of our boates with the Admirall [Philip Amadas] was sent to Aquascococke to demaund a siluer cup which one of the Sauvages had stolen from vs, and not receiuving it according to his promise, we burnt, and spoyled their corne, and Towne, all the people being fledde." "The voyage made by Sir Richard Greenuile, for Sir Walter Ralegh, to Virginia, in the yeere, 1585," in Hakluyt, *Principall Navigations* (1589), 736; idem, *Principal Navigations* (1598/9–1600), 3: 253.

102 I owe this suggestion to Professor Karen Ordahl Kupperman.

103 Guy; "Iournall," 71; see also Crout to Willoughby, *Newfoundland Discovered*, 84; however, Crout records that the Englishmen actually took away two or three children's shoes; Nottingham University, Middleton

Only "a little piece of fleshe"—"a beaver cod," that is, the inguinal sac of the beaver—was "brought away," he says. The leaving of the biscuit and beads, which in effect represented the English offering recompense for the beaver cod they had taken, was done, as we already mentioned, "to beginne to winne them by fayre meanes" and thereby initiate trade. Further exchanges then followed, as we have also seen.[104] However, when natives witnessed Europeans helping themselves to natural products of their lands, they sometimes seem to have concluded, as did the Beothuks in Newfoundland, that tools and weapons found in the absence of their owners were left as recompense for the taking.[105]

Although the Europeans and the native peoples they encountered each possessed their own modes of gift exchange and mechanisms for friendship, their practices arose within markedly different systems of kinship, social status, honor, property relations, law, natural knowledge, and religion, to name only the most obvious areas of difference. In consequence, not only were there numerous instances of misunderstanding, but the possibility of violence was always close to the surface.[106] In 1613, for example, the efforts of the Newfoundland Company to reopen trading relations with Beothuks were thwarted because the colonists found no trace of the Beothuks, since, according to a later report, they had fled the area after a violent chance encounter with some fishermen and from thence continued to attack European vessels, regardless of origin, whenever they approached Trinity Bay.[107] There were a number of murderous attacks on the French, and on more than one occasion, the Beothuks also clashed with English settlers in reprisal for earlier incidents with English fishermen.[108] These incidents reduced considerably the hope of conducting peaceful

MSS, Mi X 1/66, fol. 4, cited in *Newfoundland Discovered*, 71n1; for a related example, see Cartier, *Voyages*, 17; Cartier, *Relations*, ed. Bideaux, 108.

[104] Guy, "Iournall," 71–76; see also Crout to Willoughby, *Newfoundland Discovered*, 84–86.

[105] See Whitbourne, *Discourse*, 3–4 sig. P3r–v; *Newfoundland Discovered*, 118, 192–194. For similar evidence from Tidewater Virginia during the starving times faced by the first setters in what Edmund S. Morgan called "the Jamestown fiasco," see Edmund Sears Morgan, *American Slavery, American Freedom: The Ordeal of Colonial Virginia* (New York: W. W. Norton, 1975), 44–107; Kupperman, *The Jamestown Project*, 210–240; Horn, *A Land as God Made It*, 99–130.

[106] See, e.g., Cartier, *Voyages*, 70–72; Cartier, *Relations*, ed. Bideaux, 163–164. Crout to Willoughy, in *Newfoundland Discovered*, 84; see also *Newfoundland Discovered*, 86; David Kirke to Archbishop Laud, September 29, 1639, TNA, CO 1/10, fols. 97–115; excepted in Henry Kirke, *The First English Conquest of Canada, with some Account of the Earliest Settlements in Nova Scotia and Newfoundland*, 2nd ed. (London: Sampson Low, Marston & Co. Ltd., 1908), 139–142; James P. Howley, *The Beothucks or Red Indians: The Aboriginal Inhabitants of Newfoundland* (Cambridge: Cambridge University Press, 1915), 24; see Marshall, *History and Ethnography of the Beothuk*, 38; Cell, "Introduction," 11–12; Cell, *English Enterprise*, 69.

[107] Howley, *The Beothucks*, 22; Kirke, *English Conquest of Canada*, 139–142.

[108] Whitbourne, *Discourse*, 3–4 sig. P3r–v; *Newfoundland Discovered*, 118, 192–194; Cell, "Introduction," 35. Marshall, *History and Ethnography of the Beothuk*, 38.

trading ventures with them. As Whitbourne stressed, the Beothuks "are a people that will seeke to reuenge any wrongs done vnto to them."[109]

Severe conflicts arose elsewhere along North America's Atlantic coast in this early period as European settlements grew and their inhabitants increasingly encroached on lands, woods, and waters long in use by the indigenous populations. In Virginia, for example, there was trouble almost from the very start of the Jamestown settlement in 1607 and, in 1622, 347 settlers were killed in attacks on the Jamestown colony. This "great massacre," as it was called, set off a decade-long war.[110] Those events defeated the high hopes of the English in Virginia for the creation of a social order based on the blessings of exchange and the power of friendship and benevolence.

The founding documents and promotional literature for most of the early English colonies in North American were grounded, like those of Virginia, in the image of society as a peaceable kingdom in which natives and newcomers would come to live together in productive exchange and Christian charity.[111] However, it is not one that could easily withstand the dissonance between European expectations and the actual behaviors they encountered from their indigenous neighbors or that they exhibited themselves, let alone the growth of permanent European settlements in lands that once had belonged exclusively to the original inhabitants. Trust, essential as we have seen for the conduct of all forms of exchange, could not be consistently sustained on either side under these conditions.

CONCLUSION

According to a standard definition, the maintenance of trust implies the existence of confidence between the parties. It is performative, "an obligation of conscience," as the lawyers said, at once signifying the parties' intention or will to do what they say they will do, and their ability to do so.[112] Trust can break down on either score,

---

[109] On clashes between English settlers and the native population of Virginia, see Beverley, *The History of and Present State of Virginia*, 34, 50–55, 60–62; see also Horn, *A Land as God Made It*, 157–191, 249–278.

[110] Hakluyt, "Discourse of Western Planting," 1584, in *Original Writings and Correspondence of the Two Richard Hakluyts*, 2: 214–218, 257–265; Harriot, *A briefe and true report*, 24–30; Sacks, "Discourses of Western Planting," 436–446.

[111] *Fides est obligatio conscientiae unius ad intentionem alterius* ("Trust is an obligation of conscience of one to the will of another"); Francis Bacon, *The Learned Reading of Sir Francis Bacon, One of her Majesties learned Counsell at Law, upon the Statute of Uses: Being his double Reading to the Honourable Society of Grayes Inne* (London, 1642), 8. Bacon's readings took place in Gray's Inn during 1600–1601.

[112] See, e.g., David Harris Sacks, "The Promise and the Contract: *Slade's Case* (1602) in Perspective," in *Rhetoric and Law in Early Modern Europe*, ed. Lorna Hutson and Victoria Kahn (New Haven, CT: Yale University Press, 2001), 28–53; see also idem, "Parliament, Liberty, and Commonweal," in *Parliament and Liberty from the Reign of Elizabeth I to the Long Parliament*, ed. J. H. Hexter (Stanford, CA: Stanford University Press, 1992), 111–112.

but is most vulnerable when the parties misapprehend their counterparts' outlooks and purposes and do not share the same understandings, customs, and habits regarding personal and collective duties, as happened in the early Atlantic world. For the English, obligations arose voluntarily as matters of choice. A breach was conceived as an offense or sin for which the wrongdoer was understood or judged to be personally culpable and guilty. Among the indigenous peoples of North America, obligations arose largely from already existing status ties or dependencies, or were the product of newly created fictive forms of kinship or association. Breaches here resulted in the wrongdoer's disgrace or shame before his community.

These differences in norms and habits deeply affected the conduct of cross-cultural exchange in North America during the first age of European exploration and settlement. But they did not prevent it, since trade across cultural boundaries also held out the opportunities on both sides for the acquisition of knowledge of what the world had to offer that might prove useful for maintaining their respective ways of life or improving it.

Although cross-cultural trade has not made friendship a necessary feature of commercial society or produced a more tranquil and harmonious world, it has become an aspect of the processes of globalization whose antiquity we have been tracing. In this context the blessings of exchange have resulted primarily in the discovery of new commodities, new markets, and new trade routes, and the creation of new forms of political dominion and economic organization, often locked in conflict with one another, not in the promotion of universal peace. In this new world, the establishment and maintenance of trust among individuals and between peoples remains as important as ever, if harder and harder to attain.

ACKNOWLEDGMENTS

Earlier versions of this essay were presented at the European Social Science History Conference, in Ghent, Belgium, April 13, 2010, at the John Carter Brown Library, Providence, Rhode Island, May 26, 2010, and at the History Department Seminar, Johns Hopkins University, October 18, 2010. I am grateful to those attending each of these presentations for their comments and questions.

3

Trading with the Muslim World

RELIGIOUS LIMITS AND PROSCRIPTIONS IN THE

PORTUGUESE EMPIRE (CA. 1480–1570)

Giuseppe Marcocci

CROSS-CULTURAL TRADE IN A CATHOLIC MERCHANT EMPIRE

The legacy of a scholarly tradition that tended to present religion and commerce as separate, if not opposite, forces continues to influence current scholarship on the overseas empires established by the Iberian monarchies in the early modern period.[1] This persistent commonplace preserves the widespread opinion existing in Christian Europe, especially before the Reformation, that merchants were often identified with sinners and were thus limited in their political and economic influence.[2] In this

---

[1] I am thinking here of the long-lasting influence, explicit or not, of classic and fundamental works like Huguette Chaunu and Pierre Chaunu, *Séville et l'Atlantique, 1504–1650* (Paris: Armand Colin, 1955–1960), Carlo M. Cipolla, *Guns and Sails in the Early Phase of European Expansion, 1400–1700* (London: Collins, 1966), and Vitorino Magalhães Godinho's *L'Économie de l'émpire portugais aux XVe et XVIe siècles* (Paris: SEVPEN, 1969) and *Os Descobrimentos e a economia mundial*, 2 vols. (Lisboa: Presença, 1981–1982). Among recent works, see Carla Rahn Phillips, "The Growth and Composition of Trade in the Iberian Empires, 1450–1750," in *The Rise of Merchant Empires: Long-Distance Trade in the Early Modern World, 1350–1750*, ed. James D. Tracy (Cambridge: Cambridge University Press, 1990), 34–101. Even if partially revised, this idea still brims in Anthony John R. Russell-Wood, *The Portuguese Empire, 1415–1808: A World on the Move* (Baltimore: The Johns Hopkins University Press, 1998), Jorge Nascimento Rodrigues and Tessaleno C. Devezas, *Pioneers of Globalization: Why the Portuguese Surprised the World* (Vila Nova de Famalicão: Centro Atlântico, 2007), and Anthony R. Disney, *A History of Portugal and the Portuguese Empire: From Beginnings to 1807*, 2 vols. (Cambridge: Cambridge University Press, 2009).

[2] Odd Langholm, *The Merchant in the Confessional: Trade and Price in the Pre-Reformation Penitential Handbooks* (Leiden: Brill, 2003). For an alternative interpretation of the relation between religion and

chapter, I wish to revisit this truism and shed new light on the relationship between religion, commerce, and the state during the first century of the Portuguese overseas expansion.

In the past two decades, we have witnessed a renewed interest in early modern overseas empires.[3] Today, many consider the world that emerged between the fifteenth and seventeenth centuries as an early global system of connected empires.[4] Unlike an older imperial historiography, which was centered on the metropole and emphasized the military and economic power of the state, this new emphasis on connectivity has brought to light a variety of organizational structures that were only loosely connected to sovereign authorities. For example, it has shown that in the Atlantic and the Indian Oceans, regional trade long predated the arrival of European powers and, after the establishment of European settlers, it often depended on unofficial settlements of escapees, captives, and renegades, who developed their own commercial networks.[5]

There are good reasons to stress the weakness of government institutions (as António Manuel Hespanha has done throughout his work) in the Portuguese case, the specific context to which this chapter is devoted.[6] However, we must not underestimate the role that the Iberian Crowns played in the beginnings of European colonialism. During the initial phase of exploration and expansion along Africa's Atlantic coast, the Europeans organized their main commercial ventures "as an extension of the state."[7] Navigators and merchants coming from all over Europe

economics among medieval canon lawyers and theologians, which emphasizes a variety of moral justifications of economic activities, see Giacomo Todeschini, *I mercanti e il tempio: La società cristiana e il circolo virtuoso della ricchezza tra Medioevo ed età moderna* (Bologna: Il Mulino 2002).

[3] For an introduction, see Linda Colley, "What Is Imperial History Now?," in *What Is History Now?*, ed. David Cannadine (New York: Palgrave Macmillan, 2002), 132–147.

[4] Sanjay Subrahmanyam, "Holding the World in Balance: The Connected Histories of the Iberian Empires, 1500–1640," *The American Historical Review*, 112 (2007): 1359–1385.

[5] Anthony J. Disney, "Contrasting Models of 'Empire': The Estado da Índia and East Asia in the Sixteenth and Early Seventeenth Centuries," in *The Portuguese and the Pacific: Proceedings of the International Colloquium*, ed. Frank Dutra and João Camilo dos Santos (Santa Barbara: Center for Portuguese Studies, University of California, Santa Barbara, 1995), 26–37; Malyn Newitt, "Formal and Informal Empire in the History of Portuguese Expansion," *Portuguese Studies*, 17 (2001): 2–21. See also Linda Colley, *Captives: Britain, Empire and the World, 1600–1850* (London: Jonathan Cape, 2002).

[6] António Manuel Hespanha, *As vésperas do Leviathan: Instituições e poder político; Portugal, séc. XVII* (Coimbra: Almedina, 1994). For the specific case of the empire, see his essays "Estruturas político administrativas do Império português," in *Outro mundo novo vimos*, ed. Ana Maria Rodrigues and Joaquim Soeiro de Brito (Lisboa: CNCDP, 2001), 23–41, and "A constituição do Império português: Revisão de alguns enviesamentos correntes," in *O Antigo Regime nos trópicos: A dinâmica imperial portuguesa, séculos XVI–XVIII*, ed. João Fragoso, Maria Fernanda Bicalho, and Maria de Fátima Gouvêa (Rio de Janeiro: Civilização Brasileira, 2001), 163–188. James Muldoon criticizes the centrality of the concept of state in the history of European empires in his *Empire and Order: The Concept of Empire, 800–1800* (New York: Palgrave Macmillan, 1999).

[7] James D. Tracy, "Introduction," in *The Political Economy of Merchant Empires: State Power and World Trade, 1350–1750*, ed. James D. Tracy (Cambridge and New York: Cambridge University Press, 1991), 1–13, 2.

(mostly from Venice, Genoa, Florence, Flanders, and Germany) sailed under the Portuguese flag, while the Crown mobilized considerable resources to man their expeditions. From the start, these ventures led to an unprecedented increase in commercial exchanges that infringed on the rules set by the church concerning the goods in which and the people with whom Christians were allowed to trade. In Morocco and in West Africa, Europeans bought and sold a variety of commodities with non-Christians, especially with those Muslims who controlled internal trade routes and coastal markets. These transactions caused trouble for two reasons. The official rhetoric of the Portuguese monarchy incessantly called for Holy War and total destruction of the Muslims, reviving the spirit of the Iberian Reconquista. Moreover, canon law had long prohibited selling "infidels" arms or any items, such as horses, timber, or metals, that could be used to fight against Christians. Unlike Islamic jurists, who denounced trading in all impure and forbidden products, not only weapons, Christian theologians feared only the threat of war.[8]

When we examine carefully the early legal justifications of Portuguese and Spanish colonialism, we find that fifteenth-century pontifical bulls granted to the Iberian Crowns paid significant attention to trade, in spite of their general warlike tone.[9] They reasserted the traditional limits imposed on the trade with "infidels," but implicitly recognized the commercial aims of the overseas Iberian empires insofar as they reminded Portugal and Spain that their claims to exclusive rights on conquering lands and exchanging goods outside Europe were inseparable from their duty to spread the Gospel.[10]

In the pages that follow, I will define cross-cultural trade as all commercial exchanges between Christians and non-Christians, highlighting the complex role that these exchanges played in the institutional and economic history of the Portuguese Empire from its inception to about 1570. This chapter will focus in particular on the issue of free trade with non-Christians, that is, the trade in all goods, including those prohibited by church doctrine. This issue has wide-ranging implications, from the active role of the state in regulating foreign commerce to the coexistence of trade and violence in many areas where the Portuguese maintained contact with Muslims and other non-Christians. My aim is to reflect on the pride of place that theology held in official Portuguese policies and the consequences that theological debates had on the shaping of rapidly emerging global commercial networks.

---

[8] An in-depth discussion of Islamic legal tradition is provided by Leor Halevi, "Christian Impurity versus Economic Necessity: A Fifteenth-Century Fatwa on European Paper," *Speculum*, 83 (2008): 917–945.

[9] A. C. de C. M. Saunders, "The Depiction of Trade as War as a Reflection of Portuguese Ideology and Diplomatic Strategy in West Africa, 1441–1556," *Canadian Journal of History*, 17 (1982): 219–234.

[10] James Muldoon, *Popes, Lawyers and Infidels: The Church and the Non-Christian World* (Liverpool: Liverpool University Press, 1979).

Rather than positing a natural convergence or a constant conflict between the interest of the state and the interest of the church, I will focus on instances in which the royal power marshaled specific theological arguments in defense of its prerogatives. I will thus show how the weapon of commercial proscriptions proved useful to maintain and even expand the state's control over private merchants before the Portuguese Empire began to relinquish parts of its monopolies as part of a new economic policy initiated in the 1570s. But first, I will elucidate the terms of the intimate relationship between Catholicism and trade that existed in the early modern Portuguese world.

COMMERCE AND CONVERSION: THE PORTUGUESE EMPIRE AND THE SANCTITY OF TRADE

Portuguese colonial discourse incessantly emphasized the link between religion and commerce. Most famously, Vasco da Gama was said to have reached India in order "to seek Christians and spices."[11] This expression shows that it was possible to cloak a trading enterprise under the mantle of a missionary obligation. As a classic example of early modern monarchic capitalism, the economic system of the Portuguese Empire hinged upon the Crown's monopoly on strategic trades, including pepper and other Asian spices.[12] Of course, state control did not prevent a widespread free circulation of men and goods. Russell-Wood even characterized the Portuguese Empire as "a world on the move."[13] This characterization is captivating and largely accurate, but should not overshadow the fact that the sixteenth-century Portuguese primacy in intercontinental trade was based on a state of permanent war, often justified by religious arguments.

It was in order to dismiss growing European polemics against the royal monopoly on spices that, in 1539, the humanist Damião de Góis published a remarkable defense of the Portuguese Empire. Blessed by the papacy, the Portuguese advantage over other competitors (first and foremost, the Venetians) guaranteed necessary funds to sustain a worldwide fight against non-Christians "for the holy Catholic faith."[14] Following this argument, spices were primarily a tool of conversion. Commerce had

---

[11] "Vimos buscar cristãos e especiaria." The first Portuguese sailor who disembarked in Calicut would have said these words. I am quoting the English translation from Sanjay Subrahmanyam, *The Career and the Legend of Vasco da Gama* (Cambridge: Cambridge University Press, 1997), 129.

[12] Manuel Nunes Dias, *O capitalismo monárquico português, 1415–1549: Contribuição para o estudo das origens do capitalismo moderno* (Coimbra: Faculdade de Letras da Universidade de Coimbra, 1963).

[13] Russell-Wood, *The Portuguese Empire.*

[14] "Pro sacrosancta fide catholica." Damião de Góis, *Commentarii rerum gestarum in India citra Gangem a Lusitanis, anno 1538* (Lovanij: ex officina Rutgeri Rescij, 1539), fols. E IIIr–IVv. The book was dedicated to the Venetian cardinal Pietro Bembo.

thus gained a special religious significance. This significance was such that a participant in the debate on the spice trade promoted by João de Castro, governor of India
(1545–1548), in Goa in the mid-1540s declared that the issue of the state monopoly
over the commercial routes linking Goa to Lisbon "should be so sacred that even
talking about it could be forbidden."[15]

As far as I know, the topic of the sanctity of trade appeared for the first time in connection with the exchanges conducted at Castelo da Mina (also known as Elmina
Castle, as the Dutch named it later on), the notorious trading post on the Gold
Coast in West Africa (in present-day Ghana) that the Portuguese built in the 1480s.
Black slaves and gold sailed from there to Europe and, later, to the Americas. In his
oration of obedience to Pope Innocent VIII in 1485, the diplomat Vasco Fernandes
de Lucena extolled the fortress that had made it possible to initiate "such a holy,
such an assured, such a great commerce with people in regions where they never
heard the name of the Saviour, not even in passing mention, has now become much
more frequent."[16] Portuguese merchants frequently purchased the black slaves that
Muslim dealers brought to the coast. Evidently, the frontier between Christendom
and Islam was not a sealed one.

If we look beyond the rhetoric of Holy War, in the early modern colonial context
commercial exchanges marked the Christian-Muslim relationship in a way similar
to that noted by David Abulafia in the medieval Mediterranean.[17] There, commercial exchanges between Christians and Muslims developed alongside incessant calls
for crusades and enabled the transfer of both material goods and ideas. European
merchants, in particular, opened up new markets in the Levant and North Africa.
Similarly, the interaction between religion and commerce played a central role in the
early modern slave trade on the West African coast. Even if rarely acknowledged by
scholars, the goal of converting enslaved Africans—usually presented as "Moors" by
fifteenth-century Portuguese sources, even though they were "animists"[18]—justified

---

[15] "Tão sagrado avia de ser que té o falar se poderia haver por defeso." Opinion expressed by the fiscal officer
Bastião Luís on November 19, 1545, transcribed in Luís Filipe F. R. Thomaz, *A questão da pimenta em meados
do século XVI: Um debate político do governo de D. João de Castro* (Lisboa: Universidade Católica Portuguesa,
1998), doc. 5.

[16] "Tam sanctum, tam certum, tam magnum cum illis gentibus commertium instituit, ut salvatoris nomen
nunquam ne fama quidem in ea auditum, ita nunc hominum nostrorum frequentia in populorum illorum
auribus increbuerit." My English translation differs slightly from that published in *The Obedience of a King
of Portugal*, ed. F. M. Rogers (Minneapolis: University of Minnesota Press, 1958), 47.

[17] David Abulafia, "The Role of Trade in Muslim-Christian Contact during the Middle Ages," in his
Mediterranean Encounters: Economic, Religious, Political, 1100–1550 (Aldershot, UK, and Burlington,
VT: Ashgate, 2000), 1–21. See also Chapter 4 by Wolfgang Kaiser and Guillaume Calafat in this volume.

[18] On the reasons for using the term "Moor" in the Portuguese sources, see Kenneth Baxter Wolf, "The 'Moors'
of West Africa and the Beginnings of the Portuguese Slave Trade," *Journal of Medieval and Renaissance
Studies*, 24 (2003): 449–469.

the presence of settlements in those regions. Moreover, papal bulls confirmed the most common interpretation among canonists: conversion to Christianity did not entail emancipation for slaves (this tradition dated back to the time of the Crusades).[19] It is noteworthy that in the same period, an analogous doctrine taught by the North African jurist Ahmad al-Wansharisi (d. 1508) influenced some Muslim merchants: black slaves who converted to Islam retained their social and legal position, which derived from their former condition of unbelievers.[20] Following Sanjay Subrahmanyam, one might wonder whether this cultural correspondence favored European penetration into West African slave markets, since it did not upset their balance by holding out hopes of freedom.[21]

The scant interest of King John II of Portugal (1481–1495) in conquering new lands in North and West Africa facilitated the rise of cross-cultural trade in this area. After the bloody subjugation of Arzila and the subsequent desertion of Tangier by its panic-stricken inhabitants in 1471, the following two decades saw a period of peaceful relations between Christians and Muslims. The Portuguese sought to expand their influence without escalating any open conflict. Treaties were respected, while towns in southern Morocco passed directly under the protection of the Portuguese Crown and acknowledged its sovereignty. The residents of Safi, Azemmour, and Massa became vassals and tributaries of John II. Resurrecting a terminology used for the Muslim population of Iberia during the Reconquista, the Portuguese referred to these population as "peaceful Moors" (*mouros de paz*). Their number increased rapidly, especially in the hinterland of Portuguese forts in North Africa, in part because there was no sustained effort to convert these "peaceful Moors" to Christianity. In this context, religious proselytism was less important than commerce to the Portuguese: southern Moroccan towns had a very close relationship with the sub-Saharan coastal regions where the Portuguese were used to buying black slaves and exchanging all sorts of merchandise with non-Christians, including Muslims.[22]

---

[19] James Muldonn, "Spiritual Freedom—Physical Slavery: The Medieval Church and Slavery," *Ave Maria Law Review*, 3 (2005): 69–93, 83–84. On the origin of this convention, see Benjamin Z. Kedar, *Crusade and Mission: European Approaches toward the Muslims* (Princeton, NJ: Princeton University Press, 1984), 146–149.

[20] Al-Wansharisi's fatwa on the subject is summarized by Bernard Lewis, *Race and Slavery in the Middle East: An Historical Enquiry* (New York: Oxford University Press, 1990), 57.

[21] For a general introduction to Sanjay Subrahmanyam's approach, see his "Connected Histories: Notes toward a Reconfiguration of Early Modern Eurasia," *Modern Asian Studies*, 31 (1997): 735–762.

[22] António Dias Farinha, "Norte de África," in *História da Expansão Portuguesa*, ed. Francisco Bethencourt and Kirti Chaudhuri, 5 vols (Lisboa: Círculo de Leitores, 1998–2000), 1: 118–136, 127–128.

TRADING WITH THE ENEMY: ISLAM AND THE
PORTUGUESE EMPIRE

Nearly everywhere, with the notable exception of Brazil, Muslim powers bordered the Portuguese Empire in both Africa and Asia. The Empire's expansion revived the traditional spirit of the Reconquista on a global scale, but also facilitated daily contacts between Muslims and Portuguese settlers. There is a dearth of studies on this important topic, but on the whole, the general conclusion of the well-documented book that Eloy Martín Corrales has devoted to Catalan trade with Muslims in the early modern Mediterranean seems to apply to different regions of the overseas Portuguese Empire as well: "that frontier world, where violence never disappeared, also allowed constant trade between the two sides."[23]

Portuguese imperial culture, more than its Spanish counterpart, was obsessed with the idea of pursuing the total destruction of Islam. The fifteenth- and sixteenth-century Portuguese rhetoric of conversion made a clear distinction between heathens (*gentios*), an extremely wide category which encompassed all humanity that did not belong to one of the three "religions of the Book" and who were the real object of universal evangelization, and Muslims (*mouros*), who were seen as an age-old enemy to be defeated.[24] The recurrent call for the "war against Moors" (*guerra dos mouros*) tended to exclude the prospect of converting Muslims, a factor that scholars fail to cite when explaining Muslims' expulsion from Portugal in 1497.[25] In that year, a very different fate fell upon the Jews, who were forced into mass baptism. Portugal became the first confessional state in early modern Europe (Castile had expelled the Jews, but not the Muslims, in 1492). The case of the Jews diverged from that of the Muslims, since the former had no choice but to convert, but the latter were banned. Among the reasons for this divergent policy, historians have recently invoked the fear of possible reprisal against Christian minorities living in Islamic countries.[26] In my opinion, the need to assure the persistence of trading relations in North and West Africa also influenced the decision made by

---

[23] Eloy Martín Corrales, *Comercio de Cataluña con el Mediterráneo musulmán (siglos XVI–XVIII): El comercio con los "enemigos de la fe"* (Barcelona: Edicions Bellaterra, 2001), 50.

[24] New horizons are opened up by *The Religions of the Book: Christian Perceptions, 1400–1660*, ed. Matthew Dimmock and Andrew Hadfield (New York: Palgrave Macmillan, 2008).

[25] Portuguese official documents from the fifteenth century do not advocate proselytism among Muslims. Only in the late sixteenth century did the Crown and the Inquisition develop a conversionist strategy. See José Alberto R. S. Tavim, "Educating the Infidels Within: Some Remarks on the College of the Catechumens of Lisbon (XVI–XVII Centuries)," *Annali della Scuola Normale Superiore di Pisa: Classe di Lettere e Filosofia*, 5 (2009): 445–472.

[26] L. P. Harvey, "When Portugal Expelled Its Remaining Muslims (1497)," *Portuguese Studies*, 11 (1995): 1–14. For a factual reconstruction, see François Soyer, *The Persecution of the Jews and Muslims of Portugal: King Manuel I and the End of Religious Tolerance* (Leiden: Brill, 2007).

King Manuel I (1495–1521) and his counselors to convert the Jews but to expel the Muslims. Indeed, continued commercial relations between Christians and Muslims were of the greatest importance, particularly those with the "peaceful Moors" of Safi, Azemmour, and Massa, from whom the Portuguese bought cereals, foodstuffs, and other goods, including copper, jewels, and textiles, which were highly valued by the dealers in black slaves on the coast to the south. The protection of the Muslim inhabitants of these Moroccan towns was confirmed by an agreement signed in the same days when their coreligionists were being expelled from the kingdom of Portugal.[27]

Since the capture of Ceuta in 1415, papal dispensations enabled the Portuguese to trade in non-warlike goods with Muslims and other "infidels." Over the course of the fifteenth century, such licenses were confirmed at various times, absolving those who bought slaves in West Africa or spices in India. In addition, European merchants who sailed under the Portuguese flag often infringed on the prohibition that still pertained to specific goods, such as bronze, copper, and other metals. In 1505, Pope Julius II issued a bull to Manuel I that gave confessors the power to absolve all previous violations and allowed merchants to sell forbidden goods, including metals (but not weapons), to Muslims and other "infidels" as long as they were not at war with the Portuguese, or with other Christian powers.[28]

Trading in armaments with non-Christians, especially Muslims, was outlawed at all times because of the constant threat of religious war. Canon lawyers assumed that people whom they referred to as "enemies of faith" would take advantage of artilleries and other items in order to wage war against Christianity.[29] In reality, this proscription never stopped the commerce in prohibited goods that flourished in the medieval Mediterranean.[30] In peacetime, as we have seen, it was possible to make exceptions for metals, which were considered as any other goods. However, it was naturally difficult to make the same claim with regard to weapons. In 1496, the bull *In Coena Domini* repeated once again the ban on selling arms to "Saracens,

---

[27] The contract provided for special trading conditions: "You further agreed that none of our ships which bring merchandise to the markets of Massa shall pay tribute of any kind, nor will those which bring from there merchandise things of any kind by our order." I am quoting from the letter of King Manuel I to the inhabitants of Massa, January 11, 1497, in Malyn Newitt, *The Portuguese in West Africa, 1415–1670: A Documentary History* (Cambridge: Cambridge University Press, 2010), 32–33.

[28] Charles-Martial de Witte, "Les lettres papales concernant l'expansion portugaise au XVIᵉ siècle," *Neue Zeitschrift für Missionswissenschaft*, 41 (1985): 271–287, 274.

[29] The church prohibition on trade with Muslims might be at the origins of the legal notion of "embargo." See Stefan K. Stantchev, *Spiritual Rationality: Papal Embargo as Cultural Practice* (New York: Oxford University Press, 2014).

[30] Abulafia, "The Role of Trade in Muslim-Christian Contact," 10.

Turks and other enemies of the name of Christ." Clergymen solemnly proclaimed the bull's words every year from church pulpits on Maundy Thursday.[31] Like other serious offenses such as heresy, infringing the ban was a deadly sin whose absolution was reserved to the pope and his delegates. The collection of royal ordinances published in Portugal in 1513–1514 (a revised edition appeared in 1521) embraced and reinforced the ecclesiastical law by forbidding all residents in both the kingdom and the empire from trading in "bread, wine, olive oil, salt, wax, honey, food or any other goods" with Muslims in wartime. Those who infringed this rule were bound to suffer confiscation and exile to the Atlantic islands of São Tomé. Moreover, any subject who was discovered selling "any kind of things necessary or useful in war" in "the land of Moors" was condemned to servitude (i.e., loss of full rights).[32] The royal decree was not strictly observed, however. Across the early modern Iberian world, in open violation of canon law and royal decrees, armaments continued to be sold to non-Christians in the Mediterranean, as well as in Atlantic Africa and Asia.[33]

Under the reign of John III (1521–1557), the successor to King Manuel I, the Portuguese Empire became an increasingly expensive business for the monarchy. Meanwhile, after the Treaty of Zaragoza (1529), which assigned the Moluccas to the Portuguese sphere of influence in return for a handsome payment to Spain, diplomatic relations between the Crown and the Apostolic See grew colder and colder. Rome balked before the Portuguese efforts to obtain control of tithes and church endowments in the overseas lands as part of their royal patronage. This jurisdictional conflict led to the appointment of a permanent papal nuncio in Portugal in 1532. In response, the Portuguese Crown created a royal council of lawyers and theologians charged with spiritual matters (such as missions and conversion strategies, legislation concerning non-Christian subjects, imperial wars, and overseas commerce), called Mesa da Consciência (Board of Conscience).[34] This confessional institution had no equal in the rest of Europe. Essentially, it was a tool to make Portuguese kings more independent from the papacy, albeit in formal compliance with Catholic

---

[31] I am quoting from Charles-Martial de Witte, "Les lettres papales," 273.

[32] "pam, vinho, azeite, sal, cera, mel, sevo, nem mercadoria algua;" "em Terra de Mouros...quaesquer cousas necessarias, ou preveitosas pera feito de guerra." *Ordenações Manuelinas*, 5 vols (Lisboa: Fundação Calouste Gulbenkian, 1984), 5: tit. 81.

[33] Carlos Gozalbes Gravioto, "Andalucía y el contrabando de armas con Marruecos en el siglo XVI," *Archivo Hispalense* 192 (1980): 177–189. As Russell-Wood remarks (*The Portuguese Empire*, 133), swords, firearms, and other weapons brought from Europe were usually shipped by the Portuguese, even on the vessels sailing between Macao and Nagasaki.

[34] The Mesa was created in 1532, the same year that the papacy began to dispatch a permanent nuncio to Lisbon. On this institution, see Maria do Rosário Sampaio Temudo Barata de Azevedo Cruz, "A Mesa da Consciência e Ordens, o Padroado e as perspectivas de Missionação," in *Missionação Portuguesa e Encontro de Culturas: Actas do Congresso Internacional*, 4 vols. (Braga: Universidade Católica Portuguesa, 1993), 3: 627–647.

orthodoxy.[35] The balance between politics and religion was rapidly changing: theology gained prominence in the political sphere. The impact of this prominence was soon felt on the actual conduct of overseas trade. For example, in 1537 the Mesa da Consciência was in doubt about the amount of copper sent each year to India in exchange for spices: How much metal was it lawful to sell to "infidels"? Waiting for a resolution from his religious counselors, King John III informed the minister of finance, António de Ataíde (ca. 1500–1563), count of Castanheira, that the Portuguese fleet had loaded only the reduced amount of 600 tons of Flemish copper that year.[36] Did the Christian merchant empire have a troubled conscience?

FORBIDDEN COMMERCE: STATE AND RELIGION FOR A NEW IMPERIAL ORDER

How the Mesa da Consciência ruled in this particular case is unknown, but in the following years it continued to address questions about the trade in forbidden goods. The establishment of the Inquisition in Portugal in 1536 further complicated the relation between church and state. Even though this ecclesiastical court was officially independent from the monarchy, royal officials exerted a strong influence over it. Inquisitors were not always in full agreement with canon lawyers, theologians, and other advisors to the crown. Different voices could be heard in the midst of these mid-sixteenth-century debates about the legitimacy of trade with the Muslim world. Yet they were all seeking to strike the right balance between the needs of religion and those of commerce.

A consequential controversy erupted in the late 1540s, when Pêro Fernandes Sardinha, vicar-general of Goa (1545–1548), addressed to John III a detailed report on moral issues pertaining to political and commercial matters. The zealous prelate wrote that the most lucrative deal in India was "that of the horses coming from Arabia via Hormuz which are sold to infidels, as well as copper." In Asia, Muslim merchant communities were essential trading partners of the Portuguese, but Sardinha did not seem too worried about the souls of the latter. Rather, he shared with some Jesuit confessors a concern over their power to absolve Christian dealers of the grave sin of selling horses to Muslims. In his final proposal to the king, Sardinha expressed a basic approval of this commerce: "since Your Highness earns a lot from these horses, it would be profitable to obtain a general dispensation from the pope."[37] His call for

---

[35] On the complex meaning of "conscience" and its early modern political implications, see *Contexts of Conscience in Early Modern Europe, 1500–1700*, ed. Harald E. Braun and Edward Vallance (New York: Palgrave Macmillan, 2004).

[36] Letter of April 20, 1537, in *Letters of John III, King of Portugal, 1521–1557*, ed. J. D. M. Ford (Cambridge, MA: Harvard University Press, 1931), doc. 306.

[37] "Item o principal trato que ha na India he o dos cavalos que vão da Arabia por via d'Ormuz os quaes se vendem aos infiees e asi se vende cobre. E porque este he hum dos casos reservados na bula De Cena Domini muitas

the elimination of papal constraints on trade was an attempt to make contraband legal. This proposal, voiced by an informed official on the ground, was likely motivated by a pragmatic recognition of the risks of enforcing more intransigent policies at a time when many Portuguese and other Europeans abandoned the commercial system under the Crown's control in order to recreate merchant communities in unofficial settlements on the shores of the Indian Ocean.[38]

The metropolitan authorities listened to colonial appeals and suggestions. Sardinha's letter provoked intense debate because it hit a raw nerve. In that period, the powerful minister of finance, António de Ataíde, did not hide his opposition to the growing bureaucracy that accompanied the direct role played by the Portuguese Crown in the imperial trade system, as well as the resulting clientelism in the system of appointment to public offices, also known as "economy of reward" (*economia da mercê*).[39] In 1549, the closing of the Portuguese commercial outpost in Antwerp (*Feitoria de Flandres*) was a sign of the declining effectiveness of monarchic capitalism.[40] The negative balance of trade with Asia opened a deep economic crisis that led the Portuguese Crown to abandon temporarily the organization of expensive annual voyages between Lisbon and Goa, the so-called Carreira da Índia. From 1570 until 1597, licenses granted to private merchants replaced the traditional state-sponsored commercial organization of Portuguese intercontinental trade.[41] Sanjay Subrahmanyam and Luís Filipe Thomaz have interpreted this phase as a shift to a "semi-absolutist conception of the state's relationship to trade, in which trade was seen as beneath the dignity of royal estate."[42]

vezes no tempo das confisões os padres da Companhia e eu tivemos duvida sobre a asolvição mas porquanto Vossa Alteza tem gramdes direitos destes cavalos parece que deve ter bula e dispensação geral." Undated letter transcribed in *As Gavetas da Torre do Tombo*, ed. António da Silva Rego, 12 vols. (Lisboa: Centro de Estudos Históricos Ultramarinos, 1960–1977), 10: 703–704.

[38] Michael N. Pearson, "Markets and Merchant Communities in the Indian Ocean: Locating the Portuguese," in *Portuguese Oceanic Expansion, 1400–1800*, ed. Francisco Bethencourt and Diogo Ramada Curto (New York: Cambridge University Press, 2007), 88–108.

[39] The count of Castanheira resumed his critical remarks in a memorandum addressed to King John III in 1553, which is transcribed in Maria Leonor Garcia da Cruz, *A governação de D. João III: A Fazenda Real e os seus vedores* (Lisboa: Centro de História da Universidade de Lisboa, 2001), doc. 44. The best analysis of the "economy of reward" in Portugal is to be found in Fernanda Olival, *As ordens militares e o Estado moderno: Honra, mercê e venalidade em Portugal, 1641–1789* (Lisboa: Estar, 2001).

[40] António Augusto Marques de Almeida, *Capitais e capitalistas no comércio da especiaria: O eixo Lisboa-Antuerpia, 1501–1549; Aproximação a um estudo de geofinança* (Lisboa: Cosmos, 1993). See also Florbela Veiga Frade, *As relações económicas e sociais das comunidades sefarditas portuguesas: O trato e a família, 1532–1632* (Lisboa: Colibri, 2006).

[41] James C. Boyajian, *Portuguese Trade in Asia under the Habsburgs, 1580–1640* (Baltimore: The Johns Hopkins University Press, 1993), 29–52.

[42] Sanjay Subrahmanyam and Luís Filipe F. R. Thomaz, "Evolution of Empire: The Portuguese in the Indian Ocean during the Sixteenth Century," in *The Political Economy of Merchant Empires*, 298–331, 303.

The Portuguese debate on forbidden commerce with Muslims and other non-Christians in the mid-sixteenth century must be understood in light of this evolution, but also as a response to the simultaneous military threats posed by the Ottoman expansion in the Indian Ocean (Diu was besieged twice, in 1538 and 1546) and the military pressure of the Saadian army on the Portuguese strongholds in Morocco (crowned by the conquest of Ksar Seghir in 1549, a notable achievement in the strategy of the Saadi family that ruled Morocco from 1554 to 1659).[43] In this context, Sardinha's argument drove the acclaimed canonist Martín de Azpilcueta, better known as Doctor Navarrus, to give a solemn lecture (*relectio*) on the subject of the religious limits to free trade at the University of Coimbra, where he was a renowned professor.[44] In 1550, he published the polished draft of his lecture.[45] In the prologue, preceded by a papal printing privilege dated January 1548, Navarrus stated that he had received other letters from Jesuits in Africa and Brazil, who solicited his opinion on matters connected to the specific issue under discussion: the sale of horses to Muslims in India. As a typical canonist, he began by commenting on a decretal by Gregory IX (bk. 5, tit. 6, ch. 6). His opinion was quite different from that of the Spanish theologian Juan de Medina, who just four years earlier had reasserted a sweeping condemnation of any trade with the "Saracens" in "armaments, metal, galleys, ships, timber for ships and galleys, horses, provisions and any other item" that "could be useful to wage war on Christians."[46] Navarrus agreed that all Christian merchants and soldiers who sold forbidden goods to "Saracens" should be excommunicated, but stated that not all "Saracens" were equal. He distinguished between those who were presumed to attack Christians, like the Ottoman Turks and other enemies of the Church, and all other Muslims living in peace with Christians—"as there are many, I have heard, who are now subjects of the Portuguese Empire in

---

[43] On the Ottoman expansion, see Salih Özbaran, *The Ottoman Response to European Expansion: Studies on Ottoman Administration in the Arab Lands during the Sixteenth Century* (Istanbul: The Isis Press, 1994), Id., *Ottoman Expansion toward the Indian Ocean in the 16th Century* (Istanbul: Istanbul Bilgi University Press, 2009), and Giancarlo Casale, *The Ottoman Age of Exploration* (Oxford and New York: Oxford University Press, 2010). On the Portuguese Morocco, see Maria Luisa Garcia da Cruz, "As controvérsias ao tempo de D. João III sobre a política portuguesa no Norte de África," *Mare Liberum*, 13 (1997): 123–199, and Otília Rodrigues Fontoura, *Portugal em Marrocos na época de D. João III: Abandono ou permanência?* (Funchal: Centro de Estudos de História do Atlântico, 1998).

[44] On Doctor Navarrus's biography, see Vincenzo Lavenia, "Martín de Azpilcueta (1492–1586): Un profilo," *Archivio italiano per la storia della pietà*, 16 (2003): 15–148.

[45] Martín de Azpilcueta, *Relectio cap. Ita quorundam. de Iudaeis, in qua de rebus ad Sarracenos deferri prohibitis, & censuris ob id latis non segniter disputatur* (Conimbricae: Ioannes Barrerius & Ioannes Alvarus typographi Regij excudebant, 1550).

[46] "De christianis, qui vendunt sarracenis arma, ferrum, galeas, naves, lignamina pro navibus, vel galeis aedificandis, equos, victualia aut etiam quaecumque alia… satis est quod vendentes sciant talia posse sarracenis deservire ad christianos impugnandum." Juan de Medina, *De restitutione & contractibus tractatus* (Salamanticae: excudebat Andreas Portonariis, 1550), fl. 106v. I have used the second edition. The first is dated 1546.

India."[47] While he acknowledged as legitimate the occasional licenses granted by the king, his prohibition concerned "all and only" sales of forbidden goods to the former group of "Saracens."[48] By contrast, he condoned free trade with the latter group, that is, with those Muslims who lived in peace with Christians, especially considering that in Asia and in North Africa, the Portuguese "are said to help some Saracens fighting other Saracens."[49] In any case, concluded Navarrus, the Indian horse trade had to be condemned. Finally, his innovative treatise took into consideration the "barbarians" of Brazil. Heathens were thus becoming part of the Portuguese imperial moral theology. Navarrus held Native Americans in higher esteem than Muslims, even if he advised against selling armaments to Brazilians—an instruction that he would have recommended "were I a member of the royal council of a Christian king."[50]

Navarrus's position was deeply ambivalent. On the one hand, his permissiveness could be invoked to obtain from the Apostolic See the general dispensation applying to all free trade that the vicar-general of Goa, Sardinha, had advocated. On the other hand, Navarrus's final embrace of an inflexible policy matched the expectations of John III's religious counselors to whom the Coimbra professor addressed his remarks. In sum, he reiterated the validity of canon law proscriptions, but also left room for a more lenient interpretation of those proscriptions. This ambivalence implied that he supported giving Portuguese theologians discretionary power over the issue of commerce with the Muslims, since the Mesa da Consciência had the prerogative of interpreting papal decisions relative to Portugal and its empire. I think it is fair to read this influential treatise by Navarrus as part of a broader strategy engineered by the Crown in order to preserve its ability to control investors and traders who would have otherwise profited from the gradual liberalization of commerce in the Portuguese Empire. It does not seem a coincidence that the written version of Navarrus's lecture went to press just a month after the Portuguese Inquisition issued a provision claiming jurisdiction over everyone who traded in forbidden goods with "Moors and infidels, enemies of our faith."[51]

This provision was made following a criminal investigation conducted by Lisbon's secular court (Juízo do Crime). Upon request of John III, the judge Brás Soares had questioned two witnesses who denounced a group of dealers for trading with Muslims

---

[47] "Quales sunt multi, ut audio, nunc circum terras Indiae Lusitano imperio parentes." Martin de Azpilcueta, *Relectio*, 43.

[48] "Omnes et solos." Azpilcueta, *Relectio*, 34.

[49] "Alijs sarracenis contra alios sarracenos favere auditur." Azpilcueta, *Relectio*, 33.

[50] "Si a consilijs regum Christianorum essem." Azpilcueta, *Relectio*, 54.

[51] "Mouros e infiees imigos da nossa santa fee." Provision of the general inquisitor, Cardinal-Infant Henry, 25 September 1550, in Arquivo Nacional da Torre do Tombo (henceforth ANTT), Inquisição de Lisboa, livro 840, fols. 6v–7r. Curiously, in the same years the Spanish Crown charged the inquisitors of Aragon with the task of overseeing the smuggling of horses into France; William Monter, *Frontiers of Heresy: The Spanish Inquisition from the Basque Lands to Sicily* (Cambridge: Cambridge University Press, 1990), 86.

in North Africa.[52] These men were commercial agents of a powerful Florentine merchant, Luca Giraldi, who was among the Portuguese king's closest partners and larg-
est creditors. A businessman with strong ties to other Italian financial clans, such as
the Affaitati family in Antwerp and the Cavalcanti in Rome, Giraldi was an active
supporter of free trade across the Portuguese Empire, as were his court allies, including António de Ataíde and the descendants of Vasco da Gama, to whom Giraldi was
linked by means of his daugther's marriage to Gama's grandson, the count of Vimioso,
Francisco de Portugal.[53]

Although in 1551 Giraldi was honored with the title of knight (*fidalgo*) of the
House of King John III, less than two years later the Lisbon Inquisition put him on
trial under the charge of trading with "Moors." The affluent merchant's direct participation in these networks emerged as part of an investigation into the traffic with
southern Morocco managed by agents of Giraldi and of another renowned merchant,
Vicente Reinel, a New Christian who had lived for a long time in Safi, where he had
learned Arabic (he was dead by the time of Giraldi's trial).[54] The inquisitorial investigation intensified in 1552, after John III transferred the royal jurisdiction over these crimes
to the Holy Office in order to allow Lisbon inquisitors to judge the commercial agent
Pedro Martínez, another New Christian, and two sailors, all on the payroll of Giraldi,
who were charged with selling thousands of pikes and other forbidden goods to the
Muslims of Taroudant, another Moroccan town not far from Safi.[55] Giraldi's trial, incidentally, ended without judgment.[56]

It was relatively easy to target Giraldi's trading group, especially since the
Portuguese still had a vivid memory of Taroudant as the base from which the

[52] Isaías da Rosa Pereira, "Lucas Giraldi, mercador florentino, na Inquisição de Lisboa," *Anais da Academia da História Portuguesa*, 28 (1982): 287–314, 291–292. The judge also interrogated an agent of the merchant and nobleman Rui Lourenço de Távora, *Ibidem*, 309.

[53] Virgínia Rau, "Um grande mercador-banqueiro italiano em Portugal: Lucas Giraldi," in her *Estudos de História* (Lisboa: Verbo, 1968), 75–129. On Gama family's position regarding the imperial trade system, see Sanjay Subrahmanyam, "Making India Gama: The Project of Dom Aires da Gama (1519) and its meaning," *Mare Liberum*, 16 (1998): 33–55.

[54] On Vicente Reinel's life, see António Manuel Lopes Andrade, "De Ferrara a Lisboa: Tribulações do cristão-novo Alexandre Reinel, preso no cárcere do Santo Ofício," *Cadernos de Estudos Sefarditas*, 7 (2007): 81–131, 90–91.

[55] Royal decree, February 1, 1552, transcribed in Isaías da Rosa Pereira, *Documentos para a história da Inquisição em Portugal* (Lisboa: Cáritas Portuguesa, 1987), doc. 21. On the Jews as brokers between Christians and Muslims in North Africa, see *Entre el Islam y Occidente: Los judíos magrebíes en la Edad Moderna*, ed. Mercedes García-Arenal (Madrid: Casa de Velázquez, 2003). On the participation of Portuguese New Christians in forbidden trading with Muslims in North Africa, see José Alberto R. S. Tavim, *Os Judeus na expansão portuguesa em Marrocos durante o século XVI: Origens e actividades de uma comunidade* (Braga: APPACDM, 1997), 320–330.

[56] The full trial against Giraldi is published in Isaías da Rosa Pereira, "Lucas Giraldi," 303–308. It is not mentioned by Stefano Tabacchi, "Giraldi, Luca," in *Dizionario biografico degli italiani* (Roma: Istituto dell'Enciclopedia Italiana, 2001), 56: 455–457.

Saadian troops had reclaimed Agadir (the Portuguese Santa Cruz do Cabo de Gué) after a bloody attack on March 12, 1541.[57] These inquisitorial trials that opened in the middle of the sixteenth century were few and far between but carried considerable symbolic power.[58] Above all, we should connect this inquisitorial campaign against a host of powerful merchants with a parallel diplomatic development that in 1552 led to the promulgation of a papal brief allowing horses, copper, and bronze to be sold to non-Christians, expressly including Native Brazilians (possibly, a demonstration of Doctor Navarrus's influence).[59] However, as the Holy Office was conducting these trials, the deputies of the Mesa da Consciência rejected the Roman document.[60] This apparent contradiction is actually illuminating. John III's religious counselors purposefully refused the papal brief and instead obtained a general and perpetual concession of free trade from the Apostolic Penitentiary in 1556.[61] It was a triumph for the Crown, because the regulation of all dispensations was now permanently in the hands of the Portuguese monarchy. As free trade was spreading across the Empire, the Crown preserved moral authority over merchant communities by means of religion. The threat of the Inquisition hung over every businessman, and the opportunity to trade legitimately with non-Christians depended on the king alone: this was the new imperial order. Giraldi was aware of it. Not so surprisingly, in 1570 he became the first private merchant to take over the management of the Carreira da Índia.

CONCLUSION: MAPPING THE MORAL LIMITS OF GLOBAL TRADE

The state strategy of controlling commerce by means of religious arguments conformed to the Counter-Reformation tendency to consolidate the alliance between state and church powers in Catholic countries. But even in this context, the interests of the state and the church did not always align. The redefinition of the terms on which Christian merchants could conduct cross-cultural trade across the Portuguese Empire was part and parcel of the process of balancing the relations between secular and ecclesiastical authorities. Theology occupied a privileged place in this process. In 1560, the Mesa da Consciência sought to redefine the boundaries within which it

---

[57] An impressive description of the Portuguese vengeance on the Saadian camp outside Safi is to be found in the letter of Captain Rodrigo de Castro to John III, July 8, 1541, in *As Gavetas*, 1: 770–775.

[58] Francisco Bethencourt, "A administração da Coroa," in *História da Expansão Portuguesa*, 1: 387–411, 387–392.

[59] Charles-Martial de Witte, "Les lettres papales," 275–276.

[60] See the undated memorandum of the *Mesa da Consciência*, in ANTT, Colecção de São Vicente, livro 3, fols. 402r–407v.

[61] Charles-Martial de Witte, "Les lettres papales," 276.

was legitimate to trade in weapons with Muslims. A member of the missionary church, the vicar of Arguin (an island off the western coast of Mauritania that was then under Portuguese control), brought the problem to the board's attention. In response to the vicar's inqiuiry and two other connected but anonymous questions, the Mesa drew up a map of legal trade with "infidels." Not only did it determine that Portuguese were forbidden from selling arms to Muslims in Arguin, but it also ruled that even if merchants who shipped iron from Portugal or Sierra Leone to Brazil were not excommunicated, they were in breach of royal legislation. The Mesa da Consciência concluded that, "despite the bull granted to the king, it is not permissible to export iron, arms or sulfur [used to make explosives] to the land of the Moors or Indians, while if the sale of horses is not harmful, the faculty of selling them to infidels can be requested from the pope."[62] This order adapted former religious limits to a new imperial trade system. In spite of the reference to papal authority, all power now lay in the hands of the king and his religious counselors. The state role in the economy remained strong, as the reform of the ministry of Finance in 1560 confirmed.[63]

This cartography of legal trade with non-Christians depicts a shift from the sanctity of trade to the moralization of commerce. Although subjected to regulation, cross-cultural trade gained strength from the developing codification. Religious proscriptions became a meaningful tool of political and economic control of overseas commerce, rather than an anachronistic homage to the church doctrine concerning trading with non-Christians that was never wholly in force. Theology did not rule over politics in the least, but it held a hegemonic place in the public discourse of a confessional state, as Portugal indeed was.

To conclude, religion and commerce were an inseparable couple in the Portuguese Empire, as shown first by the justifications of royal commercial monopolies and then by the use of canon law proscriptions to limit and regulate free trade with Muslims and other non-Christians. Even so, strict observance of Catholic orthodoxy and missionary impulses coexisted with a commercial dynamism that, supported by war and human exploitation, made a decisive contribution to the origins of that peculiar amalgam of peoples and cultures that Serge Gruzinski has called the "Iberian globalization."[64]

---

[62] "À terra de mouros e indios não se pode levar ferro, nem armas, nem enxofar, não obstante a bulla que Elrey tem, mas da venda dos cavalos a infieis se nam segue damno se pode pedir faculdade ao papa para se venderem a infieis." This is the summary of three different sentences passed in 1560. They are recorded in Biblioteca Nacional de Portugal, cod. 10.890: Lázaro Leitão Aranha, *Meza das tres ordens militares de Cristo, S. Thiago e Aviz. Bullas, & decretos, & rezoluçoens e assentos desde a sua creação thé o anno de 1731*, vol. 3, fol. 21v.

[63] Maria Leonor Garcia da Cruz, *A governação de D. João III*, 74–81 and doc. 47.

[64] Serge Gruzinski, *Les quatre parties du monde: Histoire d'une mondialisation* (Paris: La Martinière, 2004), 246–247.

ACKNOWLEDGMENTS

This study was supported by funding from the Italian MIUR/FIRB research project RBFR08UX26 titled "Beyond the Holy War: Managing Conflicts and Crossing Cultural Borders between Christendom and Islam from the Mediterranean to the extra-European World—Mediation, Transfer, Conversion, 15th–19th Century," of which I am the principal investigator.

4

The Economy of Ransoming in the Early Modern Mediterranean

A FORM OF CROSS-CULTURAL TRADE BETWEEN SOUTHERN EUROPE AND THE MAGHREB (SIXTEENTH TO EIGHTEENTH CENTURIES)

Wolfgang Kaiser and Guillaume Calafat

THE RANSOMING OF captives was an important economic sector of the early modern Mediterranean, not only because the total amount of ransoms was very high, but above all because trading captives allowed merchants and ship captains to establish commerce with political and religious enemies.[1] Captives' trade and ransoming were not an exclusively early modern phenomenon. Prisoners or captives had been enslaved or ransomed since ancient and medieval times.[2] Nor was ransoming specific to the Mediterranean. We find similar practices in early modern times in the Hungarian borderlands dividing

---

[1] About high prices in the economy of ransoming, see Jean Mathiex, "Trafic et prix de l'homme en Méditerranée aux XVIIᵉ et XVIIIᵉ siècles," *Annales: Économie, Sociétés, Civilisations,* 9 (1954): 157–164; Robert C. Davis, "Slave Redemption in Venice 1595–1797," in *Venice Reconsidered: The History and Civilization of an Italian City-State, 1297–1797,* ed. John J. Martin and Denis Romano (Baltimore: Johns Hopkins University Press, 2002), 454–487, 468.

[2] Pierre Ducrey, *Le traitement des prisonniers de guerre dans la Grèce antique des origines à la conquête romaine* (Paris: E. de Boccard, 1968; rev. ed., Athens: École française d'Athènes, 1999); Anne Bielman, *Retour à la liberté: Libération et sauvetage des prisonniers en Grèce ancienne* (Athens and Lausanne: École française d'Athènes and Université de Lausanne, 1994); Francisco Vidal Castro, "Le rachat de captifs en al-Andalus (VIIIe–XVe s.): Théorie et pratique du droit et des institutions islamiques," *Hypothèses,* 1 (2006): 313–327; James W. Brodman, "Municipal Ransoming Law on the Medieval Spanish Frontier," *Speculum,* 60.2 (1985): 318–330; Kathryn A. Miller, *Guardians of Islam: Religious Authority and Muslim Communities of Late Medieval Spain* (New York: Columbia University Press, 2008), chap. 7; Youval Rotman, *Byzantine Slavery and the*

the Habsburg and the Ottoman Empires, as well as in the Great Lakes region of North America, which Richard White famously called the "middle ground."[3] Furthermore, to ransom a captive did not necessarily mean to free him or her. Roman law stated that ransomed persons returned to the status they held before their captivity (*postliminium*), although it remained uncertain whether the ransomed belonged to the ransomer until full reimbursement (*retentio*).[4] In sixteenth-century Brazil, the Portuguese bought prisoners from Indian tribes, such as the Tupinambi, in order to make them into their own slaves—a practice known as *rescate*, which could mean both ransoming and rescue.[5] This connection between war and enslavement is still present in John Locke's definition of slavery as "a State of War continued, between a lawful Conquerour, and a Captive."[6]

Warfare was also an economic affair with promising gains. These included plundered goods (among which was live booty), ransoms of prisoners, and "ransoms of the country" (the *appatis* paid by peasants or the *sauvegardes* negotiated by villages and towns for immunity or to avoid occupation and plundering).[7] The economics of warfare followed specific codes: high ransom signified the recognition of high status, a ranking visible, for example, in the difference between the ransom for an officer and a simple soldier as they appeared on official price lists. Warfare was also accompanied by non-economic rituals. In addition to gracious liberation, the exchange of prisoners by "quarter" or *Kartell* after a battle was a question of honor and a sign of mutual respect.[8] A whole literature has described the process of increasing state

---

  Mediterranean World (Cambridge, MA: Harvard University Press, 2009); Adam J. Kosto, *Hostages in the Middle Ages* (Oxford: Oxford University Press, 2012).

[3] Richard White, *The Middle Ground: Indians, Empires, and Republics in the Great Lakes Region, 1650–1815* (Cambridge: Cambridge University Press, 1991); Géza Dávid and Pál Fodor, eds., *Ransom Slavery along the Ottoman Borders (Early Fifteenth–Early Eighteenth Centuries)* (Leiden and Boston: Brill, 2007).

[4] Alberto Maffi, "Le butin humain dans le monde ancien: Normes et pratiques de la guerre et de la rançon," *Hypothèses*, 1 (2006): 307–312.

[5] Martha A. Works, "Creating Trading Places on the New Mexican Frontier," *Geographical Review*, 82.3 (1992): 268–281. However, the Portuguese agreed to manumit (*alforriar*) most of the Tupinambi for services rendered either for specific periods (5, 10, or 15 years) or until the death of the buyer. After manumission, many of the Indian former slaves were unable to return to their tribe and family clans. See Pedro Puntoni, *A Guerra dos Bárbaros: Povos indígenas e a colonização do sertão Nordeste do Brasil, 1650–1720* (São Paulo: Editora Hucitec, 2002).

[6] Locke, *Two Treatises of Government*, II, § 24, in John Locke, *Two Treatises of Government [1690]: A Critical Edition with an Introduction and Apparatus Criticus by Peter Laslett*, 2nd ed. (Cambridge: Cambridge University Press, 1967), 302.

[7] Maurice H. Keen, *The Laws of War in the Late Middle Ages* (London: Routledge and K. Paul, 1965), 137–155; Fritz Redlich, *De Praeda Militari: Looting and Booty 1500–1815* (Wiesbaden: F. Steiner, 1956); Idem, *The German Military Enterpriser and His Work Force: A Study in European Economic and Social History*, 2 vols., 2nd ed. (Wiesbaden: F. Steiner, 1964–1965).

[8] Daniel Hohrath, "'In Cartellen wird der Werth eines Gefangenen bestimmet': Kriegsgefangenschaft als Teil der Kriegspraxis des Ancien Régime," in *In der Hand des Feindes: Kriegsgefangenschaft von der Antike bis zum Zweiten Weltkrieg*, ed. Rüdiger Overmans (Cologne: Publishing House, 1999), 141–170.

control and "civilizing" warfare between European powers, and recent research, mainly concerned with intra-European wars, has shed new light on the reality of warfare, stressing the fact that violence in the early modern period was not random, brutal, and irrational, but followed highly ritualized practices in wartime.[9] Captivity and ransoming were part of these written and often unwritten rituals.

In the Mediterranean, corsairing shaped the commercial and diplomatic relations between southern Europe (Iberia, the French kingdom, and the Italian regional states) and North Africa. Fernand Braudel called this endemic activity the "secondary form of war" and placed its flourishing in the period between the battle of Lepanto (1571) and the end of the seventeenth century, which he labeled the "century of corsairing."[10] Of course, this "little war" added to the difficulties inherent in cross-cultural commercial interactions between regions controlled by Muslim and Christian powers. We argue, though, that far from just constituting an obstacle for mercantile exchanges (a mere economy of booty and plunder), corsairing in the Mediterranean, with its concomitant trade in captives, furnished a trading framework that crossed religious, legal, and normative boundaries. This apparent paradox comes with a corollary argument: in order to reconstruct the history of the economic relations between Muslim and Christian regions in the early modern period, we need to take into consideration a broad array of primary sources, which illuminates the mercantile and maritime practices that structured commercial flows and which is not confined to diplomatic sources and commercial treatises. In this chapter, for example, we will make ample use of legal documents.

The Mediterranean, in short, stands out both as an area with distinctive common characteristics and as a region filled with political conflict and cultural diversity. It thus enriches our understanding of what historians and anthropologists have called, following Philip D. Curtin, "cross-cultural trade." By "cross-cultural trade," scholars mean a variety of phenomena. We will resort to this concept in very specific terms. To start, we posit that agents involved in cross-cultural trade shared neither the same mother tongue nor the same religion, and they lived in distinct political and normative contexts. Consequently, we define cross-cultural trade, at one and the same

---

[9] Philippe Contamine, "Un contrôle étatique croissant: Les usages de la guerre du XIVᵉ au XVIIIᵉ siècle: rançons et butins," in *Guerre et concurrence entre les Etats européens du XIVᵉ au XVIIIᵉ siècle*, ed. Philippe Contamine (Paris: Presses universitaires de France, 1998), 199–236; Jean-François Chanet and Christian Windler, eds., *Les ressources des faibles: Neutralités, sauvegardes, accommodements en temps de guerre (XVIᵉ–XVIIIᵉ siècles)* (Rennes: Presses Universitaires de Rennes, 2009).

[10] Fernand Braudel, *The Mediterranean and the Mediterranean World in the Age of Philip II*, 2 vols. (Berkeley and Los Angeles: University of California Press, 1995), 2: 865–891. See also Michel Fontenay, "Course et piraterie méditerranéennes de la fin du Moyen Age au début du XIXᵉ siècle," *Revue d'Histoire Maritime*, 6 (2006): 173–228, and Lemnouar Merouche, *Recherches sur l'Algérie ottomane II: La course, mythes et réalité* (Paris: Bouchène, 2007).

time, as a *cross-religious, cross-political*, and *cross-legal* trade. Francesca Trivellato rightly warned historians not to use "cross-cultural trade" as a generic expression. "An instantaneous transaction between two strangers" is not, she reminds us, "an instance of cross-cultural trade," in particular because "such exchanges [...] involve no credit and limited risks because traders usually can inspect the merchandise."[11] However, we can legitimately consider that a finite transaction bringing two strangers face to face as part of a more regular flow of exchanges (which is precisely the case of the commerce of captives) can entail risks, in particular abuses by agents in a position to exert violence, more or less legally. So we add two further criteria to the definition of cross-cultural trade. The first is the risk inherent in the nature of the transaction, in a context of hostility or latent violence; the second is the frequency and the regularity of this type of transaction.

Cross-cultural trade is not the equivalent—although this is often how it is portrayed—of long-distance trade. The geographical proximity of the Ottoman Empire and Morocco to many Christian states produced intense commercial exchange but did not lead in any automatic fashion to the creation of a common legal system; in fact, the difficulty of crossing existing cultural boundaries persisted over time. Furthermore, if corsairing and the commerce of captives were ancient activities, common to both the Christian and Islamic worlds, they did not necessarily give rise to uniform practices. For instance, the rules about captures at sea—crucial in the corsairing context—could vary considerably between the Maghreb and the European countries of *jus commune*.[12] We can thus approach the Mediterranean as a laboratory that allows us to analyze the historical processes that generated both dense commercial networks and a persisting cultural and legal separation between Islam and Christendom. In seeking to unravel this apparent paradox, we follow the noted Norwegian anthropologist Fredrik Barth and approach these processes as the fruit of constant interactions between distinct groups and states.[13]

A LUCRATIVE BUSINESS

Capturing and ransoming in the Mediterranean took place mainly (but not exclusively) in the context of the confrontation between Christian and Islamic powers, such as the Crusades, *jihad*, or the Reconquista. Violence was thus at the core of

---

[11] Francesca Trivellato, *The Familiarity of Strangers: The Sephardic Diaspora, Livorno, and Cross-Cultural Trade in the Early Modern Period* (New Haven, CT: Yale University Press, 2009), 1–2.

[12] Christian Windler, "Diplomatie et interculturalité: Les consuls français à Tunis, 1700–1840," *Revue d'Histoire Moderne et Contemporaine*, 50.4 (2003): 63–91, 63.

[13] Fredrik Barth, "Introduction," in *Ethnic Groups and Boundaries: The Social Organization of Culture Difference*, ed. Fredrik Barth (Bergen/Oslo and London: Universitetsforlaget and Allen & Unwin, 1969), 9–38.

captives' trade in the Mediterranean. Following Janice E. Thompson, corsairing was a form of extraterritorial violence practiced as part of a commercial politics of violence conducted by privateers, military orders, and North African "state corsairs" that were issued an official license by sovereign or another legitimate authorities.[14] Stressing the difference between corsairing and piracy proves to be important: corsairs were official and legitimate warriors, who acted under the formal supervision of a state and according to the laws of war and peace; they carried on themselves either passports or commissions, and were supposed only to attack enemy ships in wartime, like the so-called "privateers" in the North European and Baltic seas, as well as in the Atlantic. By contrast, pirates were "the enemies of all nations" (*hostes humani generis*): they acted for themselves and did not obey any sovereign.[15] In the Mediterranean context, the term "Barbary pirates," used in European discourse up to the twentieth century, casts doubt on the legitimacy of the Maghrebi authorities. Formally under Ottoman sovereignty, the rulers of Algeria and Tunisia were denounced by European diplomats as violent usurpers of power and, consequently, the corsairing activities that they sponsored were portrayed as mere piracy.[16]

On both sides of the Mediterranean, captives were made to serve on galleys, in mines and mills, in agriculture and domestic service;[17] when they possessed specific skills,

---

[14] Janice E. Thompson, *Mercenaries, Pirates and Sovereigns: State-Building and Extraterritorial Violence in Early Modern Europe* (Princeton, NJ: Princeton University Press, 1994). Frederic C. Lane, "Economic Consequences of Organized Violence," *Journal of Economic History*, 18 (1958): 401–417; idem, *Profits from Power: Readings in Protection Rent and Violence-Controlling Enterprises* (Albany: State University of New York Press, 1979); Jan Glete, *War and the State in Early Modern Europe: Spain, the Dutch Republic and Sweden as Fiscal-Military States, 1500–1660* (London: Routledge, 2002). See also Lauren Benton, *A Search for Sovereignty: Law and Geography in European Empires, 1400–1900* (Cambridge: Cambridge University Press, 2010), chap. 3. It seems misleading to refer to the Knights of St. John at Malta as pirates, as in Molly Greene, *Catholic Pirates and Greek Merchants: A Maritime History of the Mediterranean* (Princeton, NJ: Princeton University Press, 2010). Michel Fontenay has proposed the term "corso," which we find in primary sources, to delineate a specific Mediterranean form of extraterritorial violence based on religious hostility, but not all scholars accept this use. See Michel Fontenay, *La Méditerranée entre la Croix et le Croissant: Navigation, commerce, course et piraterie (XVIe–XIXe siècle)* (Paris: Éditions Classiques Garnier, 2010).

[15] Daniel Heller-Roazen, *The Enemy of All: Piracy and the Law of Nations* (New York: Zone Books, 2009).

[16] For the use of the term "piracy" in various contexts in order to question the legitimacy of those involved in such activities, see Benton, *A Search for Sovereignty*, 112.

[17] Alessandro Stella, *Histoires d'esclaves dans la Péninsule Ibérique* (Paris: Éditions de l'École des hautes études en sciences sociales, 2000); Alexis Bernard, "Le logiche del profitto: Schiavi e società a Siviglia nel Seicento," *Quaderni Storici*, 107.2 (2001): 379–389; Maria Teresa Ferrer I Mallol and Josefina Mutgé i Vives, ed., *De l'Esclavitud a la Llibertat: Esclaus i lliberts a l'edat mitjana* (Barcelona: CSIC, 2000); Antonio Dominguez Ortiz, "La esclavitud en Castilla durante la Edad Moderna," *Estudios de Historia Social de España*, 2 (1952): 369–428; Moulay Belhamissi, *Les captifs algériens et l'Europe chrétienne (1518–1839)* (Algiers: Entreprise nationale du livre, 1988); Claude Meillassoux, "Esclaves, vénacles, captifs et serfs," in *Esclavage et dépendances serviles: Histoire comparée*, ed. Myriam Cottias, Alessandro Stella, and Bernard Vincent (Paris: L'Harmattan, 2006), 367–373.

they were employed in shipbuilding or customs offices; on rare occasions, they were even forced to work as translators, as in the case of al-Hasan al-Wazzan, alias Leo Africanus, who in the 1520s was put to work on the Arabic manuscripts of the Vatican library.[18]

Virtually all primary sources refer to captives indistinctively as "slaves." It is thus not surprising that captives also called themselves "slaves" in their letters and petitions. Captives were also considered as part of the traditional workforce of servile labor. Slaves were a presence in most Italian, Spanish, and Portuguese cities. If in the European literature Algiers and Tunis are often cited for their large slave population, we ought to remember that Lisbon, Seville, Genoa, Messina, and Livorno also had flourishing slave markets and numerous resident slaves during the early modern period.[19] European consuls in overseas ports were important slave traders in the Mediterranean. Thus the correspondence of the French consul François Cotolendy in Livorno with the French secretary of state of the navy tells us about the competition between the French and the Spanish consuls for the purchase of Muslim slaves in the Tuscan port. Cotolendy complained to his superior about the order to buy slaves for no more than 110 piasters each, while in 1683 the minimum price on the market was 120 piasters. The Spanish consul spent as much as 150 piasters to buy a slave.[20]

Several European and non-European languages distinguished between a slave and a captive: *esclave/captif* in French; *schiavo/cattivo* in Italian; *esclavo/cautivo* in Spanish; *escravo/captivo* in Portuguese; *slaaf/gevangene* in Dutch. A similar distinction was also made in early modern Algiers between ·*ilj* (the European slave) and *asîr* (the captive).[21] The difference did not refer to the type of servile status, but to the possible outcome of that status, that is, liberation through the payment of a ransom in the case of captives.[22] The economic logic of owning slaves and captives also differed. Ransoming normally yielded a higher profit to the owner than the price

[18] Natalie Zemon Davis, *Trickster Travels: A Sixteenth-Century Muslim between Worlds* (New York: Hill and Wang, 2006).

[19] Special issue "La schiavitù nel Mediterraneo," *Quaderni Storici*, 107.2 (2001); Special issue "L'esclavage en Méditerranée à l'époque moderne," *Cahiers de la Méditerranée*, 65 (2002); Salvatore Bono, *Schiavi musulmani nell'Italia moderna: Galeotti, vu' cumprà, domestici* (Naples: Edizioni Scientifiche Italiane, 1999); Henri Bresc, ed., *Figures de l'esclave au Moyen Âge et dans le monde moderne* (Paris: L'Harmattan, 1996); Steven Epstein, *Speaking of Slavery: Color, Ethnicity, and Human Bondage in Italy* (Ithaca, NY: Cornell University Press, 2001); António de Almeida Mendes "Les réseaux de la traite ibérique dans l'Atlantique nord (1440–1640)," *Annales: Histoire, Sciences Sociales*, 63.4 (2008): 739–768; Maria Manuel Ferraz Torrão, *Tráfico de Escravos entre a Costa da Guiné e a América Espanhola: Articulação dos Impérios Ultramarinos Ibéricos num Espaço Atlântico (1466–1595)*, Ph.D. thesis, IICT/University of the Açores, 2000, 2 vols.

[20] Archives Nationales Paris (hereafter ANP), A.E. B1, 698, f. 79 (Livorno, December 3, 1683). See also Mathiex, "Trafic et prix de l'homme," 160.

[21] Lemnouar Merouche, *Recherches sur l'Algérie ottomane I: Monnaies, prix et revenus 1520–1830* (Paris: Bouchène, 2002), 211.

[22] See also Maura Fortunati, "Captivi, riscatti ed assicurazione alla vigilia dei Codici," in *Corsari e riscatto dei captivi: Garanzia notarile tra le due sponde del Mediterraneo*, ed. Vito Piergiovanni (Milan: Giuffrè, 2010), 113–134.

that sellers thought they could obtain on the slave market. Slaves had a price determined by their value of use, their productive and reproductive capacities, and their skills; by contrast, captives had a value of exchange, their ransom being based on an estimation of how much others—family or friends, religious charity organizations or political authorities—would be able or willing to pay for their freedom.[23] Moreover, ransoming was open-ended; its final amount did not always correspond to the initial proposal, which frequently began as a "test"[24] based on the parties' expectations in a process of negotiations in which the object (the live booty) could take part, and often did so in a consequential manner. The historical and analytical difference between captives and slaves should be stressed to avoid an improper analogy between the European Atlantic slave trade and Mediterranean "white slavery," or "white captivity."[25] To insist on this distinction is not to use an excessively (politically) correct language; it is to take stock of a distinction that contemporaries made.

Not every captive was worth the same amount, and not every captive was used for the same goal. The instructions given by the grand-master of Malta to the Knights of Saint John departing on a corsairing venture (the *corso*) in 1608 distinguish carefully between various groups among the live booty. They specify that women and children should be sold at the best price on the slave market (for instance, in Messina); that rich captives able to raise large funds may be liberated immediately against payment of ransom; and that only strong men, who could serve in the galleys, should be brought to Malta.[26] Similarly, in Tunis, Algiers, and the Hungarian borderlands, the Ottomans classified captives into groups according to rank and wealth. Spanish sources call *cautivos de rescate* (captives to be ransomed) those for whom Muslim masters in Algiers expected to obtain a substantial ransom;[27] these men were held separately from other captives who were designated as workers. Along the Hungarian

---

[23] Michel Fontenay, "Routes et modalités du commerce des esclaves dans la Méditerranée des temps modernes (XVIᵉ, XVIIᵉ et XVIIIᵉ siècle)," *Revue historique*, 640.4 (2006): 813–830; idem, "Le Maghreb barbaresque et l'esclavage méditerranéen aux XVIème-XVIIème siècles," *Les Cahiers de Tunisie*, 43 (1991): 7–43; idem, "Esclaves et/ou captifs: préciser les concepts," in *Le commerce des captifs: Les intermédiaires dans l'échange et le rachat des prisonniers en Méditerranée, XVᵉ–XVIIIᵉ siècles*, ed. Wolfgang Kaiser (Rome: École française de Rome, 2008), 15–24.

[24] *Sondierungsgröße*, in the words of Niklas Luhmann, *Die Wirtschaft der Gesellschaft* (Frankfurt am Main: Suhrkamp, 1994), 111.

[25] This erroneous parallelism is argued vigorously by Robert C. Davis, *Christian Slaves, Muslim Masters: White Slavery in the Mediterranean, the Barbary Coast, and Italy, 1500–1800* (Houndmills: Palgrave Macmillan, 2003). In the Iberian Peninsula, the expression "white slaves" or "white captives" referred to North African slaves and captives. In Italy, by contrast, "white slaves" were those who came from the Black Sea.

[26] Anne Brogini, *Malte, frontière de Chrétienté (1530–1670)* (Rome: École française de Rome, 2006), 308–309.

[27] Miguel de Cervantes, *Don Quijote de la Mancha*, ed. Francisco Rico (Barcelona: Galaxia Gutenberg/Círculo de Lectores, 2004), 507 [Part 1, chap. 40]. Diego de Haëdo, *Topografía, e historia general de Argel, repartida en*

frontier, captives considered too poor to be ransomed were immediately sent to the slave markets in the Ottoman Empire.[28]

The distinction between captives and slaves was made here along social lines. Slavery was a possible destiny for the poor and the humble, and a decisive step downward on the ladder of dependent and servile labor. Family solidarity, religious charity, and political reasoning sometimes cut across social hierarchy and came to the aid of the most humble.[29] But in those instances, liberation could mean imprisonment for debt until the entire contracted loan was repaid.[30] Maddalena Bindi was a widow ransomed with her two children at Tunis through the charity of the Roman *Arciconfraternita del Gonfalone* in 1789. A year later she petitioned the officers of the confraternity, asking for financial support because she could not earn a living after her liberation and return to Rome.[31]

Ransoming followed a variety of customary and institutionalized practices ranging from the enforcement of individual written contracts (certainly the principal form), ransoming on the spot on the shore (at the *spiaggia* or *playa*) after a raid (a practice called *alafía* in Andalusia),[32] and up to the mediation of religious orders, confraternities, charity organizations, royal or municipal institutions, and diplomatic and military missions.[33] It is primarily through the documentation produced by formal institutions that we learn about the realities of ransoming and acquire

---

cinco tratados do se verán casos extraños, muertes espantosas y tormentos exquisitos que conviene se entendian en la Cristiandad [...] (Valladolid, 1612).

[28] Dávid and Fodor, eds., *Ransom Slavery*.

[29] On charity and captive redemption in Muslim countries, see Miller, *Guardians of Islam*, 151–175; Fatiha Loualich, "In the Regency of Algiers: The Human Side of the Algerine Corso," in *Trade and Cultural Exchange in the Early Modern Mediterranean: Braudel's Maritime Legacy*, ed. Maria Fusaro, Colin Heywood, and Mohamed-Salah Omri (London: Tauris, 2010), 69–96, 85. In the Dutch context and according to Dutch laws, private companies were forced to pay mariners' salaries for as long as the sailors or employees were held prisoners in North Africa. For the companies, it was simply cheaper to ransom entire crews back (even the poor and the humble) than to keep paying their salaries until their death was known. We thank Cátia Antunes for this information. See also Klaas Heeringa, *Bronnen tot de Geschiedenis van den Levantschen Handel (1661–1726)* (The Hague: Martinus Nijhoff, 1917), 508–510.

[30] Such a case in early modern Trapani is described in Carlo Carosi, "Redimere captivos: Appunti sugli atti notarili di riscatto (sec. XVI)," in *Corsari e riscatto dei captivi*, 47–74, 62–63.

[31] Archivio Segreto Vaticano (hereafter ASV), *Arciconfraternita del Gonfalone* (hereafter *Arciconf. Gonfalone*) 1157, fols. 24 and 71. Cf. fn. 40.

[32] Francisco Andújar Castillo, "Los rescates de cautivos en las dos orillas del Mediterráneo y en el mar (Alafías) en el siglo XVI, in *Le commerce des captifs*, 135–164. *Al'áfya* (Arabo-Spanish) or *'âfyya* (classical Arabic) signifies grace, pardon; in Spanish, the expression "pedir alafia" means to plead pardon ("gracia, perdón, misericordia").

[33] Beatrice Pasciuta, "'Mori, Turchi et altri infidili': Corsari e guerra da corsa in Sicilia fra norme e dottrina," in *Corsari e riscatto dei captivi*, 151–178; Miriam Hoexter, *Endowments, Rulers and Community: Waqf al-Haramayn in Ottoman Algiers* (Leiden: Brill, 1998); Loualich, "In the Regency of Algiers," 78–83; Magnus Ressel, "Conflicts between Early modern European States about Rescuing their own subjetcs from Barbary Captivity," *Scandinavian Journal of History*, 36.1 (2011): 1–22; and the articles of Magnus Ressel, Joachim Östlund, Eric Gøbel, and Leos Müller in *Historical Social Research*, 35.4 (2010), special issue on "Human Security."

fragments of narratives that reveal the frictions and the underlying values and cultural codes that sustained this kind of cross-cultural negotiations.

A multiplicity of forms of exchange, each following a different and sometimes
contrasting logic, coexisted in Mediterranean ransoming. The full costs of redemption, that is, the composition of the "price of liberation," also inform us about the
many actors involved in these transactions. To the ransom paid to the master (the
first payment), we have to add different taxes, customs, and transit fees due to local
authorities, the cost of documents (especially passports and safe-conducts), consular
fees (the chancellery of European consulates functioning as notary), transport costs,
middlemen commissions, and, last but not least, a variety of financial services such
as credit, insurance, and *cambio marittimo* (an elementary form of a bill of exchange
that included the transport and exchange of currency). A surviving account book
of a voyage to Algiers kept by merchants from Marseilles in 1651 shows a series of
entries concerning individually named slaves to be redeemed, but also more general
entries "for the slaves." This wording suggests that there were both clear commissions for specific persons and little sums invested for the general purpose of ransoming.[34] The price of liberation thus normally increased the sale price of the captive by
about one-third—and in some cases by much more.[35]

In 1757, the acting French consul in Algiers wanted to ransom two men from
Rome who had served on a Neapolitan galley. The *dey* (the main ruler of the Algerian
Regency) refused categorically the Frenchman's offer, arguing that the two Romans
had been on a galley and that, consequently, he wanted to make a prisoner exchange.[36]
The exchange of prisoners serving on the galleys of the enemy, part of the peace treaties between France and the Barbary powers, was a constant subject of friction and
complaint, especially from the Maghreb authorities who claimed that Europeans
regularly reneged on their commitments. Prisoners were often not brought back but
were sold on enemy galleys; moreover, a prisoner's health or rank was sometimes
disputed.[37] What was at stake in all cases of prisoners' exchange was not only money
or tribute, but also reciprocity and respect, according to a supposed code of warfare
that was shared across the religious divide, even in time of open hostilities.[38]

---

[34] Archives départementales des Bouches du Rhône (hereinafter ADBdR), 9 B 173, "Caier de compte et sentence arbitralle..." (Marseilles, September 6, 1651).

[35] Fontenay, "Esclaves et/ou captifs," 18.

[36] ANP, A.E. B1, 129, f. 161r–166r (Algiers, April 11, 1757).

[37] For several examples, see Wolfgang Kaiser, "Négocier la liberté: Missions diplomatiques françaises
pour l'échange et le rachat des captifs avec le Maghreb au XVIIᵉ siècle," in *La Mobilité des personnes en
Méditerranée: Procédures de contrôle et documents d'identification*, ed. Claudia Moatti (Rome: École française de Rome, 2004), 501–528.

[38] See Wolfgang Kaiser, "Suspendre le conflit: Pratiques de neutralisation entre Chrétiens et Musulmans en
Méditerranée (XVIᵉ–XVIIᵉ siècles)," in *Les ressources des faibles*, 277–290.

Quite often, as in the 1580s, the Spanish, Portuguese, and Neapolitan missions of religious orders and confraternities that came to Algiers in order to ransom captives were required to pay taxes on the money they brought with them. The so-called "Redemptions" of Portugal and Spain, that is, religious orders specialized in the redeeming of captives, paid 11.5 percent upon entrance and 3 to 4 *scudi* per redeemed slave upon exit; the Redemption of Naples only paid 6.5 percent at the entrance and nothing on departure.[39] Political pressure could reduce dramatically the funding available to redemptions. In 1748 the agent and middleman of the Roman *Arciconfraternita del Gonfalone* in Tripoli (Libya) told the superiors of the confraternity that he had been forced by the *bey* (provincial governor) of Bengazi to sell a charge of grain for a very low price; he was thus asking the superiors to send him new funds via Malta or Livorno.[40]

The *cliché* of the cruel Barbary corsairs that dominated the European discourse of the time included a notion of the corsairs' greed. In reality, the mere lure of profit— "l'interesse del denaro," in the words of the Roman redeemers in Algiers in the 1580s—was not the only element that determined a captive's price.[41] The redeemers had to deal with Arnaut Mami (Māmī Arnawūt), the Albanese corsair who converted to Islam and the famous *ra'is* who captured Cervantes.[42] Mami sold a number of his slaves at scandalously high prices, according to the Roman board of governors (*cancellieri*).[43] But Roman redeemers did not know much about the local habits and customs, or how to negotiate with the great and powerful in Algiers.[44] The high prices they eventually paid had to be considered as a recognition of Mami's high status and accepted as an offer and a grace. In return, the famous *ra'is* agreed to liberate the captives without prior payment, on the word of honor of the redeemers. For the Spanish legal scholar Bartolomé Clavero, these exchanges would represent transactions occurring in the world of *antidora*, an economic and symbolic system dominated by honor, gift, and grace, in which the buyer may accept a high price (though not necessarily pay it) in recognition of the seller's social position.[45]

Practices inspired by warfare customs compensated for the frequent lack of trust among masters, captives, and redeemers, and the fear of arbitrary decisions and

---

[39] ASV, *Arciconfr. Gonfalone*, 7, fols. 104r–105r (February 26, 1585).

[40] ASV, *Arciconfr. Gonfalone*, 1157, fol. 10r (January 10, 1748).

[41] ASV, *Arciconfr. Gonfalone*, 7, fol. 167v (April 5, 1587): "Con questa gente non si trova pietà dove ne [h]a l'interesse dil denaro" (with this people, there is no pity when it is possible to earn money).

[42] On him, see Merouche, *Recherches sur l'Algerie II*, 191–192, 209–210.

[43] ASV, *Arciconf. Gonfalone*, 1145, nos. 202, 474, 596, 598, 599, 620, 621, 624, 627, 634, 689, 707, 708, 709, 711, 723, 740, 788, 913; ASV, *Arciconf. Gonfalone*, 8, fols. 49r–52r, 155r–156r.

[44] ASV, *Arciconfr. Gonfalone*, 7, fol. 240r.

[45] Bartolomé Clavero, *Antidora: Antropología católica de la economía moderna* (Milan: Giuffrè, 1991). For a discussion of the redemption of Mami's slaves, see Wolfgang Kaiser, "Una missione impossibile? Riscatto e comunicazione nel Mediterraneo Occidentale (secoli XVI–XVII)," *Quaderni Storici*, 124.1 (2007): 19–41.

disruptive incidents. The political and diplomatic relations between European and Maghrebi authorities made frequent use of hostages. Hostages were exchanged to enforce the truce between Spain or its presidios and local authorities in the Maghreb, between Marseilles and Tunis in 1616, and as part of the peace treaties between France and Tunis in 1605 and between France and Algiers in 1619.[46] A hostage (the captive or sometimes the buyer himself) was a living bond who facilitated transactions in a context of open hostilities; sometimes that person could function as collateral and facilitate further business.[47] Anticipations or gestures of goodwill, such as the liberation of a slave, serving as a messenger or as the first move in negotiations for an exchange of captives, were also helpful. In 1598, for example, in a famous incident, Sinan Pacha Cigala, a commander of the Ottoman fleet, contacted the viceroy of Sicily and asked him to visit his old and ill mother who lived on the island. Sinan Pacha's letter was transmitted through a Christian slave liberated for the occasion.[48] These gestures of politeness or magnanimity increased one's own credibility and showed that one took the risk of being deceived.[49] "Credibility without trust" was generated through a multitude of business, military, and ritualistic relations in which the same actors were involved and in which everyone could find him- or herself in a hostage situation: in a nutshell, the threat of being taken captive helped to keep actors from reneging on their promises.[50]

MIDDLEMEN

The redeemers of the Roman *Gonfalone* confraternity or other Redemptions—and indeed all Christian institutions involved in redeeming captives—relied on merchants who were or had correspondents in North Africa. In the early modern period,

---

[46] On the career in various religious orders and in Philip II's army of those Muslim hostages in the Iberian peninsula who converted to Christianity, see Beatriz Alonso Acero, *Sultanes de Berbería en tierras de la cristiandad: Exilio musulmán, conversión y asimilación en la Monarquía hispánica (siglos XVI y XVII)* (Barcelona: Bellaterra, 2006). On Marseilles and Tunis in 1616, see Archives de la Chambre de Commerce et d'Industrie de Marseille (hereafter ACCIM), G 43, J 1887. On the peace treaties signed between France and the North African states, see Edgard Rouard de Card, *Traités de la France avec les pays de l'Afrique du Nord: Algérie, Tunisie, Tripolitaine, Maroc* (Paris: A. Pédone, 1906), 14.

[47] Diego Gambetta, *Codes of the Underworld: How Criminals Communicate* (Princeton, NJ: Princeton University Press, 2009), 54–77. On the use of human pawns in the African slave trade, see Paul E. Lovejoy and David Richardson, "Trust, Pawnship, and Atlantic History: The Institutional Foundations of the Old Calabar Slave Trade," *American Historical Review*, 104.2 (1999): 333–355.

[48] Copies of the letter and the answer of the viceroy are in Archivo General de Simancas, Estado, leg. 1158, docs. 186 and 187; Biblioteca Apostolica Vatican, Urb. Lat. 1062 fol. 565r–566r (among the collection of *avvisi* of the duke of Urbino); Biblioteca Nazionale Centrale, Florence, Fondo Nazionale II.IV.310, fol. 185r–186v.

[49] Niklas Luhmann, *Vertrauen: Ein Mechanismus der Reduktion sozialer Komplexität* (Stuttgart: F. Enke, 1968); English trans. *Trust and Power: Two Works by Niklas Luhmann* (Chichester: J. Wiley, 1979).

[50] Erving Goffman, *Strategic Interaction* (Philadelphia: University of Pennsylvania Press, 1969), 105.

there were still also *fakkak-in* or *alfaqueques*, merchants specialized in ransoming, who made a living by negotiating the liberation of Muslim slaves in Livorno or Christians in the port cities of North Africa.

This remained a risky business, but its adventurous aspects were fading away. In Spain, the redeeming of Christian slaves was an obligation fixed by the Crown for merchants trading with the Barbary Coast, the moral compensation and legitimation for trading with the so-called "infidels." In practice, this obligation allowed merchants to combine ransoming with commodity trade, including the illegal export of smuggled goods (weapons, material for shipbuilding like iron, tin, wood, or rigging). Royal licenses were sold regularly; they permitted merchants to trade in goods and slaves in North Africa upon payment of an additional indirect tax of 10 percent.[51] In the sixteenth century English merchants resident in Cadiz also acted as *alfaqueques*, organizing the transfer of money through their network of partners and agents in London and Livorno.[52] In Algiers and Tunis, in addition to the many Jewish merchants active between Livorno and North Africa, a multitude of modest merchants revolved around the French consulate and its chancellery. They came from Sicily, Corsica, Malta, or Marseilles and offered—in competition with one another—their services to newcomers, merchants, and redeemers.[53] Their services were twofold: first, they brought local knowledge because they knew with whom and how to negotiate; second, they helped European merchants and merchant-bankers to establish relations with individuals who specialized in currency trade. Middlemen and correspondents were crucial in the ransoming business. Having no correspondent in Tripoli (Libya), the Roman redeemers based in Algiers in the 1580s were unable to locate an Italian captive and to enter into negotiation with his master.[54] Networks of correspondents became particularly necessary in wartime, when regular means of communication were interrupted, as the *Gonfalone*'s correspondent in Tripoli in 1748 discovered when he desperately asked to receive money via Venice, Livorno, Malta or Tunis.[55] Mediation had its price: the standard commission rate amounted to 4 percent. When wartime led to the complete suspension of trade, the correspondent in Tripoli asked for 12 percent per transaction.[56] Competition

---

[51] Eloy Martín Corrales, *Comercio de Cataluña con el Mediterráneo musulmán (siglos XVI-XVIII): El comercio con los "enemigos de la fe"* (Barcelona: Bellaterra, 2001), 93. See also Chapter 3 by Giuseppe Marcocci in this volume.

[52] Alberto Anaya Hernández, "Simón Romero, pescador gran canario y gran almirante de la armada argelina," *Anuario de Estudios Atlánticos*, 49 (2003): 1–21.

[53] ADBdR, 9 B 171 (chancellery of the French Consulate of Algiers, 1579–1582). For the records of the French consular chancellery in Tunis, see Pierre Grandchamp, *La France en Tunisie... (1582–1705)*, 10 vols. (Tunis: Tournier, 1921–1933). For Sicily see Carosi, "Redimere captivos," 56–60.

[54] Kaiser, "Una missione impossibile?"

[55] ASV, *Arciconfr. Gonfalone*, 1157 fol. 11v (February 1748).

[56] ASV, *Arciconfr. Gonfalone*, 1157, fol. 11r (April 1748), quotation from fol. 10v (February 1748).

between ransoming partners could also increase the prices: for example, in the 1580s, the Capuchin friars of the *Gonfalone* in Algiers were worried about the arrival of wealthy Spanish and Portuguese redeemers, who aroused keen interest among local slave masters and inflated the ransoms.[57]

The redeeming of captives was a costly operation that raised the problem of financial transfers between Europe and the Maghreb. Would it be better to transport Spanish gold or silver coins to Algiers and Tunis (for which a royal permission to export money was needed), or should one prefer to borrow money locally from European merchants or via letters of exchange? The first option seemed to some more attractive: in the 1580s, to bring money from Marseilles to Algiers was—without the transport and other transaction costs, such as insurance fees—18 percent cheaper than using letters of exchange.[58] Missions organized by religious orders or charity organizations in the sixteenth century utilized a myriad of little ships and their captains, otherwise active in coastal shipping or coral fishing, in order to ship bullion and coins across the Mediterranean.[59] However, as the case of the ships and captains of the French Compagnie du Corail (founded in Marseilles in 1553) testifies, the transport of cash was a risky and costly business. Insurance costs were about 6 percent, and the captain of the transporting ship received a 2 percent commission. Once the captain arrived in Algiers with the cash, he incurred additional costs, including the percentage directly taken by the *dey*, which generally amounted to 11.5 percent in the case of the French or the Roman missions in the 1580s. Thus transport and insurance costs as well as taxation at the entry into the port eliminated the estimated advantage (18 percent) of transporting bullion or coins. Ludovico Felix, a merchant from Marseilles, made this calculation in 1584–1585 when trying to convince the Roman redeemers of the *Gonfalone*, who wanted to travel to Algiers via Genoa and Marseilles, to buy bills of exchange worth 3,000 *scudi d'oro* in Marseilles and redeem them in Algiers, rather than carry the money on board the ship.[60] But the benefits of the deal proved to be illusory: bills of exchange drawn by the merchant-bankers Bandinis of Rome, the Strozzis of Lyon, and Felix in Marseilles, as well as the financial services offered by "their merchant" (Felix's correspondent) in Algiers, Guillaume Borgal,

---

[57] ASV, *Arcivonfr. Gonfalone*, 7, fols. 191r–192v (September 1587), 223r–224r (April 1588).

[58] Kaiser, "Una missione impossibile?"

[59] Wolfgang Kaiser, "La excepción permanente: Actores, visibilidad y asimetrías en los intercambios comerciales entre los paises europeos y el Magreb (siglos XVI–XVII)," in *Circulación de personas e intercambios comerciales en el Mediterraneo y en el Atlantico, siglos XVI, XVII, XVIII*, ed. José Antonio Martínez Torres (Madrid: CSIC, 2008), 148–163; Giuliana Boccadamo, "Mercanti e schiavi fra Regno di Napoli, Barberia e Levante (secc. XVII–XVIII)," in *Rapporti diplomatici e scambi commerciali nel Mediterraneo*, ed. Mirella Mafrici (Soveria Mannelli: Rubbettino, 2004), 237–273.

[60] ASV, *Arciconfr. Gonfalone*, 7, fols. 96r–97r (10 January 1585).

ruined the Roman redeemers completely.[61] Up to 69 percent of the money engaged in the *Gonfalone*'s mission never left Europe and was absorbed by the middlemen specialized in the transfer of money.[62] In other words, the intra-European money market itself could involve as many risks as cross-cultural exchanges and, in any case, had a considerable impact on the working of Mediterranean ransoming.

Jewish merchants from Livorno, Algiers, and Tunis played a central and contested role in this trade. Accusing Jewish traders of charging exorbitant interest rates on the *cambio marittimo* (up to 15 percent of the first payment plus fixed fees) and of speculating on the exchange rates between local currencies and the Spanish pieces of eight (the silver coin of international trade, sometimes also called *piasters* or *dollars*), Catholic institutions like the Genoese *Magistrato per il riscatto* tried to avoid or at least to limit the mediation of Jewish agents and made recourse to a variety of other merchants involved in the ransoming business.[63] Compared to the above-mentioned credit instruments, the *albarano*, a type of promissory note used by the Neapolitan Santa Casa della Redenzione and Pio Monte della Misericordia, was rudimentary but very useful: a simple sheet of paper, printed by the eighteenth century, certified that the religious institutions would pay a certain amount once the captive mentioned on the document had returned.[64] The *albarano* could thus be used by a merchant or another person who had given credit to the captive, to be reimbursed in Naples.[65] The lure of profit attracted not only large merchants and institutions but also minor actors and investors to the captives' trade, in spite of its high risks. Private merchants from Sicily active in the trade with the Maghreb offered credit at 5 percent interest per month or claimed 33 percent of the captives' price (but were fined in case of unsuccessful negotiations).[66]

SECURING CROSS-CULTURAL TRADE: SHARED KNOWLEDGE AND SIMULTANEOUS TRANSACTIONS

How to secure these commercial transactions involving masters and slaves, captives and multiple creditors, often bound by a series of contracts in a cascade of

---

[61] Kaiser, "Una missione impossibile?"

[62] Ciro Manca, "Problemi aperti sul commercio e sul riscatto degli schiavi cristiani nel Mediterraneo dopo Lepanto," *Africa*, 29 (1974): 549–572; idem, *Il modello di sviluppo economico delle città marittime barbaresche dopo Lepanto* (Naples: Giannini, 1982).

[63] Luco Lo Basso, "Il prezzo della libertà: L'analisi dei libri contabili del Magistrato per il riscatto degli schiavi della repubblica di Genova all'inizio del XVIII secolo," in *Le commerce des captifs*, 267–282.

[64] Rosita D'Amora, "Il Pio Monte della Misericordia di Napoli e l'Opera della Redenzione dei Cattivi nella prima metà del XVII secolo," in *Le commerce des captifs*, 231–247.

[65] Both manuscript and printed *albarani* can be found in Archivio di Stato di Napoli, Santa Casa della Redentione, bb. 14 and 16, passim.

[66] Carosi, "Redimere captivos," 56, 60–62.

micro-credit? Legal certification and enforcement played a role. Credit contracts were sealed before the chancellery of the French consul in Tunis or Algiers, as well as before a notary in Italy or Provence. Contracts could thus be concluded according to the legal regime of the place of departure and, if necessary, they were doubled by another contract drafted or registered on the opposite shore of the Mediterranean. Their form, clauses, and guarantees shared a lot of similarities with the Islamic contract between masters and slaves used for eventual emancipation, the *mukātaba*.[67]

There was a considerable amount of shared knowledge about the organization of the redeeming of captives among Muslims, Jews, and Christians. A religious foundation in Ottoman Algiers, the Waqf al-Haramayn, had some assets endowed for the redemption of Muslim captives.[68] The redemption was organized mainly by the political authorities, but the assets endowed, for example, by janissaries, who had left the barracks for the purpose of redeeming their former companions, were not: the result was "an institution which functioned by managing assets, like a social fund at the service or a specific body of people."[69] In medieval Spain, the communities of Mudejars (Muslims living under Christian rule) had their networks for redemption of Muslim slaves based perhaps on models and formulas of Jewish communities in the medieval eastern Mediterranean.[70] The Cassa per il riscatto degli schiavi of the Livorno Jewish community (to which all members were obliged to contribute), and its equivalent in Venice and Amsterdam, may have inspired the Sklavenkasse of Hamburg (founded in 1624).[71] Ironically, when the grand duke of Tuscany reformed the Livorno's Christian fund to redeem slaves and captives in 1748, he introduced the obligation to contribute to that fund, perhaps borrowing from its Jewish counterpart in Livorno.[72]

---

[67] Sadok Boubaker, "Réseaux et techniques de rachat des captifs de la course à Tunis au XVIIᵉ siècle," in *Le commerce des captifs*, 25–46.

[68] Hoexter, *Endowments, Rulers and Community*, 158.

[69] Loualich, "In the Regency of Algiers," 85.

[70] Miller, *Guardians of Islam*, chap. 7.

[71] Giuseppe Laras, "La Compagnia per il riscatto degli schiavi di Livorno," *Rassegna mensile di Israel*, 38 (1972): 86–130; Renzo Toaff, "La 'Cassa per il Riscatto degli Schiavi' del Granduca nella Livorno del Seicento," *Studi Livornesi*, 1 (1986): 43–64; Eliezer Bashan, "La cause des juifs: Le rachat des captifs dans la société juive méditerranéenne du XIVᵉ au XIXᵉ siècle," in *La société juive à travers l'histoire*, ed. Shmuel Trigano, 4 vols. (Paris: Fayard, 1993), 4: 463–472; Magnus Ressel, "The North European Way of Ransoming: Explorations into an Unknown Dimension of the Early Modern Welfare State," *Historical Social Research*, 35.4 (2010): 125–147; see idem, *Zwischen Sklavenkassen und Türkenpässen: Nordeuropa und die Barbaresken in der Frühen Neuzeit* (Berlin: de Gruyter, 2012).

[72] Calogero Piazza, *Schiavitù e guerra dei Barbareschi: Orientamenti toscani di politica transmarina (1747–1768)* (Milan: Giuffrè, 1983), 32–35; Paolo Castignoli, "La Cassa granducale del riscatto a Livorno nel Settecento: Prime note," *Nuovi studi livornesi*, 8 (2000): 149–154.

The practice of money lending in Tunis through the (oral or written) *qirad* also seems to have been quite similar to the habit of collecting a myriad of little sums used by modest coastal captains in Marseilles and in the secondary ports of Provence in order to finance their convoys (the so-called *caravanes*). Moreover, different forms of commercial associations allowed by Islamic law—*mudharaba* or *sharika*—had parallels in Europe.[73] With respect to maritime law, there may have been borrowings between the Byzantine Empire, the Islamic world, and the European countries of *ius commune*.[74] Medieval collections of maritime customs and laws, such as the Catalan *Consolat de Mar*, could be easily adapted to the *Maliki* jurisdictions current in the Maghreb Regencies.[75]

Cross-cultural exchanges, in sum, did not necessarily need the creation of a common or a hybrid legal framework. The existence of analogous if distinct commercial customs and contracts facilitated dealings made with minimal knowledge of other normative frameworks. We find concrete examples in commercial litigation: the merchants' court of Marseilles (*tribunal de commerce*), for instance, accepted statements made before the local judge of Tunis (the *qadi*) as evidence and legal proof.[76] European consulates in the North African Regencies served in this respect as an interface. Following the European capitulations with the Ottoman Empire, consuls normally acted as judges in the first instance in commercial and civil disputes between their fellow countrymen and other protected subjects. Their legal services helped merchants find amicable solutions, and their sentences had the value of legal arbitration. For example, Claude Sévert, the French deputy consul in Tunis during the first decades of the seventeenth century, judged cases between Christian merchants and, because he charged less than the *qadi*, he was also sought after in civil and commercial disputes between Christians and Muslims.[77] In cases in which civil suits crossed religious boundaries, North African authorities tolerated the recourse to an "infidel," so long as the latter did not encroach on the *qadi*'s prerogatives and the parties agreed to his arbitration. Consuls were consequently allowed to resolve commercial and maritime disputes, especially in port cities frequented by migrants, sailors, and traders. However, according to Daniel Goffman, European merchants in

---

[73] Sadok Boubaker, "Négoce et enrichissement individuel à Tunis du XVIIᵉ siècle au début du XIXᵉ siècle," *Revue d'histoire moderne et contemporaine*, 50.4 (2003): 29–62 ; Mathias Rohe, *Das islamische Recht: Geschichte und Gegenwart*, 2nd ed. (Munich: Beck, 2009), 107.

[74] Hassan I. Khalilieh, *Admiralty and Maritime Laws in the Mediterranean Sea (ca. 800–1050): The Kitāb Akriyat al-Sufun vis-à-vis the Nomos Rhodion Nautikos* (Leiden: Brill, 2006).

[75] Hassan I. Khalilieh, *Islamic Maritime Law: An Introduction* (Leiden: Brill, 1998).

[76] ADBdR, 13 B 14, fols. 169r–170v (July 6, 1578).

[77] Grandchamp, *La France en Tunisie*, 4: 7, 17, 20.

the Ottoman Empire sometimes preferred being judged by the *qadi* if they perceived their own consul to be too partial.[78]

Consuls did not necessarily belong to the city or country they represented. In the 1620s and 1630s, the "consul of the Armenian nation" in Livorno was the Hungarian-born Andrea Signorini. He spoke Italian, Hungarian, Ottoman Turkish, and, in all likelihood, Armenian. He was therefore able not only to translate petitions, claims, and cross-examinations of Armenian merchants who settled in the Tuscan port during those years, but also to issue legal certificates, like a notary.[79] In the North African Regencies, the redeeming of Christian captives was one of the main tasks of European consuls. The importance of the ransoming business explains why the Venetian consul in Algiers was appointed by the Provveditori sopra Ospedali e Luoghi Pii (Inspectors of Hospitals and Pious Places) and not, as the other consuls of the Republic, by the Cinque Savii alla Mercanzia (the Board of Trade). His principal role clearly was to redeem slaves and captives whom Algerian privateers had taken.[80] The case of Moshe Israel, a Jewish merchant settled in Algiers in the 1590s, is a good example. He was appointed consul by the Republic of Venice in 1622 because he had long been involved in the redemption of captives in various Maghreb ports. He had a good reputation with Venetian and Christian merchants, and also with Algerian privateers. By appointing Israel consul, the Venetian Provveditori built on the preexisting expertise of a Jewish broker. We may note here that consuls of the maritime Republic of Ragusa (Dubrovnik) in Algiers and in Albania at the end of the sixteenth century were often Jewish.[81] Consuls and commercial courts also played an important role in the circulation of information about different legal customs, which they translated into local contexts and for local institutions.

The circulation of information about laws and jurisdictions between Europe and North Africa was intense. In the 1620s, Murād Bey, a Corsican convert to Islam and the only "Renegade" to become *bey* of Tunis, made recourse to the sovereign court in Livorno that had civil and commercial jurisdiction at first instance. The litigation was about money and inheritance. One of his Mamluks (a former slave converted to Islam) had died; alive, he had lent money to a Corsican merchant in Livorno, and

---

[78] Daniel Goffman, *Britons in the Ottoman Empire, 1642–1660* (Seattle: University of Washington Press, 1998), 142, see also 24, 42–67.

[79] Archivio di Stato di Livorno (hereafter ASL), *Capitano poi Governatore ed Auditore* (hereafter *GA*), Atti Civili, 75, cases 218, 228, 252.

[80] Maria Pia Pedani, "Consoli veneziani nei porti del Mediterraneo in età moderna," in *Mediterraneo in Armi (secc. XV–XVIII)*, ed. Rossella Cancila, 2 vols. (Palermo: Associazione Mediterranea, 2007), 1: 175–205, 178.

[81] Pedani, "Consoli veneziani," 181; Ivana Burdelez, "Jewish Consuls in the Service of the Republic of Dubrovnik," in *Diplomacy of the Republic of Dubrovnik*, ed. Svjetlan Berković (Zagreb: Ministry of Foreign Affairs of the Republic of Croatia, Diplomatic Academy, 1998), 337–342.

the master now claimed the money of his dead slave. The tribunal of the governor in Livorno asked for statements on the following questions: Do masters inherit money lent by dead slaves in the Abode of Islam (*dar-al-islam*)? If yes, can masters claim the money when the debtor lives in Christian countries? The court interrogated merchants and sailors familiar with the business customs of Tunis. It also received a document known as "acknowledgment of debt" sent by Claude Sévert, the French consul in Tunis. Sévert added that it was common practice in Tunis—and indeed in the whole Ottoman Empire—that "masters inherited claims from slaves in the land of Islam."[82]

A LUBRICANT OF TRADE

Trading captives was a lucrative activity in the early modern Mediterranean and involved, as we have just seen, several brokers and commercial agents. In addition to understanding the mechanisms that governed the economy of ransoming, it is important to assess the importance of trading captives within the overall exchange patterns between Mediterranean Europe and North Africa. Although peace and commercial treatises allowed European and, to a certain extent, Maghrebi ships to call at the ports of the other shore of the Mediterranean, there were a lot of interdictions and normative restrictions that hindered the business with the "infidel." For instance, the papal bulls *In Coena Domini* (1496) forbade Christians from trading in those products that could potentially reinforce the Muslim military power.[83] In 1563, Pius IV set out a number of restrictions, continuously repeated during the seventeenth and the eighteenth centuries, prohibiting in particular the commerce of horses, weapons, wire, tin, and steel.[84] The Iberian crowns and the Italian city and regional states recognized the validity of the bull, but the French monarchy never accepted it, nor did the Protestant powers, for obvious reasons.[85] In North Africa, some injunctions against trading in the land of the Christians were pronounced by Maliki jurists. For example, in a treaty of the fourteenth century with the king of Majorca, a Muslim ruler forbade Christian traders from buying weapons, leather,

---

[82] ASL, *GA*, Atti Civili, 73, case 207; Archivio di Stato di Pisa (hereafter ASP), *Consoli del Mare*, Atti Civili, 128, case 29.

[83] James Muldoon, *Popes, Lawyers, and Infidels: The Church and the Non-Christian World, 1250–1550* (Philadelphia: University of Pennsylvania press, 1979), 34 and passim. See also Chapter 3 by Giuseppe Marcocci in this volume.

[84] Géraud Poumarède, *Pour en finir avec la Croisade: Mythes et réalités de la lutte contre les Turcs aux XVIᵉ et XVIIᵉ siècles* (Paris: Presses universitaires de France, 2009), 315. See also Natividad Planas, "La frontière franchissable: Normes et pratiques dans les échanges entre le royaume de Majorque et les terres d'Islam au XVIIᵉ siècle," *Revue d'histoire moderne et contemporaine*, 48.2–3 (2001): 123–147.

[85] Poumarède, *Pour en finir avec la Croisade*, 318.

bread, and other strategic goods.[86] But here we must be careful.[87] If we over-interpret the impact of those injunctions to explain the modest presence of Muslims from North Africa in Christian Europe, we risk minimizing the hostility toward Muslim merchants and sailors in Christian port cities, a latent hostility that persisted even if it rarely turned into open violence, as during the so-called "massacre of the Turks" in Marseilles in 1620.[88] A great number of legal and religious safeguards existed for limiting commercial exchanges and contacts between the Maghreb and Europe. Those restrictions added to the fear of abuses in the port cities of the "infidels." As a result, merchants and sailors had to develop different strategies to circumvent the many obstacles facing the commerce between Islam and Christendom in the Mediterranean.

Trading captives offered an expedient that not only justified trafficking with the "infidels" more generally, but also provided merchants and ship captains with safeguards against potential abuses. The Spanish historian Rafael Benitez, analyzing the ransoming of captives between Valencia and Algiers in the early modern period, maintains that this activity functioned as a "lubricant" of trade and thus requires that historians pay greater attention to the central role that the trade in captives played for all economic exchanges between Europe and the Maghreb.[89] Two cases brought before Tuscan commercial tribunals in the 1620s—the courts of the governor of Livorno and of the consuls of the Sea of Pisa—confirm the importance of carrying captives as part of the cargo when searching for new commercial opportunities in the Maghreb. The first case pitched a French shipowner settled in Livorno, Origène Marchant, against several merchants who chartered Marchant's ship or insured its freight. This trial took place because a "Flemish" (i.e., Dutch) ship captain, Theodor Cornelissen, committed what is known in maritime law as a "barratry," that is, an act of gross misconduct tantamount legally to a crime. Cornelissen and his crew were supposed to go from Livorno to Algiers with merchandise and cash amounting in total to 40,000 pieces of eight—a huge sum. But they dropped their few passengers in southern Corsica and fled with the boat and cargo. Merchants and insurers filed a suit against the shipowner, whom they considered an accomplice, or at least

---

[86] Leor Halevi, "Christian Impurity versus Economic Necessity: A Fifteenth-Century Fatwa on European Paper," *Speculum*, 83 (2008): 917–945, 943.

[87] Halevi, "Christian Impurity," 939–940.

[88] Wolfgang Kaiser, "Asymétries méditerranéennes: Présence et circulation de marchands entre Alger, Tunis et Marseilles," in *Musulmans en Europe occidentale entre Moyen âge et l'époque moderne*, ed. Jocelyne Dakhlia and Bernard Vincent (Paris: Albin Michel, 2011), 417–442. For the eighteenth century, see Jean Mathiex, "Sur la marine marchande barbaresque au XVIIIᵉ siècle," *Annales: Économies, Sociétés et Civilisations*, 13.1 (1958): 87–93.

[89] Rafael Benitez, "La tramitación del pago de rescates a través del reino de Valencia: El último plazo del rescate de Cervantes," in *Le commerce des captifs*, 193–217, 217.

partly responsible for Cornelissen's barratry, because Marchant had chosen him to complete the voyage to Algiers. According to the merchants of Livorno, Cornelissen should have aroused Marchant's suspicion in the first place because he was a former privateer with a bad reputation.[90] Moreover, merchants and insurers thought it was suspicious that Cornelissen refused to take ransomed captives aboard. They explained very clearly that, in general, "it is something very wanted by captains of ships leaving from Livorno and going to Barbary to take on board ransomed slaves, and [ship captains] are very kind with them when they go aboard, because they can help both during the voyage in case of encounter with corsairs and once arrived in Barbary."[91] This statement is telling evidence of the advantage that a captain had in taking on board ransomed captives who would be welcomed in the port cities of North Africa. Furthermore, ransomed captives could certify, in case of an encounter with Algerian or Tunisian corsairs at sea, that the ship's captain was not a pirate, did not have hostile intentions against North African ships, and had the authorization to trade with the Maghreb. This very important point is evoked twice in the proceedings.[92]

Another case reveals the numerous difficulties in crossing boundaries and trading with the Maghreb in the early modern period. The galleys of the Knights of Saint John inspected and arrested the ship *Il Sole* off Malta. The Knights informed the Tuscan authorities about the inspection and about the fact that *Il Sole* transported smuggled goods. A Jewish merchant from Livorno, Judah Crespino, had two kegs of tin on board, while Joseph Franco, a Levantine Jew who had also settled in Livorno, was sending little knives and needles for making sails to a relative in Algiers.[93] The Knights of Malta consequently decided not to return the whole cargo, in accordance with the papal bull *In Coena Domini*.[94] The shipowner, now allied with the other merchants and insurers, accused the Jewish merchants of smuggling, referring as well to the papal bull (that being somewhat absurd since Crespino and Franco could not possibly be threatened with the excommunication sanctioned by *In Coena Domini*). In fact, the papal bull served, in all likelihood, to legitimate the depredation of the

[90] ASP, *Consoli del mare*, Atti Civili, 125, case 30 (hereafter 125/30), March 8, 1625, chapters of cross-examination: "né vi era notitia che havesse mutato costumi, né meno che havesse fatto attioni per le quali si potesse credere che fusse diventato huomo da bene et così" (there was no indication that he had changed his manners, nor that he had acted in ways that would have made him into a respectable person).

[91] ASP, *Consoli del mare*, Atti Civili, 125/30, February 19, 1625.

[92] ASP, *Consoli del mare*, Atti Civili, 125/30, March 8, 1625.

[93] ASP, *Consoli del mare*, Atti Civili, 125/30, March 8, 1625, petition by Camillo Paccalli, Giovanni Stefano Boccalandro, Origene Mercante, and Gualtiere Cesare; ASP, *Consoli del mare*, Atti Civili, 125/30, April 14, 1625, appearance in court of Joseph Franco; ASP, *Consoli del mare*, Suppliche, 974, no. 100.

[94] ASP, *Consoli del mare*, Atti Civili, 125/30, April 14, 1625, appearance in court of Joseph Franco.

Maltese corsairs. Eventually, the grand duke of Tuscany was asked to negotiate with the Maltese authorities to restore the goods to the merchants of Livorno.[95]

We can draw several lessons from this trial. Cross-cultural trade between Christian Europe and the Maghreb did not presuppose the existence of an informal "middle ground" that would offer the possibility to act outside formal regulations. On the contrary, trading with the Maghreb necessitated a continual transfer and inter-meshing of documents, rights, exemptions, and practices that required the organi-zation of a fitting procedure to make cross-cultural exchange possible. To reduce the uncertainty that was intrinsic to cross-cultural trade, merchants needed to obtain a license in the port of departure, to be well connected with North African traders (as was the case of the Jews in Livorno), and to transport ransomed captives and cash to remunerate local middlemen.[96] Merchants could also smuggle certain goods as a way of enhancing the trade of licit commodities such as grain, leather, gum, and sugar. But the lawful nature of exchanges depended, as we have demonstrated, on the political and economic choices of the different European states that, with greater or lesser reluctance, granted trading licenses for the traffic with North Africa.

If the transportation of captives proved central to the organization of commercial exchanges between Muslim and Christian regions, it was in part because ransoming was evidence of a successful negotiation. Thus respect for the procedures of ransom-ing turned out to be essential for maintaining good trading relations with North African or European partners. Another case brought before the civil and commercial court of the governor of Livorno in April 1624 illustrates this point. A Corsican ship captain, Bartolomeo Ambrogini, sued Pietro Corcia (Pedro Garcia?), a Portuguese surgeon and former captive in Algiers.[97] Ambrogini's ship left Algiers in January 1624, but its captain did not know that it was carrying Corcia, who had been stowed away in the boat's hold by friends, inside a big trunk supposed to contain grain and other foodstuffs. Corcia's subsequent escape, without the ship captain's knowledge, posed problems to Ambrogini, who explained to the judges that if he tried to go back to Algiers, Corcia's former master would likely oblige him to pay the total amount of the ransom. If he decided not to go back, however, he would lose the goods he had let in Algiers and his good commercial relations in the city. Against Corcia, he claimed 1,000 piasters in compensation in order to pay the ransom of the surgeon and the extras that were generally asked in such cases. The precarious

---

[95] ASP, *Consoli del mare*, Suppliche, 974, no. 100, May 11, 1625.

[96] The ship *Il Sole* and its owner obtained a license to sail to Algiers and Tunis on February 19, 1621. ASP, *Consoli del mare*, Atti Civili, 125/30, copy of the license for the ship named *Il Sole*.

[97] The following account is based on the trial records found in ASL, *GA*, 73, case 4 (hereafter 73/4), fols. 409–441.

commercial equilibrium built by Ambrogini to avoid snubs in Algiers had been jeopardized. While the transportation of ransomed captives made the exchanges with the Maghreb easier, the transportation of escaped captives was a considerable risk for the ship captain or the shipowner. Further, Ambrogini explained, he might not only lose commercial partners, but also risk being killed. In the written questions he put to Corcia and his friends who had helped him to escape, the ship captain explained that "in Algiers, to help slaves escape is punishable by death sentence and confiscation of ships and goods."[98]

Corcia and his friends answered Ambrogini, putting forward other arguments. They appealed to his sense of Christian charity. They threatened to bring the Corsican ship captain before the Holy Office of the Roman Inquisition. They accused him to favor the "law of the infidels" and to attach little importance to the "compassion of a poor Christian."[99] They described Ambrogini as a "person who tries to prevent poor Christians fallen into the hands of the Turks from gaining their freedom."[100] Such statement suggests that at the time, commercial interests and religious solidarity were perceived to be in conflict with one another when the latter aimed to favor captives' liberation regardless of the costs that it involved. In the end, the court of Livorno dismissed the case;[101] a few months later, we find captain Ambrogini trading with Tunis, and not anymore with Algiers.[102]

The maritime or commercial courts of other states did not necessarily agree with the sentence issued by the governor of Livorno in 1624, Don Pietro Medici, who was also a knight of Malta. For instance, at the end of the seventeenth century, in France, a trial against a captain shows how strong the will to respect regular procedures in the ransoming of captives was. A ship captain from Capbreton arrived in Algiers in 1699 and left the North African port city with two escaped Christian captives. Once in Marseilles, the ship captain was arrested, questioned, and fined for 1,500 *livres*. The two captives were sent back to Algiers to be ransomed according to the rules. As they were from Genoa, one asked the Genoese Republic to pay the customary sum of money for their ransom.[103]

In a context of religious and military conflict between the Muslim and the Christian regions of the Mediterranean, European commerce with the Maghreb required expedients: captives were certainly pitied, but they also served to justify mercantile exchanges and cooperation with the "infidels." The official function of

---

[98] ASL, *GA*, 73/4, fol. 437.
[99] ASL, *GA*, 73/4, fol. 409.
[100] ASL, *GA*, 73/4, fol. 409v.
[101] ASL, *GA*, 73/4, fol. 415.
[102] ASL, *GA*, 73, case 262.
[103] ACCIM, G 47.

corsairing was to damage the economic activities of the enemy. But in practice, corsairing also contributed to intensify exchanges between Christian, Muslim, and Jewish merchants in the western Mediterranean. The circulation of merchant letters and a variety of contracts discussed and signed before notaries, *qadi*, chancellors, and religious authorities did not create a hybrid law common to all parties involved. Rather, we find evidence of a widespread knowledge of different local rules and customs and the existence of practices and formal standards that could be transferred, applied, and adapted from one religious and geopolitical context to the other. Legal procedures remained different, but local brokers provided translations, not only into other languages but also into other normative frameworks. The centrality of customary knowledge and legal procedures to the organization of cross-cultural trade shows the extent to which the secular and economic actors in particular tried, in the early modern period, to suspend the religious conflict on which the very business of ransoming depended. At the same time, the latent religious conflict always rose to the surface whenever warriors and merchants took new captives by force.

5

Reflections on Reciprocity

A LATE MEDIEVAL ISLAMIC PERSPECTIVE ON CHRISTIAN-MUSLIM COMMITMENT TO CAPTIVE EXCHANGE

Kathryn A. Miller

THE CAPTIVE TRADE was one of the flourishing businesses along the coasts of North Africa and eastern Spain during the Middle Ages. Part sport, part commerce, it was a risky profession, although it offered the satisfactions of playing out long-standing friction between Muslims and Christians without, in most cases, actual bloodshed. The relative peacefulness in a commerce that, given its wares, spoke of conflicts should not be seen as the cause or consequence of growing tolerance, or intolerance, between religious groups. Rather, it was owed in part (as Guillaume Calafat and Wolfgang Kaiser argue in the previous chapter) to a combination, on the ground, of interests, ideal and real, and in part (as I shall try to show here) to the existence of norms that were the product of long-term, historical practice, and of an awareness of what modern scholars call "diffuse reciprocity."

Medieval Mediterranean captivity was the product of religious warfare, piracy, and violence between Christians and Muslims. In some cases, captives were taken out of fear: an enemy traveling in foreign lands, for example, posed a security risk. In battle, the victors imprisoned the vanquished—for prize and for profit. Thousands of Christians and Muslims found themselves in enemy hands in the Middle Ages as prisoners of war. Pirates and corsairs routinely intercepted pilgrims as they sailed eastward; others were snatched from their homeland along the shores of North

Africa or Spain. Village people in coastal towns were taken as captives. Even merchants conducting commercial business in foreign ports ran the risk of being seized and detained if relations between their homeland and host country soured.

Yet, while war, fear, or profit was behind the detainment and enslavement of Christians and Muslims, the act of rescuing these captives proved to be a distinctly different form of interaction between these communities. Ironically, the relationship of captives to their captors, to families and communities that came to their rescue, and to the middlemen (*fakkak* in Arabic; *alfaqueque* in Spanish) who negotiated their release can be shown to have often been collaborative, and even personal.

The medieval western Mediterranean (the Iberian Peninsula in particular) is distinguished by the close proximity of religious communities to one another and their respective institutions, living side by side for centuries. In captive exchanges, actors frequently knew each other well, and in many surviving sources it is not unusual to see the same individuals appear again and again, engaged at some level in redemptive activity. It was not an occasional practice but a professional specialization for which *fakkak* in particular cultivated reputations and exchange networks over the years.[1]

Muslim and Christian agents engaged in captive redemption (in Arabic, *fida*ʾ) certainly had reasons to suspect each other. Either party might be tempted to cheat the other, increase the ransom amount unexpectedly, alter the conditions of the written contract or spoken agreement, or even recapture a captive after he or she had been ransomed. Opportunities abounded for post-contractual high-jinks. Eager for profit, a Christian, Muslim, or Jewish agent might always pocket the ransom money without completing the exchange.

Despite such a priori handicaps, however, captive commerce flourished in the western Mediterranean region—and with it the formal and informal institutions that supported these redemptive practices. Agents from both sides crossed frontiers, transporting, depositing, and collecting money, and shuttling captives back and forth across borders. These middlemen, belonging to various social groups, cultivated a reputation of trustworthiness. Ambassadors were sometimes dispatched to royal courts to negotiate exorbitant sums; they had to prove themselves to both sides as trusted emissaries. For their intervention to be effective, these diplomats had to recognize the protocol of the rival power and to ascertain what offers would most

---

[1] Like medieval mercantile activity, to which they were obviously related, the mechanisms of captive exchange were governed by the reputation, or notoriety, of individual agents, their respective skills in negotiation and diplomacy, and market conditions. Reputation did work to establish conformity in ransoming and redemption practices and good behavior, but the motivation was not exclusively economic or profit-minded. Muslims and Christians alike worked to gain social and religious merit as well. I examine several case studies of these middlemen in my *Business with Infidels: Christian-Muslim Exchanges of Captives across the Mediterranean* (Oxford: Oxford University Press, forthcoming).

please kings and sultans. Men of Christian religious orders, such as the Trinitarians and Mercedarians, also negotiated for captive release and traveled to foreign lands on missions of mercy. They, too, saw the need to compromise and collaborate with local officials and Muslim captors. Independent middlemen (belonging to the three religions, and with different status or profession) negotiated settlements between parties. These agents performed a variety of tasks (transporting captives, negotiating bribes, paying shipping and emigration fees or government taxes, mediating between parties, establishing price and credit terms by which a captive would be exchanged or sold). In all scenarios, communication and some forms of trust and cooperation had to be established.[2]

Captive trade ran at a fairly brisk rate, and communities, leaders, and agents were constantly compelled to intercede on behalf of their coreligionists. Shared assumptions and a common language emerged. The ecumenical, international business sensibility of the middlemen defined religious boundaries more cogently, and trade agents from all communities maintained channels of information (conditions under which a captive was apprehended, ransom price, etc.) that spanned the Mediterranean. Captives, their families, and their communities posted letters and appeals for aid. An unremitting flow of correspondence between sultans, kings, and high-ranking officials shows persistent prompting on both sides to adhere to bilateral treaties and mutually agreed-upon conventions of ransom and redemption.

As a rule, captive exchanges were successful, although deals could fall through. At some point in the mid-fifteenth century, one exchange involving a young Christian man held in Muslim-controlled Malaga did, in fact, collapse, although in this case with unusually dramatic consequences. The young man had been ransomed by a Christian agent, and a contract documenting the transfer of funds and the redemption had been drawn up. The Muslim captor, however, then declared that his captive had converted to Islam. He voided the negotiation for the young man's release but he did not return the ransom money to the Christian *fakkak*.

Below I elaborate on why this particular case, as well as the document that discusses the breach in contract, is noteworthy in terms of its legal implications. Modern

---

[2] The field of study in trust and distrust is rapidly expanding, buoyed largely by interdisciplinary contributions from sociologists, psychologists, business scholars, and economists all interested in conceptual applications within their particular field. See, for example, Karen S. Cook, ed., *Trust in Society* (New York: Russell Sage Foundation, 2001); Karen S. Cook and Roderick M. Kramer, eds., *Trust and Distrust in Organizations: Dilemmas and Approaches* (New York: Russell Sage Foundation, 2004); Akbar Zaheer, Bill McEvily, and Vincenzo Perrone, "Does Trust Matter? Exploring the Effects of Interorganizational and Interpersonal Trust on Performance," *Organization Science*, 9.2 (1998): 141–159; Bill McEvily, Vincenzo Perrone, and Akbar Zaheer, "Trust as an Organizing Principle," *Organization Science*, 14.1 (2003): 91–103; Lenard Huff and Lane Kelley Names, "Levels of Organizational Trust in Individualist versus Collectivist Societies: A Seven-Nation Study," *Organization Science*, 14.1 (2003): 81–90.

scholars study captive trade and the respective legal institutions that Christians and Muslims developed in the medieval western Mediterranean to regulate the flow of exchange through a range of sources. The *fatwa* (an Islamic legal opinion) stands as a rare reflection by a Muslim writer on the tensions that the practice of captive exchange provoked, but sources for the Middle Ages, as for the early modern period, are asymmetrically distributed. We know much more about the Christian side of the story. Letters penned by Muslim captives, for example, rarely survive, and diplomatic records, especially those preserved in Spanish and Italian archives, largely document Christian interests.[3] However, the source here for the failed exchange, interestingly, is not Christian. As much as Christian officials might complain to their Muslim counterparts about policy violations—and many such complaints survive—this Muslim perspective on the Malaga incident is documented only in a *fatwa*. The text thus offers us a rare candid account of the norms of captive ransoming from a contemporary religious and legal Islamic viewpoint.

Several chapters in this volume explore how legal systems operated in a cross-cultural environment and ask how actors from different religious groups could, or could not, rely on these legal systems. Here we see a fifteenth-century Islamic scholar clearly state that, in the context of late medieval Iberia, it is fundamental to the well-being of the Muslim community and its captives that inter-religious redemption transactions be approached and monitored according to standards sanctioned by Muslims and Christians over the centuries. Significant to our purposes, this jurist elaborates on the rationale behind these exchange practices. The blatant violation of a redemption contract had evidently caused a furor in Muslim circles. Regional norms of exchange had been contravened, as the author of the *fatwa* wrote, "in a shameful way."[4] Yet, despite the current hostile relations between Granada and Christians to the north, the author stresses the negative consequences if these norms were ignored or blatantly violated by Muslims.[5]

Before turning to what the Malaga *fatwa* can tell us about an Islamic interpretation of medieval redemption practices, we must describe the local norms of exchange about which we do know something from other sources.

---

[3] There are valuable exceptions, however. See, for example, the memoir of the captive al-Fasi in Mikel de Epalza Ferrer, "Dos textos moriscos bilingües (árabe y castellano) de viajes a Oriente (1395 y 1407–12)," *Hespéris-Tamuda*, 20.2 (1982–1983): 25–112.

[4] See Aḥmad al-Wansharīsī, *Al-Miʿyār al-muʿrib wa-al-jāmiʿ al-mughrib ʿan fatāwā ʿulamāʾ Ifrīqiyā wa-al-Andalus wa-al-Maghrib*, 13 vols. (Rabat: Wizārat al-Awqaf wa-al-Shuʾūn al-Islāmiyya lil-Mamlaka al-Maghribiyya, 1981–1983), 2: 158–206, 189.

[5] In the second half of the fifteenth century, presumably when this *fatwa* was issued, towns in Granada suffered from repeated incursions by Christian militias. For an overview of Christian advances on Granada and the Muslim response, see Leonard Patrick Harvey, *Islamic Spain, 1250 to 1500* (Chicago: University of Chicago Press, 1990).

Over the years, Christians and Muslims had built up formal and informal institutions to regulate exchange, institutions that were recognized by both sides as distinctive in their laws and the ways in which they were governed. The exchange of captives—then as now—could take many forms, including ransoming, captive-to-captive exchange, and release through treaty. The process was rarely simple. More often than not, it proved a lengthy, trying affair that involved steps and stages, half-ransoms, guarantees, and alms collection. A surprisingly broad range of sources, notably from Christian-Spanish archives in particular, survives to record these processes. We now have many excellent studies on the charitable efforts of Christians and Mudejars and on the financial challenges they entailed as well as on the communal solidarity that lay behind these efforts.[6]

By the fourteenth and fifteenth centuries, regulatory processes and relatively stable institutions had long been put into place by Christians and Muslims of the western Mediterranean. The *aman*, or safe conduct, had been recognized as one of the fundamental agreements by which agents could freely cross borders and not be

---

[6] The scholarship on medieval captivity and captive exchange has expanded over the last few decades, especially on the institutions that support Christian redemption, such as the Mercedarians and Trinitarians. For the later Middle Ages, notable studies include María Teresa Ferrer i Mallol, "La Redempció de captius a la corona Catalano-Aragonesa (Segle XIV)," *Anuario de estudios medievales*, 15 (1985): 237–297; James William Brodman, *Ransoming Captives in Crusader Spain: The Order of Merced on the Christian-Islamic Frontier* (Philadelphia: University of Pennsylvania Press, 1986); María Teresa Ferrer i Mallol, "Els redemptors de captius: mostolafs, eixees o alfaquecs (segles XII–XIII)," *Medievalia*, 10 (1990): 85–106; Giulio Cipollone, *La liberazione dei 'captivi' tra Cristianità e Islam: Oltre la crociata e il ğihād; Tolleranza e servizio umanitario* (Città del Vaticano: Archivio Segreto Vaticano, 2000); Jarbel Rodriquez, *Captives and Their Saviors in the Medieval Crown of Aragon* (Washington, DC: Catholic University of America Press, 2007); Debra Blumenthal, *Enemies and Familiars: Slavery and Mastery in Fifteenth-century Valencia* (Ithaca, NY: Cornell University Press, 2009). For Muslim and Mudejar redemption practices, see Mark D. Meyerson, "Slavery and the Social Order: Mudejars and Christians in the Kingdom of Valencia," *Medieval Encounters* 1 (1995): 144–173; idem, "Slavery and Solidarity: Mudejars and Foreign Muslim Captives in the Kingdom of Valencia," *Medieval Encounters*, 1.2 (1996): 286–343; Pieter Sjoerd van Koningsveld, "Muslim Slaves and Captives in Western Europe During the Late Middle Ages," *Islam and Christian-Muslim Relations*, 6 (1995): 5–24; Francisco Vidal Castro, "Poder religioso y cautivos creyentes en la Edad Media: la experiencia islámica," in *Fe, cautiverio y liberación: Cristianos con Dios en la pasión; Actas del I Congreso Trinitario de Granada* (Cordoba: Secretariado de Trinitario, 1996), 73–96; Manuela Marín and Rachid El Hour, "Captives, Children and Conversion: A Case from Late Nasrid Granada," *Journal of the Economic and Social History of the Orient*, 41.4 (1998): 453–473; Andrés Díaz Borrás, *El miedo al Mediterráneo: La caridad popular Valenciana y la redención de cautivos bajo poder musulmán, 1323–1539* (Barcelona: Consejo Superior de Investigaciones Científicas Institución Milá y Fontanals, 2001); Kathryn A. Miller, *Guardians of Islam: Religious Authority and Muslim Communities in Late Medieval Spain* (New York: Columbia University Press, 2008). James Brodman and Yvonne Friedman have pointed to the distinction between eastern and western Mediterranean ransoming practices. These studies focus on communal solidarity and moral-religious obligation within a religious community, but not across sectarian lines. James William Brodman, "Community, Identity and the Redemption of Captives: Comparative Perspectives across the Mediterranean," *Anuario de estudios medievales*, 36 (2006): 241–252; Yvonne Friedman, *Encounter between Enemies: Captivity and Ransom in the Latin Kingdom of Jerusalem* (Boston: Brill, 2002).

taken prisoner.[7] Christians and Muslims had also been routinely using contracts and other legal documents to record the funds transferred from individuals, communities, and pious foundations to agents, and then on to captors. Treaties between kings and sultans almost always included a section on captive exchange, linking in complicated ways the release of captives on either side to truces and trade agreements. In the first half of the fifteenth century, for example, we see the complicated scenario that arose when a long-standing trade treaty between the Crown of Aragon and the North African Hafsid ruler had to be renegotiated. In 1413, the Hafsid Amir Abu Faris tried to engage Ferdinand of Antequera, deploying a range of tactics to attract him to the bargaining table.[8] Using his Catalan captives as a means to pressure the Crown of Aragon, the sultan tried repeatedly to engage the king in negotiations. When repeated attempts proved futile, Abu Faris declared that he would not release any captives, and his instruction "o tots ich exirets o tots ich estarets ("either you will all go or you will all stay") meant that he was holding out for a comprehensive, high-political settlement.[9]

International relations—and Abu Faris's reputation—rested largely on peace treaties agreed upon by both parties, and captive exchange was a fundamental part of these agreements.[10] These treaties, in fact, enumerated many stipulations that demanded

---

[7] John Wansbrough, "The Safe Conduct in Muslim Chancery Practice," *Bulletin of the School of Oriental and African Studies*, 34.1 (1974): 20–35. Muslim and Christian rulers were only too aware that safe-conduct was an essential aspect of the exchange or ransom of captives. For example, in his *rihla*, Ibn Basit recounted how he had boarded a French merchant vessel to observe the redemption of Muslim prisoners. Almost all of the captives had been ransomed, with the exception of one captive, a Turk who, speaking no Arabic, had been unable to communicate to would-be North African redeemers that he was a Muslim. A captive's fate could be indeed capricious, dependent as it was on the choices, capacities, and efforts of local Muslims, and their rulers, to rescue the thousands of kidnapped captives sailing the Mediterranean Sea. See Robert Brunschvig, *Deux recits de voyage inédits en Afrique du Nord au XVᵉ siècle* (Paris: Maisonneuve & Larose, 2001).

[8] These included engaging diplomats and merchants to work as redemption agents. For the amir's efforts with Ferdinand as well as the role of the Catalan merchants in the negotiations, see Roser Salicrú i lluch, "Cartes de captius cristians a les presons de Tunis de regnat de Ferran d'Antequera," *Miscel.lània de Textos Medievals*, 7 (1994): 549–590.

[9] Salicrú i lluch, "Cartes de captius cristians," 559.

[10] A bustling maritime port, Tunis derived its economic vibrancy in large part from the commercial activity of its merchant and foreign community of Italians (Pisans, Genoese, and Venetians) and Catalans, and their ability to move in and out with relative ease with their goods. See, for example, Robert Brunschvig, *La Berbérie orientale sous les Hafsides: Des origines à la fin du XVᵉ siècle* (Paris: Adrien-Maisonneuve, 1940); Alberto Sacerdoti, "Venezia e il regno hafsida di Tunisi: Trattati e relazioni diplomatiche 1231–1534," *Studi Veneziani*, 8 (1966): 303–346; Bernard Doumerc, *Venise et l'émirat hafside de Tunis (1231–1535)* (Paris: L'Harmattan, 1999); Georges Jehel, *L'Italie et le Maghreb au Moyen Age: Conflits et échanges du VIIᵉ au XVᵉ siècle* (Paris: Presses Universitaires de France, 2001); Olivia Remie Constable, *Housing the Stranger in the Mediterranean World: Lodging, Trade, and Travel in Late Antiquity and the Middle Ages* (Cambridge: Cambridge University Press, 2003). And for the peace treaties, see M. Louis de Mas-Latrie, *Traités de paix et de commerce et documents divers concernant les relations des Chrétiens avec les Arabes de l'Afrique septentrionale au moyen âge*, 2 vols. (Paris: Henri Plon, 1866).

accountability and cooperative behavior from all parties in exchange for cessation of hostilities. With the Venetians, for example, who persistently inquired of him the whereabouts of Venetian captives, Abu Faris equivocated.[11] With the Catalans, with whom he wished to renew a treaty, he held on to his captives as leverage.[12] Or Abu Faris agreed to find and return any captive Pisans to the Pisan consulate in Tunis if Pisans in turn would agree to cease and desist from corsair raids on Muslim boats and travelers.[13] Such were the principles, but they could be gamed: an agreement to release captives might not specify a date of return, allowing Abu Faris to hold on to his captives until the opportune moment.

Economic self-interest governed the behavior of cross-cultural agents involved in ransoming captives. It is not surprising that governmental and other regulating institutions, both Christian and Muslim, learned how to profit from the market of captive exchanges. Yet ideological pressures also determined the behavior of Muslim and Christian actors in the transactions.[14] Informal and formal settlements made between captors and liberators were based as much on religious considerations as on economic incentives. Many ransoms were motivated by familial concerns. Obviously, relatives did not want the captives to suffer or to abandon their religion, and might risk considerable sums to redeem a loved one. More critically perhaps, Christians and Muslims deemed it their obligation to liberate their coreligionists.[15] Community members frequently volunteered funds to finance captive redemption.[16] Social status and reputation could

---

[11] Sacerdoti, "Venezia e il regno hafsida di Tunisi," 328–334.

[12] Salicrú i lluch, "Cartes de captius cristians," 559.

[13] Michele Amari, *I Diplomi arabi del R. archivio fiorentino*, 1st series (Arabic) (Florence: Le Monnier, 1863-67), 131–136.

[14] Abu Faris was strategic, but he was also respected as a pious leader. A sultan's generosity in redeeming Muslim captives determined, in part, his place in history. To this end, biographical literature and chronicles highlighted rulers' contributions and efforts to liberate Muslims from enemy hands. The chronicler to the Almohad caliph Abu Yaʿqub Yusuf typically praised him for having redeemed 700 Muslim inhabitants of Seville (they had been taken captive by the army of Alfonso VIII of Castile). His words conveyed one of the stakes in redemption: "He saved them from the ensnaring adoration of Unbelief [and led them] to the liberty of Islam." The fear of apostasy motivated rulers' diligence. On this incident, see van Koningsveld, "Muslim Slaves and Captives," 6–7.

[15] Medieval Jewish communities also placed captive redemption as a high priority. Goitein published a letter of Moses Maimonides appealing to Jews to contribute to the ransom of Jewish captives "as befits your generosity and your [renown] as seekers of merit [through] kindness and love." As cited by Mark R. Cohen, *The Voice of the Poor in the Middle Ages: An Anthology of Documents from the Cairo Geniza* (Princeton, NJ: Princeton University Press, 2005), 69–70, doc. 33. Cohen gives other examples of Jewish efforts to rescue imprisoned coreligionists.

[16] Contributing funds for ransoming was regarded as a meritorious deed—in fact, a duty—in the Islamic community. Numerous bequests survive, mainly from Christians but a few from Muslims, which designate funds to captives—not only for their ransoms but also for their post-captivity recovery. For two bequests from the fifteenth century, see Luis Seco de Lucena, ed. and trans., *Documentos árabigo-granadinos* (Madrid: Instituto de Estudios Islámicos, 1961), 102 (Arabic) and 109 (Spanish). See also Vidal Castro, "Poder religioso y cautivos creyentes en la Edad Media," 95, and Marín and El Hour, "Captives, Children and Conversion," 456. For a discussion of Christian bequests, see Rodriquez, *Captives and Their Saviors*.

be boosted in this way and, simultaneously, credit gained before God. In fact, we can sometimes witness pointed, conscious competition between potential redeemers, for the sake of honor and religious merit.[17]

ISLAMIC LAW: THE CONDITIONS AND CONTEXT OF EXCHANGE

For centuries, Islamic legal scholars had put their minds, and pens, to an effort to regulate the laws of warfare, captivity, prisoners of war, rules of engagement, truces, and treaties. The four schools of law—Maliki, Hanafi, Shafi'i, and Hanbali—had long debated a multitude of issues of principle. Under what conditions could non-Muslim captives be imprisoned? How should they be treated? Should these captives be ransomed, or perhaps exchanged for Muslim captives? Was it risky to liberate non-Muslim captives and allow them to return to their communities, especially if they were brave soldiers or perhaps spies? And conversely, under what conditions, if any, was it permissible not to rescue Muslim captives or allow for the redemption of Christian captives, and what principles would guide such a decision?[18] A key debate, of course, was the distinction made between redemption through direct exchange and redemption by means of financial payment or promissory notes. Islamic scholars who disapproved of ransom payments argued that these funds fed the coffers of the enemy, as well as encouraging the reprehensible practice of putting a market price on a Muslim captive.

In theory, Muslim authorities attempted to regulate practice and produced rulings on how a *fakkak* was to handle sums of money. Jurists articulated the laws of *fida'* (redemption) that should guide the *fakkak*, and these regulations were expanded, adjusted, and fine-tuned over the centuries to accommodate new needs and contexts. As early as the twelfth century, Islamic scholars delineated the rules

---

[17] In the mid-fourteenth century, for instance, after Genoese corsairs had kidnapped inhabitants of Tripoli, neighboring towns and the sultan Abu 'Inan Faris (d. 1358) rivaled to pay the ransom. The Genoese had demanded 50,000 coins in pure gold to ransom Muslim captives. A local Muslim lord asked Sultan Abu 'Inan to lend the sum "while keeping the merits of this pious deed," but Abu 'Inan did not respond quickly enough. The Genoese refused to wait, so Ibn Mekki (lord of Gabès) "gathered all that he owned, and obtained the remainder of the sum from the inhabitants of Gabès, El-H'amma and the Djerid as a pure charity." Meanwhile, Abu 'Inan came forward with the sum, offered to reimburse the inhabitants of the three towns, and added that he [the sultan] left to him [Ibn Mekki] all the merits of the deed. But the inhabitants of the three communities preferred not to share the merit for their good deed and refused the money. *Chronique des Almohades & des Hafçides attribuée à Zerkechi*, French trans. by Edmond Fagnan (Constantine: A. Braham, 1895), 147–148.

[18] See, among other sources, Fred M. Donner, "The Sources of Islamic Conceptions of War," in *Just War and Jihad: Historical and Theoretical Perspectives on War and Peace in Western and Islamic Traditions*, ed. John Kelsay and James Turner Johnson (Westport, CT: Praeger, 1991), 31–70; Majid Khadduri, *War and Peace in the Law of Islam* (Baltimore, MD: Johns Hopkins University Press, 1955).

for transactions, within the framework of Islamic contractual law, taking into account the many opportunities for corruption, misunderstanding, and mishandling of funds.[19] Other source-genres, notably chronicles, reveal the kind of potential conflicts that could arise in exchanges.[20] Problems could hinge on whether Muslim contractual agreements with Christians should be honored in the same way as those with Muslims. Scores of letters sent between Muslim and Christian officials of this period complain of violations of bilateral treaties by the opposite side. A port official in Valencia might intentionally imprison Muslims arriving from merchant and corsair ships who were protected by these treaties, or by safe conducts.[21] Equally, a Granadan sultan would be accused of similar contractual breaches when Christian traders, with their legitimate safe conducts, were taken captive.[22] Such complaints must have overflowed on local officials' desks. They provided, however, both sides with a means of communication— monitoring, threatening, and cajoling. Equally, the correspondence reflects the diplomatic conventions of respect, honor, and reputation between Christians and Muslims. The risks of business combined with religious values to make the process an emotionally charged one. Islamic scholars' production of legal manuals, *fatwas*, and contract formularies kept the business smooth-running and religiously correct.

It was real-life problems that occasioned *fatwas*. Muslims would approach a *mufti* and ask for a legal opinion on how to handle a thorny situation. A Muslim captive marries a Christian in Christian territory. Is the marriage legal? Muslim captives escape a Christian ship in a Muslim harbor. Should they be returned? And what about monetary inflation in the captive trade? Who absorbs the loss if ransom depreciates in value before the exchange is made?[23]

---

[19] The Islamic manuals (*watha'iq*) that contain formularies for contracts and survive from Andalusian times. The *fiqh* (Islamic jurisprudence) appended to these manuals points to specific legal challenges that arose in captive exchange.

[20] Al-Zarkashi's *Chronique des Almohades and des Hafçides attribuée à Zerkechi* presents one example. Other Muslim historians, like Ibn Khaldun and Lisan ad-Din ibn al-Khatib, record the political intrigue and diplomatic complexities that Andalusian and Maghrebi rulers confronted in their dealings with captivity. See, for example, Ibn Khaldun, *Histoire des Berbères et des dynasties musulmanes de l'Afrique septentrionale*, trans. Baron de Slane (Paris: n.p., 1934); Lisan Al Din Ibn Al Khatib, *Tarikh Isbaniya Al Islamiya* [History of Muslim Spain], ed. Levi-Provencal, new ed. (Cairo: n.p., 2004).

[21] Manuel Sánchez Martínez, "Comercío nazarí y pirateria catalano-aragonesa (1344–45)," in *Relaciones de la Península Ibérica con el Magreb siglos XIII–XVI*, ed. Mercedes García-Arenal and María Jesús Viguera (Madrid: Instituto Hispano-Arabe de Cultura, 1988), 41–86.

[22] *Los documentos árabes diplomáticos del Archivo de la Corona de Aragón*, ed and trans. Maximiliano A. Alarcón y Santón and Ramon García de Linares (Madrid-Granada: Impr. de E. Maestre, 1940); Sacerdoti, "Venezia e il regno hafsida di Tunisi"; Roser Salicrú i lluch, *Documents per a la història de Granada del regnat d'Alfons el Magnànim, 1416–1458* (Barcelona: Consell Superior d'Investigacions Científiques, 1999).

[23] For the fifteenth and early sixteenth century, these *fatwas* are located in *Al-Mi'yar* by Ahmad al-Wansharisi (d. 1508) and in unpublished manuscripts in the Moroccan archives. For Abu l-Qasim b. Ahmad b. Muhammad al-Burzuli (d. 1438) and 'Abdul 'Aziz al-Zayati (d. 1656), see Bibliothèque Générale, Rabat, nos. 66 and 1694 and the Bibliothèque Royal, Rabat, nos. 2500 and 3862.

FATWA: A DISPUTE OVER A MUSLIM CAPTIVE

The *fatwa* pertaining to the Malaga incident, though, stands out from such rulings. As mentioned above, a Christian source recording this failed ransom exchange has not surfaced. We do not know what events or circumstances prompted the anonymous jurist to compose his opinion.[24] Perhaps an imam or sultan engaged in negotiations elsewhere appealed to this Muslim scholar's authority and compelled him to compensate for broken trust. Perhaps even the Christian *fakkak* involved sought legal remedy through Islamic courts.[25] In any case, the self-interested Muslim captor's refusal to hand over the converted captive was an uncooperative act in an exchange process that depended heavily on cooperation between Muslims and Christians. The captor violated Islamic contract law, or at least took advantage of a perceived loophole.

Significantly, the captor's refusal to reimburse the Christian *fakkak* made waves in the Muslim community.[26] Some local authorities stepped in, and a legal council was convened in Granada to judge whether the breach of contract could be justified. The Granadan ruling came as a shock: ransoming Christian captives by Muslims should stop entirely. Such exchanges should not be permitted. Cooperation with the infidel must cease.

A GRANADAN JURIST'S INTERPRETATION

This sweeping ruling provoked wider scandal. Eventually a prominent Maliki jurist, also in Granada, entered into the fray and wrote the long *fatwa* with which we are concerned. The *fatwa* itself is difficult. It offers a lengthy legal discussion of the Islamic treatment of captives and prisoners of war and of the conversion of Christian

---

[24] *Fatwas* are legal opinions, and thus it is often difficult to know whether rulings were enacted. Another limitation of *fatwas* as source material is that they characteristically omit the identities of the individuals involved, and in some cases relevant locations and dates. On the genre and methodology of reading *fatwa* literature, among other studies, see Muhammad Khalid Masud, Brinkley Messick, and David S. Powers, eds., *Islamic Legal Interpretation: Muftis and Their Fatwas* (Cambridge, MA: Harvard University Press, 1996); David S. Powers, *Law, Society, and Culture in the Maghrib, 1300–1500* (Cambridge: Cambridge University Press, 2002).

[25] Muslims living in Christian territory (Mudejars) often appealed to Christian courts, and Christian sources for the period survive to document this process. While the inverse may well have occurred in Islamic Iberia, unfortunately Muslim court records do not survive. For a concise overview of the legal rights and administration of Muslims in Christian territory, see Mark Meyerson, *The Muslims of Valencia in the Age of Fernando and Isabel: Between Coexistence and Crusade* (Berkeley: University of California Press, 1991), 184–224. On the role of Islamic legal scholars as middlemen for Christian and Muslim courts of law, see also Miller's *Guardians of Islam*. See Chapter 3 in this volume on the coexistence and parallelism of Mediterranean legal systems.

[26] As is the case with many *fatwas*, we are not informed of what happened to the Christian agent after the Muslim captor refused to hand over his captive. Chances are that he absorbed the financial loss.

captives.[27] The arguments it adduced range considerably—from the Islamic juris-prudence on just war mentioned above, to earlier Andalusian legal literature and precedent-setting cases on captive exchange. Significantly, however (and we will see this in more detail below), the jurist provides what he deems as "extra-legal" evidence to demonstrate just how harmful it would be to the Muslim community's interests, and to Muslim captives in particular, if Muslims refused categorically to redeem captives or cooperate with Christians in setting any terms for exchange.

The *fatwa* allows us to address a series of broad questions. Namely, how did the Muslims in Granada view cooperation with Christians? Given the Qur'anic emphasis on captive ransoming, was there any moral obligation for Muslims to cooperate with Christians? How did Muslims perceive their obligations to the exchange process, as well as the Christians' obligations and/or willingness to cooperate?

What stands out for our purposes are the jurist's comments on cooperation and commitment, and his wholesale embrace of reciprocity between Muslims and Christians in late medieval Iberia. He expressed his deep concern that the barriers were thin that prevented the bilateral processes from disintegrating into a tit-for-tat retributive chaos of violated conventions, safe-conducts, and contracts. The jurist's notable negative views of Christian kings and of their vindictive politics come into play here.

I will not expand on each of the arguments by means of which this anonymous jurist dismantled the earlier ruling. Suffice it to say that he upholds the Muslim obligation to respect contracts made with Christians, in particular those which allow for captive redemptions. In a robust argument, he defends the ransoming of Christian captives. He underscores the obligation of his Muslim contemporaries to respect conventional and current practices of captive exchange, regardless of any breaches of trust committed by Christian counterparts. The *fatwa* became authoritative; it was popular enough to circulate in Muslim territory and came to be included a few decades later in the *Mi'yar*, a compendium of useful *fatwas* compiled by the famous jurist al-Wansharisi.

The controlling concept in the jurist's *fatwa* is respect for tradition. But his was a pragmatic view that also took account of differences in region and context; correspondingly, he rejected the notion of a "one size fits all" policy on ransoming, while insisting that Muslims honor the institutions and conventions of captive exchange long established between Christians and Muslims, and providing justifications for their doing so. A contract was a contract, as he saw it, even if drawn up between

---

27 See Ahmad al-Wansharisi, *Al-Mi'yar*, 2: 158–206.

enemies.[28] Violating the terms of such an agreement was unconscionable: "for if we were to follow" these "bizarre and grievous" arguments

> and make effective the prohibition of ransoming Christians in accordance with his [the earlier/wayward jurist's] opinion…then we would have heinously contravened what we agreed to in a covenant with the Christians and the ones who came seeking the release and freedom. We would have contradicted in a shameful way what conditions we agreed to and what the Muslims generally have agreed over the years with them. We would have undone what our kings and their ancestors have sanctioned, approved, and ordered now and in the past—a solution that is abhorrent for the sensible and wise to contrive and innovate.[29]

THE IMPORTANCE OF COOPERATION ACROSS RELIGIOUS BOUNDARIES

The jurist correctly underscored that redemption institutions and practices such as the contract between captor and redeemer had existed for centuries.[30] The laws of war were enshrined in the Qur'an, but especially in the legal thought that had been developed following the seventh- and eighth-century Islamic expansion. Thus, he was stressing both religious and historical precedent in his respect for established institutions. His theoretical defense of contract dovetailed with a pragmatic appreciation for an old relationship involving both reciprocity and antagonism and for his emphasis on time and place in assessing risks and options. The captive trade throughout the western Mediterranean showed no signs of ever diminishing, let alone ending. Both sides needed to redeem their coreligionists, and in order to do so, had to trust that contracts and safe-conducts would be honored.

Respect for contracts probably did not blind the jurist to their frailty. As discussed above, the institutions or conventions developed and refined over the years to monitor captive-taking and exchange were far from perfect, reflecting all the weaknesses,

---

[28] Although few contracts from the captivity trade survive, there is enough documentation from other sources to support the central place that they held. In general, contracts served as an important regulating mechanism in the exchange of captives, documenting a range of financial transactions as well as logistical details within and across Christian and Muslim communities.

[29] Ahmad al-Wansharisi, *Al-Mi'yar*, 2: 189.

[30] The drafting of *fida'* contracts were common as early as the twelfth century in al-Andalus, as evident in the formularies of the jurist al-Jaziri, for instance. Although al-Jaziri's notarial formularies were composed in the twelfth century, they were clearly popular three centuries later, attested to by their wide circulation among fifteenth-century Muslim communities. On this notarial formulary and others that circulated in Iberian Muslim communities, see Miller, *Guardians of Islam*, 66–67, 88.

self-interest, and capriciousness of the people who employed them. Perhaps it was the very frailty, as well as the profound importance, of such interfaith agreements that led the anonymous jurist to stress recourse to authority. The jurist threw his legal weight behind the argument that the local ruler, the sultan or imam, should determine the regional policies regarding the ransoming of Christian prisoners. Indeed, these should be crafted to benefit to the maximum the local Muslim community and to increase opportunities to redeem Muslim captives from Christian hands.[31] The sultan would best be able to consider the multiple factors and the most efficacious way to get Muslim captives liberated.

LEGAL OPTIONS ACCORDED TO MUSLIM RULERS

Furthermore, the *fatwa* argued that while scholars may have disagreed whether to ransom captives for money (and many Maliki scholars did so), the sultan (or imam) had the right to decide among five legal options for the treatment of a captive. He cited Ibn Rushd and enumerated them: ransoming, killing, enslaving, or liberating a captive, or placing him or her in a tributary status.[32] A Muslim leader need not restrict "himself to any of these five options," declared our jurist. "He is free to deviate from any of the ordinary interests, such as to approve the ransom of one who is famous for courage and hurting Muslims, or to do something else that he sees fit."[33] The jurist also readily conceded that there might be good reasons not to ransom a captive—reasons pointed out by other legal scholars.[34] A captive, for instance, might be a spy who, if ransomed, would return to the infidels with potentially hurtful information about the Muslims. Or, the captive might be an excellent soldier who,

---

[31] Ahmad al-Wansharisi, *Al-Mi'yar*, 2: 178, 181.

[32] For a translation of Ibn Rushd's legal doctrine of *jihad*, see Rudolph Peters, *Jihad in Classical and Modern Islam* (Princeton, NJ: Markus Wiener, 1996), 27–42.

[33] Ahmad al-Wansharisi, *Al-Mi'yar*, 2: 178. The imam, and Muslim captors, should keep the public benefit of the Muslim community in mind in considering options. Accepting ransom funds, for example, could result in Muslims "becoming stronger by remuneration or compensation they get from their enemies and by generating the conditions for the release of their Muslim brethren who are captives in the hands of the infidels, and other benefits private or public. If the imam changed his mind, ignored an option he allowed before, and then opted for another one of the five options in view of an interest that occurred at the time of a particular case, then this option that was allowed is transformed from being allowed to being banned, from being permitted to being prohibited, such as the case concluding a truce with the warring people."

[34] Muslim captors could exercise a range of options—far more than five—in handling their captives. A skilled or educated captive was a prized commodity. Such a captive could be used to negotiate treaties, to copy manuscripts, or to help build palaces. Captives could be exchanged for other captives, or freed as a strategic gift to the infidel. Usamah ibn Munqidh, in his memoirs, recounted an episode where a legal scholar condoned not rescuing Muslim soldiers held as hostages by Christians because the effort to do so would undermine the Muslims' military position. See *An Arab-Syrian Gentleman and Warrior in the Period of the Crusades: Memoirs of Usāmah ibn-Munqidh*, trans. Philip K. Hitti (New York: Columbia University Press, 2000).

if ransomed, would return to the infidel, only to fight again. The sultan or imam was also duty-bound to change his mind according to his assessment of the best interests of the Muslim community at any given time: "And as such the affairs of the people of Andalusia concerning the issue of ransoming are run today. They are limited and restricted by what their kings had seen as their interest and benefit, and this is exactly what has been truly intended by the rite of Malik."[35]

POLITICAL AND PRACTICAL APPROACHES TO REDEMPTION

In terms of time and place—fifteenth-century Muslim Granada—ransoming Christian captives was the best option, and, in fact, sometimes the only recourse. One recommended alternative to ransom for money, for instance, was direct exchange of captives. But, as a blanket policy, this was not viable there and then. While captive exchange might be ideal, it was logistically challenging.[36] Looking at the complicated political landscape and the shifting alliances of the late medieval western Mediterranean, our anonymous jurist saw a motley assortment of Christian captives in Granadan and North African prisons, a "scattering of captives in outstretching lands," whose loyalties to different Christian kings often made direct captive exchange "impossible" to pull off.[37] It was unlikely that, he observed, a Mallorcan Christian would be ransomed by an Aragonese noble, and vice versa.[38] And, more to the point, Christians "were not well-disposed ['much displeased" was his phrase] toward their own captives." Christians could be grossly indifferent to the fate of Christian captives when ransom money was not part of the equation.

---

[35] Ahmad al-Wansharisi, *Al-Mi'yar*, 2: 179.

[36] With direct exchange, Muslim redeemers did not aid and abet the enemy by feeding their coffers with ransom funds.

[37] It is important to note that shifting alliances between Muslim and Christian states, as well as regional variations—Granada, North Africa, Aragon, and Mallorca—often had an impact on redemption practices. States who had signed a truce and agreed to refrain from taking captives obviously handled captive exchange differently from hostile states whose aims might be to collect high ransoms or fan the flames of existing conflicts.

[38] Ahmad al-Wansharisi, *Al-Mi'yar*, 2: 199: "It was aforementioned that Christians and other nations are working hard to counterattack their enemies for what they do to them. So if the Muslims were to forbid the ransoming of Christians for money, then the Christians would do the same...for the ones who look into the nations remunerating each other are the kings, and the Christian kings and others do not take into consideration concern for money of those who have a captives in their hands, if this serves a purpose in his kingdom. Moreover, the Christians are so arrogant when they have Muslim captives and ask for high prices for they trust that Muslims pay large amounts of money to buy their freedom. Also, they are much displeased regarding their own captives; they show indifference enough to prevent them from ransoming. Concerning the scattering of captives in outstretching lands that might not be obedient to their kings, this is something impossible and does not allow the ransoming of Muslim captives for Christian captives. The interest and benefit in ransoming them for money is done in accordance with what has been chosen by our kings and followed by our forefathers and scholars."

Furthermore, a general policy shift against ransoming, as proposed by the council, would have been highly impractical, since as the anonymous jurist points out, contexts and particular situations dictated their own local decisions.[39] Frontier regions of Granada made their own local arrangements for captive exchanges—and their ransoming negotiations were notably successful. They had their own *fakkak* agents and were generally in close communication with their Christian neighbors.[40] Inland towns and port cities operated under different pressures and opportunities. Treaties stipulating numbers of captives to be liberated might be more appropriate in some cases, while in other cases specific guarantees and payments were arranged.

While our jurist recognized the need to be flexible with policy, he opposed impulsive behavior in the treatment and redemption of captives. The option to ransom was not confined to authorities. It was possible—in fact, only practical—for individual Muslims to demand ransom of their Christian prisoners if they adhered to these guidelines and avoided behaving "arbitrarily" in their dealings with Christians.[41] Simply "imitating" one of Ibn Rushd's five options was too facile. Good judgment and wisdom were necessary, as well as a deep and broad understanding of the needs of the Muslim community. In the jurist's view, a sultan or imam had this capacity. The rest of good Muslims should follow suit, working within the institutions that existed to facilitate these policies.

A DANGEROUS PRECEDENT AND LONG-TERM CONSEQUENCES

Our anonymous jurist was from late fifteenth-century Granada. In this context, and in light of Granada's relationship with Christians further north at the time, the jurist wanted his audience to fully realize the implications of prohibiting ransoming. It was misguided, from a legal point of view, but it was also dangerous policy. He made it clear that their Christian contemporaries and counterparts would retaliate. Make no mistake, he seemed to say, we are dealing with a tit-for-tat political culture here: "for it is quite known for all that Muslim kings and others still face their enemies and peers, even if they were friendly, with the same kind of actions and penalties and respond in kind."[42] Experience had shown that Christians not only retaliated for acts

---

[39] Ahmad al-Wansharisi, *Al-Mi'yar*, 2: 178.

[40] M. García Fernández, "La Alfaquequería mayor de Castilla en Andalucía a fines de la Edad Media: Los alfaqueques reales," in *Estudios sobre Málaga y el reino de Granada en el V centenario de la conquista* (Málaga: Servicio de Publicaciones, Diputación Provincial de Málaga, 1987), 38–50; Carmen Argente del Castillo Ocaña, "Los cautivos en la frontera entre Jaen y Granada," in *Relaciones exteriores del Reino de Granada: IV Coloquio de historia medieval andaluza*, ed. Cristina Segura Graiño (Almería: Instituto de Estudios Almerienses, 1988), 211–225.

[41] Ahmad al-Wansharisi, *Al-Mi'yar*, 2: 176.

[42] Ahmad al-Wansharisi, *Al-Mi'yar*, 2: 197. On the notion of tit-for-tat in economic exchanges, see Robert Axelrod, *The Evolution of Cooperation* (New York: Basic Books, 1984).

of violence and ill will but tended to up the ante. Thus when Muslims killed Christian guides, the jurist noted, Christians responded by killing Muslim guides—after heinously maiming them, too.[43] In these times, the jurist pointed out, the Christians were stronger than their Muslim enemies and felt no compunction against severe retribution. He adds, "especially with the Christian kings of Andalusia, whose cruelty and arrogance are quite known. [And when] they see the Muslims conquered and are unable to resist because of their proportionally small number."[44]

His dismissal of other options than ransoming proposed by Ibn Rushd for "these times" also underscored reciprocity. If Muslims killed captives, so would the Christians. If they enslaved Christians, their own captives would be enslaved. If tit-for-tat was the political reality for Muslims and Christians, the jurist nevertheless emphasized the logistical and strategical nightmares of resorting to non-ransoming methods of dealing with captives. The sheer numbers of enslaved captives would overwhelm Muslims, he argued, and it would be impossible to feed them. Killing them, while allowable in Islamic law, would constitute "a great damage, horrible indignation to the Christians and a deviation from the custom of past nations irrespective of their religions and principles."[45]

THE JURIST'S VERDICT

At the very end of his long *fatwa*, the jurist ruled upon the case at hand: the Muslim captor who had broken his contract with the Christian *fakkak* must pay the ransom. He must free his captive, who can then opt to return to Christian territory or remain

---

[43] Ahmad al-Wansharisi, *Al-Mi'yar*, 2: 197: "If we were to stop the ransoming of those Christian captives in our hands, then this would be a reason enough for them to stop the ransoming of the Muslim captives that they have in their hands." Then he said: "this is not necessary, for they might want to ransom the Muslim captives that they have, for their desire to have the money. And this is a sheer lie, for it is quite known for all that Muslim kings and others still face their enemies and peers, even if they were friendly, with the same kind of actions and penalties and respond in kind. Even go beyond or transcend them in the meaning that is invented, especially if it can constitute a damage or injury, and there is no damage greater than this, especially with the Christian kings of Andalusia, whose cruelty and arrogance are quite known. Then they see the Muslims conquered and unable to resist because of their proportionally small number. The most indicative thing of this, and the greatest proof is what they did to a Muslim guide or anyone who might constitute a threat when was captured. They would skin his face and heinously maim him. And that is because the Muslims got into the habit of killing the Christian guides that they get in their hands. And that which was mentioned in the said modification was not intended by us to be a proof for allowing ransoming, for there is no proof in it, and it is not within our terms of reference to do so. But we mentioned what we did in justification of what our kings did, namely their choice of ransoming and dropping other options, for the interest they found therein."

[44] During the final decades of the fifteenth century, Granada's forces, and resources, were considerably weakened after years of intermittent siege and attack from the Christian north.

[45] Ahmad al-Wansharisi, *Al-Mi'yar*, 2: 197.

in Muslim lands as a convert. The jurist referred to a precedent, a case judged by an earlier authoritative jurist, al-Hajj.[46] After a Christian captive had been ransomed (but not yet freed), he was discovered to be a distinguished military leader who could ultimately do future damage to the Muslims. Nevertheless, he was liberated because breaking the redemption contract was considered even more damaging to Muslim long-term interests.

Clearly, both our jurist and al-Hajj believed it was important for Muslims to adhere to ransoming practices, to build trust, to honor commitments—to respect the "custom of past nations irrespective of their religions and principles." Even if a specific exchange might seem dubious, long-term "diffuse" reciprocity and cooperation would best serve the interest of the Muslim community in an environment in which the requirements of both the captive trade and international relations prevailed.

DIFFUSE RECIPROCITY: MEDIEVAL TO MODERN

In his 1986 article, "Reciprocity in International Relations," Robert Keohane elaborated a distinction between "'specific' forms of reciprocity and a more general concept of 'diffuse reciprocity.'"[47] While specific reciprocity can be exemplified by international trade negotiations or treaties, diffuse reciprocity "points to a wider institutionalisation of trust." Diffuse reciprocity is the atmosphere of cooperation and mutual interest in which many acts of specific reciprocity can take place.

Transactions dealing with the exchange of captives—like the ransom contract—involve specific reciprocity. That is, both parties have expectations of an equivalent exchange. The Christian agent pays the ransom, draws up a contract with the captor, and the captor theoretically hands over the captive. The exchange is not exact, but it is approximate. Muslims and Christians establish a base price in many cases, but they also assess the value of any particular captive, typically based on his social status. It is a business transaction, complete with haggling.

What is compelling about our *fatwa* is that it has a conception of diffuse reciprocity, in which the immediate expectations for the exchange are vague, although the goal is a long-term equivalence. No single negotiation or agreement can bring about diffuse reciprocity; it is the cumulative result of a series of transactions and

---

[46] Abu 'Abdallah Ibn al-Hajj (d. 737/1336–1337).

[47] Robert O. Keohane, "Reciprocity in International Relations," *International Organisation*, 40.1 (1986): 1–28, 4. Keohane's premise can be traced to the fundamental studies of Niklas Luhmann and others on trust. See in particular Niklas Luhmann, "Familiarity, Confidence, Trust: Problems and Alternatives," in *Trust: Making and Breaking Cooperative Relations*, ed. Diego Gambetta (Oxford: Basil Blackwell, 1988), 94–107.

exchanges taking place over time. This form of reciprocity is distinctive in that the mechanisms that work to insure cooperation, especially long-term cooperation, lean toward moral obligation and social forms of exchange.

What does the Malaga incident *fatwa*, viewed through the prism of a modern international trade model, suggest about captive ransoming in general? I would argue that it usually functioned owing to both diffuse and specific reciprocity. The jurist's emphasis on precedent is not only standard practice in his profession; it is also an argument for the maintenance of a delicate political balance built up over years. Legal agreements with Christians are to be met. As he reminds us, prominent Islamic scholars in al-Andalus had forcefully ruled on this issue:

> Now and in the past, their contracts still reach us, written in their own hand-writing and the handwriting of their predecessors and forefathers, scholars, sheiks and their religious scholars and those entrusted with religious edicts or *fatwas*; contracts that bear witnesses and carry the judges comments. Received also are the contracts from all over the land, so the judges accept what they dic-tate and rule accordingly and the students record what is received. No one of them had forbidden any of the sort, and no one remembers that they stopped the practice or denied it, so how could they do what is proscribed and consid-ered wrong to them and issue religious edicts contrary to it? And anyone who does such a thing, how could his edicts be accepted as right?[48]

CONCLUSION

The reasoning points to tradition and to legal authority—"scholars, sheiks, and their religious scholars"—which ordinary Muslims are morally obliged to respect. Diffuse reciprocity summons a sense of moral obligation toward the other parties involved, in the hope that they will ultimately reciprocate in kind.

The focus of many studies of Mediterranean captive ransoming and its institu-tions has been on forms of specific reciprocity and the regulations put into place to ensure (either successfully or not) against corruption or lack of cooperation. When we can access individual cases, though, and follow the dealings of one single agent (functioning as a *fakkak*, diplomat or, in this case, a *mufti*), we see a seasoned profes-sional, relying on relationships with other Christians and Muslims that are char-acterized by a history of encounters, a reliance on past behavior and a promise of future good behavior. The role of the *fakkak* is a perfect example of specific and

---

[48] Ahmad al-Wansharisi, *Al-Mi'yar*, 2: 197.

diffuse reciprocity at work—long-term trust, reputation, and networking ultimately make him a more successful agent.

Future scholarship will explore these exchanges in terms of trustworthiness or commitment or moral obligation. But what is notable for our purposes is that the jurist intended to advertise diffuse reciprocity and its importance by pointing toward historical continuity. He thus wrote: "Now and in the past, their contracts still reach us, written in their own handwriting and the handwriting of their predecessors and forefathers, scholars, sheiks, and their religious scholars and those entrusted with religious edicts or *fatwas*; contracts that bear witnesses and carry the judges' comments." The jurist is committed to one type of obligation—specific reciprocity—in his insistence that contracts between Muslims and Christians involving captives be honored. But in emphasizing historical patterns ("Now and in the past, their contracts still reach us, written in their own handwriting and the handwriting of their predecessors and forefathers"), he is also strongly urging his community's and, arguably, an entire legal system's commitment to diffuse reciprocity—whereby moral obligation is at work to ensure that captive exchange does not lead to violent reprisals or war. Interestingly, though, for this Muslim scholar at least, centuries of dealing with Christians had not produced any affectionate bonds or positive understanding of Christianity. Iberia's infidel rulers were to be regarded as equal partners in exchange. And, if they were not treated as such, paradoxically perhaps, they were not to be trusted.

Exploring Muslim-Christian exchanges in light of the notion of reciprocity, and its multiple forms, makes sense, whether we look at diplomatic gift-giving or contract fulfillment or a standard prisoner of war swap. The model of specific and diffuse reciprocity used by modern scholars—largely in a contemporary context of international trade regulations—should find resonance among medievalists. Medieval sources, especially Islamic sources, do not offer the historian the record of redemption transactions that we would like to have and that might verify how successful exchange was statistically. But the *fatwa* offers a rare glimpse of an Islamic understanding of the merits of normative relations with Christians. The *fatwa* strongly endorses the Muslim investment in the ransoming process and the maintaining of forms of commitment and trust. Islamic law provided options other than ransoming Christian captives, as well as justifications to break off cooperation with the infidel. Nevertheless, the jurist makes clear that Iberian past practices had shown that adhering to cross-cultural institutional norms of redemption exchange was in the best interest of the Muslim community. When these norms were disregarded or undermined, in Granada at least, it was Muslims who ultimately paid a penalty.

6

Cross-Cultural Business Cooperation in the Dutch Trading World, 1580–1776

A VIEW FROM AMSTERDAM'S NOTARIAL CONTRACTS

Cátia Antunes

⌒⎯⎯⎯

THE CONVENTIONAL WISDOM among historians is that the cheapest and safest way of doing business before the Industrial Revolution was within kinship groups and religious communities. These entities were efficient institutions, as the argument goes, because they punished cheaters and defectors and, by doing so, they considerably decreased the risk and therefore the costs of conducting trade. Ina McCabe, for example, holds that "family-based networks built on trust among partners are thought to have supplied the most effective governance structure as a solution to principal/agent problems and curbing agency and transaction costs."[1] According to Avner Greif, in the absence of effective legal enforcement, closed groups could exert reputational control over their members and thus decrease agency problems and transaction costs.[2] The statements by Greif and McCabe echo a long-standing scholarly tradition, according to which specific religious and ethnic groups are deemed economically successful because of their social cohesion and religious ties.

---

[1] Ina Baghdiantz McCabe, "Introduction," in *Diaspora Entrepreneurial Networks: Four Centuries of History*, ed. Ina Baghdiantz McCabe, Gelina Harlafits, and Ioanna Pepelasis Minoglau (Oxford: Berg, 2005), iv–xxxii, xx.

[2] Avner Greif, "Cultural Beliefs and the Organization of Society: A Historical and Theoretical Reflection on Collectivist and Individualist Societies," *Journal of Political Economy*, 102.5 (1994): 912–950; Avner Greif, "Impersonal Exchange and the Origins of Markets: From the Community Responsibility System to Individual Legal Responsibility in Pre-modern Europe," in *Communities and Markets in Economic Development*, ed. Masahiko Aoki and Yujiro Hayami (Oxford: Oxford University Press, 2001), 3–41.

Monographs about the Jewish, the Armenian, the Chinese, the Scottish, or the Quaker diasporas offer a handful of examples of this tradition.[3]

However suggestive, this body of literature neglects two key issues. First, historians assume but rarely demonstrate that an intrinsic inclination to cooperate reigned among members of the same family or religious group.[4] Second, historians overlook the fact that businessmen faced considerable limitations when working only with relatives and religious counterparts. Entrepreneurs ran into the problem of accessing production outlets and consumption markets in places where their affiliates were not represented. In most cases, they were also limited in the capital they could raise from friends and family. In order to solve these problems, early modern businessmen often looked beyond their kin and ethno-religious communities and ventured into business with partners from different religious, linguistic, or ethnic backgrounds. Business contracts between such parties are the basis of my definition of cross-cultural trade.

In this chapter, I will combine anecdotal and statistical evidence to emphasize the significance of cross-cultural commercial and financial cooperation between merchants who sealed their contracts in Amsterdam between the late sixteenth and late eighteenth centuries. I will bring forward two complementary arguments. I will show that different types of cross-cultural contracts stand for different levels of cross-cultural engagement between economic partners. I will also demonstrate that, in cross-cultural exchanges, financial rather than commercial cooperation became statistically more significant by the end of the eighteenth century.

The study of private commercial activities during the early modern period relies primarily on three types of sources, namely, administrative and institutional records (such as taxation lists), personal papers (including merchants' correspondence and account books), and notarial deeds that recorded commercial and financial transactions between different parties. In the context of Amsterdam commercial

---

[3] Jacob M. Price, *Capital and Credit in British Overseas Trade: The View from the Chesapeake, 1700–1776* (Cambridge, MA: Harvard University Press, 1980); Michel Aghassian and Keram Kevonian, "The Armenian Merchant Network: Overall Autonomy and Local Integration," in *Companies and Trade: Europe and Asia in Early Modern Era*, ed. Sushil Chaudhury and Michel Morineau (New York: Cambridge University Press, 1999), 74–94; Jonathan Israel, *Diaspora within a Diaspora: Jews, Crypto-Jews and the World Maritime Empires (1540–1740)* (Leiden: Brill, 2002); Steve Murdoch, *Network North: Scottish Kin, Commercial and Covert Associations in Northern Europe, 1603–1746* (Leiden: Brill, 2005); Leo Suryadinata, ed., *Chinese Diaspora since Admiral Zheng He with Special Reference to Maritime Asia* (Singapore: Chinese Heritage Centre, 2007).

[4] Francesca Trivellato questions this premise in her "The Sephardic Merchants in the Early Modern Atlantic and Beyond: Toward a Comparative Historical Approach to Business Cooperation," in *Atlantic Diasporas: Jews, Conversos and Crypto-Jews in the Age of Mercantilism, 1500–1800*, ed. Richard L. Kagan and Philip D. Morgan (Baltimore, MD: The Johns Hopkins University Press, 2009), 99–120. See also David Hancock, "The Trouble with Networks: Managing the Scots' Early Modern Madeira Trade," *Business History Review*, 79.3 (2005): 467–493.

history, historians use all three types of sources either individually or in multiple permutations.[5]

The conclusions presented in this chapter derive from my analysis of a large sample of notarial contracts preserved in the Amsterdam municipal archives. This sample includes all types of commercial and financial contracts, but excludes deeds of a personal nature such as testaments, sales and leases of urban or rural properties, and marriage contracts. Since Amsterdam's notarial collections are voluminous, I have opted to collect all contracts that were registered during the months of March and September of every year between 1580 and 1776, for a total of over 25,000 entries.[6] I have classified these deeds according to the juridical typology used by the notaries themselves, the region of the world they refer to, the type of business they registered, and the ethno-religious origin of the actors involved in the contract. Since Amsterdam was a city characterized by ethnic diversity and religious variety, I simplified the religious classification by distinguishing only between Christians (a group that includes different Protestant denominations as well as Catholics and a few Armenians) and non-Christians (Jews, whether of Sephardic or Ashkenazim background, Muslims, and others).[7] For the purpose of this chapter, I will only use

---

[5] Jan Willem Veluwenkamp, *Ondernemersgedrag op de Hollandse stapelmarkt in de tijd van de Republiek: de Amsterdamse Handelsfirma Jan Isaac de Neufville & Comp., 1730–1764*, Ph.D. thesis, Leiden University, 1981; Jan Thomas Lindblad, *Sweden's Trade with the Dutch Republic, 1738–1795: A Quantitative Analysis of the Relationship between Economic Growth and International Trade in the Eighteenth century* (Assen: Van Gorcum, 1982); Marie-Christine Engels, *Merchants, Interlopers, Seamen and Corsairs: The 'Flemish' Community in Livorno and Genoa (1615–1635)* (Hilversum: Verloren, 1997); Oscar Gelderblom, *Zuid-Nederlandse Kooplieden en de Opkomst van de Amsterdamse Stapelmarkt, 1578–1630* (Hilversum: Verloren, 2000); Jan Willem Veluwenkamp, *Archangel: Nederlandse ondernemers in Rusland, 1550–1785* (Maastricht: Bureau InterPunct, 2000); Cátia Antunes, *Globalisation in the Early Modern Period: The Economic Relationship between Amsterdam and Lisbon, 1640–1705* (Amsterdam: Aksant, 2004); Maartje van Gelder, *Trading Places: The Netherlandish Merchants in Early Modern Venice* (Leiden: Brill, 2009).

[6] I chose March and September because of the seasonality of the use of the harbor and of the annual business cycle.

[7] After the Reformation and the outbreak of the Dutch Revolt, Catholics experienced periods of relative peace and tolerance and periods of persecution and discrimination. In Amsterdam, they were allowed freedom of conscience but not freedom of worship. In this respect, they were in a lesser position than the Jews, who enjoyed freedom of both conscience and congregation. For this reason, elsewhere in my work I treat Catholics as a separate group from the other Christians. On the status of the Catholics in the Dutch Republic, see Judith Pollmann, "From Freedom of Conscience to Confessional Segregation?: Religious Choice and Toleration in the Dutch Republic," in *Persecution and Pluralism: Calvinists and Religious Minorities in Early Modern Europe, 1550–1700*, ed. Richard Booney and D. J. B. Trim (Oxford: Lang, 2006), 123–148; Benjamin Kaplan et al., eds., *Catholic Communities in Protestant States: Britain and the Netherlands, 1520–1635* (Manchester: Manchester University Press, 2009); Judith Pollmann, *Catholic Identity and the Revolt of the Netherlands, 1520–1635* (Oxford: Oxford University Press, 2011). Specifically on Amsterdam, see Joke Spaans, "Stad van Vele Geloven," in *Geschiedenis van Amsterdam, 1578–1650: Centrum van de Wereld*, ed. Willem Frijhoff and Maarten Prak (Amsterdam: SUN, 2004), 385–467, esp. 402 and 404; S. A. C. Dudok van Heel, "Amsterdamse Schuil- of Huiskerken?" *Holland*, 25 (1993): 1–10; S. A. C. Dudok van Heel, "Waar Waren de Amsterdamse Katholieken in de Zomer van 1585?" *Jaarboek Amstelodamum*, 77 (1985): 13–53.

the contracts in which Christians and Jews are mentioned. Among the latter, the majority were Sephardim of Portuguese and Spanish origin or descent.

I will begin by looking into the typology of the notarial deeds and exploring the possibility that differences in the type of contracts reflect different levels of cross-cultural engagement. For instance, a freight contract and an insurance agreement entailed a different intensity of cross-cultural linkage between the social actors. The nature and duration of commercial and financial contracts also reflect different spans of cross-cultural interconnectedness, as defined by David Held, Anthony McGrew, Jonathan Perraton, and David Goldblatt in their explanation of the process of globalization in historical perspective. For these authors, interconnectedness is a measure of the intensity, range, frequency, and impact of relations between individuals, communities, regions, and continents. This approach is commonly known as transformationalist and stands for the understanding of historical processes according to the principle that globalization existed before the twentieth century and as such took up different forms and intensities throughout history.[8]

CROSS-CULTURAL COOPERATION AND THE TYPOLOGY OF NOTARIAL CONTRACTS

Notarial contracts concerned with economic activities can be divided between commercial and financial ones. I classify commercial contracts as those in which the regulation of trading activities was central. Freight contracts, insurance policies, commercial credit, and powers of attorney enabled or facilitated the exchange of goods even over considerable distances. Financial contracts, by contrast, were those that recorded capital investments, whether private or public—personal loans, mortgages, bills of exchange, purchasing notes for shares, and state bonds.

Obviously, this distinction is partially artificial. Bills of exchange were used both to remit payments for goods purchased abroad and as speculative financial tools. Similarly, commercial credit and powers of attorney could be connected with commercial activities or used in short- to medium-term financial transactions. They could be drafted for the purchase or sale of products or for the financing of shipping activities in the short run, but they could also record medium-term personal loans for the procurement of houses, landed assets, shares in commercial companies, or state bonds. This complexity notwithstanding, the analysis of my sample shows that most powers of attorney were indeed directly or indirectly linked to commercial activities, as were contracts of commercial credit. By contrast, especially after the

---

[8] David Held, Anthony McGrew, Jonathan Perraton, and David Goldblatt, *Global Transformations: Politics, Economics and Culture* (Stanford, CA: Stanford University Press, 1999), 16–17.

late seventeenth century, bills of exchange became primarily instruments of financial transactions divorced from commodity trade. Therefore, in what follows, I consider powers of attorney and commercial credit as commercial contracts, and notarized bills of exchange as financial contracts.

CROSS-CULTURAL COMMERCIAL COOPERATION

Cross-cultural commercial cooperation appears in four types of contracts: freight contracts, insurance policies, powers of attorney, and notes of commercial credit. Freight contracts are the legal instrument through which one or more freighters hired a skipper to take his ship from a predetermined departure point to a specific destination. The goal of the voyage was the transport of specific products. Therefore, a significant portion of freight contracts is used to describe the quantity of the products to be transported, the price to be paid for every ton of transported produce, and the bonus to be paid to the skipper and crew for unusually rapid voyages or efficient unloading of the cargo. Sometimes, freight contracts also specify the responsibility of freighters and skippers regarding damages caused to ship and cargo by bad weather conditions, pirates, or privateers. Very often, these clauses are also the basic premises used for the settlement of insurance policies in case of disputes.

Freight contracts registered in Amsterdam over the period under consideration offer a double insight into cross-cultural partnerships. A consistent rule emerges: skippers were always Christians, and usually residents of the Dutch Republic. Therefore, Portuguese Sephardic merchants depended on Christian skippers. They had no other choice but to register a cross-cultural contract. In this respect, a freight contract between a Sephardic merchant and a Christian skipper was not a matter of choice, but a matter of necessity.

But some freight contracts were sealed by multiple freighters. In those cases we detect a clear trend toward a well-informed business selection. Christian and Sephardic merchants joined forces to ensure that their cooperation would result in the most effective transport and commercialization of the cargo. The Christian partners often knew the production outlets of the transported products and the skipper (or had worked with him before), while the Sephardic merchants seem to have possessed the knowledge and information needed to place the products in the appropriate consumption markets at specific times of the year.[9] This pattern is particularly

---

[9] On May 11, 1609, Volkardus Overlander, as representative of Manuel Ximenez from Antwerp (agent of João Moreno in Lisbon) freighted the ship *De Witte Swaen*, under the responsibility of skipper Cornelis Jacobsen. Jacobsen was to take *De Witte Swaen* from Amsterdam to the Algarve (Portugal) with a cargo of grain and other products. After unloading in the Algarve, he was supposed to take a return cargo of salt from Setubal (Portugal) and unload part of it in Amsterdam, Danzig, or Konigsberg (the choice was left to the skipper).

visible along the Atlantic, where Sephardic freighters had knowledge and information of the colonial production outlets. By contrast, the Christian partners knew not only the skippers, but also the European destination markets for sugar, tobacco, tropical woods, ivory, or African spices.[10] We can thus argue that the cross-cultural collaboration among freighters improved the management of a large flow of knowledge and information about products, markets, and transport routes, and simultaneously spread the risk of the journey among a religiously diverse body of business associates.

A similar pattern applies to insurance policies, which more often than not were part and parcel of the freighting activities. Insurance policies bound together two (often collective) parties.[11] A group of merchants would insure ships, crews, and cargos belonging to a second group of merchants for a certain venture or a certain period of time. In the Amsterdam sample, the contracting parties usually remained within their business community of origin. That is to say, insurers were often Christian financiers, while the insured were often Sephardic merchants.[12] Only in very few instances do we see members of one or the other group cross lines, as it were, to assume the inverse function. Therefore, although insurance policies may reflect a cross-cultural contractual agreement (insurers were normally Christian and insured were normally Jewish), the role that the two groups played in the agreement was circumscribed to their respective specialized role.[13] Moreover, in almost all

---

If the salt was unloaded in Amsterdam, the freight would be paid 11¾ *carolus guilders* for every *last* of salt taken to Amsterdam and 14¾ *carolus guilders* for every *last* of salt taken to Danzig or Konigsberg. Stadsarchief Amsterdam (henceforth SAA), Notarieel Archief (henceforth NA), 116, fols. 33–33v.

[10] On February 2, 1595, Jan Groenewegen (merchant in Delft), Lambert de Haen (merchant in Amsterdam), and Manuel Rodrigo Vega (merchant in Amsterdam) hired skipper Dick Jansz Melcknap (from Venhuizen) to take *De Blauwe Duijff* from Amsterdam to Porto (Portugal) with ballast. Once in Porto, skipper Melcknap was asked to load the ship with merchandise to be taken to the island of Madeira and from there to Pernambuco in Brazil. In Pernambuco, skipper Melcknap was supposed to await instructions by Manuel Rodrigo Vega's cousin before committing to a new trip to Setubal and Porto, and from there back to Holland. The trip from Porto should only take place after the skipper had taken advice from Vega's son-in-law in Porto concerning the prices of sugar and salt. Vega's son-in-law would also appoint a pilot to take skipper Melcknap and *De Blaeuwe Druijff* in its outbound journey to Brazil in order to circumvent the limitations imposed by the Spanish administration. The pilot would be paid for by Vega, although the skipper needed to agree to bring one of Vega's agents in Brazil to Porto and two passengers from Pernambuco to Holland. SAA, NA, 32, fol. 176.

[11] J. P. van Niekerk, *The Development of the Principles of Insurance Law in the Netherlands from 1500–1800* (Johannesburg: Kenwyn, 1998); C. F. Trenerry, *The Origin and Early History of Insurance, Including the Contract of Bottomry* (Clark, NJ: Lawbook Exchange, 2009); Sabine Go, *Marine Insurance in the Netherlands, 1600–1870: A Comparative Institutional Approach* (Amsterdam: Aksant, 2009).

[12] Cátia Antunes and Filipa Ribeiro da Silva, "Cross-Cultural Entrepreneurship in the Atlantic: Africans, Dutch and Sephardic Jews in Western Africa, 1580–1674," *Itinerario: European Journal of Overseas History*, 35.1 (2011): 49–76; Filipa Ribeiro da Silva, *Dutch and Portuguese in Western Africa: Empires, Merchants and the Atlantic System, 1580–1674* (Leiden: Brill, 2011).

[13] In December 1613, Jan Jansen Smit & Co. and Barent Sweerts & Co., merchants in Amsterdam, provided Antonio Lopes Pereira, a Sephardic Jew, with an insurance for the sugar he was to import from Brazil, via

the instances in which Christian insurers backed the Sephardim's commercial endeavors, those endeavors were directly connected to commercial activities in areas of the globe in which the Dutch did not hold a firm commercial or territorial supremacy, as was the case in the South Atlantic, the Caribbean, and certain Mediterranean routes.[14] What these routes have in common is that they connected territories often disputed by the Dutch and the Spanish (or the Spanish and the Portuguese) and where numerous members of the Sephardic diaspora operated as merchants, agents, or representatives of families, companies, states, or cross-cultural firms located in cities like Antwerp, Hamburg, Bordeaux, London, or Amsterdam.

Toward the end of the seventeenth century, we witness a growing number of insurance policies that conform to the cross-cultural typology. That is to say, a mixture of both Christian and Jewish merchants began to compose the group of insurers as well as the group of insured. The result was a transformation of the insurance activity from a hierarchical to a horizontal cross-cultural association. Rather than agreements between Christians and Jews, insurance contracts brought together religiously diverse groups of merchants on both sides of the contracting agreement. By spreading the risk evenly among and throughout both business communities, one could gather more capital and insure a higher number of ventures than if the capital of the insurers was entrenched in the financial capacity of one religious group alone. The reason for this transformation was the growing stabilization of the Dutch process of expansion in Asia and the Atlantic. Sephardic businessmen who until then had to operate within the grey areas of the territorial and maritime routes that the United Provinces and the Iberian empires disputed during most of the seventeenth century could now trade in the open across all of the Dutch overseas dominions.[15]

Lisbon. The clauses of the insurance included coverage for any accident at sea due to weather, piracy, privateering, and confiscation by the Inquisition. (In a later protest it is clear that the sugar was confiscated by the Inquisition in Lisbon and that the Christian insurers refused to pay the insurance before Pereira presented them with a copy of the confiscation sentence.) SAA, NA, 113, fols. 112v–113.

[14] On December 4, 1612, Diogo da Silva, merchant of the Portuguese Nation of Amsterdam, Claes Andriessen, Jaspar Grevenraet, and Jan Janssen Smits, merchants in Amsterdam, insured the *St. Jacob*, whose skipper was Harpert Martens (from Rotterdam). The insurers allowed for the insurance to cover several products coming from the Cape Verde Islands and Guinea, such as hides, ivory, gold, and other precious goods. The *St. Jacob* was taken by privateers to a free port in Ireland and the insurers commissioned Jan le Clercq in London to claim the goods back before they would consider paying the insurance to the freighters. SAA, NA, 129, fols. 163–164. See, more generally, Cátia Antunes, "Portuguese Jews in Amsterdam: An Insight on Entrepreneurial Behaviour in the Dutch Republic," in *Trade, Migration and Urban Networks in Port Cities, c. 1640–1940*, ed. Adrian Jarvis and Robert Lee (St. John's: International Maritime Economic History Association, 2008), 15–31; Jessica Roitman, *The Same but Different? Inter-Cultural Trade and the Sephardim, 1595–1640* (Leiden: Brill, 2011); Ribeiro da Silva, *Dutch and Portuguese in Western Africa*.

[15] On June 20, 1704, a witness (whose name is not mentioned in the contract) claimed to have found in the business papers of Philip de Flines, who had passed away recently, many maritime insurance contracts, including several ones sealed with members of the Portuguese Nation of Amsterdam, whose names are not mentioned. These

Freight contracts and insurance policies were highly specific in time and content. They bound together parties from different religious groups into temporary commercial endeavors. However, sometimes these casual relationships developed into long-standing business associations that lasted several years; in those cases, the cross-cultural relationship was charted by a multitude of powers of attorney that served numerous goals. Powers of attorney cemented the association between cross-cultural partners by establishing a relationship of agency, according to which one of the partners would represent the other in various regions of the world. Powers of attorney thus served the overall purpose of bringing cross-cultural partners economically and socially closer together.

If the first powers of attorney between long-standing partners were normally limited to the transaction of only one specific, often cheap bulk product or the sailing of a specific itinerary along the European maritime routes, over time powers of attorney could become materially substantial.[16] This evolution suggests a period of trial and buildup of experience that could be personal if the cross-cultural business partners were solely involved in the function of agency, but could also extend to the entire religious network of the partner receiving the agency. This process implies the existence of an individual degree of responsibility for the actions of the collective.[17] Moreover, it was not uncommon for members of a religious group to resort to powers of attorney to appoint someone who was not a coreligionist as their legal representative, especially for conflicts debated before a court in a faraway location.[18]

---

insurance contracts concerned the following maritime routes: Goa-Lisbon, West Indies (probably Spanish West Indies)–Lisbon, Cartagena de las Indias–Lisbon, Coast of America (North America)–Amsterdam, Africa-Amsterdam, St. Thomas–Copenhagen, Buenos Aires–Cadiz, and Livorno-Amsterdam. For all these routes the witness saw lists of insurance premiums that still had to be partially paid for. SAA, NA, 5672/1455. This example illustrates a somehow different reality from the one portrayed by Jonathan Israel concerning the role of Sephardic merchants as brokers between the Dutch Republic and the Iberian worlds. It is plausible that this function of brokerage was only made possible by deep and long-term cross-cultural engagement with Christian merchants and fellow investors. Jonathan I. Israel, *Empires and Entrepots: The Dutch, the Spanish Monarchy and the Jews, 1585–1713* (London: Hambledon, 1990); Jonathan I. Israel, *Conflicts of Empires: Spain, the Low Countries and the Struggle for World Supremacy, 1585–1713* (London: Hambledon, 1997).

[16] On October 4, 1605, Manuel Lopes and Francisco Nunes Homem, Sephardic merchants in Amsterdam, gave power of attorney to Pieter Marcus, Matheus de la Palma, and Balthasar van der Voorde, merchants in Middelburg, to claim in their name the sugar taken by privateers from Zealand when the latter took hold of a Portuguese *caravela*, which was sailing from Bahia (in Brazil) to Portugal under the command of skipper Antonio Nunes. Lopes and Homem hoped that their representatives in Middelburg would be as successful as they had been seven months before, when they had rescued ten boxes of sugar and brazil wood from those same privateers. SAA, NA, 101, fols. 110–110v. Manuel Lopes and Francisco Nunes Homem will use these agents in Middelburg for the coming 12 years for the purpose of salvaging and reclaiming lost cargoes, ships, and papers to different Zealand's privateers.

[17] Eric M. Holmes, "A Contextual Study of Commercial Good Faith: Good-Faith Disclosure in Contract Formation," *University of Pittsburgh Law Review*, 39.3 (1978): 381–452, esp. 411–415.

[18] On May 9, 1740, Dingeman Broen, legal representative of the widow at the head of the firm Marcelles Broen & Son in Amsterdam, received from Abraham Costa & Son 4497.8.8 guilders for selling coffee and sugar from Suriname. This money was to be used by Dingeman Broen to defend the interests of the Jewish

Finally, powers of attorney were useful as instruments to contract cross-cultural commercial credit. Commercial credit took three principal forms: delayed payments, return payments, and capital loans. In the case of delayed payments, two partners agreed to wait for the payment of a certain cargo until it was sold. This mechanism allowed merchants short of capital to keep trading. However, the fact that delayed payments depended upon the future price at which a cargo would be sold meant that this mechanism was quite risky. If the cargo lost value between the production outlet and the consumption market, or if it simply did not arrive at its destination because of an accident at sea, the merchants were still indebted and with little chances of getting their capital back.[19]

Return payments implied even higher risks. Cross-cultural partners would agree to buy a certain product in one place and sell it elsewhere. Assuming they would make a profit from the transaction, they would use the profit to ask the skipper or their local representative to buy a new cargo, which they would then sell upon arrival in Amsterdam. Only then would they settle their profits (or losses), and use them to honor the delayed and the return payment.[20]

Commercial capital loans simplified the mechanisms described above, as they could be used when cross-cultural partners partook in broad commercial networks that demanded the movement of capital over long distances. Commercial capital loans can be better explained by the lending of small or large sums of capital in Amsterdam for the acquisition of commercial cargo abroad. These loans were usually short-term (no longer than six months) and were subject to an interest rate and a penalty rate. The latter only applied if the borrowing party did not follow through with the payments.[21]

---

community of Suriname in their dispute against Joseph and Isaac Pardo (also members of the community) taking place in Amsterdam. SAA, NA, 10217, fol. 229. More generally, see also Phanor James Eder, "Powers of Attorney in International Practice," *University of Pennsylvania Law Review*, 98 (1949–1950): 840–864.

[19] On October 10, 1618, João Peres da Cunha, a Sephardic merchant in Amsterdam, gave power of attorney to Henk Snel and Jacob Belt, Dutch merchants in Porto (Portugal), to claim from the Portuguese Inquisition the sugar boxes confiscated after the arrest of Alvaro Gomes Bravo. Snel and Belt were instructed to retrieve eight boxes, four of which had been loaded on the ship of skipper Claes Willemse Gort and others from the ship of skipper Jan Martsen. SAA, NA, 625, fol. 83.

[20] On August 8, 1652, Simão Rodrigues de Souza and Luis Rodrigues de Souza, Sephardic merchants in Amsterdam, freighted the vessel *De Lieffde* under the command of Willem Jacobsz Spangiaert (a citizen of Monnikendam). According to the original freight contract, Spangiaert was to take his ship to the Canary Islands and after that to Recife (Brazil). The skipper also received a power of attorney with a description of his delegated powers. He was to load wine at the Canary Islands (for a minimum of 150 barrels) and take it to Recife. The profit made by selling the barrels of wine should correspond to about 3,000 guilders. All income above this sum belonged to the skipper, who would receive his payment in Recife either in cash or merchandise. If the skipper was to be paid in merchandise, then he was owed a 20 percent commission on the goods sold during the inbound journey to the Canary Islands and another 5 percent on the cargo he would bring to Amsterdam. SAA, NA, 1536, fols. 18.

[21] Harold R. Weinberg, "Commercial Paper in Economic Theory and Legal History," *Kentucky Law Journal*, 70 (1981–1982): 567–592.

Commercial capital loans often circulated in the form of bills of exchange that could be discounted in Amsterdam or sent to the parties' representatives in different parts of the globe. The exchange and transaction of bills of exchange within cross-cultural networks demanded a certain degree of cohesion within the network, on the one hand, and the liquidity necessary to pay the bills upon request of the lending party, on the other.[22]

The complexity of commercial capital loans made them a viable resource only for cross-cultural networks built on long-standing relationships between groups with strong family and religious ties. Strong family and religious ties functioned as insurance for the partner outside the group. A group's collective business reputation would force its members to honor or renegotiate any bills of exchange between the "outsider" and the "insider" in an attempt to maintain personal and collective business repute. According to Abraham Ledesma and Joseph Abraham de Parra, leaders of the Portuguese Jewish Nation in Suriname in 1750, the community was there to "respect and honor contracts and arrangements between honorable men of business [. . .] and make sure that our brother[s] and fellow merchants will keep their names, families, and reputation intact."[23] However, the Amsterdam notarial archives also document innumerable instances in which commercial capital loans were not honored. In those instances, protracted legal conflicts usually followed.

CROSS-CULTURAL FINANCIAL COOPERATION

Bills of exchange enabled commercial capital loans to be used extensively throughout the globe between business partners of different religious and cultural backgrounds.[24]

---

[22] For the exchanges and commercialization of bills of exchange in the Atlantic, see Ana Crespo Solana, *Mercaderes Atlánticos: Redes del Comercio Flamenco y Holandés entre Europa y el Caribe* (Córdoba: CajaSur, 2009), 58–61 and 84–89.

[23] The notarial archives in Amsterdam offer multiple examples of collective groups who came to the rescue of one of their members in order to safeguard the reputation of the entire group within a cross-cultural network. On October 30, 1749, Isaac Uziel de Avelar, living in Suriname, borrowed 180 guilders to rent slaves for seasonal work. According to the bill of exchange issued at the time, Avelar had six weeks to pay his debt or allow for the discount of the bill in Amsterdam, at the office of his lifelong partner and investor in Suriname, Jacob Fruyt. The original bill of exchange was endorsed to A. Mauricius and Adriaan de Bree in Paramaribo on January 12, 1750, and three months later, Dingeman, Broen & Co. tried to discount it in Flushing. Since the partners of the company were not able to obtain the liquidation of the bill, Jacob Fruyt traveled from Amsterdam to Flushing to inquire about the case. He soon concluded that Isaac Uziel de Avelar in Suriname had to be informed that the merchant community in Flushing and Amsterdam were about to declare him insolvent, since he had no funds to cover his bills of exchange. The answer to Jacob Fruyt's pleas and warnings arrived from Abraham Ledesma and Joseph de Abraham de Parra, leaders of the Portuguese Jewish Nation in Suriname, who guaranteed the payment of all Avelar's bills of exchange and added the passage cited in the text. SAA, NA, 8892, akte 516, June 15, 1750.

[24] J. A. F. Wallert, *Ontwikkelingslijnen in Praktijk en Theorie van de Wisselbrief, 1300–2000* (Amsterdam: Nederlands Instituut voor het Bank- en Effectenbedrijf, 1996).

Their primary function was to enable or facilitate the transfer of capital between business partners separated by short and long distances. By the seventeenth century, the capital transferred via these bills, in turn, was used not only for commodity trade, but also to purchase shares in chartered companies or bonds in public debt.[25]

The use of bills of exchange as means of capital transfer and of credit between cross-cultural parties within the orbit of the Amsterdam market does not seem to have been different from the use of the same instruments by parties belonging to the same group. The use of bills of exchange was widespread among Christian and Jewish, Dutch and foreign businessmen residing in Amsterdam, a city known for its liquidity and the policing of businessmen's reputation. The extensive use of bills of exchange was facilitated by the existence and orderly operations of the Wisselbank, created in 1609 as a deposit bank where merchants could liquidate their bills. For bills of exchange amounting to 600 guilders or more, the Wisselbank was the only institution that could legally discount those commercial papers. Most businessmen accepted and even welcomed this financial and regulatory body because it sustained the money market by standardizing the process of bills' liquidation, especially in the cases of large bills.[26] Therefore, the abundance of bills of exchange in the notarial archives does not arise from the need to notarize them as legal instruments. They appear in the notarial collection when parties protested the clauses of the bill, either by default of one of the parties or by common agreement in the renegotiation of the bill. In both cases, bills and protests had to be notarized.

When we analyze the geographical reach of cross-cultural commercial loans, specific zones of influence of different religious groups emerge. Merchants belonging to the Portuguese Jewish community of Amsterdam provided capital to Dutch (or other Christian) settlers in the Dutch colonies in the Atlantic, and particularly in Suriname. However, these loans were only provided when the borrower came well recommended by a member of the Jewish community in Suriname or by a long-standing Christian business partner in Amsterdam. Personal loans were extended only to persons of proven reputation, although the degree of anonymity in

---

[25] Willem D. H. Asser, "Bills of Exchange and Agency in the Eighteenth Century Law of Holland and Zealand: Decisions of the Supreme Court of Holland and Zealand," in *The Courts and the Development of Commercial Law*, ed. Vito Piergiovanni (Berlin: Duncker & Humblot, 1987), 103–130.

[26] J. G. van Dillen, *De Amsterdamsche Wisselbank in de Zeventiende Eeuw* (n.p., 1928); Natascha van Trotsenburg, *Van Amsterdamse Wilsselbank tot Europese Optiebeurs, 1609–1820* (Amsterdam: Optiebeurs, 1987); Marius van Nieuwkerk and Cherelt Kroeze, eds., *De Wisselbank: Van Stadbank tot Bank van de Wereld* (Amsterdam: De Nederlandsche Bank, 2009); Odette Vlessing, "Twee Bijzondere Klanten van de Amsterdamse Wisselbank: Baruch Spinoza en Francisco Lopes Suasso," *Amstelodamum: Orgaan van het Genootschap Amstelodamum*, 96.4 (2009): 155–168.

the credit market increased after the 1740s and the development of the *negotiaties* as a financial instrument, as will be explained below.[27]

Members of the Portuguese Nation in Amsterdam also used bills of exchange to purchase shares in the Dutch chartered companies in their own name or together with non-coreligionsits. Herbert Bloom maintains that the participation of Sephardic capital in the years after the creation of the Dutch East India Company (henceforth VOC) and the Dutch West India Company (henceforth WIC), chartered in 1602 and 1621, respectively, was very low. This pattern changed between 1650 and 1680 with a dramatic increase in the number of Sephardic investors, although the amount of capital invested by Jews remained low relative to the total. A full-scale participation of the Sephardim in the Dutch stock market only occurred between 1680 and 1700. During the last two decades of the seventeenth century, both the number of Sephardim who invested directly or through cross-cultural agreements in the VOC and the WIC and the amount of Sephardic capital committed to the stock market increased.[28]

Bloom's findings for the early seventeenth century can be explained in light of a trend identified by Antonio Dias. Dias contends that only older, well-established Sephardic businessmen of the Portuguese Nation of Amsterdam, who had dealt successfully for several years with Christian partners and agents, were able to recur to bills of exchange in order to purchase shares in the VOC and the WIC.[29] By contrast, younger and less experienced Sephardim, who were also less well-versed in cross-cultural transactions, were bound to deal in the semi-legal and morally condemned investments in futures pertaining to the companies they so much wished to participate in, but whose access was made difficult by members of the community and by the lack of cross-cultural contacts outside the Nation.[30]

Bills of exchange served yet another purpose. Christian (mostly Dutch) businessmen invested in the emergent market of the English East India Company (henceforth EIC), especially after the Glorious Revolution.[31] To move large sums from

---

[27] On January 28, 1764, Gerrit Blaauw declared to have borrowed 10,000 guilders from Joseph de la Penha, a Sephardic merchant in Amsterdam, in order to start a new life in Suriname. The loan had a maturity date of 12 months and a 4 percent annual interest rate. Before leaving Amsterdam, Blaauw provided 1,000 pound sterling in English state bonds as collateral. SAA, NA, 11543, fol. 100.

[28] Herbert I. Bloom, *The Economic Activities of the Jews of Amsterdam in the Seventeenth and Eighteenth Centuries* (Port Washington, NY: Kennikat, 1969 [1937]), 118; Jonathan I. Israel, "The Economic Contribution of Dutch Sephardi Jewry to Holland's Golden Age, 1595–1713," *Tijdschrift voor Geschiedenis*, 96 (1983): 505–535.

[29] A. M. V. Dias, "De Deelname der Marranen in het Oprichtingskapitaal der Oost-Indische Compagnie," *Jaarboek van het Genootschap Amstelodamum*, 33 (1936): 43–58; A. M. V. Dias, "Over den Vermogenstoestand der Amsterdamsche Joden in de 17e en de 18e eeuw," *Tijdschrift voor Geschiedenis*, 51 (1936): 165–176.

[30] Lodewijk Petram, *The World's First Stock Exchange: How the Amsterdam Market for Dutch East India Company Shares Became a Modern Securities Market, 1602–1700*, Ph.D. thesis, University of Amsterdam, 2011, 128.

[31] See Marjolein 't Hart's "The Merits of a Financial Revolution: Public Finance, 1550–1700," Piet Dehing and Marjolein 't Hart's "Linking the Fortunes: Currency and Banking, 1550–1800," and Wantje Fitschy and René

Amsterdam (and other major Dutch towns) to London was risky. A solution was found in the close cross-cultural collaboration that developed through most of the eighteenth century between Dutch Gentiles and Portuguese Sephardic merchants from Amsterdam, who took upon themselves to transfer funds to Christian partners in London via the growing number of influential Portuguese Sephardic financiers who operated there after the crowning of William III.[32] The use of cross-cultural networks to relocate capital investments from Amsterdam to London contributed significantly to the integration of both financial markets. Evidence of this network relocation does not invalidate Larry Neal's argument that printed gazettes played an important role in the integration of the Amsterdam and London financial markets. However, notarial evidence shows that Neal grossly understated the role of personal, especially cross-cultural, capital transferences from one market to the other.[33]

The cross-cultural networks and community circuits that were used to transfer funds to be invested in the EIC also allowed Dutch merchants to purchase English state bonds. With the rise of warfare costs during most of the eighteenth century, England was forced to borrow large sums of domestic and foreign capital to finance its military enterprises in Europe and overseas. This rising English public debt coincided with a time when options for profitable investment in Amsterdam were declining consistently. Again, Christian and Jewish businessmen in Amsterdam pooled their capital together, issued bills of exchange to be withdrawn by Portuguese Sephardic merchants in London, and used the sums to purchase bonds issued by the Bank of England or to trade in the London Stock Exchange.[34]

To a smaller extent, the Amsterdam business elite also turned to the French financial markets. Although the French public debt was less opened to foreigners than the

---

van der Voort's "From Fragmentation to Unification: Public Finance, 1700–1914," all in *A Financial History of the Netherlands*, ed. Marjolein 't Hart, Joost Jonker, and Jan Luiten van Zanden (Cambridge: Cambridge University Press, 1997), 1–36, 37–63, 64–93, respectively.

[32] Albert Montefiore Hyamson, *The Sephardim of England: A History of the Spanish and Portuguese Jewish Community, 1492–1951* (London: Methuen, 1951); Daniel M. Swetschinski and Loeki Schönduve, *De Familie Lopes Suasso: Financiers van Willem III* (Zwolle: Waanders, 1988); Yosef Kaplan, "The Jewish Profile of the Spanish-Portuguese Community of London during the Seventeenth Century," *Judaism: A Quarterly Journal of Jewish Life and Thought*, 41 (1992): 229–241.

[33] Larry Neal, *The Rise of Financial Capitalism: International Capital Markets in the Age of Reason* (Cambridge: Cambridge University Press, 1990), 20–43 and 141–165. On March 20, 1724, Jacob Machado da Veiga, a Sephardic merchant in Amsterdam, accepted 10,000 guilders from Jan Beerend Bicker, secretary of the city of Amsterdam, to invest in EIC shares. Veiga sent the funds to Joseph Rodrigues, his representative in London, and received a commission of 3.5 percent for 12 months, although he expected the transfer to be cleared within six weeks. SAA, NA, 7175, fol. 22.

[34] On May 30, 1741, Charles de Dieu, magistrate in the town of Purmerend, gave power of attorney to Moses and Jacob Pereira, Sephardic merchants in London, to buy 2,000 pound sterling worth of English state bonds on his behalf. SAA, NA, 8654, fol. 598.

English one, many cross-cultural contracts signed in Amsterdam aimed to purchase French bonds. Here too, Portuguese Jews acted as intermediaries by transferring bills of exchange from Amsterdam to their family members and business representatives in Rouen and Bordeaux, who bought the bonds and paid their interests back to Amsterdam. However, the status of the Portuguese Jewish communities in France was far more precarious than in England. To be safe, some Amsterdam businessmen chose to channel their business through the Portuguese or Dutch ambassadors or their French business representatives in Paris, even if the latter generally charged a higher commission than the Portuguese merchants living and operating outside Paris.[35]

In sum, bills of exchange sustained the transfer of personal loans as well as the purchase of shares and bonds among cross-cultural associates. These three financial operations forced businessmen into long-term commitments that were only possible among businessmen who had cemented their relationship over many years of collaboration in regions near and far. Yet, no other financial instrument demanded a greater commitment from parties of different religious background than mortgages.

During the eighteenth century, the Dutch commercial sector slowed down after the loss of several European, Atlantic, and Asian routes to the British. Although this commercial decline brought the Golden Age of Amsterdam and the Dutch Republic to an end, it gave way to new forms of financial investments.[36] One of the new financial investment possibilities that developed in this context of economic decline was the issuing of mortgages.

Mortgages were often used for the purchase of plantations in the Caribbean islands (both Dutch and non-Dutch) and in Suriname. Settlers often borrowed from Amsterdam financiers the capital to acquire large plots of land. The land itself was used as collateral to finance these mortgages. At the beginning of the eighteenth century, most mortgages were issued by Christian and Jewish investors alike and were handed to settlers regardless of their religious background or even country of origin.

Soon enough, however, most settlers-turned-planters realized that to purchase land was only the first step, while larger sums were needed to start up and manage

---

[35] On April 20, 1763, David Pereira, Jr., a Sephardic merchant living in the Keizersgracht in Amsterdam, gave power of attorney to Jean Cottin and Louis Cottin, bankers in Paris, in his own name and on behalf of unspecified Dutch partners, so that the Cottins could demand the already delayed payment of their investments in the French East India Company and the French public debt. Pereira proposed that if the Crown was unable to satisfy the payments, the firm would accept in their place a tax farming contract, which would, in turn, rent out to the Cottins. SAA, NA, 11426, fol. 92.

[36] Jan de Vries and Ad van der Woude, *The First Modern Economy: Success, Failure, and Perseverance of the Dutch Economy, 1500–1815* (Cambridge: Cambridge University Press, 1997), 207–208.

a plantation as a whole.[37] In response to this need, during the eighteenth century a system of bundled borrowing developed within the Amsterdam market, popularly known as *negotiaties*. In regular mortgages, a plot of land was used as collateral for the mortgage. In the case of the bundled *negotiaties*, the same collateral that was used for the mortgage was also used to vouch for personal loans (disguised within the mortgage) that financed the purchasing of seeds, slaves, the provisioning of the plantation, and the hiring of skippers and ships to export the plantation's goods. This bundling of different loans under the banner of a mortgage was then sold in shares in the Amsterdam market.[38]

The *negotiaties* presented two serious problems. First, the collateral that was meant to cover the mortgage for the plot of land also hid personal loans. This bundling would not have posed a problem if the value of the collateral (the plot of land turned into plantation) increased proportionally to cover the personal loans. That was, in fact, not the case, although the system survived for more than 50 years because investors assumed that the value ascribed to the plantations was real and not grossly overstated by borrowers and lenders (as appears to have been the case). Close to the stock exchange crash of the 1770s, the value of some plantations was indexed at more than 200 percent of their real value (taking into account the plot of land, slaves, houses, and prospects for the output of next year's crop). The second problem of the *negotiaties* was their accessibility. They were sold and resold for large and small amounts of money and therefore made available to ordinary people, at least in the major Dutch towns. The ever growing belief that the value of the plantation complex in Suriname was accurately assessed by the market encouraged many to invest considerable portions of their savings in this venture.

The *negotiaties* provided borrowers in the Atlantic colonies with enough capital to maintain, extend, and optimize the plantation system, and lenders in Amsterdam with new investment opportunities that were opened to all social strata. Even though the *negotiaties* worked well for most of the eighteenth century, the collateral's over-valuation, together with a series of bad crops due to weather conditions, brought the *negotiatie* scheme to a dangerous zone and contributed to the crash of the Amsterdam stock exchange in the early 1770s and the bankruptcy of some

---

[37] Philip Curtin, *The Rise and Fall of the Plantation Complex: Essays in Atlantic History* (Cambridge: Cambridge University Press, 1990); David Eltis, *The Rise of African Slavery in the Americas* (Cambridge: Cambridge University Press, 2000).

[38] J. P. van de Voort, *De Westindische Plantages van 1720–1795: Financiën en Handel* (Eindhoven: Drukkerij de Witte, 1973); Gert Oostindie, *Roosenburg en Mon Bijou: Twee Surinaamse Plantages, 1720–1870*, Ph.D. thesis, University of Utrecht, 1989, esp. 289–297 and 342–344; Alex van Stipriaan, *Surinaams Contrast: Roofbouw en Overleden in een Caraibische Plantagekolonie, 1750–1863* (Leiden: KITLV Drukrije, 1993), 220; de Vries and van der Woude, *The First Modern Economy*, 474.

planters.[39] For cross-cultural businesses operating in the Amsterdam market, *negotiaties* served to compensate for the increasingly less profitable commercial enterprises. They also contributed to tie metropolitan and colonial interests and to strengthen the cooperation of merchants from different religious groups in Amsterdam and the colonies.[40]

COMMERCIAL AND FINANCIAL CROSS-CULTURAL
COOPERATION: THE LONG-TERM VIEW

While the notarial archives reveal that cross-cultural cooperation occurred frequently across the Dutch trading world during the early modern period, a statistical analysis of the records shows that the nature and character of such cooperation changed over time. Figure 6.1 indicates the proportion of cross-cultural contracts for the periods before and after the Glorious Revolution in England. The year 1688 marked the moment when the fortunes of the Dutch Republic and England would be forever linked by the political and military intervention by the Dutch Stadholder, the future king of England, William III following two Anglo-Dutch wars for the control of the European and Asian commercial routes. These wars culminated with the Dutch losing significant commercial ground to the English in what historians have called the end of the Republic's Golden Age. It makes sense, therefore, to divide the data around this turning point.

The sample of circa 25,000 notarial deeds collected from 1580 to 1766 reveals the statistical significance of cross-cultural business cooperation within the Amsterdam market. If before 1688 roughly one-quarter of the contracts were between Jews and Christians, after that date the proportion increased to almost 60 percent (see Figure 6.1). This increase can be ascribed to two simultaneous processes. On the one hand, the Sephardic community in Amsterdam grew larger and more autonomous and at the same time its members integrated more and more into the local society, as demonstrated by the studies of Jonathan Israel, Yosef Kaplan, Odette Vlessing, and others.[41] On the other hand, many members of the Amsterdam business elite

---

[39] P. C. Emmer, "The Dutch in the Atlantic Economy, 1580–1880: An Introduction," in *The Dutch in the Atlantic Economy, 1580–1880: Trade, Slavery and Emancipation*, ed. P. C. Emmer (Aldershot: Ashgate, 1998), 1–10, 5–6.

[40] On March 15, 1760, Maria Catharina van Tuijll, widow of the Baron Van Lockhorst, gave the management of the mortgage taken by David Moses Cardoso Baeça on February 24, 1752, on his plantation, called *Mahanaim*, in Suriname, to Jan and Theodore van Marselis, directors of the *negotiatie* fund for the planters of Suriname. Baroness Isabella Agneta van Lockhorst, daughter of Maria Catharina and the Baron Van Lockhorst, approved of this transference. SAA, NA, 10512, fol. 526. Little is known about the social and economic consequences of the *negotiaties* and the crash of the stock exchange in 1773. Further research is needed to illuminate their impact on Dutch credit markets and on cross-cultural economic relations more specifically.

[41] See, in particular, the following essays by Jonathan I. Israel: "The Economic Contribution of Dutch Sephardi Jewry"; "The Changing Role of the Dutch Sephardim in International Trade, 1595–1715," in *Dutch Jewish*

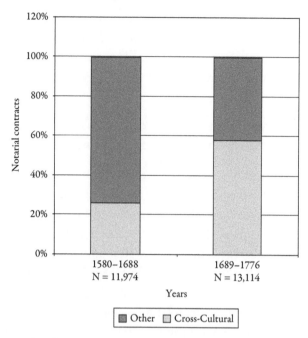

FIGURE 6.1 Cross-cultural cooperation in Amsterdam, 1580–1776.
Source: SAA, NA, based on a sample of 25,088 contracts.

(Christian and Jewish alike) wished to diversify their investments into geographical areas where the Sephardic diaspora thrived and where they could rely on its knowledge and information networks, as was the case in the financial markets of London and Hamburg, throughout the Iberian Peninsula, and more broadly around the Mediterranean and the Atlantic.

The increase in the proportion of cross-cultural cooperation was also accompanied by an evolution over time in the types of contracts between Christians and Jews, as Figure 6.2 illustrates.

After 1688, cross-cultural cooperation occurred primarily in contracts that I have classified as financial rather than commercial. This shift from broadly commercial cross-cultural associations to purely financial cross-cultural contracts reflects

History: Proceedings of the Symposium on the History of the Jews in the Netherlands (November 28–December 3, 1982, Tel-Aviv–Jerusalem), ed. Jozeph Michman (Jerusalem: Tel-Aviv University, Hebrew University of Jerusalem, The Institute for Research on Dutch Jewry, 1984), 31–53; and "The Final Suppression of Crypto-Judaism in Spain and the End of the Sephardi World Maritime Networks (1714–40)," in his *Diaspora within a Diaspora*, 567–584. See also Yosef Kaplan, "Gente Politica: The Portuguese Jews of Amsterdam *vis-à-vis* Dutch Society," in *Dutch Jews as Perceived by Themselves and by Others: Proceedings of the Eighth International Symposium on the History of the Jews in the Netherlands*, ed. Chaya Brasz and Yosef Kaplan (Leiden: Brill, 2001), 21–40; Odette Vlessing, "The Jewish Community in Transition: From Acceptance to Emancipation," *Studia Rosenthaliana*, 30.1 (1996): 195–211.

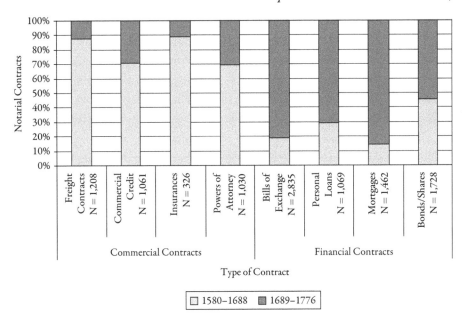

FIGURE 6.2 Cross-cultural cooperation in Amsterdam: Contractual typology, 1580–1776.
Source: SAA, NA, based on the 10,719 contracts in the sample of 25,088 that are classified as cross-cultural.

a reallocation of Dutch economic interests from trade to finance. After losing its primacy in many commercial routes in the Baltic, Western Europe, and the Mediterranean during the second half of the seventeenth century, the Amsterdam business community was left with large sums of accumulated capital that originated from their commercial enterprises during the period before 1688, but with fewer trading activities to go around; this capital was then channeled to financial investments in the Dutch Republic and abroad, especially to the London and Paris financial markets.

The dramatic increase in financial cross-cultural cooperation in Amsterdam presents a historical paradox. Financial commitments between partners of different religious backgrounds bonded parties for longer periods of time than freight or insurance contracts. This was particularly true in the case of personal loans and mortgages. Christian and Sephardic businessmen were forced into relationships that lasted as long as the financial contract took to mature or be liquidated. At the same time, financial instruments like bills of exchange and financial schemes like the *negotiaties* allowed for an increase in the number of potential participants in the financial market. These participants, Christian and Jewish alike, could choose the level of their engagement (how much they invested) and their level of commitment (the depth and frequency of their contacts with the other investors). The result was an ever growing anonymity within the financial markets. The persistence of personal credit relations between Jews and Christians and a substantial growth in the number of anonymous credit relations needs to be understood in light of a structural transition from early modern forms of financial exchanges to modern instruments of finance, some of them used nowadays, in the late eighteenth century.

Cross-cultural cooperation within the Amsterdam market grew from one-quarter of the total number of notarized acts between 1580 and 1688 to 60 percent between the Glorious Revolution and the War of Independence of the United States. Economic relations between Christians and Sephardim shifted from commercial to financial transactions in parallel with an overall change in the economic structure of the Dutch Republic. After losing ground to English shipping and trade during the second half of the seventeenth century, businessmen operating from major Dutch towns were forced to invest their liquid assets into financial ventures.

The evidence presented in this chapter demonstrates the willingness and ability of Christians and Sephardim to contract with partners and acquaintances who belonged neither to their kinship networks nor to their ethno-religious community. Contrary to the business environments of the medieval Mediterranean and the Armenian diaspora analyzed by Greif and McCabe, that of early modern Amsterdam was characterized by a high degree of cross-cultural economic cooperation. This cross-cultural economic cooperation was rooted in a multiplicity of contractual relations between individuals and communities that prospered together economically, but remained socially divided.

In some respects, cross-cultural dealings in early modern Amsterdam were not only a matter of choice, they were inevitable. This inevitability is further evidenced by the fact that neither structural economic change (from commercial to financial activities) nor alterations to the social composition of the money market (growth in the anonymity of financial markets and greater participation from diverse social strata in financial mechanisms) halted cross-cultural business contracting. On the contrary, the growth of the financial sector, the broadening of financial activities to new segments of the urban population, and the lack of alternatives to invest accumulated capital brought Jews and Christians into more intensive, closer contacts. If nothing else, Amsterdam economic shifts during the early modern period stimulated cross-cultural business exchanges.

7

Trade across Religious and Confessional Boundaries in Early Modern France

Silvia Marzagalli

ON THE EVE of the 1789 Revolution, France played a key role in international maritime trade. The country was a traditional major wine and salt producer and an importer of wood, naval stores, and cereals. Its large population—one European in five was a Frenchman—and its relatively high level of urbanization (18 percent) boosted both production and consumption. A lively shipping activity between the country and neighboring foreign ports, and among French ports themselves, sustained maritime commerce. Merchants in France, however, had also secured a prominent position in trade with extra-European regions throughout the past two centuries. By 1789, colonial imports from the West Indies represented a third of French total imports. Half of the sugar and most of the coffee shipped to Europe was produced in the French Caribbean and was redistributed to European and Mediterranean consumers through French ports. French ships forcibly transported more than a million slaves across the Atlantic throughout the eighteenth century. Other branches of long-distance trade had expanded, too. French shipowners carried to Marseille half of the Levant exports to Western Europe and successfully penetrated the Spanish-American trade in Cadiz, where they played a prominent role. Franco-Baltic commercial exchanges were relevant, although dominated by non-French shipping. The French East Indian Company carried a considerable trade with Asia, even if not on the same level as its British and Dutch counterparts. French interests in Newfoundland were still important, if no longer dominant as they had been during the first century and a half of the history of European cod fisheries. The loss of territorial holdings in North America in 1763 did not modify contemporary representations of France's major role in overseas markets. In short, throughout the eighteenth century, France traded worldwide.[1]

This chapter suggests that the emergence of early modern France as one of the greatest commercial powers was predicated upon the daily interactions between merchants of different religious denominations within the boundaries of the kingdom. International and colonial trade relied on a dense web of local, regional, and national exchanges, which gathered and redistributed goods bound to, and arriving from, distant places. These exchanges occurred between merchants living in France, who followed different religious affiliations. Unfortunately, the current state of the secondary literature makes it impossible to determine the share of cross-religious and trans-confessional trade that took place in France because this topic has been largely neglected by the historiography.[2] Despite numerous studies of the different branches of French trade, of French port cities, and of their merchants, historians of French commerce have not paid systematic attention to its confessional aspects and implications.[3] In this, they are not alone. The scholarship on trade involving people of different religious groups has largely privileged exchanges in luxury goods occurring in faraway lands over the daily commercial intercourse and business relations of people of different religious denominations that occurred within the same city. Moreover, when historians have focused on religious minorities that were disproportionally represented in early modern French commerce and banking, such as the Jews, New Christians, and Huguenots, they have generally taken for granted that religious groups and merchant communities were coterminous. This assumption has further hampered our understanding of when and how religious affiliation affected the ways in which merchants contracted with members of other groups in the cities of the kingdom and its colonies, or in other ports.

---

[1] The literature on French foreign and colonial trade is extensive. For an overview, see Wim Klooster, "The Northern European Atlantic World" and Silvia Marzagalli, "The French Atlantic World in the Sventeenth and Eighteenth Centuries," both in *The Oxford Handbook of the Atlantic World, c. 1450–c.1820*, ed. Nicholas Canny and Philip Morgan (Oxford: Oxford University Press, 2011), 165–180 and 235–251, respectively; Alain Cabantous, André Lespagnol, and Françoise Péron, eds., *Les Français, la terre et la mer XIIIᵉ–XXᵉ siècle* (Paris: Fayard, 2005).

[2] The expression "trans-confessional" is used in this chapter with regard to interactions between Catholics and Protestants or between Protestants belonging to different churches. By contrast, "cross-religious" is used to designate economic exchanges between Christians and Jews, including New Christians whenever contemporaries recognized them as Jews.

[3] For a very extensive, although not exhaustive, bibliography on different aspects of French maritime history, see *Revue d'histoire maritime*, 10–11 (2010): 423–457, and Cabantous, *Les Français*, 847–872. On coastal shipping and trade, see the special issue on "Histoire du cabotage européen aux XVIᵉ–XIXᵉ siècles," *Revue d'histoire maritime*, 8 (2008).

Certainly, merchant families generally married with people of the same religion and tended to engage in general business partnership with members of their kin.[4] Most of the firms, therefore, were mono-confessional. However, both trans-confessional and cross-religious trade can be documented simply by looking at existing literature and sources with fresh eyes. In what follows I will pursue this goal, while asking what logics informed merchants' choices of the range of agents with whom they did business.

Early modern France represents a particularly interesting case study because merchants of different confessions lived in the country since the middle of the sixteenth century, and later migrated to its colonies, and because of the tumultuous history of religious wars and changing toleration practices in the two and half centuries following the Reformation. Interactions with merchants of another religious group were not restricted to the exchange of luxury goods of exotic provenance, which were handled by a few select agents living in distant places. In several French cities and ports, they could be daily experiences for most of those active on the marketplace, from mid-ranking traders to the wealthiest shipowners and merchant-bankers. I suggest that such interactions might have been much more frequent than is usually assumed by the historiography, which generally insists on the religious uniformity of commercial networks and overlooks cross-religious and trans-confessional trade relations. The coexistence of merchants with different religious and confessional affiliations constituted a structural feature of French trade, a factor that had considerable institutional, cultural, and political implications. This reality also prompts us to question the validity of the explanations that are generally put forward to elucidate why trade networks were generally composed by coreligionists, and to suggest an alternative interpretative frame.

The first part of this chapter examines how the existing historiography has approached the issue of religious networks and trans-confessional trade. The second part of the chapter questions the common assumption according to which trade in early modern France involved a series of religiously homogeneous networks and suggests that we take into consideration the nature of different types of economic transactions and the degree of risk that each implied, which possibly affected the intensity of recourse to coreligionists. The last part of the chapter concentrates on Bordeaux and examines the multi-religious and multi-confessional character of its merchant community, which grew out of both entrepreneurial decisions and specific policies initiated by the Crown. My analysis of eighteenth-century Bordeaux

---

[4] Paul Butel speaks of "a very selective socio-religious endogamic strategy" in his *Les dynasties bordelaises de Colbert à Chaban* (Paris: Perrin, 1991), 128.

confirms the necessity of reassessing the question of the frequency and nature of cross-religious and trans-confessional trade.

THE STATE OF THE ART: HISTORIOGRAPHICAL AND METHODOLOGICAL BIASES

In analyzing the merchant communities of France's principal ports, historians have unanimously maintained that social and confessional endogamy was the norm.[5] As most commercial partnerships in early modern Europe were formed by blood relatives and in-laws, they were also, in general, made up by coreligionists.[6] But there is more. According to the existing literature, family partnerships also conducted most of their business with coreligionists. J. F. Bosher, for instance, a leading scholar in the field, writes: "Patterns of kinship are keys to business connections [...] in an age when merchants lived and traded in groups drawn together by ties of kinship and religion. Only in a network of relatives and fellow Roman Catholics, fellow Protestants or fellow Jews did a merchant normally feel that his contracts and funds, ships and merchandise, were in good hands."[7]

The reasons historians advance for the mono-confessional nature of early modern merchant networks rest on the tendency of past approaches to social history to group people according to a single characteristic, which is often presented as self-explanatory, as well as on more recent social scientific approaches. The latter stress the risks involved in extending credit in the absence of effective legal institutions that oversee the enforcement of business contracts behind national boundaries—risks that merchants tried to curb by building fiduciary relations with their partners and agents.[8] Today most scholars insist on the fact that trust was generally

---

[5] In Bordeaux, fewer than 10 percent of the Jews married outside their community from 1793 to 1820: Jean Cavignac, *Les Israélites bordelais de 1780 à 1850: Autour de l'émancipation* (Paris: Publisud, 1991), 88–97. Guy Saupin stresses the same phenomenon concerning the Dutch and the Flemish in Nantes, who married within Protestant and Catholic networks, respectively: Guy Saupin, "Les Hollandais à Nantes dans la première partie du règne de Louis XIV," in *D'un rivage à l'autre: Villes et protestantisme dans l'aire atlantique, XVIᵉ–XVIIᵉ siècles*, ed. Guy Martinière, Didier Poton, François Souty (Paris: Maison des Sciences de l'Homme et de la Société 1999), 129–137.

[6] The emergence of joint-stock companies to finance intercontinental trade and later insurance policies is an important exception to this trend.

[7] John Francis Bosher, "The Lyon and Bordeaux Connections of Emmanuel Le Borgne, c. 1605–1681," in his *Business and Religion in the Age of New France, 1600–1760* (Toronto: Canadian Scholar's Press, 1994), 141–163, 143.

[8] The renewal in social history approaches came both through network analysis and micro-history. For a discussion of the new paradigms, see Maurizio Gribaudi, ed., *Espaces, temporalités, stratifications: Exercices sur les réseaux sociaux* (Paris: Éditions de l'EHESS, 1998), and notably Gribaudi's "Introduction," 5–40. For the framework set by social scientists, see Janet Landa, "A Theory of the Ethnically Homogeneous Middleman

greater within kinship and religious networks not because of any inherent moral value attached to given ethnic or religious criteria, but because members of these networks had ampler possibilities of sanctioning opportunistic behavior of kin and coreligionists.[9]

Recent research also suggests that the ability to establish durable trade relations outside religiously homogenous networks was key to the success of the most entrepreneurial private merchants.[10] The success of a prominent merchant and banking house like the family firm of David Gradis, a Jew of Iberian descent, in eighteenth-century Bordeaux owed a lot to its capacity to contract not only with immediate relatives and other New Christians and Jews, but also with the French Crown, and to its participation in the colonial and slave trade, in which Catholic agents and sea captains dominated.[11] The same holds true for those Huguenot merchants who traded with Canada, a branch of trade in which they developed close interactions with Catholic agents, particularly in wartime, when the Crown's need of supplies dramatically increased demand and profit margins.[12] Put simply, and following what sociologist Mark Granovetter calls "the strength of weak ties," the capacity of building reliable credit and business relations extending beyond one's own immediate circle opened up new possibilities for members of a network, resulting in a competitive advantage for them.[13]

According to the picture painted by the existing literature, the vast majority of early modern French merchants operated in networks that were composed of coreligionists; only a few select and prominent merchant houses involved in faraway trade entertained a certain degree of cross-religious and trans-confessional ties. This

---

Group: An Institutions Approach to Contract Law," *Journal of Legal Studies*, 10.2 (1981): 349–362; and Edna Bonacich, "A Theory of Middleman Minorities," *American Sociological Review*, 38.5 (1973): 583–594.

[9] Moravian merchants offer a good example of the entanglement between business and religion: Katherine Carté Engel, "'Commerce That the Lord Could Sanctify and Bless': Moravian Participation in Transatlantic Trade, 1740–1760," in *Pious Pursuits: German Moravians in the Atlantic World*, ed. Michele Gillespie and Robert Beachy (New York: Berghahn Books, 2007), 113–126.

[10] See, for example, the contributions edited by Anthony Molho and Diogo Ramada Curto as "Les réseaux marchands à l'époque moderne," in *Annales: Histoire, Sciences Sociales*, 58.3 (2003): 569–672.

[11] Richard Menkis, *The Gradis Family of Eighteenth-Century Bordeaux: A Social and Economic Study*, Ph.D. thesis, Brandeis University, 1988; Silvia Marzagalli, "Limites et opportunités dans l'Atlantique français au 18ᵉ siècle: Le cas de la maison Gradis de Bordeaux," *Outre-Mers: Révue d'histoire*, 362–363 (2009): 87–110.

[12] See, for instance, the cases of Pierre Desclaux, a Bordeaux Protestant, and his links to Joseph Cadet, the official purveyor-general for Canada; or the partnership between Pierre-François Goossens (a French-naturalized Dutch) and Nicolas Beaujon (the famous financier, whose grandfather was Huguenot), in John Francis Bosher, *The Canada Merchants, 1713–1763* (Oxford: Clarendon Press, 1987), 174–180. Bosher, like other historians studying religiously defined merchant networks, documents trans-confessional trade and even, incidentally, a few trans-confessional partnerships. He stresses, however, that "Catholic, Protestant, and Jewish merchants traded freely together, but they seldom formed partnerships and even more rarely intermarried" (43).

[13] Mark Granovetter, "The Strength of Weak Ties," *American Journal of Sociology*, 78.6 (1973): 1360–1380.

picture is largely unsatisfactory. First, it appears to be the result of a bias in our ways of studying trade networks: influenced by the idea that there is an explanatory connection between religion and capitalism, historians have looked for (and thus found) evidence of religious homogeneity more than they have searched for evidence of cross-religious and trans-confessional interactions (which exists, but has been overlooked). Second, no scholar provides a good explanation for why Catholics, Protestants, New Christians, and Jews in early modern France, who shared a common set of rules and customs about commercial transactions and who had access to the same legal institutions, should not do business together on a regular basis.

In fact, evidence of regular cross-religious and trans-confessional business inter-actions abounds, both in the very studies that emphasize the closed confessional character of trade networks in early modern France and in studies that are not con-cerned specifically with this issue, not to mention the primary sources. The fact that it has been overlooked seems to be due largely to historians' widespread assump-tion that networks were structured around religion. My view is that networks were largely shaped by kinship, and that for this reason, they were also largely composed of coreligionists.[14] Networks were built and expanded by recommendations pro-vided by relatives and correspondents: the chances that the new contacts belonged to someone's kinship (and thus, given the low religious exogamy, to the same confes-sional group) were high.[15] Rather than representing a conscious positive choice, the religious uniformity of a given network reveals its intrinsic limits, because of its rela-tive inefficiency in promoting access to a varied spectrum of agents, and thus of pro-viding occasions to establish "weak ties" with respect to one's religious network. But coreligionists did not exhaust the range of agents in a merchant's network, which also included non-coreligionists. In fact, the greater the share of the latter was, the greater the range of potential useful connections and contacts a merchant could establish with friends of his friends.[16]

---

[14] Charles Carrière contests the prevalent view, according to which commercial networks of Protestant mer-chants in Marseille relied on confessional affinity, and emphasizes instead the role of kin and common geographical origins. Charles Carrière, *Négociants marseillais au XVIIIᵉ siècle*, 2 vols. (Marseille: Institut Historique de Provence, 1973), 2: 944.

[15] In his study of the French merchants in Cadiz, Arnaud Bartolomei shows that their commercial net-work was extended by "capillarity," by establishing contacts with their correspondents' partners. Arnaud Bartolomei, *La Bourse ou la vie: Destin collectif et trajectoires individuelles des marchands français de Cadix, de l'instauration du comercio libre à la disparition de l'empire espagnol (1778–1824)*, Ph.D. thesis, Université d'Aix-Marseille I, 2007. Although his study does not take into consideration the religious nature of com-mercial networks, the arguments that are advanced in the vast literature on "national" networks rely on assumptions that are very similar to those evoked for religious networks.

[16] The question of the costs of belonging to a network has been raised by David Hancock, who stressed that the network imposed upon its members a series of implicit and explicit duties that were not necessarily eco-nomically rational. David Hancock, "The Trouble with Networks: Managing the 'Scots' Early-Modern Madeira

EVIDENCE OF CROSS-RELIGIOUS AND TRANS-CONFESSIONAL
TRADE IN EARLY MODERN FRANCE

In a few instances, scholars have explicitly challenged the notion that religiously based trade networks were the norm in early modern France. Jacques Bottin and Pierre Jeannin demonstrate that Jean Heufft (also spelled Hoeufft), a Huguenot from Liège who moved to Rouen in 1600 at the age of 22, began his career by interacting mainly—though not exclusively—with other Protestant merchants of northern France and northern Europe, but that his network rapidly lost "the smooth confessional homogeneity of its early days" when Heufft started furnishing arms and munitions to Charles de Gonzaga, duke of Nevers, who needed his assistance in the early 1620s for his crusade against the Ottoman Empire. Heufft later became a financier of the Crown at the time of Cardinals Richelieu and Mazarin.[17] More recently, Évelyne Oliel-Grausz's preliminary exploration of documents concerning New Christians' and Jews' trading networks linking eighteenth-century Bordeaux to the Iberian world has also pointed to the existence of trans-religious relations on a regular basis.[18]

It is nonetheless fair to claim that most scholars, when they do take at all into account the religious or confessional identity of the merchants whom they study, implicitly or explicitly assume that merchant networks in early modern France were essentially, if not entirely, made up of coreligionists. Very few of them have actually analyzed the business network of any given firm in order to test this assumption.[19] More frequently, scholars tend to emphasize the importance of confessional business networks. They also display a predilection for the study of non-Catholic merchants in a predominantly Catholic France, in a move that, implicitly, echoes the Weberian assumption of the entrepreneurial inferiority of Catholics. Paradoxically, the few studies that include an analysis of the religious profile of a merchant group (which is not necessarily an analysis of the mono-confessional character of their business

---

Trade," *Business History Review*, 79.3 (2005): 467–491. A homogenous network could add another disadvantage: if its members shared a common characteristic—be it religious affiliation, geographical origin, or nationality—their opportunities for establishing new links with outsiders were reduced.

[17] Jacques Bottin and Pierre Jeannin, "Entre conviction et réalisme: Deux hommes d'affaires protestants du premier XVIIᵉ siècle," in *D'un rivage à l'autre*, 157–171, 165.

[18] Évelyne Oliel-Grausz, "Communication, marchandise et religion: Les négociants séfarades au XVIIIᵉ siècle," in *Commerce, voyage et expérience religieuse, XVIᵉ–XVIIIᵉ siècles*, ed. Albrecht Burkardt (Rennes: Presses Universitaires de Rennes, 2007), 145–159, 153.

[19] Two notable exceptions are Menkis, *The Gradis Family*, and José do Nascimento Raposo, *Don Gabriel de Silva, a Portuguese-Jewish Banker in Eighteenth-century Bordeaux*, Ph.D. thesis, York University, Toronto, 1989. Menkis affirms that the Gradises' success derived from their cross-religious networks. Raposo insists on the importance of family ties and ethnicity, but also shows that the Portuguese Jewish banker Gabriel Da Silva (who went bankrupt in 1762) maintained close credit relations with Parisian Protestant bankers and Catholic firms, and intensified them over time (249–261).

networks) cite evidence that suggests the frequency of cross-religious trade.[20] J. F. Bosher's study of the Catholic merchant Emmanuel La Borgne in La Rochelle, for instance, begins by postulating the confessional nature of trade networks, but mentions that La Borgne relied on his son-in-law Jacques de Lamothe, who settled in Bordeaux in 1669 and became one of the most important merchants fitting out to New France *because* Jacques had close contacts with Dutch, English, and Huguenot merchants.[21] Similarly, other studies that Bosher devoted to Huguenot merchants in Canada point to the existence of mono-confessional firms, but also demonstrate that Huguenots increasingly extended their commercial relations beyond their confessional networks and were encouraged to do so by the changing attitude of the French monarchy, which, according to this historian, gave up "a policy of Catholic imperialism" by the mid-eighteenth century.[22]

More evidence of trans-confessional business peppers the secondary literature, even when that literature is not directly concerned with the issue. French historians have not paid much attention to the interactions that non-Catholic merchants maintained with their Catholic homologues. And yet, their research invariably mentions such interactions, at least in passing. Thus, discussing the role of Dutch merchants in Nantes between 1660 and 1685, Guy Saupin stresses the difficulty of distinguishing Dutch from Flemish merchants, and prefers to speak of a single group of foreign Northerners that included both Catholics and Protestants, although the confessional question is raised when discussing the effects of the revocation of the Edict of Nantes.[23] By looking more closely at the merchants he cites, however, evidence of trans-confessional business partnerships emerges.[24]

---

[20] The authors of most of these studies are not French: Perry Viles, *The Shipping Interest of Bordeaux, 1774–1793*, Ph.D. thesis, Harvard University, 1965; Jonathan Webster, *The Merchants of Bordeaux in Trade to the French West Indies, 1664–1717*, Ph.D. thesis, University of Minnesota, 1972; Bosher, *Business and Religion*; Bosher, *The Canada Merchants*.

[21] Bosher, "The Lyon and Bordeaux Connections of Emmanuel Le Borgne." For the statement on the confessional nature of merchant networks, see fn. 7 above.

[22] "Huguenots families remained discretely in touch with merchant bankers of both religions," that is, with both Catholics and Huguenots: John Francis Bosher, "Identifying Huguenots in the Canada Trade, 1663–1763," in his *Business and Religion*, 213. For the evolution of these patterns over time, see 215.

[23] Saupin, "Les Hollandais à Nantes." It is indeed difficult to distinguish Catholics from Protestants, either because adequate sources have not survived or because all French Protestants were nominally Catholic after the revocation of the Edict of Nantes in 1685. The same difficulty exists with regard to the nominal and genuine confessional identity of Bordeaux's New Christians until 1723.

[24] Saupin cites, for instance, the business venture for the fitting out of a ship, *La Fortune*, between some foreign Northerners (an Irishman and a few French merchants), but glosses over its trans-confessional nature (Saupin, "Les Hollandais à Nantes," 134). We know the religious identity of at least one of the Northerners because Saupin refers to him as a Protestant in a previous footnote (130n); we can also identify the Irishman as a Catholic thanks to Patrick Clark de Dromantin, *Les réfugiés jacobites dans la France du XVIIIᵉ siècle* (Pessac: Presses Universitaires de Bordeaux, 2005), 417.

In my own research on the trade networks connecting Bordeaux and the United States between 1793 and 1815, I found some evidence of trans-confessional partnerships among merchants born in the United States and living in Bordeaux.[25] Jona Jones, a wealthy Quaker of Philadelphia, married the daughter of a prominent Bordeaux Huguenot merchant, Texier, in 1785 and subsequently prospered in the West Indian trade.[26] During the French Wars (1793–1815), he owned at least two ships together with another merchant house based in the United States, Fenwick & Mason, and occasionally freighted Fenwick's ships for his own ventures. Catholic Joseph Fenwick and Anglican John Mason—the son of the Founding Father George Mason—had formed a general partnership in Bordeaux in 1788. They relied on Joseph Fenwick's brother James, in Georgetown, Maryland, for their supply of tobacco, but starting in 1793 the European conflict offered them a unique opportunity to expand their trade in West Indian goods. Fenwick & Mason dissolved their Bordeaux partnership in 1793 in order not to be considered as French by the British and created a new business firm known as "Fenwick Mason & Company" of Georgetown. In this case, the two partners belonged to different confessions, and regularly interacted with Jona Jones, a merchant of yet a third confession.

This scattered evidence does not allow us to generalize about the incidence of cross-religious and trans-confessional trade in early modern France, but it is enough to question the validity of current assumptions. We know that Catholic, Protestant, and Jewish merchants lived and conducted business in the same cities.[27] They met not only on the floor of the Exchange, where goods and financial instruments were traded, but also in many institutions of eighteenth-century urban sociability, including local cultural associations and Masonic lodges.[28] If we accept that, in many

---

[25] Silvia Marzagalli, "Establishing Transatlantic Trade Networks in Time of War: Bordeaux and the United States, 1793–1815," *Business History Review*, 79.4 (2005): 811–844.

[26] Archives départementales de la Gironde, Bordeaux (hereafter ADG), 3E 20603, January 21, 1785. At the beginning of the French Wars, Jones signed a power of attorney to recover his money in Saint-Christophe, Saint-Eustache, Saint-Martin, Sainte-Croix, and Saint-Thomas, that is, in all the centers of West Indian interlope trade, as well as in Martinique and Guadeloupe: ADG, 3E 31354, February 12, 1793.

[27] Protestants—both French and foreigners—made up approximately 15 percent of the merchants of Le Havre in 1660 and 8 percent of those of Nantes: Édouard Delobette, "Les marchands protestants du Havre à la fin du XVIIe siècle (1685–1720)," in *D'un rivage à l'autre*, 139–156; Saupin, "Les Hollandais à Nantes." There are no good sources to estimate their numbers in the century following the revocation of the Edict of Nantes, but by the 1780s there were as many Protestants in Nantes as a century earlier, and they were predominantly involved in trade: Yves Krumenacker, "Les minorités protestantes dans les grandes villes françaises de l'époque moderne," *Analele Universităţii Bucureşti* (2008): 101–114. In the 1780s, over a third of merchants fitting out ships in Bordeaux were Protestant, and two-thirds of the banking houses were Jewish: Viles, *The Shipping Interest of Bordeaux*, 70 and 76. On the persistent importance of Protestant and Jewish merchants in Bordeaux, see also Jean Cavignac, *Les vingt-cinq familles: Les négociants bordelais sous Louis-Philippe* (Bordeaux: Cahiers de l'I.A.E.S. no. 6, 1985).

[28] The French Masonic lodges excluded Jews, with a notable and controversial exception in Bayonne. On the limits of the assimilation of Jews, Muslims, and confessional minorities in the European freemasonry,

instances, merchants in France did business with non-coreligionists, we should then try to understand when and why this occurred, and when, by contrast, merchants privileged exchanges within networks constituted by coreligionists.

If we admit that recourse to coreligionists was not an absolute norm or a fate, but the product of specific choices, the French case allows us to test empirically the prevailing theoretical explanation for the predominance of confessional networks. Inspired by the new institutional economics, most scholars maintain that kinship and religious networks were able to sanction opportunistic behavior at a time when international law was not.[29] However, the efficiency of social ostracism within a confessional group is more often postulated than demonstrated. There is, for instance, no evidence that Étienne/Stephen Girard, who became one of the first millionaires in the United States, was ever ostracized by his Catholic French colleagues, despite a dubious start in his career, which led him to migrate to the United States.[30] Of course, if one of the parties deliberately emigrated in order to avoid the consequences of an opportunistic behavior or misfortune, the possibilities of legal recourse were scarce, even if the French consular system was alerted and consuls were asked to intervene against fugitives, should the latter show up in their cities of residence. But was social ostracism any more available when a merchant moved to another country and started a new life there?

In France, trans-confessional and cross-religious trade occurred between merchants who were subject to the same legal regime, and not between actors residing in distant regions or bound to different legal systems. Therefore, there is no reason to assume that merchant networks in France relied exclusively on sanctions imposed by one's own religious community. The difficulty of obtaining legal recourse, which is generally advanced in order to account for the predominance of religiously uniform networks, cannot be invoked to explain why two merchants belonging to different religious groups but living in the same kingdom would not do business together.

---

and the differences between various lodges, see Pierre-Yves Beaurepaire, *L'Autre et le frère: L'Étranger et la Franc-maçonnerie en France au XVIIIᵉ siècle* (Paris: Champion, 1998), 539–605. Jews were admitted in the Bordeaux Musée, a cultural association of public utility in which Bordeaux freemasons were a majority. On the composition of French cultural institutions more generally, see Daniel Roche, "Négoce et culture dans la France du XVIIIᵉ siècle," *Revue d'histoire moderne et contemporaine*, 25.3 (1978): 375–395.

[29] Mark Casson and Mary B. Rose reconstruct the fertile encounters between the new institutional economics and business history and how they led to an increased attention to family firms as efficient ways of reducing transactions costs and the uncertainty of business investments. See their "Introduction" to the special issue on "Institutions and the Evolution of Modern Business," *Business History*, 39.4 (1997): 1–8. This special issue also was published as a book (London: Frank Cass, 1998).

[30] Girard was a native of the Bordeaux region who sailed to the West Indies, did not come back to France because he was unable to reimburse the money he had borrowed, and finally settled in Philadelphia. During the French Wars (1793–1815) he reactivated his contacts with France and Bordeaux, including some with Catholic merchants. On his life, see John B. MacMaster, *The Life and Times of Stephen Girard, Mariner and Merchant,*

In early modern France, as in other European countries, legal recourse was available even to foreigners. When Jona Jones and Joseph Fenwick disagreed on who should carry the £3,800 loss provoked by the British capture in 1794 of a ship Jones had freighted from Fenwick for a voyage from Bordeaux to the French island of Mauritius, and from thence to New York and back to Bordeaux, they engaged in a costly 13-year-long legal suit that ended in 1807 in front of the Cour de Cassation in Paris, after having being discussed in the Tribunal de Commerce and the Cour d'Appel in Bordeaux.[31] More often, merchants agreed to accept the arbitrage of a third party, or the sentence of the merchant consular jurisdiction (Tribunal of Commerce after 1790), a tribunal composed of elected merchants, which rendered rapid and cheap decisions. The sum involved in this case, however, demanded the intervention of higher courts.[32] Incidentally, it is thanks to this lawsuit that we know that Jones was a Quaker, as he refused to take the oath in front of the tribunal—an argument that Fenwick tried to exploit in a final, desperate attempt to reverse the judgment that condemned him. Religion had clearly not factored into Fenwick's decision to lend his American-flagged ship to Jones, who wished to engage in Bordeaux's colonial trade together with two other French merchants. We can only speculate that the outstanding reputation of the two firms, their solid trade networks in the French colonies and the United States, as well as the invaluable chance of discussing business directly without leaving any written trace of the risky nature of their dealings in times of war, played a much more relevant role than their respective religious congregations.[33]

Once we admit that there was no a priori reason why two merchants living in France should not seal a partnership because they belonged to different religious or confessional groups, we still have to find an explanation for the evidence that merchant networks were indeed largely religiously uniform. It is possible that many merchants sought to evaluate the relation between the perceived degree of risk involved in a specific business venture and the possibilities of sanctioning opportunistic behavior that existed in that venture before deciding with whom to enter into contract. When merchants sealed unlimited liability partnerships, they customarily

2 vols. (Philadelphia & London: Lippincott, 1918) and Harry Emerson Wildes, *Lonely Midas: The Story of Stephen Girard* (New York: Farrar & Rinehard, 1943).

[31] The Bibliothèque Municipale in Bordeaux holds a series of printed arguments of the two parties, which amount to over 1,000 pages (D 71214, D 71215, D 71217 to D 71221).

[32] Consular jurisdictions were created in the sixteenth century and met with immediate favor among merchants: see Ernest-Désiré Glasson, "Les juges et consuls des marchands," *Nouvelle revue historique de droit français et étranger*, Jan.–Feb. (1897): 5–38.

[33] Any written trace of arrangements aiming at circumventing belligerents' restrictions on maritime trade was risky. In this case, as the cargo was condemned and sold in Halifax, Fenwick dispatched his partner to buy the cargo in order to prevent the discovery of papers that would cause the condemnation of the ship as a

chose a close relative whom they knew well and who likely belonged to the same ethnic and religious group (although the general partnership between Fenwick and Mason offers a counter-example). Kin (and thus common religious backgrounds) prevailed in the choice of faraway agents, when legal recourse was extremely complicated, if possible at all.

But there were many exceptions to this rule. It is reasonable to assume that, as in Amsterdam (see Chapter 6 in this volume), religious and confessional heterogeneity varied by type of contract. When freighting a ship or underwriting an insurance policy at the local exchange, kin and religion counted less, as legal recourse was possible, the procedure highly standardized by the eighteenth century, and liability was limited. When the Catholic partners of the Gramont, Chegaray, & Company in Bordeaux insured a cargo on the American ship *Suffolk* for a journey from Cayenne to Bordeaux, both Jews (Fonseca & Pereire, Roget junior, and D. A. Rodrigues & sons) and Protestants (Faure frères) undersigned the policy.[34] Both the legal system and the social monitoring among merchants living in the same place could provide acceptable equivalents to blood, kin, and religious affiliation. In sort, when other conditions were in place and when merchants of different religious groups shared a common way of doing business, religious differences could fade away.[35]

In order to understand the complexity of early modern European trade, it is not helpful to oppose closed, religion-based networks to the open market, and thus propose a linear, almost teleological evolution over time toward an economic world in which religion ceases to matter. Religion did matter, but not equally in all circumstances of life or in different kinds of business.[36] I find it more appropriate to conceive of the possibility that merchants selected their partners and agents according to a multiplicity of criteria, which encompassed religious affiliation, kinship ties, and

---

good prize. The purchase of the cargo provoked a substantial financial loss, which Jones refused to endorse, because he claimed that he had never issued the order to buy the cargo in Halifax.

[34] ADG, 3E 31401, 16 fructidor XIII (September 3, 1805), declaration of the loss of the ship.

[35] This feature seems to characterize most cosmopolitan port cities. In Hamburg, the merchant and banker John Parish expressed his deepest gratitude to one of his Jewish creditors who saved him from ruin at a delicate moment: Richard Ehrenberg, *Grosse Vermögen: Das Haus Parish in Hamburg* (Jena: G. Fischer, 1905), 25–29. More evidence on the integration of Jews within the Hamburg merchant community in Klaus Weber, "Were Merchants More Tolerant? 'Godless Patrons of the Jews' and the Decline of the Sephardi Community in Late Seventeenth-Century Hamburg," in *Jews and Port Cities, 1590–1990: Commerce, Community and Cosmopolitanism*, ed. David Cesarani and Gemma Romain (London: Vallentine Mitchell, 2006), 77–92. Note that by the seventeenth century, although anti-usury debates and legislation were still in place, Christian and Jewish merchants regularly shared the same credit instruments.

[36] In discussing the ostentatious conversion of several members of the Ashkenazi merchant family Homberg, Beaurepaire stresses the role of religion in their integration in the commercial society of eighteenth-century Le Havre: Pierre-Yves Beaurepaire, *La France des Lumières* (Paris: Bélin, 2011), 610–615.

proven reputation in business, as well as the possibility of obtaining justice through either legal or informal means.

Unfortunately, rarely are primary sources explicit about the intentions that guided merchants. Therefore, historians are compelled to infer the logic that drove merchants' decisions from records that document solely the existence and terms of specific transactions. Contemporaries did implicitly know—or believed to know— whom to trust and when, but wrote little about the information and principles that guided their evaluations. If merchants' letters often allow us to trace the monitoring processes that were employed within a network, they rarely explain why and when merchants ventured outside their usual network. A systematic study of partner- ship contracts involving one or more silent partners who provided capitals but did not intervene in the company's decisions (*sociétés en commandite*) would be useful to measure the relevance of religious affiliation in one instance where liability was clearly limited.[37] Regrettably, as of this writing, no one has engaged in such as study in order to explore the degree to which different elements played a role in merchants' strategic choices about whom to enlist as partners. Recent scholarship suggests that in major hubs such as Livorno and Amsterdam, cross-religious business relations could be built more easily through contracts about marine insurance, bottomry loans, joint ship ventures, and other instances in which liability was limited.[38] The implications of this hypothesis for trade within France and between France and its colonies still need to be explored. The case of Bordeaux shows not only that the growth of the city to a major colonial and international port relied on cross-religious and trans-confessional business relations, but also that the evolution of the commer- cial and religious policies of the French monarchy, the flexibility of local authori- ties, and the interests of merchants concurred to create a propitious context for this development.

THE CASE OF BORDEAUX

Bordeaux's merchant community in the early modern period was largely multi-confessional and multi-religious, as was the case in several other important French ports. Starting in the Middle Ages and until the end of the seventeenth century, wine was Bordeaux's primary export commodity.[39] Wine was exported on

---

[37] On the legal framework in which these companies developed in France, see Henry Levy-Bruhl, *Histoire juridique des sociétés de commerce en France aux XVIIIᵉ et XIXᵉ siècles* (Paris: Dumat Montchrétien, 1938).

[38] Francesca Trivellato, *The Familiarity of Strangers: The Sephardic Diaspora, Livorno, and Cross-Cultural Trade in the Early Modern Period* (New Haven, CT: Yale University Press, 2009) and Chapter 6 in this volume.

[39] Christian Huetz de Lemps, *Géographie du commerce de Bordeaux à la fin du règne de Louis XIV* (Paris: Mouton, 1975).

foreign bottoms to England and northern Europe, and cargoes in Bordeaux were handled primarily by foreign merchants who operated in the city as commission merchants. Given the fact that most of these merchants came from northern Europe, a large majority of them was Protestant.

Other branches of Bordeaux's trade yielded major profits to a few, influential merchants and allowed for the city's integration in larger European and Atlantic commercial networks. From the late fifteenth century, the trade of pastel, which was produced in the region of Toulouse and forwarded down the Garonne River to Bordeaux, from where it was shipped to northern Spain, Flanders, and England, was significant and was dominated by Italian and Spanish merchants.[40] After the decline in the demand of pastel in the 1560s, Bordeaux found in the Newfoundland fisheries another major set of opportunities.[41] Bordeaux's merchants reduced their participation in the fisheries during the seventeenth century, but did not abandon it.[42] By the 1660s, a few wealthy ones sponsored mercantile ventures to both Newfoundland and the West Indies, where France began to have a colonial presence in the 1630s. Some of these merchants were Catholic, like François Saige and Pierre Cornut; others were Huguenots, like Étienne Dhariette. The latter fitted out the first known expedition from Bordeaux to Quebec in 1671, as well as the first triangular shipping venture from Bordeaux to Quebec and to the West Indies in 1672. For the latter voyage, Dhariette freighted the ship of his Catholic colleague, Saige. Most of the funds for these Newfoundland ventures were obtained through bottomry loans granted by a naturalized Dutch merchant living in Bordeaux, Jean de Ridder, and his relative, the British wine merchant Thomas Arundell. Between 1660 and his death in 1671, Ridder's father financed 86 bottomry loans in Bordeaux for expeditions to the Newfoundland fisheries, often in partnership with the Catholic Everhard Jabach,

---

[40] Gilles Caster, *Le commerce du pastel et de l'épicerie à Toulouse de 1450 environ à 1561* (Toulouse: Privat, 1962). Italian merchants, who dominated French trade and finance in the second half of the sixteenth century, were predominantly Catholic, but the merchants of Lucca, who were mostly Protestant, were just as successful and interacted daily with both French and other Italian merchants in France: Bernard Allaire, *Crépuscules ultramontains: Marchands italiens et grand commerce à Bordeaux au XVIᵉ siècle* (Pessac: Presses Universitaires de Bordeaux, 2008).

[41] Robert Boutruche, ed., *Historie de Bordeaux*, vol. 4: *Bordeaux de 1453 à 1715* (Bordeaux: FHSO, 1966), 91–138. Bordeaux's merchants first reached the Newfoundland fisheries in the 1520s, both with their own ships and by financing fishing expeditions leaving from other southwestern French ports. In 1560, Bordeaux fitted out 61 cod-ships. In spite of the disruption caused by the wars of religion, in 1585 the city still sent off 47 of those ships. Laurier Turgeon, "Pour redécouvrir notre 16ᵉ siècle: Les pêches à Terre-Neuve d'après les archives notariales de Bordeaux," *Revue d'histoire de l'Amérique française*, 39.4 (1986): 523–549. See also Jacques Bernard, *Navires et gens de mer à Bordeaux (vers 1450–1550)* (Paris: SEVPEN, 1968).

[42] Little is known about Bordeaux's trade in the first half of the seventeenth century. See Bertrand Gautier, *Contribution à l'histoire de l'économie maritime et de la société marchande à Bordeaux dans la première moitié du XVIIᵉ siècle: 1630–1650*, Unpublished dissertation (Travail d'étude et de recherche), Université de Bordeaux III, 1987–1988.

a banker who settled in Paris, who was also director of the French East Indian Company.[43] Jabach's father had made a fortune as banker in Antwerp, before settling back in Cologne and converting to Catholicism in order to be accepted in the local Senate.[44]

These same group of wealthy merchants was at the origin of Bordeaux's increasing involvement in the West Indian trade, which developed from the 1660s onward.[45] Huguenot merchant Étienne Dhariette participated, alone or in partnership with others, in a quarter of the 343 voyages fitted out to the West Indies from the 1660s to 1685.[46] Out of 65 merchants organizing these voyages, 60 percent were possibly Protestants. Out of the 20 merchants who participated at least in two ventures to the West Indies from 1680 to 1685, 14 were Protestant, 2 were Jewish, and 4 were Catholic.[47] Among them, the most prominent Catholic merchant was François Saige. As mentioned, Dhariette and Saige conducted business together, as did Dhariette and the Catholic merchant Cornut. The first phase of Bordeaux's involvement in colonial trade thus relied on constant interactions between merchants of different confessions. Within a generation, French merchants in Bordeaux were able to bypass Dutch capital and financial infrastructure and to fit out to the West Indies using their own capital. This evolution was encouraged by the French state.

The progressive emergence of Bordeaux as an Atlantic port developed in parallel with a major shift in French colonial and religious policy. In 1662, a report presented to the minister of finance Jean-Baptiste Colbert estimated that out of 150 ships trading with the French Caribbean, no more than 3 or 4 were French owned. The minister spent the rest of his life trying to reverse this situation.[48] Colonies were put under direct state control, instead of under the control of chartered companies or private landlords who were granted regalian rights (*propriétaires-seigneurs*). In 1671, foreign ships were excluded from colonial ports, and French exports to the colonies were exempted from all duties. Duties on French colonial imports were reduced from 5 percent to 3 percent. These decisions laid the basis of what was later labelled as the "exclusive system," a policy excluding foreigners from colonial trade and obliging the

---

[43] On Jean de Ridder, see Webster, *Merchants*, and Peter Voss, "L'exemple d'un 'bourgeois et marchand de Bordeaux' au milieu du XVIIᵉ siècle," *Bulletin du Centre d'Histoire des Espaces Atlantiques*, 4 (1988): 73–109.

[44] Vicomte de Grouchy, "Everhard Jabach, collectionneur parisien," *Mémoires de la société d'histoire de Paris et de l'Ile de France*, 21 (1894): 217–248.

[45] Éric Saugera, *Bordeaux, port négrier: Chronologie, économie, idéologie, XVIIᵉ–XIXᵉ siècles* (Paris: Karthala, 1995).

[46] Webster, *Merchants*, 125–160; Silvia Marzagalli, "Le négoce bordelais et ses hommes," in *Histoire des Bordelais*, vol. 1: *La modernité triomphante (1715–1815)*, ed. Michel Figeac (Bordeaux: Mollat, 2002), 85–115.

[47] Webster, *Merchants,* 207.

[48] Webster, *Merchants,* 36.

colonists to trade exclusively with the ports and merchants of the mother country. French shipping and shipbuilding were boosted.[49]

In 1685, two major laws were passed in France. In March, the *Code Noir* provided a comprehensive reorganization of the French colonies. Its first article banned non-Catholics from all the colonies subjected to the king of France, thus condemning both Jews and Protestants to expulsion within three months. In October, the Edict of Nantes was revoked, ending an era of relative toleration for the French Calvinist minority that had started in 1598 after 30 years of religious civil wars. All subjects of King Louis XIV had to be Catholics. While banning foreigners from its overseas trade in order to implement a mercantilist goal, the French Crown was thus also promoting confessional uniformity within the kingdom and its colonies. Both decisions should be understood in the context of the economic war opposing Louis XIV and the Dutch since the 1660s. Fighting the Dutch and promoting Catholicism were, from the point of view of the French king and his minister Colbert, two facets of the same struggle.

The implementation of these policies proved challenging. By the time the *Code Noir* banned non-Catholics from the colonies, Jewish settlers had already proved useful there in providing commercial and credit services to planters and administrative authorities. Connected as they were to the Sephardic diaspora, Iberian New Christians in the French Caribbean had access to important business contacts in Amsterdam and were thus able to acquire timely information on the fluctuations of world markets directly from the most important European commercial and financial hub—a veritable asset at a time when part of the French cargoes was still exported directly from the West Indies to northern Europe and when Sephardim were extremely active in the Dutch and English Caribbean. By 1680, 16 Jewish colonists were reported to be living in Martinique, and at least four of them owned slave-run sugar plantations. In spite of repeated expulsions, Jews settled in the French West Indies throughout the eighteenth century with the complicity of colonial authorities, who found their presence and their credit services to be extremely useful.[50] The same pragmatic acceptance of non-Catholic settlers extended to Protestants,[51] just as

---

[49] Jean Tarrade, *Le commerce colonial de la France à la fin de l'Ancien Régime*, 2 vols. (Paris: PUF, 1972).

[50] For a synthesis on this issue, see Silvia Marzagalli, "Atlantic Trade and Sephardim Merchants in Eighteenth Century France: The Case of Bordeaux," in *The Jews and the Expansion of Europe to the West, 1493 to 1800*, ed. Paolo Bernardini and Norman Fiering (Providence: Berghahn Books, 2001), 268–286.

[51] In 1777, Johan Jacob von Bethmann, a successful merchant and banker of Frankfurt living in Bordeaux, acquired together with the Sephardi David Gradis of Bordeaux a plantation in Saint-Domingue: Wolfgang Henninger, *Johann Jacob von Bethmann, 1717–1792: Kaufmann, Reeder und kaiserlicher Konsul in Bordeaux*, 2 vols. (Bochum: Brockmeyer, 1993), 1: 342–343. Klaus Weber, *Deutsche Kaufleute im Atlantikhandel, 1680–1830* (München: Beck, 2004), 370–380, provides a list of German merchants based in Bordeaux (all of them being Protestant) who traveled to, or died in, French colonies and mentions a few examples of German firms

in La Rochelle in the 1630s.[52] If in the first half of the seventeenth century French merchants in Nantes petitioned against the presence of Jewish and Protestant merchants in their city, this did not prevent them from doing business with non-coreligionists; one century later, Protestant merchants were well integrated into the local merchant community.[53]

In the mother country, too, confessional uniformity was no longer on the agenda once it became clear that the promotion of French shipping and trade was not only compatible with, but also dependent on, the presence of non-Catholic bankers and merchants in France. The pragmatism of the local authorities contributed to make trade between people of different confessions and religions in France a daily experience. Two exceptions prove this rule. Unlike other eighteenth-century French ports, Marseille and Saint Malo did not have a religiously and confessionally diverse population, but geopolitical reasons and the power of local merchant elites, rather than an innate aversion to trans-confessional and cross-religious business, explain their policies. In Marseille, inhabitants massacred the Algerian ambassador in 1620 and repeatedly enforced xenophobic policies against Armenians and Jews, despite Richelieu's and Colbert's efforts to facilitate the latter's presence in the city. Integration of Jews and Armenians continued to be difficult within the city in the eighteenth century, whereas Protestants represented a significant part of the local merchant community. Marseille merchants and captains, however, interacted extensively with Muslim, Jewish, and Greek Orthodox merchants and brokers in their Levant trade, notably in the *caravane*, the shipping services that Marseille provided to and within the Ottoman Empire and that represented a profitable branch of its long-distance ventures during eighteenth century. The banning of Jews and Armenians from Marseille, in other words, stemmed from the determination to prevent competition, rather than from a reluctance to engage in trans-confessional,

---

from Bordeaux that owned plantations in the French West Indies (284–285). For a detailed study of the Bordeaux Protestant firm Romberg, Bapst & Co. and its plantations, see Françoise Thésée, *Négociants bordelais et colons de Saint-Domingue: "Liaisons d'habitations"; La maison Henry Romberg, Bapst et Cie 1783–1793* (Paris: Société Française d'Histoire d'Outre-Mer, 1972).

[52] Bosher wrote that, despite the siege of the Huguenot bastion of La Rochelle by royal forces, after 1628 Huguenots there "were tolerated as sources of financial capital and foreign ships" because of their links with "relatives and partners in Holland and England"; J. F. Bosher, "La Rochelle and New France, 1627–1685," in his *Business and Religion*, 133.

[53] Xenophobic riots exploded against Jews and Protestants in Nantes in the 1630s and 1640s: Guy Saupin, *Nantes au XVIIe siècle: Vie politique et société urbaine* (Rennes: Presses Universitaires de Rennes, 1996), 247–249. Since the late sixteenth century, Portuguese, Spanish, and Dutch had increased their share in Nantes' export trade. I have argued elsewhere that the development of colonial and slave trade from the mid-seventeenth century allowed for a division of tasks between French and foreign merchants that proved profitable for both groups and made the presence of foreign merchants not only tolerable, but also welcomed. Silvia Marzagalli, "L'évolution de la politique française vis-à-vis des étrangers à l'époque moderne: Conditions, discours, pratiques," in *Les étrangers dans les villes-ports atlantiques (XVe–XIXe siècle): Expériences allemandes et françaises*, ed. Mickaël Augeron and Pascal Even (Paris: Les Indes Savantes, 2010), 45–62.

cross-religious, and inter-ethnic (in the case of Catholic Armenians) trade as such.[54] In Saint-Malo, the geography of eighteenth-century shipping, trade, and privateering, which extended from the Newfoundland fisheries to Cadiz, did not require the presence of foreign merchants in the city, as they did not initiate a massive re-export trade to northern Europe, as colonial trade did.[55]

If the share of Protestant merchants in the trade between Bordeaux and the French Caribbean diminished from 82 percent in 1680–1685 to 66 percent in 1686–1689, the revocation of the Edict of Nantes in 1685 did not provoke a sudden, drastic change in the organization of colonial trade in terms of the role that non-Catholic minorities played in it. Although many Huguenot merchants emigrated, in most instances, at least one family member converted to Catholicism (if only nominally) and remained in France, thus protecting his family estates and business's interests.[56] Moreover, whereas the king enforced confessional uniformity among his subjects, he did not ban foreigners of Protestant persuasion. As a matter of fact, in 1686 Louis XIV explicitly reiterated that foreigners were welcomed in France, irrespective of their religion, although they were not granted the right to worship in public.[57]

This policy was not as contradictory as it may appear at first sight: the king expected his subjects to be Catholics, but did not force foreigners to convert. In fact, he encouraged whatever immigration seemed beneficial to the French economy.[58]

---

[54] Pierre Échinard and Émile Temime, *Migrance: Histoire des migrations à Marseille* (Aix-en-Provence: Édisud, 1989), 41–45; Carrière, *Négociants marseillais*, 1: 275 and 282; Daniel Panzac, *La caravane maritime: Marins européens et marchands ottomans en Méditerranée, 1680–1830* (Paris: CNRS, 2004).

[55] Lespagnol argues that the fact that business in Saint-Malo was in the hands of its local Catholic merchant dynasties might have contributed to the city's growing economic difficulties in the eighteenth century. André Lespagnol, *Messieurs de Saint-Malo: Une élite négociante au temps de Louis XIV*, 2 vols. (Rennes: PUR, 1997), 1: 94–100. The limited hinterland of the port might explain why the city's merchants were not competitive in the colonial trade, which is considered the most dynamic sector of eighteenth-century French trade.

[56] Webster, *Merchants*, chapter 3. The author is extremely prudent in assessing the effects of the revocation of the Edict of Nantes on Bordeaux's Atlantic trade and attributes the relative decline that followed the peak of 1685 less to the expulsion of Huguenots than to the ongoing wars and to the death of some prominent local merchants. Both Saupin's "Les Hollandais à Nantes" and Delobette's "Les marchands protestants du Havre" are equally cautious in tracing causal links between the effects of the Edict's revocation, the continuing warfare, and the natural inter-generational change. On the strategies adopted in La Rochelle, see Bosher, *The Canada Merchants*, 114–117 and, on the international business network created by the Huguenot emigration, 168–173. On the impact of the Huguenot diaspora on the French wine trade to the Netherlands, see Anne Wegener Sleeswijk, "Une affaire huguenote? Les immigrés français et le commerce du vin à Amsterdam (fin du XVIIᵉ et XVIIIᵉ siècle)," in *Les étrangers*, 287–308. See also Yves Krumenacker, "Des négociants protestants dans la France catholique," in *Commerce, voyage et expérience religieuse*, 304–305.

[57] Peter Sahlins and Jean-François Dubois, *Et si on faisait payer les étrangers? Louis XIV, les immigrés et quelques autres* (Paris: Flammarion, 1999), 43.

[58] Unlike the French soil, where the king had to take into account established privileges and local interests, colonies were conceived as experimental laboratories for political decisions and administrative innovations, and were thus supposed to be kept entirely free of non-Catholics and of foreign merchants all together.

The Crown, moreover, tacitly tolerated an extensive participation of non-Catholics in colonial trade, as long as they were based in France and thus beneficial to the economic interests of the mother country. According to a 1734 report by the royal official (*intendant*) of Bordeaux, five or six Jewish shipowners were trading at that time with the American colonies and were responsible for a "very considerable business."[59] Nothing was done to prevent them from conducting such business. The need to boost the re-export of colonial goods made authorities equally lenient toward the constant immigration of Protestants from northern Europe to Bordeaux, where, by all counts, they integrated well into the local merchant community.[60] Ultimately, these explicit and tacit policies contributed to further blurring of the confessional frontiers here, as in most eighteenth-century French port-cities. Though J. F. Bosher dates this evolution to the mid-eighteenth century as far as the exchanges between France and Canada were concerned, all of Bordeaux's colonial trade was a multi-confessional and cross-religious affair since the beginning.

Mercantilist legislation and the restoration of peace in 1713 proved favorable to the growth of Bordeaux's overseas trade. By the late 1730s, the city emerged as the main French port importing colonial goods, which were increasingly re-exported to northern Europe. The value of its maritime trade multiplied tenfold over the course of the century, and its population grew threefold.[61] Northern European merchants based in Bordeaux dominated the export of local wines and the re-export of colonial commodities to their home ports. In the 1780s, 240 vessels left Bordeaux every year for the West Indies and 20 to 30 for Africa, where they embarked slaves destined to

---

On the way the French Crown conceived the administration of the colonies, see Marzagalli, "The French Atlantic World," 242–243.

[59] Cited in Théophile Malvezin, *Histoire des Juifs de Bordeaux* (Bordeaux: Lefebvre, 1875), 179.

[60] On the German merchant community in Bordeaux, see Alfred Leroux, *La colonie germanique de Bordeaux*, vol. 1: *de 1462 à 1870* (Bordeaux: E. Feret, 1918); Paul Butel, "Les négociants allemands de Bordeaux dans la deuxième moitié du XVIIIᵉ siècle," in *Wirtschaftskräfte in der europäischen Expansion*, ed. Hermann Kellenbenz and Jürgen Schneider (Stuttgart: Klett-Cotta, 1978), 589–613; Wolfgang Henninger, *Studien zur Wirtschafts- und Sozialgeschichte von Bordeaux im 18. Jahrhundert unter besonderer Berücksichtigung der deutschen Kaufleute: Schriftliche Hausarbeit für die Erste Staatsprüfung*, Unpublished dissertation, University of Köln, 1986; Michel Espagne, *Bordeaux-Baltique: La présence culturelle allemande à Bordeaux aux XVIIIᵉ et XIXᵉ siècles* (Paris: CNRS, 1991); Henninger, *Johann Jacob von Bethmann*; Peter Voss, *Bordeaux et les villes hanséatiques, 1672–1715: Contribution à l'histoire maritime de l'Europe du Nord-Ouest*, 2 vols., Ph.D. thesis, Université de Bordeaux 3, 1995; Alain Ruiz, ed., *Présence de l'Allemagne à Bordeaux du siècle de Montaigne à la veille de la Seconde Guerre mondiale* (Pessac: Presses Universitaires de Bordeaux, 1997); Weber, *Deutsche Kaufleute*. Dutch merchants were very influential in Bordeaux in the late seventeenth century, but ceased to play a major role in the city's overseas trade in the eighteenth century, except for their continued interest in wine: Peter Voss, "Une communauté sur le déclin? Les marchands hollandais à Bordeaux, 1650–1715," *Bulletin du Centre d'Histoire des Espaces Atlantiques*, 7 (1995): 33–57. .

[61] The city had 45,000 inhabitants in 1700 and 110,000 in 1790. On Bordeaux's rapid economic growth in the eighteenth century, see Paul Butel, *Les négociants bordelais, l'Europe et les Iles au XVIIIᵉ siècle* (Paris: Mouton,

the American plantations. These commercial branches were exclusively in French hands, but not exclusively in Catholic hands. Between 1782 and 1789, 324 different Bordeaux merchant houses fitted out a total of 1,597 ships to the West Indies. Of these, a mere 32 firms (10 percent of the total) fitted out at least 10 ships, totaling 588 voyages, or 37 percent of the total. Among this merchant élite, there were French Huguenots (Boyer, Barthez, and Bonnaffé), French Catholics (Lavaud, Testard & Gachet, and Cochon & Troplong), a naturalized Portuguese Jewish firm (the Raba brothers), and naturalized Northern Protestants (Draveman, Eyma frères, and Romberg, Bapst, & Co.).[62] Naturalization—but not a full embrace of Catholicism—was required to trade with the colonies.[63]

If colonial trade absorbed the entire capacity of Bordeaux's merchant fleet and most of the city's commercial capital, re-export trade to northern Europe was carried on foreign ships, as in the previous centuries.[64] The city's prosperity relied on extensive international trade, which in turn was sustained by the many foreign and non-Catholic merchant communities that resided in Bordeaux and their connections to other European ports. In the 1780s, Sephardim, Germans, Dutch, and Irish (some Catholic and some Protestant) made up a third of Bordeaux's overall merchants. Moreover, a significant portion of the French firms were run by crypto-Huguenots, who, until the Toleration Act of 1787, had to hide their religious persuasion but often inter-married with the families of openly Protestant merchants from northern Europe residing in Bordeaux. The latter grew increasingly conscious

---

1974); Figeac, *Histoire des Bordelais*, vol. 1: *La modernité triomphante*; François-Georges Pariset, ed., *Histoire de Bordeaux*, 8 vols., vol. 5: *Bordeaux au XVIIIᵉ siècle* (Bordeaux: FHSO, 1968).

[62] Viles, *The Shipping Interest of Bordeaux*, 215–217. The five Raba brothers arrived in Bordeaux in 1763 from Lisbon. Shortly thereafter, they were circumcised; in 1779, they obtained a certificate of Catholicism and French naturalization before sailing to Saint-Domingue. A letter of naturalization was necessary because New Christian merchants in the colonies were not protected by the 1550 patents that applied to them within the jurisdiction of Bordeaux's *parlement*.

[63] All persons born in France—and, by the mid-sixteenth century, children born abroad from French parents—were considered French subjects (*régnicole*). All other individuals living in France could suffer from legal, economic, and political restrictions. Particularly aggravating was the king's right to seize the inheritance of all foreigners who died on French soil (*droit d'aubaine*). Economic restrictions concerned access to specific positions. Most (but not all) of other restrictions affecting foreigners could be levied by a letter of naturalization, a costly procedure by which the king granted his protection to a foreigner. The letter of naturalization was granted to an individual and did not apply to other family members. This norm varied from place to place, as some cities and provinces were exempted from the *droit d'aubaine*, and some groups of foreigners, or people who benefited from bilateral treaties between their countries or other legal decisions, could be exempted. This was the case, among others, in Bordeaux. See Marzagalli, "L'évolution de la politique française"; Peter Sahlins, *Unnaturally French: Foreign Citizens in the Old Regime and After* (Ithaca, NY: Cornell University Press, 2004).

[64] For example, of the 221 ships leaving Bordeaux for Amsterdam, Bremen, or Hamburg in 1787, only 6 were French. Data extracted from the database Navigocorpus, a project financed by the French Agence Nationale

of their importance, as demonstrated by the report they addressed to the king in 1765 asking for permission to build a temple.[65]

Foreign merchants in Bordeaux, most of whom were not Catholics, enjoyed favorable conditions. They were exempted from the *droit d'aubaine*, a traditional privilege according to which the French Crown inherited the estates of all foreigners who died in the kingdom. Immigrants from the Hanseatic towns, the United Provinces, Denmark, and Sweden also benefited from a reduction of import and export duties. Jews—referred to as Portuguese New Christians since 1550, but officially recognized as Jews after 1723—enjoyed virtually the same rights as native Frenchmen as far as trade was concerned.[66] They could also obtain the title of *bourgeois de Bordeaux*, which conferred additional commercial privileges, notably in the wine trade.[67] This relatively tolerant policy toward Jews in Bordeaux and Bayonne—an exception compared to other parts of France—was inspired by economic reasons, just as in other major port-cities like Amsterdam or Livorno.

Some of these privileges extended to French Huguenots as well, although in theory no subject of the French king was supposed to be a Calvinist after 1685 and until the Toleration Act of 1787. Exceptions, however, were made. Louis XV, for instance, elevated the affluent Bordeaux merchant and shipowner Jacques-Alexandre Laffon de Ladebat to noble status in 1773, even though he was a Huguenot. After 1767, every year the French king ennobled two individuals who had distinguished themselves for their commercial entrepreneurship. In doing so, the monarchy stressed the utility of trade for the French state and society and promoted the compatibility of wholesale trade and noble status—a principle that the French Crown sought to advance since the 1620s, with moderate success as far as the conversion of ancient noble families to shipping and trade was concerned. The fact that the Crown occasionally conferred noble titles on Protestant merchants proves that in the eighteenth century confessional concerns were increasingly subordinated to the principle of

---

de la Recherche and coordinated by Silvia Marzagalli (sources: Archives Nationales, Paris, G5, 50). The database can be accessed at http://navigocorpus.org/.

[65] They wrote that Bordeaux could only compete in international trade thanks to foreigners who enjoyed the trust of their compatriots and were the only ones to receive commissions. See Bruno de Coulon de Labrousse, *Le statut juridique des protestants de Bordeaux (1598–1787)*, Unpublished Thèse d'État, Université de Bordeaux I, 1974, 844.

[66] On the history of the Jews of Bordeaux, see Frances Malino, *The Sephardic Jews of Bordeaux: Assimilation and Emancipation in Revolutionary and Napoleonic France* (Tuscaloosa: University of Alabama Press, 1978).

[67] This status was hereditary and granted to propertied citizens who resided in Bordeaux for a number of years. In order to become a *bourgeois*, one had to be Catholic. Before 1679, however, a number of Sephardim acquired the title because they were officially New Christians, that is, nominally Catholic. Between 1722 and 1752, out of a total of 350 new *bourgeois*, there were only four Portuguese, all merchants, likely Jews of sufficient reputation to be admitted in spite of their religious affiliation. Other prominent Jewish merchants already possessed the title of *bourgeois*, having inherited it from their fathers before Judaism was recognized in 1723. See

public utility. The case of Laffon is not unique.[68] Most of the financiers who enabled the French monarchy to survive multiple fiscal crises were Protestants.[69] The king, moreover, repeatedly granted colonial and military supply contracts to Jewish and Protestant commercial houses in Bordeaux, notably during the Seven Years' War.[70]

Restrictive colonial and religious policies, in sum, did not prevent the development of a largely multi-confessional and multi-religious merchant community in Old Regime Bordeaux. This is hardly surprising, as it conforms to a trend visible in most Atlantic port-cities, including Cadiz, Nantes, London, Amsterdam, and Hamburg, but is also common to cities beyond the Atlantic World, such as Livorno or Saint Petersburg. The specificity of the French case lies in the commercial influence of French Protestants, although their existence was officially forbidden for over a century. In this sense, economic realities fostered a de facto toleration. Far from hindering the growth of overseas colonial trade and the Caribbean plantation economy, and of the French economy more generally, "the most Christian king" sought to strike the right balance between religious orthodoxy and fiscal and commercial pragmatism. Under these circumstances, and given the considerable presence of non-Catholic merchants in France, the case of Bordeaux urges us to reconsider the assumption that French merchants traded essentially with members of their own confessions and religious groups. The point is not so much to demonstrate that colonial and international trade was a multi-confessional business, but to rethink the implications of the coexistence in the same city of merchants who did not share the same religious affiliations. Transactions across confessional and religious lines were a daily experience on the floor of the Exchange, where goods changed hands, insurance contracts were underwritten, and shipping ventures were planned; these transactions were essential to reach many of the suppliers in the city's hinterland, who were French Calvinists. The problem is that historians have been attracted by

Georges Cirot, *Les Juifs de Bordeaux, leur situation morale et sociale de 1550 à la Révolution* (Bordeaux: Féret, 1920), 35–37.

[68] Xavier Caron, "Images d'une élite au XVIIIème siècle: Quarante négociants anoblis face à la question sociale," *Histoire Économie Société*, 3.3 (1984): 381–426, lists 14 Protestant merchants who were ennobled out of a total of 40.

[69] On the decisive role that Protestant bankers played in both the general French economy and the royal finances in particular, see Herbert Lüthy, *La Banque protestante en France de la Révocation de l'Édit de Nantes à la Révolution*, 2 vols. (Paris: SEVPEN, 1959–1961).

[70] J. F. Bosher, "Financing the French Navy in the Seven Years War: Beaujon, Goossens and Compagnie in 1759," *Business History*, 28.3 (1986): 115–133; Silvia Marzagalli, "Bordeaux et le Canada, 1663–1773," in *Champlain ou les portes du Nouveau Monde: Cinq siècles d'échanges entre le Centre-Ouest français et l'Amérique du Nord (XVIᵉ–XXIᵉ s.),* ed. Mickaël Augeron and Dominique Guillemet (La Crèche: Geste, 2004), 207–212; idem, "Limites et opportunités"; idem, "De Grateloup à l'Élysée, en passant par Bordeaux: Ascension sociale et mobilité de la famille Beaujon aux XVIIᵉ–XVIIIᵉ siècles," in *Négoce, Ports et Océans: Mélanges offerts à Paul Butel,* ed. Silvia Marzagalli and Hubert Bonin (Pessac: Presses Universitaires de Bordeaux, 2000), 15–28.

transoceanic and international trade much more than by the nature of business that happened in the city itself and in its immediate surroundings.

CONCLUSION

Recent research has pushed the conceptual and empirical boundaries of our understanding of cross-cultural trade, but we are far from understanding how cross-religious and trans-confessional trade really worked among merchants operating within the same legal system. In most early modern French port cities, merchants had the opportunity to enter into contractual relations with members of other confessions and religions on a regular basis. This chapter has discussed scattered but ubiquitous evidence indicating that cross-religious and trans-confessional business was more common than is currently assumed.

More in-depth research than the one I have discussed here is needed to confirm, nuance, or refute my preliminary conclusions. In the absence of solid studies that examine the trans-confessional and cross-religious nature of French business, I have drawn upon the evidence currently available for Bordeaux and have examined it in light of the general features of the religious, commercial, and colonial policies adopted by the French state during the last century or so of the Old Regime. I have concluded that the French Crown and local authorities tolerated the presence of non-Catholic merchants both in the kingdom and in the colonies as long as it proved economically beneficial, and thus multiplied the occasions for trans-confessional and cross-religious business ventures. Moreover, economic actors manipulated and reinterpreted the existing legislation and ultimately shaped an original, pragmatic commercial world in which religious and confessional concerns could become secondary.

We still need to understand better when and why merchants chose to do businesses with coreligionists and when they were open to alternatives. This chapter has suggested some hypotheses, which await further substantiation. If it turns out that cross-religious and trans-confessional interactions were not confined to a few commercial houses involved in long-distance trade but were an ordinary phenomenon, we will need to shelve current assumptions (which, I fear, are close to becoming orthodoxy) about the intra-confessional nature of early modern French business networks. In pursuing this line of research, we will also be able to promote truly comparative studies of major European cities and ports and assess their respective openness or closure to a multi-confessional and cross-religious commercial society.

8

Coins and Commerce

MONETIZATION AND CROSS-CULTURAL COLLABORATION IN THE WESTERN INDIAN OCEAN (ELEVENTH TO THIRTEENTH CENTURIES)

Roxani Eleni Margariti

After the value is specified, turn everything into cash, gold and silver, nothing else, divide it among various merchants, our associates (*aṣḥābinā*) or others, as long as they are well-known and reliable, and send it on.[1]
(A prominent Jewish merchant from Aden, writing to his brother-in-law in Cairo, twelfth century)

Scripture has said: Never trust Gentiles.[2]
(Another Jewish merchant from Aden, complaining to his Jewish business partner, twelfth century)

---

[1] Bodleian Library (hereafter Bodl.), MS Heb a3 (Cat 2873), fol. 19, lines 41–44: "*fa idhā ṣāra dirham maʿlūm kāna al-awḍ naqd dhahab wa-fidda lā ghayr qasama dhālika wa-anfadha minhu shay maʿ baʿḍ al-tujjār aṣḥābinā aw ghayrihim al-maʿrūfīn al-thiqāt.*" For a full translation that differs from mine slightly and analysis, see S. D. Goitein and Mordechai Akiva Friedman, *India Traders of the Middle Ages: Documents from the Cairo Geniza; "India Book"* (Leiden: Brill 2008), 374–375.

[2] Cambridge, Taylor Schechter Collection (hereafter T-S), 18J5, f. 5, line 3: "*wa-qad qāla al-kitāb lo emuna ba-goyim.*" See Goitein and Friedman, *India Traders,* 445–446 and note 40; previously discussed and quoted in S. D. Goitein, *A Mediterranean Society: The Jewish Communities of the Arab World as Reflected in the Documents of the Cairo Geniza,* 5 vols. (Berkeley: University of California Press, 1967–1993), 2: 275, 586n3.

INDIAN OCEAN MERCHANTS, STATES, AND COINAGES

Expansive, straddling a number of political divides, and linking the Indian Ocean with the Mediterranean, the so-called India trade of the early second millennium C.E. relied on an intricate concatenation of cross-regional merchant networks.[3] It entailed numerous, long-lasting, and diverse cross-cultural encounters, which varied in scale, transactional mechanics, and goals, as well as in the group and individual identities of their participants. Focusing on the period of increasing integration of the Mediterranean and Indian Ocean worlds between the tenth and the fifteenth century (conventionally referred to here as the medieval period), this chapter explores the role of coins in long-distance trade and specifically in the transactions between merchants who belonged to different ethnic and religious communities; these merchants were often based in different polities and operated under separate, and sometimes multiple, political authorities.[4]

The point of departure for this inquiry is the testimony of such businessmen, preserved serendipitously in the document repository known as the Cairo Geniza. Between the tenth and the thirteenth century, several generations of Arabic-speaking Jewish businessmen operating across the extended Islamic world left behind an invaluable paper trail of correspondence, legal documents, and other writs of everyday life.[5]

---

[3] The term "India trade" has been used to describe the commercial continuum that saw great expansion in the centuries following the unification of the Middle East by the Muslim conquests of the seventh and eighth centuries and that brought eastern spices, textiles, dye stuffs, and various other goods to the cities of the Islamic and Mediterranean worlds while channeling gold and some western products eastward. See, for example, Wilhelm Heyd, *Histoire du commerce du Levant au Moyen-Âge* (Leipzig: Harrassowitz, 1885); Eliahu Ashtor, *Social and Economic History of The Near East* (Berkeley: University of California Press, 1976), 108–109, 147–148, 197; André Wink, *Al-Hind: The Making of the Indo-Islamic World*, 3 vols. (Leiden: Brill, 1991–2003), 1: 25–64.

[4] The application of the term "medieval" to the histories of places around the Indian Ocean has been rightly criticized, yet none of the critics has proposed a workable alternative. See Daniel Martin Varisco, "The Study of 'Medieval' Yemen: Recent Work and Future Prospects," *Yemen Update* 32 (1993), 10–13, 34; Marshall G. S. Hodgson, *The Venture of Islam: The Classical Age of Islam*, 2 vols. (Chicago: University of Chicago Press, 1977), 1: 48–56. For broader criticism, see Lee Patterson, "On the Margin: Postmodernism, Ironic History, and Medieval Studies," *Speculum* 65 (1990), 92–93. For an application of the term in an Indian Ocean context, see Hermann Kulke and Dietmar Rothermund, *A History of India* (New York: Routledge 2010), xvi–xvii, 72.

[5] The bulk of the documentary material in the remarkable anti-archive of the Cairo Geniza relates to the economic and social lives of Mediterranean Jews, but a sub-corpus of some 460 documents is now in the process of becoming extensively published thanks to the efforts of Mordechai Freedman (and, recently, Amir Ashur), who edited, updated, and largely supplemented more than three decades of work on Geniza documents and the India trade by S. D. Goitein; see Goitein and Friedman, *India Traders*; eidem, *India Book I: Joseph al-Lebdi, Prominent India Trader* [Hebrew] (Jerusalem: Ben Zvi Institute, 2009); eidem, *India Book II: Madmun Nagid of Yemen and the India Trade* [Hebrew] (Jerusalem: Ben Zvi Institute, 2010); eidem, *India Book III: Ben Yiju, India Trader and Manufacturer* [Hebrew] (Jerusalem: Ben Zvi Institute, 2010); Mordechai Akiva Friedman, *India Book IVA: Halfon and Judah ha-Levi, the Lives of a Merchant Scholar and a Poet Laureate According to the Cairo Geniza Documents* [Hebrew] (Jerusalem: Ben Zvi Institute, 2013); and S.D. Goitein and Mordechai Akiva Friedman with the assistance of Amir Ashur, *India Book IVB: Halfon the Travelling Merchant Scholar, Cairo Geniza Documents* [Hebrew] (Jerusalem: Ben Zvi Institute, 2013).

Among other topics, the sub-corpus of this material that relates to the India trade illuminates some of the dynamics of merchants' encounters as experienced by members of this particular "trade diaspora."[6]

The epigraphs to this chapter, both excerpts from letters exchanged between Jewish traders in the twelfth century, offer two telling examples. The first one concerns assets belonging to the author, a leading Jewish merchant of Aden, which were dispatched to Egypt as part of a partnership between himself and the South Arabian port city's powerful Muslim governor. This Jewish-Muslim partnership mentioned explicitly earlier in the document showcases the possibility of business collaboration across lines of religion, while the particular quote highlighted here intimates the readiness of the author to entrust the transfer of funds—albeit on the crucial condition of familiarity and reliability—to individuals outside his and his correspondent's primary business network, which consisted primarily of coreligionists. These entrusted individuals could be fellow Jews, but the several documented instances in which Muslim and other non-Jewish traders were also entrusted with similar dispatches demonstrate that religion was not a barrier to being considered "well-known" and "reliable."

This same document also hints at the mechanics and goals of the circulation of cash. The author expects that the sale of the partnership assets will produce a specified monetary value, *dirham ma'lūm* (literally, "a known dirham," or silver coin). As Abraham L. Udovitch has demonstrated, the insistence on definition and transparency of partnership assets was a strong mandate in medieval Middle Eastern commercial legal theory.[7] Determination of value by reference to coinage was a method to achieve such specificity, and our document and others that utilize this expression serve as illustrations of this principle in practice.[8] "Gold" and "silver" here stand not for bullion but for gold and silver coin issues, expressed in the original by the term *naqd*. These would have been the gold and possibly silver issues struck in the name of the Fatimid sovereigns of Egypt; or, given the apparent deterioration in silver

---

[6] For Philip Curtin's discussion of this extended community as a trade diaspora engaged in cross-cultural trade, see his classic *Cross-Cultural Trade in World History* (Cambridge: Cambridge University Press, 1984), esp. 112–115, 158. Religious bonds constitute one of the classic characteristics of trade diasporas as these have been defined by Abner Cohen in "Cultural Strategies in the Organization of Trading Diasporas," in *The Development of Indigenous Trade and Markets in West Africa*, ed. Claude Meillassoux (London: International African Institute, 1971), 266–281, esp. 266–267 and 270.

[7] A. L. Udovitch, *Partnership and Profit in Medieval Islam* (Princeton, NJ: Princeton University Press, 1970), 180–181.

[8] The expression also appears as *dīnār ma'lūm*. See Bodl. MS Heb a3, f. 19, lines 40–44, instructions about selling merchandise and disposal of proceeds once they become *dirham ma'lūm*; T-S 6J3, f. 12, line 10, a transaction resulting in *dīnār ma'lūm*; and T-S 16.288, line 39, a dispatch of *dirham ma'lūm*.

coinage in the eastern part of North Africa in this period, the silver coins intended here may have been those struck by the Almoravid authorities of Morocco.[9] Copper, the third component of the theoretically tri-metallic currency system of the medieval Islamic world, is implicitly excluded from the transaction, and so are other items that might have taken the place of currency. This exclusion is not surprising. Gold and silver currency had a widely recognizable intrinsic value and a concomitant wide circulation and constituted the acceptable monetary medium in overseas trade; copper, on the other hand, was a fiduciary coin with very low and variable intrinsic value, for the most part limited to the monetization of local economies, and in any case very scarce in this period.[10] The overall effect of the transaction at hand is that precious metal coinage struck by Muslim authorities in the Mediterranean and frequently employed in the long-distance trade of the region is used to liquidate a range of commercial assets and will subsequently travel eastward to become part of what we might call the multi-denominational currency system of the Indian Ocean, a system in which discrete currency zones intersected and overlapped.

The second epigraph points in a different direction. Writing in Aden and accounting for a business loss, the details of which unfortunately remain unknown to us, the author resorts to a rhetorical summary dismissal of non-Jewish business associates. While the collaboration between a Jewish merchant and a Muslim potentate evidenced by the document of the first epigraph encourages us to consider the strands of connection that made cross-cultural collaboration possible, here the adversarial and dismissive attitude evinced toward non-Jews—who on the strength of other usage of the biblical term *goyim* in the Geniza, are to be understood as Muslims— reminds us to take into account the separateness of the groups involved and to ask when and how that separateness caused conflict and ruptures in the collaborations.[11]

Taken together, these two passages, and the body of documents to which they belong, speak to the ramifications of business associations across physical space and communal lines. The challenges to all collaboration in the context of trans-regional trade in this period were many. Meager information, slow communications, and unsafe transportation complicated decisions and their outcomes. These circumstances

---

[9] On silver and its metrological fluctuations in the later Fatimid period and the use of Almoravid silver denominations in the eastern half of North Africa and beyond, see Goitein, *A Mediterranean Society*, 1: 233–234, 380. Debased silver appears to have been used primarily for local transactions.

[10] For a foundational analysis of the preference for gold and silver coins and the debate concerning the admissibility of copper in capital formation in the normative Islamic legal texts on partnership, see Udovitch, *Partnership and Profit*, 52–55, 177–179. See also Udovitch, "Fals," *Encyclopaedia of Islam*, 2nd ed. (Leiden: Brill, 1965), 2: 768–769.

[11] Goitein, *A Mediterranean Society*, 2: 275, 278, 587n3. See also the lengthy discussion in Goitein and Friedman, *India Traders*, 133–134n55, and 446n40.

made it necessary to collaborate with diverse partners, while enabling mechanisms for minimizing the risk of conflict. Disputes in cross-cultural collaborations, more difficult to adjudicate than internal disputes, highlighted cultural or communal differences. Speedy disbursement of credit and debt could contribute to the easing of potential tensions in collaborations, making money extremely useful. Perhaps nothing served better than minted coins—with their power to assign value to complex assets, their portability, and their eminent transferability—to facilitate risky transactions between members of different faiths.

My inquiry into this topic—the particular role of coined money in cross-cultural business collaborations—ultimately aims at contributing to our understanding of how these connections worked in a formative period of the Indian Ocean interregional arena.[12] I will argue here that from the tenth century, monetization and expertise in handling diverse but shared instruments of trade, particularly the multi-denominational currency assemblages that I describe below, facilitated in a number of ways the forging of ties across a number of real and historiographically constructed divides. Thus before delving into how coins featured in commercial and cultural interaction, I will briefly examine some of the evidence for the role of religious and diasporic identity in the formation of the Indian Ocean's business communities and its historiographical ramifications; and I will propose that the legal and political fragmentation of the region provides an additional set of divides that coins helped to mitigate.

The two epigraphs suggest that religious belonging was one of the significant factors in forming business associations, and they include two of the most visible and commonly recognized trading groups: Jews and Muslims. The authors and recipients of the documents are Jews. In the first epigraph, the expression *aṣḥābinā* (from the term *aṣḥāb*, sing. *ṣāḥib*) most likely refers to fellow Jewish business associates, and has been translated in S. D. Goitein and Mordechai Friedman's definitive work as "our coreligionists." By translating this term instead with the more literal "associates," I highlight the fact that the expression in this context also denotes a specific kind of business relationship. Thus, while the *aṣḥāb* intended here appear to be fellow Jews, that is, coreligionists of the writer of the letter, we should not forget that the term's main function in business contexts is to refer to relationships that sometimes obtained with members of other confessional communities.[13] Beyond the

---

[12] While Sugata Bose uses the term "interregional arena" to denote cultural and economic "action and interaction" but not necessarily the conflict implicit in the original sense of the word "arena" as a place of combat, I prefer to include that original sense of contest, since I see competition and conflict as important elements both of the political configuration of the maritime polities that characterized this world in the period under investigation here and of the mercantile policies they pursued. Sugata Bose, *A Hundred Horizons: The Indian Ocean in the Age of Global Empire* (Cambridge, MA: Harvard University Press, 2006), 6, 285n8.

[13] This is not to deny that, to the best of my knowledge, no individual non-Jewish business partner is ever referred to as a *ṣāḥib* by the authors of Geniza business documents and in one case, in a Mediterranean

question of the identity of the particular *aṣḥāb* invoked by the writer of the first epigraph, that writer's main partner and joint owner of the assets in question is a Muslim potentate; the unspecified outsiders ("others" than "our associates") to be entrusted with the funds may be Muslims; and if the collectively branded *goyim* of the second epigraph are Muslims (which is likely given the standard use of the term in Geniza documents as mentioned earlier), so is the writer's erstwhile associate, whom he would have mentioned differently had the particular business deal not become a source of conflict.[14]

Though the religious identity of individuals mentioned in the documents is not always decipherable, due to cultural convergences and common naming patterns in the medieval Middle East, it is fair to say that the Jewish authors of Geniza papers often distinguished between themselves and their non-Jewish, especially Muslim, partners.[15] They sometimes described such "other" business links collectively as *al-muslimūn* ("the Muslims," or perhaps more specifically intended, "the Muslim traders"). In one late eleventh-century document, the Muslim colleagues of a Cairo-based India trader are explicitly subdivided into "Egyptian" and "Indian" Muslims, adding geographical nuance to the clearly larger category of non-Jewish associates; again, association with Muslims is set apart from association with members of the Jewish traders' own community.[16] Another indication that this was so is the explicit awareness of at least one distinction between Jewish and Muslim

context of the mid-eleventh century, a Jewish businessman appears to be using this term to express the dividing line between himself and a Christian partner. Goitein translates the operative line as "He is a Christian and I am a Jew—he is not my companion (*ṣāḥibī*)," and notes that with this twice repeated statement the author tries "to make it clear that he was not responsible for the misbehavior of his Christian business friend." Goitein, *A Mediterranean Society,* 2: 275, 586n3. I discuss the identities of "non-Jewish" associates of Jewish merchants in the Indian Ocean as well as the concept of *ṣuḥba* in "Aṣḥābunā l-tujjār— Our Associates, the Merchants: Non-Jewish Business Partners of the Cairo Geniza's India Traders," in *Jews, Christians and Muslims in Medieval and Early Modern Times: A Festschrift in Honor of Mark R. Cohen,* ed. Arnold Franklin, Roxani Eleni Margariti, Marina Rustow, and Uriel Simonsohn (Leiden: Brill, 2014), 40–58.

[14] Margariti, "Aṣḥābunā l-tujjār," 47.

[15] Jews and Muslims of the extended Islamic world shared culture and a language (Arabic) and drew upon overlapping folk, literary, and scriptural traditions, and, among other things, a shared pool of personal names. These intense cultural convergences and overall cultural commensurability in turn support recent critiques against projecting hard lines of division and difference back in time to Indian Ocean peoples whose identity may have been more flexible and inclusive. See Alka Patel, *Building Communities in Gujarat: Architecture and Society during the Twelfth through Fourteenth Centuries* (Leiden: Brill, 2004); and Finbarr Flood, *Objects of Translation: Material Culture and Medieval "Hindu-Muslim" Encounter* (Princeton, NJ: Princeton University Press, 2009).

[16] T-S 13 J6, f. 32, lines 11–13. This legal document, dated to the late eleventh century, discusses the dispatch of a sum of money apparently realized in the course of an association between the subject of the document, India trader Joseph al-Lebdī, and the Muslim merchants mentioned here. See Goitein and Friedman, *India Traders,* 227, 237; Goitein and Friedman, *India Book I,* 143–144.

partnership laws, as expressed by the Judeo-Arabic term *qirāḍ al-goyim*, contextually translating into "partnership agreement according to Islamic law." The *qirāḍ* was a legal instrument of business association and risk sharing that Jews employed in its "more practicable" Islamic law variety, while acknowledging by the above expression that doing so meant crossing a line that separated them from their neighbors.[17] These and other expressions, as well as the stated and implicit preference for associating with coreligionists, suggest that the identity lines between Jews and Muslims were clear and played a role in the formation of business networks.

In addition to the testimony of the unique documentary corpus of the Cairo Geniza and the Jewish voices it represents, a number of other sources can be marshaled to support the conclusion that religious belonging mattered to merchants and affected their choice of associates. In the late tenth century, Buzurg b. Shahriyār, the author of a unique collection of Muslim sailors' tales, delights in the otherness of the "Indian" customs that those sailors encountered once they left the Arabian seaboard and the Persian Gulf.[18] Sanskrit, Tamil, and multilingual inscriptional records dating from the ninth century onward from the western coast of India collectively outline the rights, responsibilities, and special status of diverse religious communities living under the authority of brahmanic potentates.[19] Somewhat later than the period under investigation here, the terms of separateness of the established Muslim groups in western India feature prominently in the travel account of Ibn Baṭṭūṭa.[20] This kind of testimony has encouraged scholars

---

[17] On the *qirāḍ*, its equivalency with the western *commenda*, its Jewish version (*'isqā*), and the use of the expression *qirāḍ al-goyim*, see Goitein, *A Mediterranean Society*, 1: 171. On Islamic legal discussions about the issues with "interdenominational" *commenda*, and the legal instrument of the *qirāḍ* in theory and practice, see Udovitch, *Partnership and Profit*, 170–248.

[18] Buzurg b. Shahriyār, *The Book of the Wonders of India: Mainland, Sea, and Islands*, ed. G. P. S. Freeman-Grenville (London: East West Publications, 1981), esp. 1–3, 69, 86, 91.

[19] An example of the ambiguities that these records entail is the so-called Ravi Sthanu inscriptions of the city of Quilon (Kūlam), dating to sometime in the tenth century. The Tamil text mentions privileges extended by the local Kerala ruler to a group that has been identified with a Christian church spatially separated from the city, and is witnessed by signatures in Arabic, Hebrew, and Pahlavi. Identified tentatively with Christians, Muslims, Jews, "Arab Jews," and Zoroastrians, the signatories in question are all witnesses of a document that grants trade and other economic and social privileges to a certain Christian group, and must therefore benefit from the arrangement and be connected with the group in question; yet the very identities and boundaries of the groups are hard to define. Thus, Meera Abraham concludes rather vaguely that "the signatures appended to the grant including those of Zoroastrians and Muslims and also possibly Jews and Christians tell us something of the composition of this group of foreigners, traders who were either established in Quilon or who had commercial links with the city in the 9th and 10th centuries"; see Meera Abraham, *Two Medieval Merchant Guilds of South India* (New Dehli: Manohar 1988), 21–33, 36. In the subsequent centuries, study of trading groups thought to have come to dominate trading activity in India by the fifteenth century tends to focus on groups defined by a complex of religion and geography. The Muslim Mappilas and Pardesis of Malabar, and the Hindu Chettis and Banyas of the Coromandel and Gujarat, respectively, emerge as the dominant trade groups and appear to have monopolized overseas commerce in their respective territories; see Wink, *Al-Hind*, 74–75.

[20] Ibn Baṭṭūṭa, *The Travels of Ibn Baṭṭūṭa, A.D. 1325–1354*, ed. H. A. R. Gibb (London: Hakluyt Society, 1994), 4: 807–813.

of the social and economic history of the Indian Ocean to describe the loosely defined trans-regional economic system in terms of diasporic merchant groups aligned primarily along lines of religious affiliation.[21]

What has not been adequately addressed in this literature is how associations and transactions worked across these lines in the medieval period, how long-distance merchants of different faiths and different diasporic identities entered into short- and long-term agreements with each other. In addition to religious and diasporic identity itself, there are two other factors to consider with respect to what we might call cross-cultural interaction. The first has to do with the legal structures under which these merchants operated. In the context of the medieval Indian Ocean, different communities of faith meant theoretically separate systems of rules governing transactions and associations. The sway of personal, as opposed to territorial, law in the context of medieval Islamic states meant that the adjudication of relationships was first and foremost situated within the purview of the religious community. In the non-Islamic polities of the western coast of India, corporate groups of various kinds, including both elite (brahmanic) groups and what have been described as the "intermediate corporate groups" of traders and merchants, exercised discrete legal authority, an authority that appears to have increased in the period in question.[22] The trading and mercantile groups included clusters of foreign merchants, several of which appear to have been incorporated on the basis of religious affiliation (examples of Christian, Jewish, Muslim, Jain, Hindu, Parsee merchants). Witnessing, documentation, confirmation of transactions, and adjudication of disputes between members of different communities are not well understood but must have necessitated the creation of mercantile space and of instruments and mechanisms of transactions that were recognized by everyone.

The second factor that impacted identity, personal allegiances, and interaction pertains to political authority. Between the tenth and the thirteenth century, the merchants of the Indian Ocean not only belonged to a wide variety of confessional

---

[21] I am thinking of Patricia Risso's work on Muslim merchants across the Indian Ocean, André Wink's survey of diasporic communities on the Indian littoral, S. D. Goitein's and now Mordechai Friedman's work on the Arabic-speaking Jewish traders, and even older works, such as George Hourani's survey of Arab Muslim maritime history and trade in the Indian Ocean. See Patricia Risso, *Merchants and Faith: Muslim Commerce and Culture in the Indian Ocean* (Boulder, CO: Westview Press 1995); André Wink, *Al-Hind*, vol. 1; Goitein and Friedman, *India Traders*; and George F. Hourani, *Arab Seafaring In the Indian Ocean in Ancient and Early Medieval Time* (Princeton, NJ: Princeton University Press, 1995).

[22] On the "intermediate-level corporate groups," their "increased prominence...in the creation and administration of law," the interaction of these laws with the normative brahmanic legal discourse, and the implications of these phenomena for the dynamism of medieval India, see Donald Davis, "Intermediate Realms of Law: Corporate Groups and Rulers in Medieval India," *Journal of Economic and Social History of the Orient* 48 (2005), 92–117.

communities, but also operated in a very fragmented geopolitical landscape: a series of port city-states that dominated the western Indian Ocean littoral and maintained complex relationships with polities in their hinterlands. Earlier, the rise and development of a powerful caliphate in the Middle East and North Africa between the seventh and tenth centuries had erased the tumultuous frontier between the two rival empires of the Byzantines and the Sassanians and had unified the space that had previously been divided between them, signaling a new era in the conduct of trade linking the Indian Ocean and the Mediterranean. With the disintegration of the Abbasid caliphate, this unity was disrupted but trade continued to flourish and accelerate, partly thanks to a string of port cities along the coasts of Arabia, Persia, East Africa, and western India, which served as hubs and where markets and services made it possible for traders to make a variety of choices about the scope and volume of their enterprises. Thus, in the period under investigation here, the scene was dominated not by the relatively large and unified territorial states that developed later (the trade-oriented Rasulids of Yemen from the second quarter of the thirteenth century onward, and to some extent the Delhi Sultanate in the north and west of India, and the Vijayanagaran kingdom in the south slightly later), but by autonomous or semi-autonomous trade-oriented city-states that controlled much of the maritime traffic involved in trans-regional commerce: the Swahili states of the African seaboard, autonomous and semi-autonomous port city polities such as Aden in the Arabian peninsula, Siraf, Sohar, and later Kish in the Persian Gulf, and a variety of similarly semi-independent entities controlling the port cities of the western Indian seaboard.[23] In social and economic terms, these could be described as "polyglot emporia containing ethnically and religiously heterogeneous populations."[24] While the political nature of these polities has not been fully understood yet, it is clear that each asserted some kind of authority over parts of trade routes, levied customs duties, and imposed a variety of regulations on the merchants who traded there. These impositions but also networking opportunities offered by the existence of trade-oriented states made collaboration between resident and non-resident merchants crucial to the success of trading ventures for all.

---

[23] For East Africa, see Chapurukha Kusimba, *The Rise and Fall of the Swahili States* (New Delhi: Altamira, 1999); Mark Horton and John Middleton, *The Swahili: The Social Landscape of a Mercantile Society* (Oxford: Blackwell, 2000). For the Gulf of Aden, see Margariti, *Aden*. For Oman and the Persian Gulf, see Valeria Piacentini, "Merchant Families in the Gulf: A Mercantile and Cosmopolitan Dimension, the Written Evidence (11th–13th Centuries A.D.)," *ARAM Periodical* 11 (1999-2000): 145–159. For the Indian seaboard, see Wink, *Al-Hind*, 1: 73–78; Brajadulal Chattopadhyaya, *Coins and Currency Systems in South India, c. A.D. 225–1300* (New Delhi: Munshiram Manoharlal 1977), 126–127.

[24] I borrow the phrase from Finbarr Flood, who applies it more specifically to the cities on the Abbasid frontier with the non-Muslim polities of medieval India; see Flood, *Objects of Translation*, 17.

This same fragmented political configuration produced a wide array of coins, which the activities of Indian Ocean merchants brought into intersecting monetary orbits. I suggest that the skill to recognize and utilize this constellation of coinage was one that helped to integrate the merchants into a single network, thus transcending the very divisions that the issuing of coins represented. Coins were inscribed with the symbols of the political authority under which they were issued. For the eponymous authority coinage actively fulfilled two important functions: it asserted that authority's claims of sovereignty and broad allegiances and it served as an economic tool that allowed the state to meet its payment and tribute obligations and to participate in trade.[25] In its former function, coinage accentuated difference as the distinct affiliations and ideology of each sponsoring authority were literally inscribed on the coin. Thus coins could be seen as delineating boundaries between the states and cultures that produced them and that included ideologies with rival claims of political and moral authority. As David Wasserstein posits, Islamic coins bore discourse that rendered them "boundary markers in the symbolic universe of Islam."[26]

While the Arabic legends of Islamic coins asserted differences both among Islamic states and between Islamic and non-Islamic polities, their mode of production and their wide circulation transcended these same boundaries. The production of coins was sponsored but not micromanaged by the authorities named on them, and their circulation was effected primarily through the activities of merchants in zones much broader than those controlled by these authorities. As Michael Bates has eloquently and convincingly argued from the vantage point of Islamic numismatics, the first of these realities resulted in a variety of legends and metrological characteristics that ultimately cautions us not to privilege the message-bearing capacity of the coins.[27] Circulation, by contrast, was a result of the coins' more important, economic role.

---

[25] In Islamic contexts, *sikka,* or the making of coins, was a theoretical correlate and prerogative of political power, and presented as such in Islamic political theory. On the ground, the striking of coins required more than the sanction of a ruler. Michael L. Bates provides a lucid corrective to the notion that rulers issued coins, and explicates the relationship between eponymous authorities and the entrepreneurial production of coins; see his "Methodology in Islamic Numismatics," *As-Sikka: The Online Journal for the Islamic Coins Group* 2–3 (2000) http://web.archive.org/web/20110707064710/http://islamiccoinsgroup.50g.com/. See also John Meloy, "Money and Sovereignty in Mecca: Issues of the Sharifs in the Fifteenth and Sixteenth Centuries," *Journal of Economic and Social History of the Orient* 53 (2010): 712–738, 712–713. In broader terms, and as Keith Hart argues in his seminal paper on the anthropology of money, thinking of money as only one thing—i.e., an impersonal means of exchange that reduces interpersonal relationships to their bare minimum of economic transactions—or as only its opposite—i.e., as instruments of the state that issues it and as tokens of relationships between that state and its participants—does not do justice to the plurality of functions and meanings money can acquire; see his "Heads or Tails? Two Sides of the Coin," *Man* 21 (1986): 637–656.

[26] David Wasserstein, "Coins as Agents of Cultural Definition in Islam," *Poetics Today* 14 (1993): 303–322, 305.

[27] Bates, "Methodology in Islamic Numismatics."

A particularly strong effect of coin circulation in the region, under way by the tenth century, is the infiltration of Islamic coinage, both Mediterranean and indigenous Indian Ocean issues of the new mints of the region, into discrete currency zones all around the western Indian Ocean, which blurred the boundaries between coining states and cultures. Moreover, the "hybrid" nature of the material cultures, including the coinages, of the littorals and hinterlands of the Indian Ocean world demonstrates that in reality the boundary-marking capacity of coinage was often complicated and overshadowed by the capacity to both transfer and absorb motifs and ideas.[28] In their purely transactional function, these same coins unified the politically fragmented Indian Ocean realm. Their Islamic legends were commonly recognized across lines of difference within the Islamic world, while beyond those borders the less discursive characteristics of their metrology (metal type, weight, and fineness) allowed them to pass everywhere. The agency and cross-cultural association of the merchants that handled the coins and communicated their value created and sustained this system.

In short, evidence of robust and sustained collaboration between members of different religious communities supports the prevalent view of the pre-modern Indian Ocean as a space of cultural harmony and hybridity; at the same time, evidence of assertion of difference hint at possible fault lines that contribute to the shape of conflict. It is therefore important to attempt to define what strands held together cross-cultural collaborations, a necessarily speculative task, as these types of collaborations were far less well documented and understood than those that remained within the fold of religious-communal axes of belonging. I contend that the attested mutual assistance and the few cases of formal partnership across cultural lines engendered in themselves another "axis of belonging," a kind of merchant identity bolstered variously by additional non-religious bonds such as general geographical provenance and specific urban affiliation.[29] Merchant identity involved, among other things, expertise in handling money, and it is with the aim to elucidate how this expertise contributed to interactions with merchants of different communities that I raise the following questions. What was the extent of monetization of the Indian Ocean seaborne trade? Given the diverse jurisdictions and spheres of influence of

---

[28] The best work on this topic is by Finbarr Flood, who addresses Wasserstein's points on boundary marking; see Flood, *Objects of Translation*, 39–59.

[29] Alka Patel has demonstrated the intersecting axes of belonging that allowed for Indian craftsmen building in the Maru-Gurjara tradition—that evolved partly in temple building patronized by Hindu elites in medieval Gujarat—to apply their skills to commissions by Muslim merchant communities for the building of the earliest Islamic buildings in the region. The lack of insular and monolithic identities produced shared sacred space architecture and fostered bonds between members of heterodox groups that are now beginning to be described; see Patel, *Building Communities in Gujarat*.

medieval Indian Ocean states and the multiple associations of merchants active in this system, how did the use of coins facilitate the crossing of multiple boundaries (including culture)? Finally, what kinds of conflict potential did coins generate, and how can we conceptualize the ways in which coin usage not only obviated such conflict potential but actually contributed to a blurring of cultural lines? In what follows I address the first two questions, and will return briefly to the last question in my conclusions.

MONETIZATION AND MULTI-DENOMINATIONAL CURRENCY ZONES: EVIDENCE AND PROBLEMS

Implicitly or explicitly, the common assumption regarding the monetary profile of medieval Indian Ocean trade is that significant monetization of the trans-regional economy begins in earnest only in the course of the thirteenth century. This assumption tends to overshadow the evidence for earlier use of coinage in trade and to sidestep the question of the degree and significance of monetization in a formative stage of trans-regional economic integration. In one of the few studies devoted specifically to networks of monetized exchange in the pre- and early modern Indian Ocean and to the numismatics of the region as a whole (rather than those of one of its constituent parts), monetary historian Najaf Haider argues that after the thirteenth century, "a surge in the circulation of metallic and bill money to finance exchange" promoted the integration of the Indian Ocean system and the region's nexus with the Mediterranean world.[30] This conclusion appears to be based partly on the surge *in direct evidence* for coins and monetized transactions starting in the early thirteenth century but does not address the methodological dilemmas posed by indirect evidence and evidentiary gaps concerning earlier stages of monetization.

The challenge in deciphering the nature of monetary exchange in the region before the thirteenth century is partly due to the less explicit, or simply less abundant and more fragmentary, evidence. In the context of Indian economic history, scholars have met this challenge by revisiting the neglected numismatics of this period, producing systematic corpuses of the relevant evidence, and combining the study of direct and indirect evidence of coinage; the result has been at the very least a new awareness of the significance of monetized exchange before the thirteenth century. The traditional view of the economy in early medieval India has been that there was a contraction of economic activity; economic life was dominated by agrarian

---

[30] Najaf Haider, "The Network of Monetary Exchange in the Indian Ocean Trade, 1200–1700," in *Cross Currents and Community Networks: The History of the Indian Ocean World*, ed. Himanshu Prabha Ray and Edward A. Alpers (New Delhi: Oxford University Press, 2007), 181–205, 181.

production with slow and localized rhythms, exchange was characterized by barter, and cash was scarcely used. Starting in the mid-1970s, however, this view has been challenged. Economic historian Brajadulal Chattopadhyaya published the first detailed account and analysis of South Indian currency systems between the third and the fourteenth centuries, and by utilizing a wide variety of sources, pointed to the fact that from the tenth century onward, coin usage surfaces at all levels of economic activity—local, regional, and trans-regional.[31] Almost two decades later, John Deyell's study of northern India in the period between the eighth and the thirteenth century also highlighted the evidence for monetary exchange in the context of what had previously been understood as a money-starved landscape.[32] "Living without silver," Deyell suggests, does not mean trading without coins. On the contrary, acute shortages in bullion and the concomitantly declining quality and quantity of recorded coins are not necessarily signs of a slow, inward-looking, non-monetized economy; they can also signal an "excess of demand over supply."[33] In addition, to help us think about visible and invisible monetization for the region as a whole, these two studies also offer remarkable insights into the importance of mixed currency systems, an aspect of pre-modern Indian Ocean monetization that this chapter seeks to establish and explain.

A related difficulty is presented by the compartmentalized record of coins and coinages, with disparate studies rooted in discrete and discretely examined parts of the ocean. To the geographical and political boundaries, one needs to add a marked historiographical segmentation that develops along perceived cultural lines. Thus Islamic numismatics are treated separately from Indian numismatics, again not without solid methodological and practical reasons but also not without attendant blindspots. Michael McCormick's imposing work on the early medieval Mediterranean economy reveals that long-standing and sophisticated discussions of intersecting currency systems play a major role in the understanding of mobility and exchange in European and Mediterranean medieval economies.[34] A comparably

---

[31] Brajadulal Chattopadhyaya, *Coins and Currency Systems,* esp. 124ff. To borrow Michael McCormick's useful methodological distinction, Chattopadhyaya relied on "virtual coins" (that is, coins attested in textual sources) to make inferences about the use of the scarcer "real coins" (that is, actual coin finds). Michael McCormick, *Origins of the European Economy: Communications and Commerce A.D. 300–900* (Cambridge: Cambridge University Press, 2001), 319ff.

[32] John Deyell, *Living Without Silver: The Monetary History of Early Medieval North India* (Delhi: Oxford University Press, 1990).

[33] Deyell, *Living Without Silver,* 2.

[34] Michael McCormick, *Origins,* 319–387. It seems to me that Horden and Purcell's bibliographic note that "much discussion has focused on the role of Muslim coinage in commercial relations between Islam and Europe, less on what the few individual finds can tell us about possible networks of exchange" has been expertly addressed by McCormick for the Carolingian period; see Peregrine Horden and Nicholas Purcell, *The Corrupting Sea: A Study of Mediterranean History* (London: Blackwell, 2000), 569.

sophisticated discussion has yet to develop with respect to the currency flows of the Indian Ocean in the pre-modern period. Yet the painstaking work of numismatists on the coinages of different parts of the ocean now amounts to a substantial, if still dispersed, corpus and presents an opportunity to address the "movement of coinage in the lands bordering the Indian Ocean" as well as the implications of that movement for the history of business associations across the region.[35]

The above-mentioned studies of medieval Indian currency systems succeed in unearthing a number of symptoms of monetization. These include the expansion of minting activity and the undertaking of coinage by new polities, the assessment of a variety of taxes in terms of cash, and the usage of a wide variety of coins (coins minted in different places and times) within identifiable currency zones. Similar indices of monetization can be traced around the shores of the western Indian Ocean. First, numismatists and archaeologists have pointed to expanded activity at a number of Islamic mints not previously attested at different port cities of the western Indian Ocean. The earliest coins to be minted in East Africa were excavated at the site of Shanga in the Lamu archipelago and dated stratigraphically to the eighth or ninth century. They comprise silver coins that bear Arabic and Islamic legends but are otherwise unique and unlike the standard Islamic coin types both in terms of their metrology, especially their very small weight, and in terms of the content of their legends—single names with accompanying short pious statements. In other words, here we have what Timothy Insoll calls the "indigenization" of the basic format of Islamic coinage current in the region.[36] The coins of Shanga are followed by similar silver issues found in a hoard from the site of Mtembwe Mkuu, in Mafia, Tanzania, and dated to the second half of the eleventh century by their association—significant for our discussion below—with datable Fatimid dinars.[37] The other mints of the Swahili and Somali coast, Kilwa, and Mogadishu follow suit in the next couple

---

[35] The quote comes from Helen Brown's and Mark Horton's seminal study of the coins of the Swahili site of Shanga, the earliest local issues of Islamic coins discovered so far in East Africa. At the time of publication in 1996, the authors remarked that "the transmission of ideas and the movement of coinage in the lands bordering the Indian Ocean, are still very far from being understood." See Helen Brown, "The Coins," in *Shanga: The Archaeology of a Muslim Trading Community on the Coast of East Africa*, ed. Mark Horton (London: The British Institute in Eastern Africa, 1996), 377.

[36] Timothy Insoll, *The Archaeology of Islam in Sub-Saharan Africa* (Cambridge: Cambridge University Press, 2003), 177. Put simply, "a typical Islamic coin bears the name and titles of a ruler (or several rulers), several religious statements, and the place and date of the coin's making"; Michael L. Bates, *Islamic Coins*, American Numismatic Society Handbook 2 (New York: The American Numismatic Society, 1982), 3. In her study of the Shanga coins, Helen Brown points out that the coins in question "observe none of the canons of regular Islamic coinage and breach the Caliph's prerogative of *sikka* (the right to strike coins)." Brown, "The Coins," 372.

[37] Mark Horton, "The Mtambwe Mkuu Hoard," *Azania* 21 (1985): 115–123; idem, "Artisans, Communities, and Commodities: Medieval Exchanges between Northwestern India and East Africa," *Ars Orientalis* 34 (2004): 62–80.

of centuries.[38] Along the Gulf and Arabian Sea shores, a number of coastal mints, among them ones at the major hubs of Siraf in Iran and Sohar in Oman, issue standard Islamic coins from the ninth century on, and simultaneously in the early tenth century appear rightly attributed to "the unprecedented traffic in luxury goods."[39] As Abbasid fragmentation advanced and the emphasis of transit trade shifted to the west of the Gulf area, these mints ceased their production while Aden, the main port to benefit from that shift, produced coins that, as we shall see, became a unit of account as well as a widely circulating currency in the region.[40] Further east, in addition to the expansion of indigenous coin usage in South India mentioned earlier, new gold coinage appears in Sri Lanka between the eighth and the twelfth century.[41] From the beginning of this period there is also evidence for the development of coin types in imitation of Umayyad and Abbasid dinars in India and Burma.[42] Thus, rise of polities and growth of economies around the western Indian Ocean and the concomitant intensification of trade connections are neatly matched by expansion of minting activity around the Ocean, itself an index of monetization.

Second, Geniza documents, to date the only direct record of mercantile exchange in this period across the region produced by merchants, refer explicitly to a noteworthy range of transactions involving cash and demonstrate an adeptness in recognizing and, presumably, assaying different coin types. These transactions include liquidation of partnership assets and distribution to partners, as seen in the first epigraph to this chapter; liquidation of assets belonging to deceased foreign merchants and award of proceeds to rightful heirs; advances to agents or partners for overseas purchases; credit arrangements for remote partners overseas; ransoming of victims of piracy; payments of rent; payments of port taxes; and remuneration for labor. In addition to showing the use of cash for many different purposes, these documents detail the utilization of the Egyptian and Yemeni gold coins in India, that is, outside the jurisdiction of the specific authorities that issued them, and even well outside the realm of Islamic political authority broadly construed. In fact, the documents also reveal that several different denominations circulated in single ports and were used concurrently in single enterprises. In the period of densest documentation between

---

[38] See Helen Brown, "Coins of East Africa: An Introductory Survey," *Al-Yarmuk li'l-masku'kat* 5 (1993): 9–16.

[39] Nicholas Lowick, "Trade Patterns on the Persian Gulf in Light of Recent Coin Evidence," in *Near Eastern Numismatics, Iconography, Epigraphy, and History: Studies in Honor of George C. Miles,* ed. Dickran Koymjian (Beirut: American University of Beirut Press, 1974), 319–333, 321.

[40] Robert Darley Doran and Elisabeth Darley Doran, *History of Currency in the Sultanate of Oman* (Muscat: Central Bank of Oman, 1990), 42.

[41] Venetia Porter, "Islamic Coins Found in Sri Lanka," in *Origin, Evolution and Circulation of Foreign Coins in the Indian Ocean,* ed. Osmund Bopearachchi and D.P.M. Weerakkody (Colombo: Manohar, 1998), 229–231.

[42] See Shailendra Bhandare and Stefan Heidemann, "A Die for Imitation of Umayyad Dinars Found in India," *Oriental Numisimatic Society Newsletter* 162 (2000): 8–9; and Porter, "Islamic Coins," 229.

the late eleventh and third quarter of the twelfth century, Egyptian and Yemeni gold coins head the list of coin types used by the merchants. Other denominations also appear, including silver coins of Yemen, other Islamic silver coins of unknown provenance, and, remarkably, Indian denominations. The use of such a mixed bag of coins is paralleled by the acceptability of foreign coins in three distinct currency zones in southern India.[43]

Combining the testimony of the Cairo Geniza documents with the findings of numismatic studies, we begin to chart the monetary landscape of the early medieval Indian Ocean. In sum, numismatic and textual sources show more port cities across the western half of the region issuing coins, with gold predominating but silver also used notably along the Swahili coast, where silver would have been scarce; an expanded circulation of Egyptian gold coins in particular and Islamic coins of gold and silver more broadly; proliferation and imitation of Islamic coin types; cash used in a variety of transactions; and a variety of denominations used by businessmen in the same network and at places across the sea. Mapping these trends, we can begin to discern the development of three broad and interlinked zones of primarily gold and secondarily silver and copper coin circulation—what I refer to here as interdenominational currency zones. The Arabian seaboard was dominated by gold dinars of local mints as well as dinars imported from elsewhere in the Islamic world; although scarcer, silver is also used, with high-purity silver specifically designated for long-distance transactions, while at some point a number of Chinese copper coins also entered the scene, presumably used for local port transactions.[44] The Indian littoral exhibits a more diverse currency zone that includes a number of local currencies in gold and bullion, as well as Islamic dinars and Chinese coppers. Finally, the East Africa coast was characterized by local silver Islamic issues that probably served local economies but perhaps also circulated from port to port and between merchants; while some gold, including Fatimid and earlier Abbasid issues, appear to have been imported here, too, the role of gold in this zone is unclear. These assemblages speak to the role of merchants in rendering coinages from different minting authorities and ultimately different spheres of political influence desirable, recognizable, and integrated into the local economies.

It is important to keep in mind that the integration of these economies and of the currency zones just described was far from constant or complete. Circulation of specie in these zones was uneven. The most distinct trend was the flow of bullion and cash to India, part of the overall balance of trade and similar to the trend

---

[43] Chattopadhyaya, *Coins and Currency Systems*, 141–142.

[44] On Chinese coppers in the western Indian Ocean, see John Cribb and Daniel Potts, "Chinese Coin Finds from Arabia and the Arabian Gulf," *Arabian Archaeology and Epigraphy* 7 (1996): 108–118.

in the ancient commercial system that linked the Indian Ocean with the Roman Mediterranean.[45] The demand for bullion also differed in each of the three segments of the region, both in intensity and in the kind of metal in demand. In East Africa, gold was accessible in Mozambique, but the extent of the exploitation of gold mines attested in the country's hinterland in the period in question is uncertain.[46] Some Arab geographers and travelers note the Arab traders' quest for gold at Sofāla, the southernmost reach of the Swahili coast, and scattered in Arabic and even Chinese sources are references to gold mines in southeastern Africa and gold coin circulation along the East African coast, but the extent of gold coinage remains uncertain.[47] Finally, the volume of monetary exchange also varied seasonally through the year, as bullion and coin availability would have depended on the sailing patterns and seasons.[48]

The material traces of the total volume of medieval coinage in circulation between the tenth and the thirteenth centuries are admittedly scarce compared to other periods, and thus cast some doubt as to the volume of monetized transactions.[49] Measured against the impressive quantities of Roman coins that testify to the scale of the earlier India trade, there are very few real specimens of the Fatimid coins that the merchants who appear on the pages of the Geniza documents sent across the seas, presumably into the hands of India-based partners. There are at least two broad explanations for this phenomenon. First, the modern record of lost coins is generally imperfect. As McCormick concludes in his examination of the infiltration of Arab dinars into the Carolingian Europe, gold coins are not so easily lost; the degree to which the material record tends to underrepresent the actual circulation of coins in any one realm emerges when the evidence of real coins is compared to

---

[45] This eastward flow of precious metal (specie or bullion) is a well-known trend, even if it does not fully describe the balance of trade. See Goitein and Friedman, *India Traders*, 18–21; and Éric Vallet, *L'Arabie marchande: État et commerce sous les sultans rasūlides du Yémen (626–858/1229–1454)* (Paris: Publications de la Sorbonne, 2010), 227.

[46] G. S. P. Freeman-Grenville, "A Propos of Gold at Sofala," in *Threefold Wisdom: Islam, the Arab World and Africa; Papers in Honour of Ivan Hrbek* (Prague: Academy of Sciences of the Czech Republic, 1993), 89.

[47] Freeman-Grenville, "A Propos of Gold," 94–98.

[48] Vallet, *L'Arabie marchande*, 215, 228.

[49] Two hoards with a substantial number of Islamic coins discovered in India date to a later period and include only one or possibly two issues dating to the twelfth century. On this phantom hoard, see Humphrey William Codrington, "On a Hoard of Coins Found at Broach," *Journal of the Bombay Branch of the Royal Asiatic Society* 15 (1882–1883): 339–370; and Simon Digby, "The Broach Coin Hoard as Evidence of the Import of Valuta Across the Arabian Sea During the 13th and 14th Centuries," *Journal of the Royal Asiatic Society of Great Britain and Ireland* 112.2 (1980): 129–138. Another hoard is reported from Sri Lanka: this one, too, does not appear to have included any quantity of issues dating to the period under investigation here. Hoards might not best reflect the volume of coins in circulation, especially in periods that predate the deposition of the hoard.

that of "virtual" coins, that is, coins mentioned in documents of transactions.[50] In the case of India, the effect may be exacerbated by a cataloguing bias at some of the termini of much of the gold used in the transactions in question. According to Michael Mitchiner, the "published literature does not serve the subject adequately, because most Islamic coins found in India are simply recorded as 'Caliphate coins,' or as 'Kufic coins.'"[51] Second, and more important, the dearth of remains may be related to the processes of incorporation of the western gold and silver into the Indian and East African economies, respectively. It seems likely that Fatimid coins were incorporated into local circulation zones in India, partly thanks to their metrological compatibility with the locally issued coins.[52] Incorporation and accelerated circulation meant less hoarding or transformation into adornments, and therefore a decline in the kind of withdrawal from circulation that would produce a record. A different but not necessarily incompatible scenario is that, given their exceptional fineness, some of these "western" Islamic coins were prized precisely for their metal content and were recycled into local currency both in India and to a lesser extent in East Africa, where imported silver dirhams, especially the *nuqra* type that Geniza documents show were sought after for long-distance trade, may have ended up as metal for local mints.[53] Incorporation and recycling speak to an increased circulation of coinage, not the opposite. The argument for these processes may be partly speculative, but it helps to explain the virtual Islamic coins of the Geniza traders. Thus, while it is difficult to quantify the degree of monetization in this period, it seems fair to argue that it was increasing.

A final objection to the idea that monetization played a growing role in the conduct of long-distance trade after the tenth century may stem from the collective

---

[50] McCormick, *Origins*, 381.

[51] Michael Mitchiner, *Ancient Trade and Early Coinage*, 2 vols. (London: Hawkins Publications 2004), 2: 1359. The situation seems to have improved very little since the 1970s, when Chattopadhyaya noted that "our knowledge of actual types of foreign coins imported into South India from east and west is extremely meager because of the absence of any useful inventory of such coins." Chattopadhyaya, *Coins and Currency Systems*, 142.

[52] The metrological compatibility of Islamic gold coins with indigenous types in India is noted in diverse numismatic studies. See, for example, Bhandare and Heidemann, "A Die for Imitation of Umayyad Dinars," 8–9. Chattopadhyaya speculates that foreign gold coins were widely accepted in South India from the tenth century onward, if not earlier; Chattopadhyaya, *Coins and Currency Systems*, 142.

[53] Bullion flows are an important side story to that of the monetization of the Indian Ocean. Eliahu Ashtor and others have established that the "expansion of gold" witnessed in the expanding Islamic world was primarily fed by gold from West Africa, but the role of gold deposits in East Africa and the gold trade with Sofāla (modern-day Mozambique) is less well understood; see Freeman-Grenville, "Sofāla," *Encyclopaedia of Islam*, 2nd ed. (Brill Online, 2012) <http://referenceworks.brillonline.com/entries/encyclopaedia-of-islam-2/sofala-SIM_7085>. The dearth of silver in parts of the Islamic world and the demand for it in East Africa and elsewhere also played a role in the character of the interdenominational currency zones outlined above, but the sources known to me at present do not suffice for a full discussion of these phenomena.

testimony of Geniza documents that credit arrangements were often prolonged and liquidation of assets infrequent. Goitein and Udovitch have indeed argued that the economy reflected in the Geniza documents was primarily based on credit, not cash. Credit instruments, especially the *ḥawāla* (often improperly translated into English as "bill of exchange"), were used to keep track of debts. Debts were discharged with the dispatch of merchandise, and only less frequently with cash. While this may be true for the Indian Ocean segment of this particular network's economy as well, the nature of the record may be significant. Generated in the Judeo-Arabic milieu of the Jewish communities of the Islamic world, these documents naturally record first and foremost transactions between coreligionists (who communicated primarily in Judeo-Arabic) and only secondarily transactions between Jews and non-Jewish partners, agents, and clients; communications with and among the latter would have been in Arabic or other idioms and would not necessarily have ended up in the same Jewish ritual deposit of written matter, that is the Cairo Geniza. The preponderance of credit arrangements rather than cash payments may be a consequence of this documentary bias of the Cairo Geniza corpus and thus characteristic of collaborations among coreligionists rather than a generalizable conclusion. It is reasonable to suppose that cash payments were more common among parties belonging to different religious groups. The far-flung nature of cross-cultural exchanges involved increased uncertainty of completion—an uncertainty that the use of easily transportable, easily recognizable measures of value could reduce. Moreover, the legal separateness of communities of faith, compounded by the problem of physical distance, may have reduced the facility in employing credit instruments, as it would have amplified issues of witnessing, documentation, and adjudication in case of dispute.

MONETIZED EXCHANGE AND CROSS-CULTURAL COLLABORATION

In support of the hypothesis that cash was more important in cross-cultural than in intra-diasporic agreements in this formative period of early global trade, this chapter will conclude with a close reading of four testimonies from the Cairo Geniza about the use of cash in transactions associated with long-distance trade. The first example illustrates the use of cash in advances meant to ensure the provision of merchandise in India and in the disbursement of debt in cross-cultural collaborations. The second provides a snapshot of the interdenominational character of the monetary apparatus available to merchants and their ability to handle the different currencies involved. The final two examples show the advantages offered by cash in long-distance cross-cultural relationships but also the risks that those transactions entailed.

The remarkable case of Joseph b. David al-Lebdī, whose business operations in the late eleventh century took him from Cairo to inland Nahrawāra, in the heart of

Gujarat, leaves an early trace of the use of cash in the system that linked Cairo with western India.[54] According to a subsequent court deposition, on one of his expeditions, Joseph deposited funds belonging to a fellow Jewish merchant in Aden with his contact in Nahrawāra, the "seller" Dādā, whose name suggests a respectable and possibly high-caste Hindu businessman.[55] Since al-Lebdī is known to have exported goods from India to Aden, this deposit must reflect part of the process of acquiring the goods to be transported abroad.[56] The relationship between the two parties includes long-term expectations of fiduciary preservation and delayed delivery. Cash, no doubt the fine gold dinars of the Fatimids, allowed the traveling Jewish merchant to contract local Indian suppliers beyond the specific coins' primary zone of circulation and beyond the merchant's primary business network.

The second example entails a set of accounts and missives exchanged between Abraham Ben Yijū—who had settled in India and owned a coppersmith's workshop there—and his partners in the city of Aden. The set offers glimpses of the impressive variety of coins that Abraham and his Jewish, Muslim, and Hindu associates were handling, and suggests the advantages that it may have offered, as well as the tensions that it may have produced. In a summary of dispatches of cash to Abraham by Adeni merchant Maḍmūn b. Japheth,[57] the Egyptian gold issue of the Fatimid dynasty, the *mithqāl*, heads the list.[58] The remaining coins are Yemeni issues: half dinars from Dhu Jibla, the capital of the much diminished Sulayhid state, and

---

[54] On the documents relating to Joseph's business in India, see Goitein and Friedman, *India Traders*, 204–208, 237–240. Nahrawāra is the Arabic toponym for the Chaulukya capital Anhilwara (modern-day Pattan). For cross-cultural encounters in this town, see Flood, *Objects of Translation*, 65, and Mehrdad Shokoohy, *Muslim Architecture of South India: The Sultanate of Maʿbar and the Traditions of Maritime Settlers on the Malabar and Coromandel Coasts (Tamil Nadu, Kerala and Goa)* (London: Routledge Curzon, 2003), 10.

[55] According to Goitein and Friedman, the name should be related to the Persian Jewish term for "old nursemaid"; Goitein and Friedman, *India Book I*, 110 and note 17. Yet the same name could also be related to the Hindustani word for "paternal grandfather," which is used as a respectful appellation for Brahmins. The professional designation given to this person in our document is *bayyāʿ*, a term literally meaning "seller," frequently associated with the preparation and sale of food, but also sometimes denoting a broker, albeit a female one; Goitein and Friedman, *India Traders*, 207 and note 13. For the feminine form denoting female brokers, see Goitein, *A Mediterranean Society* 1: 161 and 439n43.

[56] TS 28.22, lines 15–17: *dafaʿtuhu maʿ Dādā al-bayyāʿ*.

[57] "I sent to him [you] with Sheikh Abū Saʿīd b. Maḥfūẓ in the ship al-Mubārak to Mangalore—may God ordain its safe arrival—100 Egyptian *mithqāl*, worth 253 *dinār*, and with him also 260 Zabidi *dinār*, equivalent to *malikis* [Yemeni/Adeni dinars] in weight. I also sent to him (you) some fine Jibli *niṣāfis* (half-dinars)…my lord please take delivery of these [i.e., the money as well as consignments of copper mentioned earlier in the letter] from the above-mentioned people." T-S 20.130, lines 29–37; see also Goitein and Friedman, *India Traders*, 333.

[58] Noted for its full weight and high fineness of over 98 percent, this gold coin features prominently in the traders' documents and appears to have been acceptable everywhere. See Goitein and Friedman, *India Traders*, 18; Stephen Album, *A Checklist of Islamic Coins* (Santa Rosa, CA: Stephen Album, 1998), 45; Goitein, *A Mediterranean Society*, 1: 360.

dinars from Zabid, Aden's rival on the Red Sea coast. Significantly, Maḍmūn calculates the balance in yet a third denomination, the *maliki dīnār*, a coin type issued
by the sovereigns of Aden and clearly functioning as the "unit of account" in most
of the accounts of India traders.[59] Ben Yijū's own accounting rests on a mixture of
Maliki dinars and a number of local denominations, both in silver and in gold. The
most frequently mentioned Indian coins fall under a broad denomination that the
Judeo-Arabic authors call *fīlī*; along with two other denominations, they have tentatively been matched by Friedman with currencies mentioned in Indian inscriptional
records.[60] Thus, the multi-denominational nature of the local exchange mirrors the
variety of coins used in international trade, and the overlap between the two speaks
further of monetization.

The exchange between two Jewish merchants temporarily sojourning in India in
the middle of the twelfth century speaks to the importance of ready cash in overseas
ventures and reveals the extent to which a cross-cultural liaison could mitigate the
difficulties of procuring cash in a pinch.[61] While on a business venture in India, Adeni
shipowner Maḥrūz sought to supply cash to his brother-in-law, the Cairo-based
merchant Abū Zikrī, who had recently survived a piratical attack further north on
the western coast of India. The cash was to be delivered by one of Maḥrūz's native
contacts. The latter is described in highly respectful terms and, although there is
no other record of the connection between the two men, this single case reveals a
close and involved association. Cash would have been extended by the Indian merchant to his non-Indian partner's relative and business associate. While it is unclear
if the reference here is to actual Fatimid dinars or simply to a convenient and commonly recognized unit of account, the gist of the reference and the silence over any
exchange rate gives the impression that the equivalency was not an issue. What purposes could cash serve in this case? Maḥrūz originally proposed to have his Indian
associate remit to Abū Zikrī "21 *mithqāl*," a respectable amount. Abū Zikrī would

---

[59] This coin type was issued by Al-Malik al-Mukarram, hence its name, *maliki*. At the time, the Sulayhid sovereign ruled over a large part of Yemen from its highlands and counted the Zurayid governors of Aden among
his dependents; but the relationship was reversed in the beginning of the twelfth century. Interestingly, the
Zurayids continued striking these *maliki* dinars, leaving their design intact and later sometimes supple-
menting it with the name of their own ruler; it was only at the very end of the dynasty's tenure in Aden in
the second half of the twelfth century and shortly before the Ayyubid takeover that the issue was discon-
tinued; see 'Umāra al-Ḥakamī, *Ta'rīkh al-Yaman*, ed. Henry Cassels Kay (London: Edward Arnold, 1892),
37; Album, *Syllogue of Islamic Coins in the Ashmolean*, vol. 10, *Arabia and East Africa* (Oxford: Ashmolean
Museum Oxford, 1999), ix.

[60] The denominations include *fīlī dirham*, *fīlī mithqāl*, and *fīlī Kūlam* (the latter clearly the denomination of
the homonymous port in southern India), *faj*, *fanam*, and the Arabian *rawbaj*; see Goitein and Friedman,
India Traders, 637–638. Friedman's reference for the identification of the Indian issues is Chattopadhyaya,
Coins and Currency Systems.

[61] On this exchange, see Goitein and Friedman, *India Traders*, 473–479.

have been strapped for cash after using his own funds to extricate himself from the piratical attempt. Any cash he may have had with him may have been stolen, and if his merchandise had been lost, too, this sum may have been useful for purchasing new items and thus salvaging something of the long business expedition to India. Or he may have needed part of this amount to pay off a ransom debt. In any of these scenarios, availability of cash guarantees the safety of the "foreign" merchant, mitigates the effect of involuntary changes of plans, and allows for partial recouping of losses.

The final case concerns once again Ben Yijū and his Adeni connections: it illustrates the role of cash in creating obligations and the repercussions when such obligations are not met. The story unfolds in a series of letters exchanged between Ben Yijū and his Adeni associates Khalaf b. Isḥāq and Joseph b. Abraham concerning collaboration with a nameless associate in India identified only by an occupational title, *kārdār*.[62] Apparently instructed to procure a quantity of cardamom for the Adeni market, Ben Yijū proceeded to delegate the purchase to this man and to seal the deal. He likely gave him an advance of money for that purchase. The *kārdār*, however, did not deliver, thus putting Ben Yijū in a very awkward position indeed. Khalaf and Joseph covertly censured Ben Yijū for charging them in covering the cost of the advance, but reserve their harshest words for the *kārdār* himself.[63] The harsh words point to the absence of a formal system of adjudication for the particular dispute, and, more generally, to the absence of any formally articulated and instituted means of enforcement that could serve across religious groups when a deal was broken. Leaving aside technical details about the identities of the parties involved in this transaction, it is important to note that, in the end, the use of cash funds here appears to have been intended to facilitate a future delivery but perhaps also to avert the difficulty of sealing a formal agreement backed by a legal instrument.

CONCLUSION

In an important article about the influx of Venetian ducats in Mamluk Egypt in the end of the fourteenth century, Jere Bacharach painstakingly demonstrates that, contrary to the received wisdom about the phenomenon, the ducats did not prevail because they were better coins than the native issues (more stable in terms of fineness

[62] Amitav Ghosh examined this dispute between the Jewish merchants and their apparent supplier in India and concluded that the *kārdār* was a non-Jewish Indian partner of Ben Yijū and possibly related to him through Ben Yijū's marriage to his manumitted Indian slave; see Ghosh, "The Slave of MS. H. 6," *Subaltern Studies* 3 (1994): 207–208; cf. Goitein, *Letters*, 193. Friedman disagrees with this verdict because of the wording of the censure against the *kārdār*, the same wording that leads Ghosh to conclude that the man cannot possibly be a coreligionist; see Goitein and Friedman, *India Traders*, 639n17.
[63] T-S 12.320; Gosh, "The Slave of MS H.6," 207.

and weight) or because the Mamluk state had exceptional difficulties in securing raw metal supplies, but rather because at a time of political instability the Venetian issues were perceived as trustworthy and constant instruments.[64] McCormick's study of the circulation of Arab dinars in Europe at a formative stage of the medieval European economy finds that a similar reason accounts for the importance these "foreign" gold coins assumed in certain parts of Carolingian Italy in the end of the eighth century.[65]

In this chapter, I have attempted to sketch the joint circulation of currencies in the western Indian Ocean, a broad and politically fragmented realm. Because of this complex and expansive geographical frame and the nature of the relevant record to date, the picture I have provided is necessarily much more impressionistic than these two richly detailed studies, yet I hope that it allows us to see a pattern of joint circulation of originally discrete coinages, one more complex and more variegated than either of the two cases just mentioned. The concept of "interdenominational currency zones" is my attempt to convey that pattern, in which a distinct variety of coins were brought into joint circulations through the efforts of merchant groups belonging to a variety of cultures and engaged in cross-cultural trade. The reasons behind this distinct pattern of coin circulation are several. Bullion availability requires further investigation. The needs of merchants in an accelerating economic system undoubtedly played a role. The very multiplicity of partners and discrete cultural spheres, including cultures of law, made the use of money all that more attractive than the deployment of instruments of credit, as the latter would have required greater legal integration. Finally, I have argued that the ability to handle and deploy this interdenominational currency assemblage constituted a bond that brought merchants across cultures closer together.

A question that this essay necessarily leaves for future investigation is that of the potential ideological tensions engendered by the handling of coins across cultures. In his aforementioned article, Bacharach convincingly shows that the reasons that Mamluk authorities strived against the domination of the Venetian ducats in the domestic Egyptian market were not purely, or even primarily, economic. The maritime republic's issues bore the image of the Doge kneeling before Saint Mark, a scene that Muslim sources read as representing Peter and Paul; misunderstood in its details, this overtly Christian iconography presented a challenge to the authority of the Mamluk rulers, whose claim to legitimate sovereignty had revolved around their early championing of Muslim causes against non-Muslim enemies (Crusaders and Mongols).[66] Bacharach's conclusion that the eventual displacement of the ducat and

[64] Jere Bacharach, "The Dinar versus the Ducat," *Journal of Middle Eastern Studies* 4 (1973): 77–78.
[65] McCormick, *Origins,* 340.
[66] Bacharach, "The Dinar versus the Ducat," 81–83.

its replacement by the *ashrafi*, a fully Islamic coin, was motivated by such concerns demonstrates that ideological dimensions of coins could in certain political contexts, times, and places become decisive in popular and elite perception and decision making. Furthermore, the handling of coins bearing Qur'anic verses by non-Muslims, as well as the presence of figurative art on both Muslim and non-Muslim coins, could conceivably have presented dilemmas for legal thinkers and popular pious imaginations alike. While far from conclusive, the material presented above contains no indication that such dilemmas ever featured prominently in the Indian Ocean world of the period in question. The inscriptional character of Muslim coins entailed in itself a kind of ideological muting in contexts where Arabic legends were not directly intelligible to the viewers and users. Moreover, hybrid coins produced in the littorals and hinterlands of the Indian subcontinent themselves blurred the ideological hard lines that might have been drawn by the Islamic wariness toward representation in religious contexts. While silences do not prove the absence of such concerns for the historical subjects involved, the potential for trepidation in handling coins loaded with symbols of the "other" is likely to have been mitigated in merchants' circles accustomed to the diversity of coinages described here.

9

Crossing the Great Water

THE HAJJ AND COMMERCE FROM PRE-MODERN SOUTHEAST ASIA

Eric Tagliacozzo

IT IS A requirement of the Muslim faith that every Muslim who is able to do so must go to Mecca to perform the pilgrimage once in his or her lifetime. This is a religious duty, a compulsion that all Muslims worldwide understand and share. Yet religious devotion cannot be divorced from the ways and means of performing it, namely the financial wherewithal of undertaking a journey that may be thousands of miles from one's home. Traveling on Hajj for Southeast Asians thus has always required the accumulation of significant economic resources before such a trip could even be contemplated. These funds were earmarked for the trip of a lifetime, one that was usually performed only once. The economics of Hajj thus was serious business. The pilgrimage contributed to regional and trans-regional economies of Muslim lands in Arabia and Southeast Asia, enriched non-believers such as the English and the Dutch, who eventually established colonies in the region, and was also vital to the financial planning of thousands of individuals and their families over the course of the centuries. This chapter explores the economic history of the pilgrimage to Mecca from roughly the sixteenth to the early twentieth century, outlining its early forms as part of the early modern Indian Ocean "system," and its colonial morphogenesis, when the Hajj became an economic phenomenon controlled at least partially by non-indigenous hands.[1]

---

[1] The best overview of the Hajj generally as a historical and as a contemporary phenomenon is F. E. Peters, *The Hajj: The Muslim Pilgrimage to Mecca and the Holy Places* (Princeton, NJ: Princeton University Press, 1994). Only a tiny fraction of this book touches on the role of Southeast Asians, however.

How was the Hajj organized financially over the centuries? Who saved for these journeys, how did they do so, and what challenges were faced in the attempt to accumulate enough capital to be able to travel all the way from tropical Southeast Asia to the deserts of the Arabian Peninsula? How did local government bodies, both indigenous (in the pre-colonial period) and foreign (in the colonial era), either help or hinder these processes as the centuries passed? How much did non-Muslims benefit economically from the Southeast Asian Hajj through mechanisms of cross-cultural trade? Additionally, how much cross-cultural trade was there between various Muslim ethnic groups along the outstretched sea routes from monsoon Asia to Jeddah, the doorstep to Mecca?

This chapter examines cross-cultural commerce both when it occurred among members of different religions and when it involved different Muslim groups. It analyses a faith-driven phenomenon from an everyday, utilitarian point of view: it asks how the pilgrimage was possible not in people's minds or hearts but through evolving economic arrangements. By necessity, in most cases, I will resort primarily to narrative and anecdotal evidence, and not to large sets of data, because almost no such numerical sources exist for the Southeast Asian Hajj prior to the late nineteenth century. This contribution approaches devotion, therefore, primarily from an economic vantage. Yet this tack need not be seen as one reflecting purely *homo economicus* values, as for most Southeast Asians the decisions and priorities of Hajj were always woven together with larger concerns about a life well-lived. Economics and devotion need not be inseparable realities of pilgrimage, therefore, but rather can be seen as two sides of one coin that were both important to the average pilgrim.

I argue in this chapter that the financing of Muslim devotion as seen through the Hajj evolved from a predominantly singular or family/clan endeavor to a phenomenon primarily organized by the state. In the pre-colonial era, the ability and energy to perform the pilgrimage to Mecca was incumbent upon the individual Hajji or Hajja. Sovereigns could help these journeys along in a variety of ways, but pre-modern forms of organization, banking, transport, and travel meant the onus of Hajj primarily rested upon the pilgrim, or a small group of his or her fellows. In the colonial period of the eighteenth and especially the nineteenth centuries, the state began to take a more active role in these deliberations, directing pilgrim traffic across the Indian Ocean both in the interest of the welfare of colonial subjects, and in the very real surveilling interests of evolving imperial states themselves. Though pre-colonial states such as the Safavids and the Mughals were also interested in the Hajj, of course, they did not have the same long-distance capabilities of succor and surveillance of their subjects that colonial states evinced in the shift toward the later, "high colonial" period. The projection of influence over large, oceanic distances was one of the major transitions in the history of the pilgrimage to Mecca from a "pre-modern" to a more "modern" phenomenon. The Ottoman court also attempted to modernize its capabilities (taxation, surveillance, control) in dealing with the Hajj from the sixteenth to the early twentieth centuries, but did so with only sporadic success.[2] This contribution clarifies these policy and population undulations in the Indian Ocean, and queries how these patterns were altered over the centuries at the same time that more and more religious aspirants undertook this longest of journeys.

THE COMMERCIAL ORBIT OF THE PRE-COLONIAL PILGRIMAGE TO MECCA

Scholars do not concur with one another regarding the importance of the Hajj to the overall economy of the early modern Indian Ocean. Ashin Das Gupta, one of the foremost interpreters of commerce and society in the Indian Ocean basin during the fifteenth to eighteenth centuries, has put forward the notion that "the international market of the hajj continued to be the principal draw for trade in the Indian Ocean," thereby seeing the pilgrimage as the central axis for commerce around which all other trade functioned.[3] If weather and political conditions cooperated, merchants coming from as far away as western India could expect to make gross profits of approximately 50 percent on their trade goods in Mecca, a huge return on initial investments.[4] However, the connection between the monsoon cycle and the religious (lunar) cycle was very complex, and changed from year to year. Das Gupta saw the Hajj as the engine for this trade, attracting vessels that would have stopped farther down the coasts to offload their cargoes of textiles in return for coffee and other local products. Such was the trans-regional dependence on Hajj traffic, in Das Gupta's eyes, that "a poor haj or the expectation of one would create a profound depression from Jeddah to the farthest points of Surat's hinterland."[5] Michael Pearson, another important contributor to scholarship on the Hajj and Indian Ocean commerce, sees this emphasis on the part of Das Gupta as misguided. For Pearson, Jeddah (Mecca's feeder-port) was just another harbor way-station on the oceanic routes, and the Hajj a mere appurtenance to traffic that would have stopped there anyway. Pearson believes that Jeddah would have survived without the Hajj, but that

[2] See Stephen Dale, *The Muslim Empires of the Ottomans, Safavids, and Mughals* (Cambridge: Cambridge University Press, 2010), and Douglas Streus, *Islamic Gunpowder Empires: Ottomans, Safavids, and Mughals* (Boulder, CO: Westview Press, 2011).

[3] Ashin Das Gupta, "Indian Merchants and the Trade in the Indian Ocean, c. 1500–1750" in *Cambridge Economic History of India*, vol. 1: *c. 1250–c. 1750*, ed. Tapan Raychaudhuri and Irfan Habib (Cambridge: Cambridge University Press, 1982), 407–433, 430.

[4] Ashin Das Gupta, "Gujarati Merchants and the Red Sea Trade, 1700–1725," in *The Age of Partnership*, ed. B. B. Kling and M. N. Pearson (Honolulu: University of Hawaii Press, 1979), 123–158, 124.

[5] Ashin Das Gupta, *Indian Merchants and the Decline of Surat, c. 1700–1750* (Wiesbaden: Harrasowitz Verlag, 1979), 68–69. Das Gupta sees the Hajj as an engine *primus inter pares* among other economic phenomena

the pilgrimage actually linked Mecca, an otherwise fairly insulated city, from a financial point of view, with trade routes that prospered on their own economic terms.[6]

It is still not clear which of these two views is substantially correct. Yet contemporary eyewitness descriptions of the early modern Red Sea and its economic connections to the Indian Ocean can help us ascertain the relative importance of trade. We know from an anonymous account dating from around 1580 that 40 or 50 large ships were coming to Jeddah each year, laden with precious merchandise and sundries, and that these ships were paying large sums in customs duties to the local rulers in order to trade.[7] A few decades later, the actual size of these ships, and not just their number, starts to become apparent. Pilgrims' ships coming from India carried pilgrims, but also commodities to fund their voyages: these ships could be over 150 feet long and 40 feet wide, with depth-displacements into the water reaching around 30 feet as well.[8] These were large, blue-water vessels, in other words, and there were substantial numbers of them making the voyage to Jeddah from other ports in the Indian Ocean. "The superstitious custom of pilgrimages to Mecca made by those who follow the infamous Koran" encouraged these trips, according to another seventeenth-century chronicler, "since the ships which sailed to Juda made excellent business profits."[9] It is quite clear that the Hajj and regional and oceanic commerce were often linked, therefore, through the monsoons and other patterns—each seems to have depended on the other in a fairly mutually enhancing relationship of religious and commercial profit.

By the late seventeenth century, a more detailed narrative of how the Hajj and regional business practices intersected becomes available. A fruitful source here has

in the Indian Ocean. "The major consideration in any season at Surat was the market of the haj. A major part of the city's shipping was engaged in the Red Sea run, and they [i.e., the Mughals] took their textiles directly to the port of Mocha which was the principal trading center in the Red Sea at the time. Some of the ships would sail past Mocha and make for Jedda further up the coast, but this was probably because of the proximity of Jedda to Mecca.... The market at Mecca...functioned every year as pilgrims from all over the Ottoman empire and the Islamic world assembled at this city" (68–69).

[6] M. N. Pearson, *Pious Passengers: The Hajj in Earlier Times* (Dhaka: The University Press Limited, 1994), 158; F. E. Peters, *Jerusalem and Mecca: The Typology of the Holy City in the Near East* (New York: New York University, 1986), 70–71.

[7] Anonymous, "A Description of the Yeerly Voyage or Pilgrimage of the Mahumitans, Turkes and Moores unto Mecca in Arabia," in Richard Hakluyt, *The Principal Navigations*, (Glasgow: Hakluyt, 1903–1905), vol. 5, 340–365.

[8] This according to the early modern European traveler John Saris, quoted in Samuel Purchas, *Purchas, His Pilgrimes* (Glasgow: Hakluyt, 1905–1907), vol. 3, 396.

[9] Jeronimo Lobo, *The Itinerary of Jerinomo Lobo*, trans. Donald M. Lockhart (London: Hakluyt, 1984 [reprint from the original]), 89–90. Lobo further described Jeddah as a city "which has been made so famous in these times in all of the East by the great numbers of ships that go there and the rich trade the merchants find there.... Because of the great wealth of the universal market of people and merchandise carried out in that city,

been the writings of the Frenchman Jean-Baptise Tavernier (1605–1689), who took a great interest in the Indian Ocean traffic he saw heading toward Arabia. Tavernier sketches the mechanisms of these contacts as they related to trade, political patronage, and religious devotion between Mughal India and the holy city of Mecca:

> Every year the Great Mogul sends two large vessels there (to Surat), to carry pilgrims, who thus get a free passage. At the time when these vessels are ready to depart, the *fakirs* come down from all parts of India in order to embark. The vessels are laden with good articles of trade which are disposed of at Mecca, and all the profit which is made is given in charity to the poor pilgrims. The principal only is retained and this serves for another year, and this principal is at least 600,000 rupees. It is considered a small matter when only 30 or 40 per cent is made on these goods.... Added to which all of the principal persons of the Great Mogul's Harem, and other private persons, send considerable donations to Mecca.[10]

Dutch records from this time concur with Tavernier that the Mughal Hajj mixed the religious duty of the pilgrimage with trade on these journeys as a normal matter of course.[11] The scale of these voyages is again discernible from contemporary records. In 1662, a ship from Bijapur, India, arrived in Aden with pilgrims and merchandise on its way to Jeddah. The amount of merchandise was so great (400 bales of goods) that the cargo had to be brought into Aden via a detour, the city gates being too small. The number of Hajjis transporting this merchandise was said to be 1,500 pilgrims on this one ship alone, all of them en route to Mecca.[12] The goods were to be sold in various ports of the Red Sea in order to help finance the voyage, a common practice apparently among many Hajj ships at the time. Gifts, charity, merit-making, and the reputations of Muslim rulers in their dealings with their subjects and with other Muslim potentates thus all came into play.

Yemen, astride the Red Sea route between Asia and the Hejaz, was vital in structuring the conditions for these long-distance economies to function. Even in the

---

they (the ships) became so famous in India that when people wanted to indicate that something was very costly and valuable they would call it a ship from Mecca" (89–90).

[10] Tavernier quoted in W. H. Coates, *The Old Country Trade of the East Indies* (London: Imray, Laurie, Nurie, and Wilson, 1911), 124.

[11] Van Outhoorn, Van Hoorn, Pijl, De Haas, Van Riebeeck, XXIII, November 23, 1699 (Koloniaal Archieven [hereafter Kol. Arch.], 1503, fol. 12–237), in W. Ph. Coolhaas, ed., *Generale Missiven van Gouverneurs-Generaal en Raden aan Heren XVII der Verenigde Oostindische Compagnie* (hereafter VOC, *Gen. Miss.*) (The Hague: Martinus Nijhoff, 1960), 88, hereafter VOC, *Gen. Miss.*

[12] Suraiya Faroqhi, *Pilgrims and Sultans: The Hajj under the Ottomans, 1517–1683* (London: I. B. Tauris, 1994), 159–160.

time of the great Portuguese explorer and admiral Afonso de Albuquerque, who pulled his ship into Aden's harbor on Easter Day of the year 1513, Yemen was already making an impression on Europeans as the commercial choke-point for the entire Red Sea economy, and for the seas beyond in either direction (the Mediterranean and the Indian Ocean). An engraving in the admiral's record of his travels shows a large, prosperous city of rectangular Hejazi-type houses climbing up the steep hills of Aden's bay, which must have been then (as it is now, 500 years later) an incredible sight, given the blasted-stone quality of the landscape in the area. What could have given rise to a flourishing entrepôt such as this one? D'Albuquerque was unequivocal in expressing his opinion: the traffic of ships through the Red Sea made the city one of the best-positioned ports in the world, and a natural stopping place for vessels, despite the fact that the metropolis had no source of its own running water.[13] The flourishing commerce with other Muslim lands and Aden's strategic location was stronger than this impediment, however. Urban cosmopolitanism literally grew out of craggy stone in this case, with little soil or fresh water to help such sophistication grow. Writing only a century later, in 1609, another European traveler, John Jourdain, also landed in Aden, though his curiosity about the commercial possibilities of the place took him into the interior of Yemen as well. He eventually ascended the steep hills of the Tihama and penetrated into the interior of the country, traveling by caravan to Ta'izz, Ibb, Say'un, and finally to Sana'a. He was one of the first Westerners to become aware of the internal economies of Yemen that linked the thriving towns of the hills to the littoral systems of exchange on the coasts, a transit that was already at this early date becoming partially predicated on the steady traffic of Hajjis passing through the region.[14] Muslims from the rest of the Indian Ocean, therefore, seem to have been in a dialogue of cross-cultural trade with the interior towns of Yemen well prior to the advent of European record keeping there in the early modern age.

It was in fact during the late sixteenth century when something happened that would transform this region's economy in ways that had been previously unimaginable, and this was the lightning Ottoman campaign to subdue Yemen and bring the country under its rule between 1569 and 1571.[15] Turkish documentation on this military and political coup is extremely good, yet it was the *economic* legacy

---

[13] Walter de Grey Bird, *The Commentaries of the Great Alfonso Dalboquerque, 2nd Viceroy of India* (London: Hakluyt Society, 1884), vol. 4 (see especially Map 1 in his account).

[14] William Foster, ed., *The Journal of John Jourdain, 1608–1617* (London: Hakluyt Society, 1905), Series 2, vol. 16 (see especially Map 2 in his account).

[15] Qutb al-Din al-Nahrawali al-Makki, *Lightning over Yemen: A History of the Ottoman Campaign, 1569–1571*, trans. and ed. Clive Smith (London: I. B. Tauris, 2002).

of the campaign that was probably more important in the long-term history of this region.[16] The Ottomans fixed the roads and secured the long-distance caravan routes; they also made sure that water was available on the trade routes, and that sentry posts were stationed for many miles in every direction coming out of the country. Ports were revamped all along the coasts.[17] Trade prospered as never before, including Ottoman-Yemeni commerce across the two cultures, and the increase in Hajjis coming to the Hejaz during this time was partially dependent on these structural conditions, which made the end terminus of the pilgrimage so much safer and more reliable than it had been previously. Despite lasting images of the Ottoman Empire as the "sick man of Europe," these early decades of rule and administration in the late sixteenth century were anything but anemic.[18] The Ottomans actually made Yemen a recognizable place for intercontinental commerce outside the regions of the Middle East and the waters of the Arabian Sea for the first time since the Queen of Sheba in classical antiquity. The economy of the Red Sea eventually soared over the coming decades, though it became now very much dependent on boom and bust cycles that followed prices and surplus/scarcity in the global commercial system as a whole, especially on goods such as coffee.[19] The Hajj rode these changing economic structures to some degree, rising steadily as a diasporic phenomenon over the years, even if individual seasons or groupings of years could still be difficult.

[16] Colin Heywood, *Writing Ottoman History: Documents and Interpretations* (Aldershot, Hampshire: Ashgate, 2002).

[17] Rifa'at 'Ali Abou-El-Haj, *Formation of the Modern State: The Ottoman Empire Sixteenth to Eighteenth Centuries* (Albany: State University of New York Press, 1991).

[18] Asli Cirakman, *From the Terror of the World to the Sick Man of Europe: European Images of Ottoman Empire and Society from the Sixteenth Century to the Nineteenth* (New York: Peter Lang, 2002).

[19] Farhad Nomani and Ali Rahnema, *Islamic Economic Systems* (London: Zed Books, 1994) and Sevket Pamuk, *A Monetary History of the Ottoman Empire* (Cambridge: Cambridge University Press, 2000). For scholarship on the importance of coffee, see particularly Julien Berthaud, "L'origine et la distribution des Cafeiers dans le monde," in *Le commerce du café avant l'ère des plantations coloniales: Espaces, réseaux, sociétés (XVe-XIXe siècle)*, ed. Michel Tuchscherer (Cairo: Institut Français d'Archéologie Orientale, 2001), 364–369; Ernestine Carreira, "Les français et le commerce du café dans l'océan indien au XVIIIe siècle," in *Le commerce du café*, 333–357, 334; William Clarence-Smith and S. Topik, eds., *The Global Coffee Economy in Africa, Asia and Latin America, 1500–1989* (Cambridge: Cambridge University Press, 2003). For period Dutch notices of the ins and outs of the trade on Yemen's "coffee coast," see VOC, *Gen. Miss.*, 111: De Haan, Huysman, Haselaar, Blom, Durven, XIV, March 31, 1727 (Kol. Arch., 1933, fol. 3222–3413); VOC, *Gen. Miss.*, 209: De Haan, Huysman, Haselaar, Blom, Durven, XIV, December 8, 1728 (Kol. Arch., 1975, fol. 517–1071); and VOC, *Gen. Miss.*, 214: De Haan, Huysman, Haselaar, Blom, Durven, XIV, December 8, 1728 (Kol. Arch., 1975, fol. 517–1071).

"THE LANDS BENEATH THE WINDS" AND INDIAN OCEAN COMMERCE

Hajj aspirants journeyed to the Hejaz from all of the littorals of the ocean, encompassing Africa, India, and the distant "lands beneath the winds," the classical Arabic designation for Southeast Asia. Indeed, there are reliable records (not easy to come by) of Southeast Asians performing the Hajj even as far back as 1561, when an Acehnese ship laden with gold and a palanquin to be shipped to the Ottoman sultan made the voyage in the mid-sixteenth century. Even at that early date, commerce and the Hajj were intertwined, as the contents of this ship make clear.[20] The pilgrimage from Southeast Asia to Mecca at this early date was not entirely dependent on commerce; there was the wherewithal for the wealthiest rulers to send aspirants to the Hejaz without trading being part of the bargain. But this likely rarely happened—the distances were too great, and the opportunities too enormous, to single these voyages out for only religious purposes when so much more could be accomplished by blurring intentions. Many trading ships no doubt traversed the ocean without Hajjis on board. But it would likely have been a rare event—if it ever happened at all—for Southeast Asian ships to come all the way to Arabia without having some pilgrims involved in commerce. There simply was no need for these merchants to separate the religious and economic functions.

The Acehnese ship mentioned above was only one of many that eventually traveled these routes. From elsewhere in Southeast Asia, there were other Hajjis, including perhaps most famously the renowned Shaykh Yusuf of Makassar, who had undertaken the pilgrimage in 1644 after being initiated into a Sufi order in Aceh on his voyage across the Indian Ocean.[21] Arab traders came down to Indonesia and seem to have mixed their business voyages and their roles as missionaries at this time as well.[22] Even the *Tuhfat al-Nafis* (the Malay epic translated roughly as "The Precious Gift"), the famous chronicle of the Bugis kings of Riau (an agglomeration of small islands just south of Singapore), mentions the financial dealings of the hero Raja Ahmad, who performed Hajj as part of his wanderings.[23] Raja Ahmad first had to travel to Java in order to raise cash for the journey; he ended up accumulating 14,000 Straits dollars for the trip there through Javanese contacts (he himself was of Bugis lineage), and left on a pilgrim ship from Penang with 12 companions for the

---

[20] Pearson, *Pious Passengers*, 164.

[21] Martin van Bruinessen, *Tarekat Naqsyabandiyah di Indonesia: Survei Historis, Geografis dan Sosiologis* (Bandung: Penerbit Mizan, 1992), 34–46, and Abu Hamid, *Syekh Yusuf Makassar: Seorang Ulama, Sufi dan Pejuang* (Jakarta: Yayasan Obor Indonesia, 1994).

[22] VOC, *Gen. Miss.*, 193: Van Diemen, Van der Lijn, Maetsuyker, Schouten en Sweers, XX, January 13, 1643, (1050, fol. 1–13).

[23] For an overview, see Raja Ali Haji ibn Ahmad, *The Precious Gift / Tuhfat al-Nafis*, ed. and trans. Virginia Matheson and Barbara Watson Andaya (Kuala Lumpur: Oxford University Press, 1982).

Holy Land. It is interesting that the *Tuhfat al-Nafis* spills almost as much ink on the economic aspects of this voyage as on the spiritual dimensions: while in the Hejaz, Ahmad bought land and houses for the use of archipelago pilgrims, and gave money generally for religious purposes.[24] Philanthropy, piety, and commerce therefore mixed and mingled easily on these routes. In the career of men such as Raja Ahmad, one can see the financial and monetary necessities that went along with the devotional responsibilities of Hajj, even in the centuries well before the high colonial age.

The Dutch were important in facilitating these transoceanic connections. Because the Dutch East India Company (henceforth VOC) was active both in the Red Sea and in Southeast Asia, and was becoming increasingly involved in the commercial orbits of both regions over the course of the seventeenth century, it seems natural that Dutch records provide a crucial connective in explaining how the Indian Ocean economy started to become a more unitary space during this time. Trade corridors and segmented systems of the Indian Ocean world began to coalesce into larger fields of exchange. Where previously "arenas" of the Indian Ocean may have been in evidence, which traded and interacted with other nearby "arenas" of the same sea (such as the Red Sea, the Persian Gulf, the Arabian Sea, or the Bay of Bengal), by the seventeenth century these bailiwicks were starting to fade away into a larger, oceanic system. A Dutch servant of the VOC named Pieter van den Broeke was among the first to comment on these connections in the 1620s when he was charged with an expedition to the Red Sea by the "Gentlemen Seventeen," who ran the company from Amsterdam.[25] Van den Broeke was a keen observer of trade patterns coming in and out of Yemen and his *Resolutieboeck* provides clues as to the nature of the beginnings of sustained contact between Southeast Asia and this region. Van den Broeke already had experience in Yemeni waters for a number of years by the time of this expedition: he possessed a number of solid contacts in the region, and he knew which questions to ask in trying to figure out why and how the Tihama coasts were becoming ever more prosperous via long-distance trade. He established a small trading post on those coasts and also managed to have at least one of his crewmen, a man named Abraham Crabee, learn enough Arabic so that they could profitably deal with local people. Among the products that he brought with him to sell were cloves, benzoin, and camphor, all from the VOC's new trading posts in Indonesia.[26]

---

[24] Virginia Matheson and A. C. Milner, eds., *Perceptions of the Haj: Five Malay Texts* (Singapore: ISEAS, 1984), 15, 20.

[25] C. G. Brouwer, "Le Voyage au Yemen de Pieter van den Broecke (serviteur de la VOC) en 1620, d'après son livre de resolutions," in *The Challenge of the Middle East*, ed. F. E. Peters et. al. (Amsterdam: Institute for Modern Near Eastern Studies, University of Amsterdam, 1982), 175–182.

[26] C. G. Brouwer, "Pieter van den Broecke's Original Resulutieboeck Concerning Dutch Trade in Northwest India, Persia, and Southern Arabia, 1620–1625," in his *Dutch-Yemeni Encounters: Activities of the United*

Because van den Broeke's primary interests were commercial in nature, he noted in passing the presence of Malays on these same coasts, some of them trading in similar commodities to his own. A number of these men he surmised were trading while on mercantile-cum-pilgrimage voyages, an early example of the conjoined nature of the two activities.

Yet the most detailed records on Hajj from the "lands beneath the winds" in this early period primarily come from Java. Javanese came on Hajj for religious purposes, but they also knew that the pilgrimage was invested with political and economic opportunities as well. Certainly ethnic groups from other parts of the archipelago knew this; period records attest to merchants from Ternate in Maluku coming to Central and East Java (Rembang) for both commercial reasons and to undertake the pilgrimage as parts of the same voyage.[27] The Sultanate of Banten in West Java is another one of the earliest places we see this connection at work. It is apparent with the title of one of its rulers in the late seventeenth century, who called himself simply "Sultan Haji" (reigned 1682–1687) as a mark of his voyage to the Holy Land (he performed the pilgrimage twice before ascending the throne in Banten).[28] Other Javanese also knew the many different values of the Hajj. One of the Central Javanese sultans made vessels ready on the northern coast of the island in order to go on Hajj, but then decided not to go himself, sending others on his behalf in 1700 and 1701. It is unclear what was at work in this decision, but it seems possible that it may have even been dangerous to be away from Java during this period of early VOC aggression. Sending one's subjects therefore still conferred merit, but left the *kraton* (palace) defended in case of Dutch adventurism. When this adventurism did come a few decades later, the Surakarta Major *Babad* (the court's chronicle) says that Hajjis were at the forefront of Javanese forces in fighting the Europeans, right alongside the *ulamas* (Muslim religious teachers), who were also praised for their bravery.[29] By the middle of the eighteenth century, Sultan Mangkubumi was sending missions to provision and repair his own houses in Mecca so that they could be used by his subjects in their travels across the width of the Indian Ocean.[30] Here again we have evidence of cross-cultural trade between Javanese and Arab Muslims on the wings of the Hajj.

East India Company (VOC) in South Arabian Waters since 1614 (Amsterdam: D'Fluyte Rarob, 1999), 77–102.

[27] VOC, *Gen. Miss.*, 351: Camphuys, Van Outhoorn, Pit, Van Hoorn, De Saint-Martin, XXI, March 14, 1690 (Kol. Arch., 1347, fol. 8–228); VOC, *Gen. Miss.*: De Haan, Huysman, Hasselaar, Blom, Durven, Vuyst, IV, November 30, 1725 (Kol. Arch., 1911, fol. 541–965).

[28] Merle Ricklefs, *A History of Modern Indonesia* (Stanford, CA: Stanford University Press, 1993), 78–79.

[29] Merle Ricklefs, *Mystic Synthesis in Java: A History of Islamization from the Fourteenth to the Early Nineteenth Centuries* (Norwalk: Eastbridge, 2004), 75–76, 94.

[30] P. B. R. Carey, *Pangeran Dipanagara and the Making of the Java War*, Ph.D. thesis, Oxford University, 1975, vol. 1, 76.

On the eve of the comprehensive Dutch takeover of Java, Prince Diponegoro him-self was even having Hajjis appear to him in his dreams, as he planned and shortly afterward executed his five-year rebellion against the Dutch conquest of all of Java.[31]

The fragmentary sources that have survived the centuries suggest that the pre-modern Hajj was a significant event in the Indian Ocean world, from Zanzibar and the African littoral to the South Asian subcontinent, and even all the way to Southeast Asia. The pilgrimage was significant in a religious sense during these cen-turies to many people, and certainly among the commercial classes. Yet it was also important not just religiously but also economically for the majority of its long his-tory, as Michael Laffan and others have shown. The Hajj provided a spiritual ratio-nale for the physical agglomeration of peoples from many different societies, all at the same time.[32] These Muslim pilgrims from far-flung lands met and mingled while on Hajj, and they prayed side by side in the great mosques of the Arabian peninsula. Yet they also traded across each other's cultures while on the pilgrimage, linking the Indian Ocean orbit into a system of financial exchange that was at least partly based on their movements as religious wanderers. They did this with both co-religionists and with non-believers. In fact, and as we have seen, the arrival of Europeans into the Indian Ocean system of exchange seems to have only advanced the possibilities for Hajj among early modern Southeast Asian pilgrims, as well as for trade itself across the various ethnic actors who were swirling through the ocean's far-flung commer-cial circuits. The Dutch understood this, according to period sources, and realized that good business and devotional Islam went hand in hand.[33] Carpets, brassware, gems, spices, and other valuable commodities traveled on these circuits. Spiritual travel, therefore, was often linked with the more earthly advantages of voyaging, as pilgrims sold various kinds of merchandise from their own homelands in order to help pay for their trips. This pattern has been a phenomenon of long-standing in much of the Islamic world, but it was particularly important in the Indian Ocean because the distances that needed to be crossed were often so immense. Financing devotion in this comparatively early period of world history therefore took some concerted planning, and the numbers of devotees grew only slowly as the mechanics of going on the pilgrimage gradually evolved. It would only be in the mature colo-nial period of the nineteenth century moving forward, however, that more volu-minous records of the economic importance of the Hajj would become revealed in existing period documents.

---

[31] Carey, *Pangeran Dipanagara*, 359–381.

[32] Michael Laffan, *Islamic Nationhood and Colonial Indonesia: The Umma below the Winds* (London: Routledge, 2003). Laffan has uncovered a lot of useful material on the specifics of lodges, meeting houses, study committees, and more, not just in Mecca but in Cairo as well.

[33] Johan Eisenberger, *Indië en de Bedevaart naar Mekka* (Leiden: M. Dubbeldeman, 1928), 12–15.

THE HAJJ FROM THE BRITISH DOMINIONS OF SOUTHEAST ASIA

Large numbers of indigenous pilgrims left the burgeoning colonial empire of Southeast Asia, with or without the sanction of local imperial regimes. As in the early modern period, financial concerns helped determine who could go on these journeys, how long they might last, and the chances of pilgrims of coming back safely to their homes in the region. In British Malaya, the average Hajji was usually male, in the middle decades of his life, and fairly well-off financially. He was also, more often than not, from the west coast or from the southern states of the Malay peninsula.[34] This profile is contrary, perhaps, to expectations, which might posit pilgrims as coming from the more Malay-dominated, poor, and religiously conservative Muslim east coast states like Kelantan and Trengganu. Having a substantial nest egg of cash was essential. It cost roughly 300 Straits dollars (or 1,000 rials) to perform the Hajj in 1896, though larger sums had to be saved in order to provision one's self for the three-week trip across the Indian Ocean and subsequent months that might be spent in Arabia.[35] The cash earned from the pepper boom on the peninsula in the 1890s helped many Malays go to Mecca, but cash crops and linkage to the global economy meant boom as well as bust.[36] Peasants saved money for years in order to perform the trip, often selling possessions so that extra cash could be acquired on top of one's already pooled resources. The accumulation of vast quantities of money to perform the pilgrimage, even to the point of indigence afterward, was not uncommon. The completion of the Hajj was seen as a ticket to special prestige, so few efforts were spared to round up the necessary funds, even if this meant the potential for financial hardship upon one's return.[37]

An important institution for helping along the financial aspects of the Hajj in British-controlled Southeast Asia was that of *waqf,* or Islamic endowments. *Waqf* were established in a number of different places in the British imperium in the region, but nowhere more so than in Singapore, where there was already a great concentration

---

[34] Mary McDonnell, *The Conduct of the Hajj from Malaysia and its Socio-Economic Impact on Malay Society,* Ph.D. thesis, Columbia University, 1986, 74. Although contemporary Malaysians from all over the country go on Hajj, there is still a strong stereotype of the east coast peninsular states as being more "Muslim" than the heterogeneous west coast states. Part of this pattern is demographic—the west coast states, with their histories of tin mines, rubber plantations, and cities, were the places that received the most overseas laborers, usually from China and India. Likewise, Sarawak and Sabah, in East Malaysia (Malaysian Borneo), have large indigenous populations of "Dayaks" who have not converted to Islam.

[35] McDonnell, *The Conduct of the Hajj from Malaysia,* 75.

[36] William Roff, "The Conduct of the Hajj from Malaya and the First Malay Pilgrimage Officer," in *Kuala Lumpur: Occasional Paper #1 of the Institute of Malay Language, Literature, and Culture* (Kuala Lumpur: Universiti Kebangsaan Malaysia, 1975), 104, now in his *Studies in Islam and Society in Southeast Asia* (Singapore: NUS Press, 2009), 308–342.

[37] J. M. Gullick, *Indigenous Political Systems of Western Malaya* (London: Athlone, 1958), 139–141.

of surplus funds in Muslim hands. Powerful Arab families in Singapore, such as the Al-Sagoffs and Alkaffs, both of which had strong connections with clan-members still in the Hejaz, were particularly important in extending the benefits of *waqf* to ordinary Southeast Asian pilgrims who needed financial help in order to perform the Hajj.[38] This was done most often between ethnic Arabs, on the one hand, and Malays, on the other. *Waqf* endowments lent money, helped pay for steamship tickets, fronted cash or credit for housing in the Holy Cities, and also put forth a network of contacts and handlers so that pilgrims from the Malay world could attempt this huge journey, one that was usually far outside of the experience of local people. *Waqf* also performed these services under the aegis of what we might now call the building blocks of "Islamic banking principles."[39] This is to say that undertaking the Hajj through such endowments was supposed to insulate and protect pilgrims to a degree from some of the more rapacious members of capitalist Singapore—both indigenous and foreign, Muslim and non-Muslim—who made huge sums of money every year off the Hajj trade. In reality, the British colonial government kept a very strong watch on the *waqf* endowments, both because they were suspected of illegal transactions and abuses of their charges and because they were considered to be anti-colonial in nature on a number of occasions. Despite these concerns, many local Muslims felt safest organizing their pilgrimages through *waqf*-endowments, though reliance on these institutions did not prevent some Hajj-aspirants from being cheated or bilked of funds by some of their coreligionists as well.[40] The Hajj, in sum, necessitated a curious and complex mix of financial arrangements, whereby indigenous *waqf* payments and imperial banking arrangements vis-à-vis shipping and savings deposits (more on this latter notion in a moment) all coalesced in the undertaking of most individual pilgrimages. Colonial Europeans, of course, profited on these latter lines of commerce across cultures in the undertaking of the Hajj, making money off both transport and banking whenever they could.

Though Islamic teachings frowned upon commercial risk-taking in order to undertake the Hajj, many Malays still did go into debt in order to fulfill this fifth pillar of the faith. Statistics from the *fin de siècle* show that there were Malays who had a difficult time maintaining themselves in the Hejaz, and also returning home.[41] The *shaykhs* who controlled the pilgrim-brokerage and pilgrim-transport businesses

---

[38] Rajeswary Ampalavanar Brown, "Islamic Endowments and the Land Economy in Singapore: The Genesis of an Ethical Capitalism, 1830–2007," *South East Asia Research*, 16.3 (2008): 343–403.

[39] D. S. Powers, "The Islamic Endowment (Waqf)," *Vanderbilt Journal of Transnational Law*, 32.4 (1999): 1167–1190, 1190.

[40] Stephanie Po Yin Chung, "Western Law vs. Asian Customs: Legal Disputes on Business Practices in India, British Malaya and Hong Kong, 1850s–1930s," *Asia Europe Journal*, 1 (1993): 527–539.

[41] McDonnell, *The Conduct of the Hajj from Malaysia*, 71.

were almost uniformly seen as sharks, men who preyed on their coreligionists in an attempt to earn fast money on unsuspecting souls. This was cross-cultural commerce, as one period European observer of the system commented, but it was also cross-cultural robbery when it came to the mixing of the Hajj and the economic mechanisms that were used to run it.[42] Pilgrims were constantly extorted at each step of the journey: they were made to wait for their passage and use up funds on housing until the proper steamers arrived, were over-charged for tickets, were given passage to only the next port, and also were frequently deceived about the overall costs involved.[43] For all of these reasons, the British finally assented to the appointment of a Malay pilgrimage officer after the turn of the twentieth century, who went off with the first Malay ships of the Hajj season and who came back on the last one, tending his "flock" as a kind of officially sanctioned guardian.[44] Yet it was only after many decades of graft, including several high-profile court cases (such as one involving the famous Alsagoff family in 1881, who were accused of essentially keeping pilgrims in a position of slavery before and after the Hajj through debt-bondage), that matters were even somewhat ameliorated by the British.[45]

The problem of indigence among archipelago pilgrims was a serious one for some time in Southeast Asia. Poor Hajjis who could not pay to get back to the region came from both the British and Dutch sides of the Straits of Melaka, and there was often a stream of correspondence between the civil servants of both colonies trying to figure out how to get these pilgrims home at the least possible cost.[46] Calculated political surveillance sometimes met genuine colonial philanthropy (and paternalism) in a number of these cases. These unfortunates, who could be stranded in the Hejaz for some time, often with little or no means of supporting themselves

---

[42] Snouck Hurgronje to General Secretariat, October 7, 1893, in E. Gobee and C. Adriaanse, eds., *Ambtelijke Adviezen van C. Snouck Hurgronje* (hereafter *AASH*), 3 vols. (The Hague: Martinus Nijhoff, 1959), 2–32, 1383; Snouck Hurgronje to Director of Education, Religion, and Industry, March 10, 1891, in *AASH*, 2–32, 1371.

[43] Moshe Yegar, *Islam and Islamic Institutions in British Malaya: Policies and Implementation* (Jerusalem: Magnes Press, 1979), 228. For all of the above reasons, the British took an active interest in policing the conduct of Hajj traffic as it moved across the Indian Ocean from Britain's Southeast Asian possessions. Though it took several decades for these efforts to really bear fruit, by the turn of the century there were already some inroads being made into the coordination and control of some of the worst abuses of the Hajj. See the *Straits Settlements Government Gazette*, Ordinances #12 (1901) and #3 and #17 (1906), for changes made to the laws on pilgrim ships and pilgrim brokers.

[44] Haji Abdul Majid, "A Malay's Pilgrimage to Mecca," *Journal of the Malaysian Branch of the Royal Asiatic Society*, 14.2 (1926): 269–287.

[45] See the *Straits Times Overland Journal*, July 28, 1881, and William Roff, *The Origins of Malay Nationalism* (Kuala Lumpur: Penerbit Universiti Malaya, 1974), 39.

[46] "List of British Javanese Pauper Pilgrims Repatriated by S.S. 'Sardar,' dated the 26 September 1916," in Arsip Negara Malaysia (National Archives of Malaysia (hereafter ARNEG), High Commission, Secretary of Police Bombay to Sec., Foreign and Political Dept., December 21, 1916, #491/1917.

and their families, occasionally even traveled back across the Indian Ocean on the same ships, putting into British and then Dutch Indies ports in keeping with the sailing schedules of the main ocean passenger lines.[47] Yet not all pecuniary matters involved indigence when it came to the Hajj; there were also a number of other prosaic matters that made the entire huge system of transport and traffic run on an Asia-wide basis. Sometimes Malay elites applied for loans to the government to send family members to Mecca, like Dato Bandar of Sungei Ujong, who did just this in an attempt to get his wife to the Hejaz right at the turn of the twentieth century.[48] Financial support from non-Muslim institutions allowed the Hajj to run in many cases like this one, for example. Even more common was a vast system of remittances that developed to keep archipelago pilgrims solvent while they were in Arabia, constantly supplied with funds from their family members and associates who were still back in Southeast Asia.[49] Banking facilities in the Hejaz were still rather underdeveloped even into the second decade of the twentieth century, necessitating all sorts of arrangements to ensure that capital could move over large oceanic distances and then be available to traveling Muslims.[50] Most of the financial systems were not run by Muslims themselves, and this gradually became a matter of concern for many Muslims, who felt—especially in the advancing age of anti-colonial "awakening"—that something as important as the Hajj should not be financially controlled by non-believers. English banks and Englishmen made profits on these cross-cultural transactions, of course. Yet even certain Malay state governments (such as Kedah) used these systems, often to pay salaries to their own *shaykhs* and pilgrim agents during the months they were away from the peninsula.[51]

THE HAJJ FROM THE NETHERLANDS EAST INDIES

The smaller colonial power of Holland also took great care to exercise maintenance and control over the pilgrimage in its Southeast Asian domains. As was the case on the evolving British side of the Straits, the Dutch were mostly fine with the idea of their subjects going to Mecca, and trading and meeting a variety of people along the way, so long as these journeys did not translate into any kind of anti-colonial "militancy" when their subjects returned from the Hejaz. They also realized that this was a chance to make substantial profits on the allied trades involved with the pilgrimage, too.

---

[47] ARNEG, High Commission, Dutch Consul, Singapore to Sec. for the High Commission, March 31, 1919, #402.

[48] ARNEG, High Commission, 1905, #945

[49] See, for example, ARNEG, High Commission, 1918, #279 and 1918, #720.

[50] ARNEG, High Commission, Sec. to the Comm. to Sec. of the Resident, Perak, March 20, 1918, #279/1918.

[51] ARNEG, High Commission, Advisor to Kedah Government to High Comm., Sing., May 16, 1918, #1187/36.

Dutch record keeping on the subject of the Hajj tends to be excellent from a very early date. Local *controleurs* (mid-level civil servants, usually Dutch but often assisted by indigenous helpers) were told by their superiors to note the details of the pilgrimage to Mecca from their residencies, and much of this reporting ended up being financial in nature. The reports from a single place, the residency of Banten in West Java for the year of 1860 alone, are instructive in this regard. In a series of handwritten accounts from that year, the local resident informed Batavia of the names of local people who had returned from Mecca that same year: individuals such as Mochamad Markoem, Inam, Hadjie Djamiel, and Hadji Daham all entered the records in this manner. This piece of information is interesting in and of itself because it gives us the actual names of farmers and fishermen who would not normally have entered into colonial record (we do not usually find the names and scattered details of indigenes in the record unless they were in direct contact with the Dutch, either politically or economically). But it is also important because it informs us that 222 of these people came back to the residency that year from Mecca, a very high number if one considers the costs and difficulties of travel in 1860.[52] Since 1858, two years previously, almost a quarter of a million guilders had left the residency via these trips, as pilgrims took whatever funds they could get their hands on. This was a cause for some alarm to local officials, and the problem of "silver drain" became one commented upon in every level of government reportage examining the mechanics of the Hajj.[53]

Finally, some of these reports are detailed enough to let us know exactly how much money each pilgrim was bringing on his person for the trip. Kardja brought 150 Spanish dollars in 1860, Kaman brought 100, while Abdulah and Oesman from Petier and Dragem villages, respectively, brought 200 dollars each.[54] The level of detail in the reporting is quite astonishing, and given the fact that this was happening all across the more settled districts of the Dutch Indies, a very large cache of data exists with which to interpret the conduct of the Indonesian Hajj, even at this early date.[55]

---

[52] Arsip Nasional Republik Indonesia, Jakarta (National Archives of Indonesia, hereafter ANRI), Residentie Bantam Algemeen Verslag, Appendix: Opgave van de Personen die ter Bedevaart naar Mekka zijn Teruggekeerd (1860).

[53] ANRI, Residentie Bantam Algemeen Verslag (1860).

[54] ANRI, Residentie Bantam Algemeen Verslag, Appendix: Opgave van de Personen die ter Bedevaart naar Mekka zijn Vertrokken (1860).

[55] For an incredible example of the depth of this reportage, see the bundle titled "Rapporten Dari Perkara Hadji Hadja njang Minta Pas dan njang Baru Datang dari Mekka, 1860/61/62/63/64," in ANRI, Tegal archive, #196/5, "Laporan Pergi dan Pulang Haji." This is only one of a number of 500-page bundles of local letters and reports on the Hajj in Tegal alone—just one small residency in Java. A small book could be written on the basis of this one archival bundle alone.

Fees were charged by the Dutch for the right of going on pilgrimage, and these escalated from 110 guilders at mid-century to 200 guilders in 1873, and then to 300 guilders in 1890. Shortly after this latter date, the price was lowered to 100 guilders again, but a return-ticket on a steamer was a condition of being let out of the Indies so that pilgrims would not be stranded.[56] In both of these ways—outright fees and through shipping charges—the Dutch made large sums from the Hajj. An enormous system of brokers developed to take care of the ever-burgeoning Dutch East Indies pilgrim traffic, most of which was transited through British Singapore. In 1880 there were 180 *shaykhs* in charge of this Indies flow alone, a number that grew to 400 by the eve of World War I and to 600–700 ten years after that, according to the chronicler Haji Abdul Majid, who made the trip himself in that former year.[57] Since large numbers of these *shaykhs* were Arabs, there was a significant cross-cultural dimension to these transactions, in addition to the cross-religious dealings with the Dutch. A great many of these Indies pilgrims were leaving the archipelago for the first time and had little idea of the vagaries of international commerce on the great shipping lanes stretching all the way across the vast Indian Ocean. As a result, many of these Hajjis were charged quite a bit more than their Malay counterparts, despite the fact that they were ultimately leaving from the same Southeast Asian ports.[58] A steady stream of pilgrims found their way over to the Hejaz via these intricate connections, leaving the Indies from a series of Dutch harbors and stopping over in the British dominions (usually Singapore or Penang) before making the big jump across the sea to the Arabian Peninsula.

Yet just as with the Malay pilgrims, many Indies Hajjis suffered at the hands of a series of middlemen who took advantage of their comparative naiveté and powerlessness as they tried to complete their Hajj.[59] (Though rumors and information

---

[56] Eisenberger, *Indië en de Bedevaart*, 27, 175.

[57] Jacob Vredenbregt, "The Hadj: Some of Its Features and Functions in Indonesia," *Bijdragen tot de Taal-, Land-, en Volkenkunde*, 118 (1962): 91–154, and Haji Abdul Majid, "A Malay's Pilgrimage," 270. Keeping track of all of these *shaykhs* and the various dangers they represented to the Dutch colonial government was a small but very active group of diplomats scattered across several Indian Ocean ports. The Dutch had their own servants reporting on Hajj movements and patterns via salaried European consuls, and they also maintained a quiet network of indigenous Southeast Asian spies who reported on local movements for money. Dutch consuls and vice consuls charged with keeping an eye out on the Hajj were stationed in Batavia, Singapore, Penang, and Jeddah, so that irregularities or potential ideas of rebellion and/or dissent traveling on the religious radials of pilgrimage could be watched.

[58] McDonnell, *The Conduct of the Hajj from Malaysia*, 76.

[59] For a partial overview of the legislation against this profiteering, see Eisenberger, *Indië en de Bedevaart*, 31–37. Ann Kumar has suggested that despite widespread notices of indigence, pious men could receive generous gifts of clothes, sustenance, and other presents from benefactors when they returned to Southeast Asia; see Mas Rahmat's experiences in Ann Kumar, *The Diary of a Javanese Muslim: Religion, Politics and the Pesantren, 1883–1886* (Canberra: Faculty of Asian Studies Monographs, 1985).

circulated in villages via returning Hajjis, most pilgrims had never traveled anywhere near as far as Mecca before their own trips, and thus were vulnerable to predations of different sorts along the way.) An 1876 Dutch consular report suggested that approximately 30 percent of all Indies pilgrims eventually found themselves to be destitute in the Hejaz, a number and a percentage far higher than for Malay pilgrims.[60] Many of the archipelago Hajjis entered into contracts in order to raise cash for their journeys, agreeing to work in Singapore, Malaya, or even in Arabia itself for years so that sufficient funds could be raised.[61] The rate of return on these menial jobs (usually on plantations) was so low that some pilgrims could find themselves in a perpetual cycle of debt from which they could never hope to escape.[62] The *shaykhs* who perpetuated this cycle of indebtedness were often Arabs resident to Southeast Asia, but after several decades there were more and more indigenous archipelago returnees who were also entering this very profitable business. Since the Dutch gradually restricted the numbers of Indies pilgrims allowed to go on the pilgrimage, many started to go illegally by way of Singapore, putting themselves even more at the mercy of the *shaykhs*, as they now had little recourse to colonial laws to protect them. A report in the *Indische Gids* in 1897 catalogued some of the many deceptions that were practiced on Indies pilgrims, but offered little by way of practical solutions.[63] Ottoman Turkish officialdom was also implicated in these bad business dealings, showing that the confluence between religion and predatory commerce also happened within Islam, if still across ethnic boundaries.[64] Even if the Dutch knew their subjects were being fleeced, often on a systemic basis, doing something about these frauds seemed to be beyond the organizational powers of Batavia's administrators.

Undertaking the Hajj in the colonial Southeast Asian world, therefore, was certainly possible, despite European fears of pan-Islamic influences, and even despite global recessions such as the ones that periodically swept the region in the late colonial age. Yet it was always a difficult journey at best, filled with danger, deception, and disease, as well as the possibility of life spent in penury for the very best motives of fulfilling one's religious duties. Colonial states tried to ameliorate some of the problems facing their Asian subjects, but often these challenges were too difficult for

---

[60] Marcel Witlox, "Met Gevaar voor Lijf en Goed: Mekkagangers uit Nederlands-Indie in de 19de Eeuw," in *Islamitische Pelgrimstochten*, ed. Willy Jansen and Huub de Jonge (Muiderberg: Coutinho, 1991), 18–38, 30.

[61] See Roff, *The Origins of Malay Nationalism*, 38–39.

[62] Vredenbregt, "The Hadj," 113–115.

[63] See the *Indische Gids* (1897), 390.

[64] Snouck Hurgronje to Director of Education and Industry, May 30, 1894, in *AASH*, 2–32, 1451; Snouck Hurgronje to Minister for the Colonies, April 2, 1909, in *AASH*, 2–32, 1460; Snouck Hurgronje to Minister for the Colonies, July 2, 1910, in *AASH*, 2–32, 1461.

regimes still teetering on the brink of a kind of administrative modernity. The numbers of Britons and Dutchmen in Southeast Asia were still small in the mid- to late nineteenth century; the sustained surge of Europeans coming out to the colonies to find work would not take place for another several decades. The question of intent also needs to be raised, as there is some suggestion in many period documents that very real Western fears over the results of the Hajj (spiritual and political) may have weakened imperial resolve to fix all existing deficiencies.[65] It is not clear how much of a role this anxiety may have played, but what is certain is that Southeast Asians were able to go on pilgrimage in far larger numbers than they ever had previously, in fact by the tens of thousands each year by the *fin de siècle* period.[66] The attendant risks and difficulties were seen as part of the voyage, and the large sums of money that had to be raised were almost always viewed as resources well spent.

CONCLUSION

Prior to the colonial age, the Hajj across the Indian Ocean was undertaken by relatively few people from a total population standpoint; it might be a good year for the pilgrimage if only a few hundred souls made the journey, up until the turn of the nineteenth century. The Hajj was outside the economic reach of all but a few; sultans and nobles could hope to go if their devotion or their connections were particularly strong, but for most ordinary people, Mecca was simply too far way from the "lands beneath the winds" to be an attainable destination. Some archipelago rulers did help finance the pilgrimages of their subjects, and a few poorer Southeast Asians did indeed find their way out to the Hejaz, sometimes staying there for months or even years as part of their initial Hajj. These communities in turn acted as gatekeepers for other people from the region who followed, aiding them with their religious obligations and with their acclimatization to the holy cities of the desert. Trade between coreligionists of different ethnicities was also an important component of the system, helping it to run on an oceanic level of exchange. Despite Das Gupta's assertions to the contrary, however, it seems that the Hajj was an important—but not always a crucial—lynchpin to the economic orbit of the greater Indian Ocean. Pilgrims came and went across this vast expanse of sea, and their funds helped to invigorate a far-flung oceanic economy that transited across these maritime spaces. Yet the available sources from this early period suggest that the numbers of devotees were simply too small to have had an overwhelming effect on the early modern

---

[65] See the argument presented in Eric Tagliacozzo, "Kettle on a Slow Boil: Batavia's Threat Perceptions in the Indies' Outer Islands," *Journal of Southeast Asian Studies*, 31.1 (2000): 70–100.

[66] Tagliacozzo, "Kettle on a Slow Boil," 86.

economy of the region, even if this effect was financially important in all sorts of ways.

The imposition of concerted colonial rule over large parts of Southeast Asia from the nineteenth century changed this paradigm considerably. Subjects of British Colonial Malaya and the Straits Settlements, as well as from the Dutch East Indies, had more of an opportunity to go on Hajj now than they ever had previously.[67] Colonial steamship lines, cholera quarantines, and expanding financial services all ensured a lower cost and safer pilgrimage than had been possible in the past. These same European regimes in the colonies also worked to ameliorate debt-bondage and some of the other egregious violations of pilgrims' rights both in Southeast Asia and on the Arabian peninsula. At the same time, colonial governments were reluctant to cede too much control to Hajjis themselves in arrangements to get pilgrims out to the Hejaz and then back again to Southeast Asia. If it became economically more realistic to perform one's Hajj during these decades leading up to the *fin de siècle* than it had been previously, it also became less and less realistic to do this on one's own terms. Commerce across the Asian/Western divide, even if it was in the service of devotion, thus sometimes had its limits. Singapore and especially Batavia both saw the pilgrimage as a potentially dangerous transmitter of militancy and radical ideas to their own subject populations. In this sense, the financing of devotion was made available to the indigenous populations of the archipelago, but only through channels that colonial governments themselves could check and approve on a regional basis. This desire for absolute or near-absolute control on the part of imperial regimes in their dealings with the Hajj was, in fact, a discernible hallmark of the late colonial age.

---

[67] Pilgrims also started to come from some of the other colonies of Southeast Asia during this period, most notably the Spanish Philippines and French Indochina, but they were so small in overall number at this point that I have not treated this phenomenon here.

10

African Meanings and European-African Discourse

ICONOGRAPHY AND SEMANTICS IN

SEVENTEENTH-CENTURY SALT CELLARS FROM SERRA LEOA

Peter Mark

INTRODUCTION

In this chapter I propose a historically contextualized interpretation of ivory vessels carved in West Africa in the sixteenth and early seventeenth centuries and then sold to Portuguese merchants. These objects illustrate—indeed, they embody—cross-cultural communication and resulting cultural hybridity. Religious symbolism figures prominently on several of these salt cellars, yet the meaning associated with these symbols changed as the objects moved from African producer to European consumer. In my conclusion, and following the recent work of Hans Belting, I seek a more profound and systemic analysis and understanding of art and cultural hybridity, one that takes us beyond the iconographic interpretation identified with classic art history.

In sixteenth- and seventeenth-century Guinea of Cape Verde—the Upper Guinea Coast from Senegal through Sierra Leone—an extensive and varied commerce developed between local Africans, Portuguese merchants, some of whom settled on the coast, and middlemen composed largely of the Luso-African descendants of both groups. "Luso-African" is the descriptive term used by historians to refer to those individuals of Portuguese or mixed Portuguese and African background who constituted a hybrid cultural group, characterized by their language, profession, religion, and material culture. Luso-Africans referred to themselves and were described by their neighbors as "Portuguese," regardless of the color of their skin. They spoke Portuguese as a *lingua franca*; by the mid-seventeenth century their descendants spoke Portuguese *Crioulo*. In addition, they had a distinctive material culture, characterized by their European-style clothing and household wares and by their "Portuguese-style" houses: rectangular white-washed structures, with a veranda or *alpendre*. The Luso-Africans were also defined by their religion (they were, at least nominally, Catholics) and by their profession (they were merchants). Their cultural hybridity and their professional activity meant that the Luso-Africans were also cultural intermediaries or brokers.[1]

By the late sixteenth century, an extensive trade in blade weapons, known as *armas brancas*, played a central role in commerce between Europe and the Upper Guinea Coast. This weapons trade was depicted by ivory carvers from Serra Leoa (present-day coastal Sierra Leone and southeastern Guinea). The artists, identified as *Sapes* by contemporary Portuguese sources, were themselves working for an international clientele.

The forced conversion of Portugal's Jewish community in 1497 brought about the establishment of the category of New Christians, descendants of these converted Jews. While many New Christians continued discreetly to observe their traditional religious rituals, the creation of a Portuguese Inquisition after 1536 placed secretly practicing Jews at serious risk. Growing numbers of Portuguese New Christians subsequently sought to escape the threat of the Inquisition through emigration to outposts of the Portuguese commercial empire. An unknown number—likely several hundred—settled in the commercial hub for the Guinea Coast trade, the Cape Verde Islands. By then moving—illegally—to the mainland, individuals could escape the tentacles of the Inquisition. By the end of the seventeenth century an indeterminate, but significant, number of both Old and New Christian traders had moved to Guiné do Cabo Verde to cast their lot among the local populations as *lançados*. These *lançados* served as middlemen in the coastal trade; they were also cultural intermediaries between European merchants and local African merchants, as well as the African

---

[1] On the Luso-Africans, see George Brooks, *Eurafricans in Western Africa* (Athens: Ohio University Press, 2003); José da Silva Horta, "Evidence for a Luso-African Identity in 'Portuguese' Accounts on 'Guiné of Cape Verde' (16th–17th Centuries)," *History in Africa*, 27 (2000): 99–130; Peter Mark, *Portuguese Style and Luso-African Identity* (Bloomington: Indiana University Press, 2003); Peter Mark and José da Silva Horta, *The Forgotten Diaspora, Jewish Communities in West Africa and the Making of the Atlantic World* (New York: Cambridge University Press, 2011); Philip Havik, *Silences and Soundbytes: The Gendered Dynamics of Trade and Brokerage in the Pre-colonial Guinea Bissau Region* (Münster: Lit Verlag, 2004); Toby Green, ed., *Brokers of Change: Atlantic Commerce and Cultures in Precolonial Western Africa*, Proceedings of the British Academy, 178 (Oxford: Oxford University Press, 2012).

producers of cotton cloth, ivory, hides, wax, and of captives.[2] Those *lançados* who had emigrated in order to maintain their Jewish traditions did so, naturally, in secret. Contemporary records of their existence are, consequently, limited to rumors. There is some indirect evidence of Jewish *lançados* in mid-sixteenth century Casamance, as well as in late-sixteenth century Serra Leoa. That situation changed, however, about 1610, with the establishment of two communities of publicly declared Jewish merchants at Portodale and Joal, on Senegal's Petite Côte.[3] These communities are richly documented both in records of the Lisbon Inquisition—which never succeeded in persecuting them—and in the notary archives of Amsterdam, whose newly established Jewish community developed strong commercial and religious ties with the Portuguese Jews of the Petite Côte.

From shortly before 1610 until at least 1620, the Jews of the Petite Côte dominated the export trade from Upper Guinea of ivory and of hides. Most of the ivory was exported as tusks. However, the production for export to Europe of carved ivory spoons and elaborately decorated vessels known as salt cellars, or *saleiros*, an artistic production that began in the late fifteenth century, was still carried out by artists of the Sapi or Sape "nation" from Serra Leoa in the early seventeenth century. These ivories show a complex symbolism that conjoins cultural elements from the Guinea Coast and themes introduced by the European clients—or the Portuguese and *lançado* coastal brokers. Some of the European symbols derive from mythology or fables; some are clearly expressions of Christian themes. Religious symbols incorporated both Christian and local African imagery. In the following pages, I do not propose any additional specifically Jewish or New Christian interpretation of the salt cellars. However, the African-European commerce and intercultural contact that determined the symbolism and provided the subject matter of the ivories clearly reflect and illuminate the economic role of the Jewish traders who acquired and, undoubtedly in many cases, placed the orders for the ivory spoons and salt cellars. So these ivory vessels provide visual evidence for both trade and the production for market of a wide range of both import and export goods. Subsequent research may be able to establish the existence of a New Christian iconographic sub-stratum.

---

[2] On the *lançados*, see Jean Boulègue, *Les Luso-Africains de la Sénégambie* (Lisbon: IICT/Université de Paris I-Centre de Recherches Africaines, 1989); George Brooks, *Landlords and Strangers: Ecology, Society, and Trade in Western Africa, 1000–1630* (Boulder, CO: Westview Press, 1993); Horta, "Evidence for a Luso-African Identity"; Peter Mark, "The Evolution of 'Portuguese' Identity: Luso-Africans on the Upper Guinea Coast from the Sixteenth to the Early Nineteenth Century," *Journal of African History*, 40. 2 (1999): 173–191; Toby Green, *The Rise of the Trans-Atlantic Slave Trade in Western Africa, 1300–1589* (Cambridge: Cambridge University Press, 2011).

[3] See Mark and Horta, *The Forgotten Diaspora*.

Production of ivory carving for export raises an interesting question: How were orders conveyed to local artists, and how was the desired subject matter described? In other words, how did European and African producers and traders communicate across cultural frontiers? How were directives passed on to local producers? This chapter endeavors to answer these questions in the case of several ivory salt cellars that were produced in Serra Leoa between the early sixteenth and the mid-seventeenth century.

Contemporary Portuguese observers have left us a rich documentation of African society on the Upper Guinea Coast. Three of these men, André Alvares de Almada, André Donelha, and Father Manuel Alvares, all lived for extended periods of time in Upper Guinea. Their writings, which date from 1593 to 1625, refer directly to the production of ivory carvings and provide ethnographic information that enables us to situate the art in its immediate cultural context. Consequently, one may reconstruct some of the meaning inscribed in the ivories by their creators. At the same time, as I hope to make clear, these salt cellars had a meaning on the part of the artist and a meaning, often quite different, imputed by the person who acquired it. In other words, an object's meaning changes with translation. These early written sources are also important because they show that the Luso-African ivories were produced over a much longer period of time than earlier scholars thought. Furthermore, most if not all of the ivories came from Serra Leoa.

"SERRA LEOA": PORTUGUESE WRITTEN SOURCES

Approximately 150 carved ivory spoons, horns, and salt cellars constitute the *corpus* of so-called "Afro-Portuguese" ivories. I have argued that these pieces should more appropriately be referred to as Luso-African ivories. The latter term more accurately reflects the objects' creation by West African sculptors who were working in Africa. The works, although hybrid in inspiration, are far more African than they are Portuguese. West African artists created the sculptures within the context of their own cultures.

These artists were responding to a hybrid Luso-African cultural presence that was first established on the West African coast from Senegal to present-day Sierra Leone in the late fifteenth century (see Figure 10.1). Contemporary sources, namely Father Alvares (1615), identify their place of origin as coastal "Serra Leoa" and their producers as the constellation of ethno-linguistic groups whom the Portuguese called collectively the Sapes.

From the early sixteenth century there existed two concepts of "Serra Leoa." The more narrowly defined area comprised the present-day Sierra Leone peninsula and its mountainous hinterland. The wider "Serra Leoa," however, in the sense used by

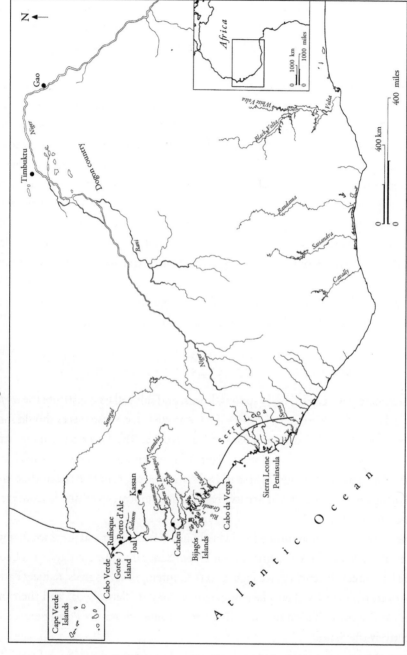

Greater Sengambia/*Guiné do Cabo Verde* in Western Africa

FIGURE 10.1 Map of Greater Sengambia or *Guiné do Cabo Verde* showing Serra Leoa, Joal, and Porto d'Ale.
Source: Peter Mark and José da Silva Horta.

Almada (1594), extended along the coast from the site of present-day Conakry in Guinea to Sherbro Island.[4] Almada, as historian P. E. H. Hair notes, "equated the limits of Serra Leoa with those of the 'Sapes.'" Donelha, too, clearly defines the Serra Leoa both as a geographical area and as a political and linguistic conglomerate. In fact, he goes farther; he associates Serra Leoa with the long-distance commerce that is carried out there. Almada and Donelha were talking about a coastal region and giving it a cultural meaning, the Sape region. Donelha writes:

> All of the country that extends for 53 leagues in a straight line, from Serra Leoa towards the north and northwest as far as Cape Verga at 10 degrees latitude, all of this territory, as I say, is called Serra Leoa. Although it is populated by people of diverse nations speaking various tongues, these nations can understand one another and they are all subjected to the Manes; and as soon as they pass Cape Vergas the navigators who come to trade and carry out commerce say that they are in the Serra Leoa.[5]

Shortly after 1600 a Portuguese Jesuit mission to Guinea was established, headquartered in the Cape Verde Islands. This missionary presence is historically important because several Jesuits left written records that are a rich source of firsthand information about coastal society at the beginning of the seventeenth century. The account written by Father Alvares complements the better-known texts of two late-sixteenth century Cape Verdean–Portuguese merchants, Donelha and Almada. Together, these authors provide a wealth of information about local African societies. Close reading of the narratives also affords insights into material culture.

The Euro-African descendants of Portuguese settlers—like Almada himself—bridged European and African culture. So, too, did some local African rulers and a few wealthy African traders. These African merchants and local rulers showed an astonishing capacity to assimilate elements of European culture. Many of them spoke European languages and lived in "Portuguese style" houses. A few had converted to Christianity. The wealthiest among them filled their houses with furniture, rugs, clothing, and table settings worthy of European royalty. Notable is the king of Bussis, a kingdom located south of the seventeenth-century Portuguese trading

---

4 André Alvares de Almada, *An Interim and Makeshift Edition of André Alvares de Almada's Brief Treatise on the Rivers of Guinea*, trans., introduction, notes on chap. 13–19 by P. E. H. Hair, notes on chap. 1–6 by Jean Boulègue (issued personally, University of Liverpool, Department of History, 1984). See also Almada, *Tratado Breve dos Rios de Guiné do Cabo Verde*, ed. António Brásio (Lisbon: LIAM, 1964). All translations from Almada, unless otherwise noted or initially given in Portuguese, are by P. E. H. Hair.

5 André Donelha, *Descrição da Serra Leoa e dos Rios de Guiné do Cabo Verde (1625)*, ed. A. Teixeira da Mota, notes by P. E. H. Hair, French trans. Léon Bourdon (Lisbon: Junta de Investigações Científicas do Ultramar, 1977), 98–99.

settlement of Cacheu. Father Alvares described this ruler's unparalleled wealth. His possessions included luxury items from all corners of the Portuguese Empire. Some of the silk and the tapestries came from Asia:

> Within his house he keeps many trunks and boxes full of different articles of clothing, such as very elaborate smocks, doublets and breeches, sheets, coverlets and canopies made in silk, and items in gold and silver…these items he has bought and continues to buy from the Portuguese who come there with their ships to obtain slaves.… he possesses tapestries, decorations in leather, carpets, a fine wardrobe. As for weapons, apart from the cannon given him by his admirer, he has muskets, swords, and daggers.[6]

The king of Bussis certainly had access to ivory. In fact, in about 1615, one Portuguese Jewish trader asked him to send ivory and other commodities north to the Petite Côte, in exchange for luxury cloth.[7] Unfortunately, virtually nothing from the material culture of this local African elite has survived—not even the architecture remains. Given the fragility of ivory spoons and vessels, and in view of the fact that even among those ivories that entered European *Kunstkammern* at an early date, only an estimated 4 to 10 percent have survived, it is hardly surprising that no physical evidence of this internal African market for ivory carvings exists today.[8]

ASIAN SOURCES OF ARTISTIC INSPIRATION

Another possible source of artistic inspiration may be found elsewhere in the Portuguese commercial empire: India. Art historian Ezio Bassani suggests that European (and possibly Indian) themes reached Sierra Leone via European engravings.[9] However, there was direct commercial contact between India and Serra Leoa, and probably also with Cape Verde during the late sixteenth century.[10] Indian cotton

---

[6] Manuel Álvares, "Etiópia Menor e Descripção Géografica da Província da Serra Leoa" [ca. 1615], Manuscript copy (eighteenth century), Sociedade de Geografia de Lisboa, Res. 3, E-7, fols. 30v–31r. See also P. E. H. Hair, trans. and annotation, Alvares, *Ethiopia Minor, and a Geographical Account of the Province of Sierra Leone (c. 1615),* transcription from an unpublished manuscript by the late Avelino Teixeira da Mota and Luís de Matos on behalf of the Centro de Estudos de Cartografia Antiga, Lisbon (Department of History, University of Liverpool, 1990).

[7] Arquivos Nacionais/Torre do Tombo, *Inquisição de Lisboa*, livro 250, fol. 294v: "nas folhas 23 esta uma carta sua para dom Sebastião Reei [sic] negro de Bosis."

[8] See Elke Bujok, "Africana und Americana im Ficklerschen Inventar der Münchner Kunstkammer von 1598," *Münchner Beiträge zur Völkerkunde,* 8 (2003): 57–142.

[9] Ezio Bassani, "Additional Notes on the Afro-Portuguese Ivories," *African Arts,* 27.3 (1994): 34–45, 44.

[10] Almada, *Brief Treatise,* 28. Almada wrote that the Serer of Sine, a kingdom on Senegal's Petite Côte, obtained Indian cloth from the Portuguese.

textiles were in great demand in Senegambia, and silk (probably embroidery) was a luxury import.[11] Some of the African horns contain hunting scenes that are nearly identical to scenes embroidered into *colchas*, large embroidered textiles from India commissioned by the Portuguese during the second half of the sixteenth century and into the seventeenth century.[12] As we now know that ivory carving continued into the seventeenth century, the later date for importation of *colchas* to Portugal and Guinea would be consistent with the appearance of Indian themes in carvings from Sierra Leone.

Recently discovered merchants' records show that Asian textiles arrived in Guinea as luxury items, a fact also implied by Father Alvares's 1615 description of the ruler of Bussis. Hence, Indian colchas may have served as inspiration for the later hunting horns.[13] Valentim Fernandes describes the Sapes as follows: "In Sierra Leone the men are extremely subtle and ingenious…Some make spoons others make salt cellars and others make handles for daggers and any other subtlety."[14] This characterization makes it clear that, at least in the first decade of the sixteenth century, there were more than a few ivory carvers. Furthermore, the artists specialized: some produced spoons, others salt cellars, and still others dagger handles or other objects. Hence the argument that there were only as many artists as could have produced the known ivories cannot be sustained.

SAPES SOCIETY AND RELIGION AND SEVENTEENTH-CENTURY IVORY CARVING

The critical information for the provenance of post-1550 Luso-African ivories must, of course, be provided by historical documentation. Such documentation exists, and it demonstrates convincingly that the so-called Sapes produced ivory carvings from the late fifteenth century to the mid-seventeenth century. ("Sapes," as suggested

---

[11] Linda Newson, in her study of the account books of the Portuguese New Christian merchant Manoel Bautista Peres, a trader who was in Upper Guinea between 1616 and 1618, calculates that 28 percent of the more than 22,000 pieces of cloth traded by Peres came from India. See Newson, "Bartering for Slaves on the Upper Guinea Coast," in *Brokers of Change*, 259–284, 271.

[12] In an unpublished study, Kathy Curnow observes the appearance of hunting motifs on *colchas*: *The Afro-Portuguese Ivories: Classification and Stylistic Analysis of a Hybrid Art Form*, Ph.D. thesis, Indiana University, 1983. However, her dating of the Sierra Leone ivories to before 1550—if correct—would effectively have ruled out the possibility of Indian influence.

[13] For the import of Indian goods to Guinea, see Newson, "Bartering for Slaves," 266. I wish to thank Dr. Barbara Karl for providing access to her comprehensive photographic archives of Indian *colchas*. Indian influence via *colchas* is only possible for hunting horns produced after 1570.

[14] *Códice Valentim Fernandes*, original manuscript, Bayerische Staatsbibliothek, *Codex hispanicus* 27, MF 1282 363 Aufn 1282 363, fol. 136r: "Em Serra Lyoa som os homens muyto sotijs muy engeniosos…hûus fazem colheyros outros saleyros outros punhos pera dagas e qualquer outra sotileza." See also fn. 36.

earlier, is an umbrella term that incorporates the ancestors of several present-day ethnic groups, including Bullom, Baga, Landuma, and possibly Temne. The term "Sapes" has not been used since the seventeenth century, which probably facilitated the mistaken assumption that, following the Mane "invasion," the people referred to by that label ceased to exist.) In Sierra Leone the Sapes continued to carve ivory into the seventeenth century. Manuel Alvares, the Jesuit missionary who lived in Sierra Leone from 1607 to 1616, describes the creation of these works in his *Etiópia Menor*. Álvares lived on the coast of Serra Leoa and was familiar with local society. His description firmly documents the survival of ivory carving, 65 years after the Mane invasion. The Manes were a Mande-speaking people who, around 1550, migrated southward into Sape territory. Initially their migration took the form of a military invasion, probably incited in part by the desire to collect taxes from the Sapes. The fighting destroyed parts of the coastal societies and led to the enslavement of several hundred Sapes.[15] Within a generation, however, the Mane invaders were transformed into settlers who lived peacefully and intermarried with the original inhabitants, leading to a thriving, hybrid Sape/Mane society.

Alvares describes the many diverse peoples living in the vicinity of the Portuguese trading center of Mitombo. Each group, including Temnes and Sapes, whose country, he writes, "only survives in part," speaks its own language."[16] He continues:

> Because of their ability and intelligence some of them have the gift of artistic imagination and they carve in wood images of their dead which they call "cerof,"…The variety of their handicrafts is due to their artistry. [They make]…tagarras, large wooden dishes in different sizes, of unusual and pleasing design, which are here used at table; spoons made of ivory, beautifully finished, the handles carved in entertaining shapes, such as the heads of animals, birds or their "corofis" [idols], all done with such perfection that it has to be seen to be believed; "betes" or "rachons" which are round and are used as low seats, and are made in curious shapes to resemble lizards and other small creatures.[17]

Alvares, writing in 1615, was absolutely clear. The Sapes were still highly skilled artists. They continued to carve ivory spoons with great skill long after the Mane invasion of the preceding century. Furthermore, the description of the decorated handles perfectly fits surviving spoons, some of which have been attributed to Benin.

---

[15] Green, *The Rise of the Trans-Atlantic Slave Trade*, 24–26.

[16] Alvares, "Etiópia Menor e Descripção Géografica da Província da Serra Leoa," P. E. H. Hair, translation, fol. 54r.

[17] Alvares, "Etiópia Menor," fol. 55v.

Alvares's description also informs us about Sape religion. The Sapes were not Muslims. Their religion centered on shrines that were the locale for prayers and accompanying libations of palm wine and animal sacrifices, marking formal ritual contact between the human and the spiritual realm. These shrines embodied or represented spiritual forces, which the Sapes called *corofis*. They took the form of natural objects such as trees; or of man-made objects such as wooden stakes, sometimes carved; or of ivory carvings of the *corofis*. Individuals, as well as village societies, gathered to make ritual offerings and to pray at the shrine. As the passage from Father Alvares implies, the Sapes venerated their ancestors, some of whom they memorialized by means of wooden carvings. By the 1570s, if not earlier, some local Sape rulers ("kings," as the Portuguese referred to them) had converted to Christianity.

Father Alvares's description of the large wooden bowls might fit salt cellars, too. The original manuscript reads: "...large dishes of wood, most unusual and beautiful, and that here are used at table; of which some are rather small, others larger."[18] Later Luso-African ivories also figure in André Donelha's 1625 account, *Descrição da Sierra Leoa e dos Rios do Guiné do Cabo Verde*. This account was based on two decades of experience as a trader at the end of the century. Donelha mentions the production of ivory trumpets.

Highly significant, because of its late date, is the account of Francisco de Lemos Coelho, a Portuguese Cape Verdean trader who frequented the coast in the middle decades of the seventeenth century. Lemos Coelho, who visited Sierra Leone in 1658, wrote an account of Guinea in 1669, which he revised and expanded in 1684.[19] He writes that "the Blacks make many curious things in ivory," and he adds "those from here being better than those from any other part of Serra Leoa."[20] This terse notation makes it abundantly clear that ivory carving in Sierra Leone continued through the seventeenth century and that pieces carved for local consumption often held religious significance.

THE WORK OF PRODUCTION

Ivory is carved with knives. Once high-quality steel blades became available to Guinea Coast artists, the refinement of carving techniques would have rapidly

---

[18] Ibid, fol. 55v: "que são hûas escudellas grandes de páo, mui curiósas, e lindas, que cá servem nas mesas; das quais hûas são mais pequenas, outras maiores."

[19] See Francisco de Lemos Coelho, *Description of the Coast of Guinea (1684)*, trans. P. E. H. Hair (Liverpool: University of Liverpool, History Department, 1985), introduction.

[20] Lemos Coelho, *Description of the Coast of Guinea (1684)*, vol. 1, Introduction and English translation of the Portuguese text by P. E. H. Hair, issued for circulation to scholars from the Department of History, University of Liverpool, 1985, chap. 9, para. 73, p. 36.

increased. So the trade in subtly carved ivory that began in the 1490s would, in fact, have facilitated the creation of these ivory salt cellars in the first place. Ivory carving would not be the highest priority use for imported blades. Priority would have gone to weapons and agricultural implements. Only as steel became more readily available via European trade would the carvers have obtained ready access to steel blades.

These ivories were produced by members of one cultural grouping, the Sape peoples. At least some of the salt cellars were ordered by Europeans, probably for use by nobility. Along the Upper Guinea Coast, many of the Portuguese and Luso-Africans traders were married to local African women. And some of the women, too, were merchants. In Sierra Leone, it was the Luso-Africans or "Portuguese" who served not only as commercial middlemen, but also as cultural intermediaries. In other words, this Luso-African community provided a channel to communicate demand to the producers. The Luso-Africans would have been responsible for passing on the commissions, including at least a broad sense of the desired subject matter, to the artists.

The carving of ivories in Serra Leoa for European clients leads us to ask: How was demand conveyed to the local artisans and how were orders placed? In other words, how did European and African merchants carry out the work of trade across cultural frontiers? How were instructions, particularly relating to subject matter, passed to the local producers? We can answer these questions in varied ways, depending on the iconography. But one group of ivory salt cellars conveys symbols that can only be understood, in the first instance, through an appreciation of the local culture's representation of power. And specific and detailed information about those sixteenth- and seventeenth-century societies is available in the contemporary descriptions of coastal society that I already have discussed, all written by men who had extensive trading experience with the peoples of the Upper Guinea Coast.

The Luso-African middlemen were ordering luxury objects for European nobility. The local Sape artists provided images of secular and spiritual power, as they understood such power from their own societies. That is, these ivories are intended as images of royal authority, expressed in local cultural terms from the Guinea Coast. A salt cellar now in the Museo Civico in Bologna may enable us to reconstruct the process whereby Luso-African middlemen conveyed commissions to the Sape artists. This sculpture comes from the Bolognese *Kunstkammer* of Ferdinando Cospi (1606–1686), the so-called Museo Cospiano, which was the nucleus of today's Museo Civico's collection. It must have been acquired in the mid-seventeenth century.

The lid of the salt cellar originally depicted three figures: two women—now broken off—kneel, one on either side of a strange horned animal. A third figure, almost entirely unclothed, rides on the back of this beast. This figure reclines, almost lying on its back, but with its head raised. In his description of the carving, Bassani identifies the animal as a goat with "sharp teeth."[21] But the short, smoothly curving horns and the thick body and neck, as well as the broad forehead, are much more bovine in form. I believe the animal represents a bull. The rider is a somewhat ambiguous, nearly naked woman. Certainly this is a strange image whose obscure meaning poses an iconographic challenge. Nevertheless, close reading of contemporary Portuguese sources may provide a plausible interpretation. I believe that a key to the artist's intended meaning of this image is provided by Almada, who lived on the Upper Guinea Coast for many years. In 1594, Almada wrote of the region between the Casamance and Geba Rivers: "The Kings of this land occasionally ride about on horses, but most of the time they use [cows and] bulls, if the journey is short."[22]

South of the Casamance, in present-day Guiné-Bissau, the Beafada also used cattle as beasts of locomotion. Almada writes:

> These Beafa[das] rarely use horses to ride; some Kings and nobles do, but rarely: most of the time [they use] cows and bulls, and in this manner, they run cords through their nostrils, much like reins, with which they control them. And they travel for many days and have quite a good ride; the Casangas, Banhuns, Buramos and Bijagós do the same.[23]

If the figure riding on the bull were a man, then the identification would be relatively straightforward: it would represent a ruler, "o Rei." However, as it depicts a woman, the interpretation is more complex. Almada's description of kings riding on bulls establishes the connection with political authority. This association was also seen in pre-colonial Casamance. At the same time, the bull is the paramount cultural symbol, in the Casamance and in much of Guiné-Bissau, of masculinity and virility.[24] In the Casamance, the *oeyi*, or sacred king of the Floup peoples, was associated

---

[21] Ezio Bassani and William Fagg, *Africa and the Renaissance: Art in Ivory* (New York: The Center for African Art, 1988), 72.

[22] Almada, *Brief Treatise*, 68: "Cavalgam os Reis desta terra algumas vezes em cavalos, e as mais das vezes em bois, sendo a jornada perto."

[23] Almada, *Brief Treatise*, 98: "E estes Beafares...usam pouco cavalgarem cavalos; alguns Reis e fidalgos o fazem, mas poucas vezes: a mais das vezes é em vacas e bois, que para isso têm mansos, com as ventas furadas, nas quais trazem uns cordeis ao modo de freio, com que os governam. E andam muitas jornadas e têm muito bom passeio; o mesmo usam Casangas, Banhuns, Buramos, Bijagós." See also Manuel Álvares, "Etiópia Menor e Descripção Géografica da Província da Serra Leoa," Sociedade de Geografia de Lisboa, Res. 3, E-7, fol. 30v, who observes that the bulls were first castrated, then fattened, after which they were perfectly domesticated by passing a rope through the nostrils and thus riding for a good number of leagues on the animals. "Ainda que este Barbaro não tem Cavállos, em seu lugar uza dos Boys, cortando lhe primeiro o sexo, e parta de geração, engrossando o animal muito,...tem por estado tão domésticos, que lhey passão ua corda pelos narizes,...e paseão nelles bom numero de léguas."

[24] On bovine symbolism among the Jola peoples, see Peter Mark, *The Wild Bull and the Sacred Forest: Form, Meaning, and Change in Senegambian Initiation Masks* (New York: Cambridge University Press, 1992).

with the bull. The symbol of the *oeyi*'s authority was his scepter, which took the form of the tail of a bull. Anything he touched with that scepter became his possession. Specifically, any woman who might please his fancy, if he touched her with the scepter, would belong to him.[25] Thus, among many cultures on the Upper Guinea Coast, from the Casamance southeast to Guinea, bovine imagery was associated both with masculinity and with royalty or political authority. The reclining figure on the back of the bull (a West African "Rape of Europa"?) would then represent a woman who belongs to the local ruler.[26] Furthermore, the figure reclines, in a position of submission. This would also provide a possible interpretation of the two now-broken female figures that kneel to the side of the bull. The implication of servile status is in itself significant, as we shall see below.

The subject matter affords insight into how the artists worked in the context of intercultural dialogue. This piece was made for European nobility. The order was communicated through the Luso-African middleman on the coast. One can readily imagine the artist asking himself: How do I portray an image fit for a powerful patron? The easiest answer must have been: by depicting locally meaningful images of Guinean kingship. This reasoning would not have been accessible to the European patron, in this case Ferdinando Cospi, who ultimately came to own the ivory once it arrived in Italy.

There is a meaning that was intended by the artist, and there is a meaning imputed by the person who acquired it. In other words, there have always been multiple meanings, which changed as the object moved from one culture to another. The work of art becomes a palimpsest, that is, a sequence of texts or a series of meanings, each of which is in turn inscribed, partially effaced, perhaps to be re-inscribed.

THE BASE OF THE BOLOGNA SCULPTURE: DOGS

The base of the Bologna salt cellar is decorated with standing figures of naked women, alternating with dogs and standing figures of men, naked above the waist.

---

[25] On the oeyi see Peter Mark, *A Cultural, Economic, and Religious History of the Basse Casamance since 1500*, Studien zur Kulturkunde, 78 (Stuttgart: Frobenius-Institut & Steiner Verlag, 1985), 77ff.. The Floups were the ancestors of the southern Jola peoples of Casamance and northwestern Guiné-Bissau. The *oeyi* was a priest of the village rain shrine, whose authority sometimes extended over a group of communities. On Floup royalty, see also Robert Baum, *Shrines of the Slave Trade: Diola Religion and Society in Precolonial Senegambia* (New York: Oxford University Press, 1999); Mark and Tomas, "Jola Traditional Peace Making; From the Perspective of the 'Historien engagé,'" in *Powerful Presence of the Past: Integration and Conflict along the Upper Guinea Coast*, ed. Jacqueline Knörr and Wilson Trajano-Filho (Leiden: Brill, 2010), 137–153.

[26] Bassani and Fagg suggest that the figural group represents a European theme, specifically a participant in a Witch's Sabbath, "transported on the back of the Devil himself in the form of a goat" (*Africa and the Renaissance*, 75). This interpretation, which is not anchored in local Sierra Leonean culture, nor convincingly connected to it by means of any thematically or compositionally similar European print that could have been carried to West Africa, can be dismissed as too conjectural.

The dogs face off against large snakes, whose heads hang down from the next register of the sculpture. Dogs are, in fact, a common theme: they appear on at least a dozen surviving salt cellars in Bassani's *catalog raisonné*; two more are known only from old engravings. It is unlikely that so frequent a motif should be purely decorative. One suspects that the animals were part of the iconography of spiritual power.

Among many of the peoples of the Upper Guinea Coast, snakes are associated with the expression of spiritual power; they are seen either as the manifestation of a deity or as a focus for important rituals. Dogs, according to Almada, were an important sacrificial animal in Casamance and northern Guinea-Bissau. The close association of snakes and dogs on the base of several salt cellars suggests that the joint representation of the two species reflects some aspect of spiritual power. In Guinea Coast societies, spiritual and temporal power are generally seen as complementary. Among non-Muslim groups the local "chief" or "king" is often also in charge of religious rituals to ensure community well-being. This, in turn, suggests, particularly in the case of those salt cellars intended as symbolic embodiments of temporal power, that the dogs and snakes alluded to the spiritual foundations of the power of the ruler depicted on the lid. A close reading of Almada supports this interpretation.

Writing of the Buramos, who lived near Cacheu, he notes: "The kings value mastiff dogs and own them as a mark of royalty. They keep them for prestige and at feasts and banquets they often eat them."[27] So the dog, like the elephant or the bull, is an animal emblematic of royalty. While Almada does not specifically mention religious sacrifice in this context, the consumption of animal flesh is often directly associated with sacrifice of that animal, and is characteristic of religious ritual. This observation points to the spiritual component that underlies local kingship in the Casamance-Bissau region. In a subsequent passage, the Cape Verdean chronicler provides a detailed description of a religious ceremony that revolves around canine sacrifice. The ceremony, which specifically refers to and confirms the king's authority, is worth citing at length:

There is another oath which kings and lords take when they swear to maintain laws and rights.... They take a solemn oath in the following way. They eat the flesh of a dog and offer the blood to their idol, called in these parts *china*.[28] ... When the oath is taken accompanied by their solemn proceedings,

---

[27] Almada, *Brief Treatise*, 82.
[28] Among the neighboring Floups [Jolas] the root word for religious shrine is *kiin* [*boekiin*]; it refers generally to the spirit embodied by the shrine, as well as to the forked stake, set in the ground, that receives blood and palm wine sacrifices to that spirit. Almada is clearly speaking of such a shrine. *Ch* in "china" is pronounced as a hard k.

all feel confident that the king will keep the established law, or whatever it is they demand the oath for.

Almada adds that he is familiar with this ceremony because many Portuguese traders—including, one presumes, himself—witnessed it. He continues:

When our people in these parts were living in towns which they shared with the Blacks [i.e. before the foundation of Cacheu in 1588], they often did not feel secure until the king had taken this oath, which they used to do each year. The same oath is taken by the Banhuns, the Buramos—otherwise called Papels—and the Chans.[29]

Dogs were certainly a symbol of royalty, but they were much more than that. As sacrificial animals, they were the embodiment of the ruler's obligation to uphold the laws of the land. They were the focal point of an annual ritual that confirmed that obligation. Just as the king's scepter/axe represented his authority to carry out justice and the potential severity of the sentences—literally, capital punishment—so too, in complementary fashion, the dog represented the legal constraints under which even the ruler operated. Together, dog and scepter embodied the privileges and the limits of royal authority. They constituted the visual expression of the social contract.

The presence of dogs calls attention to their ritual significance, specifically with regard to religious and secular authority on the northern Upper Guinea Coast. It also illustrates a fundamental characteristic of European-African relations in the sixteenth and seventeenth centuries: African kings and local elites controlled the context and the nature of commercial exchanges with Portuguese and, later, with other European traders. Among the social and cultural institutions that enabled them to exert this control were religious rituals. Portuguese merchants and Luso-African brokers were obliged to accept and sometimes to participate in these rituals. As Philip Havik has observed, "ritual factors as well as the nature of economic exchanges need to be taken into account when conceptualizing these [commercial] exchanges."[30]

Did the salt cellars that depicted spiritually powerful animals themselves embody spiritual power in their original setting? Father Alvares's comment that the animals depicted on ivory spoons represent the Sapes' corofíls, or spirit forces, implies that some spoons played a role in religious ritual. Assuming that some of the salt cellars were initially intended for local use, they may well have held spiritual power.

[29] Almada, *Brief Treatise*, 89.

[30] Philip J. Havik with Toby Green, "Introduction: Brokerage and the Role of Western Africa in the Atlantic World," in *Brokers of Change*, 1–26, 9.

Although ivory vessels are referred to as "salt cellars" in Portuguese sources as early as 1506, we cannot be certain that they were initially used in Sape society to hold salt. They may indeed have served a ritual function. While they are too small to have held the meat of ritually sacrificed animals (such as dogs), the bowls may possibly have held libations, for example palm wine.

Contemporary written documents provide little information about the Sape ivory carvers. With regard to the carving of objects of religious significance, for example, we are reduced to hypothesis. By 1600, the *métissage* of Sape society with the culture of their former invaders, the Manes, may possibly have had an impact in the religious sphere. The Manes—non-Muslims like the Sapes—belonged to the Mande cultural grouping. Among Mande of the Middle Niger valley, spiritually charged sculpture could only be carved by men who belonged to the casted groups born with *nyamakalaw*, the ability to control spiritual power.[31] Is it possible that later Sapes artists were subject to similar strictures? We can only speculate.

THE MUSEO PIGORINI SALT CELLAR

I am concerned primarily with uncovering the symbolic meaning that was initially inscribed by the ivory carver. The object's subject matter very likely reflects ideas or instructions imparted to the artist by the Luso-African middleman who initially conveyed the order for the salt cellar. However, the specific form that this visual text assumes, this iconographic "text," derives primarily from the Sape culture in which the artist lived.

The lid of a salt cellar preserved in the Museo Pigorini in Rome, for example, depicts a kneeling figure wearing a wide-brimmed hat and holding a shield. At his feet are several severed heads; beside him cowers his next victim. As Bassani and Fagg have observed, the executioner represents an African.[32] His European hat is an emblem of authority, resembling hats given to local chiefs by the Portuguese. At Cape Mount (present-day Sierra Leone) in 1617, to wear any hat at all was a sign of high rank.[33] This figure is also carved on a larger scale than are his victims, another indication of higher status. Bassani and Fagg, referring to Almada, interpret this

---

[31] On *nyamakalaw* and the creation of Mande sculpture, see, *inter alia*, Sarah C. Brett-Smith, *The Making of Bamana Sculpture: Creativity and Gender* (New York: Cambridge University Press, 1994), and David Conrad and Barbara Frank, *Status and Identity in West Africa: Nyamakalaw of Mande* (Bloomington: Indiana University Press, 1995).

[32] Bassani and Fagg, *Africa and the Renaissance*, 75ff. They also observe that the axe and the head of the victim are modern restorations.

[33] Samuel Brun, in 1617, wrote, "They also wear wide cotton knee-length breeches, but no hat, except perhaps in the case of the people of high rank." In Adam Jones, *German Sources for West African History 1599–1669* (Wiesbaden: Frobenius-Institut and Steiner Verlag, 1983), 74.

image as "a symbolic representation of the great chief endowed with the power of life and death."[34]

Thanks to the contemporary ethnographic information provided by Almada and Álvares, we can be more specific. Along the Upper Guinea Coast from Senegal's Petite Côte to Sierra Leone, there were no large states; political authority rarely extended beyond groups of neighboring villages.[35] In the absence of centralized political authority, local African rulers played an important role in trade with the Portuguese; they controlled commerce by maintaining periodic markets. Traders at these markets were beholden to the local ruler, whose judicial authority extended over everyone in the area. Royal judicial authority was expressed through the metaphor (or, often, the reality) of capital punishment. Geographer Valentim Fernandes, writing during the period when the earliest Luso-African ivories were being produced, described how the ruler of São Domingos (northern Guinea-Bissau) would mete out justice to people who broke his laws:

> The king of this land is called Jagara and he is very much feared because he carries out strong justice and if anyone should do that which he ought not, the king orders that they [his agents] cut off his head and place it on a stake in the road where they travel.[36]

Fernandes reported practically the same method of royal punishment in the lower Gambia. There, however, the Mandinka ruler himself cut off his victim's head and then confiscated the man's possessions and those of his family.[37]

Portuguese traders who resided on the African coast were themselves subject to the power of life and death that local rulers held over them. This is indicated by an episode in about 1612 that involved a community of Portuguese Jews living on Senegal's Petite Côte, north of the Gambia River. A delegation of Portuguese

---

[34] Bassani and Fagg, *Africa and the Renaissance*, 80.

[35] The Bagnun (or Kasa) "empire" that extended along the Casamance River (present-day southern Senegal) constituted an exception in the mid-sixteenth century. Even here, however, there was little evidence of centralized political authority. This ruler, the Kasa Mansa, was also distinguished by the life-and-death power he held, in the context of judicial cases, over those who lived in his realm.

[36] Valentim Fernandes, *Déscription de la Côte occidentale d'Afrique (Sénégal au Cap de Monte, Archipels)*, trans. Théodore Monod et. al. (Paris: Larose, 1938), 70: "Ho rey desta terra se chama Jagara e he muy temido porq. faz grande justiça e se alhue faz o q no deve logo el rey lhe manda cortar a cabeça e põer em hu paco pello caminho onde ha vejan." For the original manuscript, see fn. 14.

[37] Fernandes, *Déscription*, 40: "Qualquer maleficio q algu Negro fizer ou furto q seja acusado, corta lhe elrey mesmo a cabeça e lhe manda tomar toda sua fazenda a elle e a toda sua geração assy q por causa do malfeitor fica todos seus parentes destruidas." ("Whatever ill deed any Black does or is accused of, the king himself cuts off his head and orders that all his riches be taken and from all his family [lineage] and so it is that by reason of the evil doer, all of his relatives are ruined.")

Catholics from Cacheu, 160 kilometers farther south, arrived on the Petite Côte to try to convince the local ruler, the Buur Siin, to expel the Jews.[38] As a contemporary chronicler reported:

> [T]he Portuguese seeking to kill them and expel them from that place ran a serious risk. Because the king took the side of the former and he told the latter that his land was a market where all kinds of people had a right to live and that no one would cause disorder in his land, or he would have their heads cut off. If they wanted to make war they ought to make it on the sea not on his land which, as he had already said, was a market.[39]

Among the Sapes, the connection between capital punishment and civil authority in the person of the ruler was clearly articulated by Almada in 1594. In fact, Sapes kings were identified by a scepter that was presented to them upon their investiture. This scepter also served as the weapon they used to decapitate criminals. Almada writes:

> They put in his hand the weapon called *queto*, the scepter, with which the heads of those condemned are cut off. *All the kings of the Serra carry in their hands these weapons, which are royal insigniae.* When the ceremony is finished, he becomes the king and is feared by all.[40]

The Pigorini salt cellar clearly depicts a Serra Leone king with his royal scepter. For coastal communities, long-distance commerce was a major source of wealth, much of which accrued to the local rulers who controlled the markets. Such control was directly associated with the authority to impose capital punishment. The image on the lid of the salt cellar in Rome is a dramatic representation of political authority in general and, specifically, of the life-and-death power of the local ruler over his subjects and over those who came to trade in his realm. Indirectly, the image may also refer to the ruler's prerogative to regulate markets within his realm. Significantly, the twin prerogatives of local rulers applied not only to their African subjects, but also

---

[38] The Buur Siin had life and death power over his subjects, whereas in the neighboring kingdom, also predominantly Sereer, the ruler of Saloum did not have that power. See Abdou Bouri Ba, "Essai sur l'histoire du Saloum et du Rip," *Bulletin de l'Institut Fondamental d'Afrique Noire*, serie B, 38. 4 (1978): 815.

[39] Unpublished ms., circa 1607 or 1608 by Sebastião Fernandes Cação, untitled [Relacion de todo el distrito de Guinea y gouierno de Caboberde]. Biblioteca da Ajuda (Lisbon), cód. 51–IX–25, ff. 87–90v, fol. 87v. See also José da Silva Horta and Peter Mark, "Two Portuguese Jewish Communities in Early 17th-Century Senegal," *History in Africa*, 31 (2004): 233.

[40] Almada, *Brief Treatise*, 14.

to European and Luso-African merchants. In this respect, the iconography of the Pigorini salt cellar refers indirectly to the very commerce for which it was created.

Both the Bologna and the Rome salt cellars graphically represent political author-ity, by depicting recognizable attributes or prerogatives associated with rulers along the Upper Guinea Coast. While the references would in all likelihood have been lost once the ivories arrived at their ultimate destination among European aristocracy, the symbolic meaning must have been clear to the Luso-African or "Portuguese" settlers on the coast who served as cultural brokers and commercial intermediaries in the trade between Portugal and Guinea of Cape Verde.

THE VIENNA ELEPHANT RIDER

If this reading of the iconography of the ivory vessels is correct, it is likely that other salt cellars were also intended by the artists to represent, in like manner, secular/spiritual authority. Indeed, this reading helps us to interpret a salt cellar from the collection of the Weltmuseum in Vienna (Figure 10.2). The lid or upper register of the Vienna salt cellar clearly represents a man riding on an elephant (neither man nor beast is drawn to scale). If one compares this piece to the salt cellar in Rome, sty-listic similarities in the treatment of the shields on the two works appear to support the impression of iconographic parallels.

Curnow suggests that the rider may represent a Portuguese *lançado*. The *lança-dos*, as mentioned above, were Portuguese traders who settled illegally on the coast. Many of them were New Christians or even secret Jews, and not a few of them mar-ried local African women. The *lançados* were thus at the origin of the population of Luso-Africans who, during the sixteenth and early seventeenth centuries, served as cultural brokers. However, Curnow's proposed identification is unwarranted, both because the hat and shield serve generally as symbols of local political power and because the figure does not look European. Furthermore, the *lançados* did not hold any spiritual or temporal authority in the eyes of the coastal societies, including the Sapes.

It seems plausible to interpret the elephant and his rider as symbols of political and spiritual power. Such a reading of this salt cellar has already been suggested by Bassani and Fagg and by Doran Ross.[41] Indeed, even today in the Casamance region of southern Senegal, to call someone "Elephant"—*enab*—is a sign of deep respect. Furthermore, the metaphorical association of the temporal ruler with elephants is

---

[41] Bassani and Fagg write, "figures riding or standing on elephants occur in African art as a metaphor for power" (*Africa and the Renaissance*, 79). See also Doran Ross, ed., *Elephant: the Animal and Its Ivory in African Culture* (Los Angeles: Fowler Museum, 1992).

FIGURE 10.2 Elephant rider.
Source: Ethnologsiches Museum, Vienna, III C 17036.

documented in sixteenth-century Portuguese sources. Almada mentions the presence of traders at El Mina who refer to the Mandi Mansa as "O grande Elefante."[42]

In addition, the figure who rides on the elephant holds a shield in his left hand. Almada, in 1594, wrote that Wolof warriors carried shields made of elephant hide, which had been tanned to obtain a hardness that afforded the bearer protection against swords.[43] He added that the shields were round and were decorated with a diamond pattern in the center.[44] This is precisely the form not only of the shield in this salt cellar, but also of the shield borne by the executioner in the Pigorini salt

---

[42] Almada, *Brief Treatise*, 48: "The Mina people call this king the Great Elephant and he is so well known that all the Blacks respect his name for more than 300 leagues around." Almada offers a detailed description of Mande long-distance caravans linking the Middle Niger, including Timbuktu, to the Upper Gambia River. This account is based on his own experience trading for gold on the upper river in 1578, at which time he did business with Mande (almost certainly Jahanké) merchants whom he interviewed. The gold was brought by caravan, by Manding traders "who are also *bixirins*..." (47). The caravans take over six months to make the trip: "They follow a route which fringes all the Blacks of our Guinea, on the interior side, and they go by order of a black emperor whom all the Guinea Blacks we have discussed are subject to, called Mandimansa, whom none of our people has ever seen" (49).

[43] Almada, *Brief Treatise*, 13.

[44] Almada, *Brief Treatise*, 13.

cellar. We may assume, then, that both salt cellars depict men bearing elephant hide shields. These sculptures are indeed replete with elephantine symbolism.

Elephants, of course, are the source of ivory. One might say that, by depicting the elephant, this ivory, in a sense, represents itself. The artist has engaged in a complex visual pun. The salt cellar is carved out of elephant ivory; it represents an elephant; it also represents the powerful individual or ruler who is himself a metaphorical elephant; and this metaphorical elephant holds a shield that is made out of elephant hide. Each of these elements, directly or indirectly, refers to an iconography of power. The image constitutes a complex emblem of royal power, while the medium, ivory, would have been perceived as prestigious material by both the producer and the consumer.

The importance of elephant ivory to the people of the Sierra Leone peninsula and Sherbro Island is evidenced by the account of the German trader Samuel Brun, who made three commercial expeditions to the Guinea Coast. During his 1617 voyage he wrote of the inhabitants of this region, "They have nothing to sell except elephant bones and tusks, for there are many elephants there, which often come right into their dwellings."[45] At Cape Mount, the commercial situation was much the same. There, the inhabitants had only "ivory, rice, and a little gold" to sell.[46] How many hundreds of animals were killed to provide the tonnage of ivory that was exported from the Upper Guinea Coast? The slaughter continued well into the seventeenth century. This destruction is evidenced in the financial records of the Portuguese Jewish community on Senegal's Petite Côte. These men held a virtual monopoly over the trade in ivory tusks, if not in carved ivories. The scale of their commerce is reflected in the fact that one Jewish merchant, as security for a loan he had made to another member of the Sephardic community, held 2,000 pounds of tusks.[47]

The salt cellars, then, constituted part of a specialized segment of the trade in ivory. Among the goods imported to the Guinea Coast by the merchants who acquired these carvings were blade weapons: swords and daggers.[48] Whereas the Vienna piece depicts an elephant, numerous salt cellars represent soldiers carrying swords and daggers. Although the weapons trade to Muslims had long been outlawed by the papacy, as revealed by Giuseppe Marcocci in Chapter 3 of this volume, this restriction was widely ignored in late-sixteenth and early-seventeenth century

---

[45] Jones, *German Sources*, 79.

[46] Jones, *German Sources*, 74.

[47] Amsterdam, Stadsarchief, Notarial Archives 62, fol. 345 (January 12, 1612).

[48] On the trade in blade weapons, and for a discussion of artistic representations of the commerce of which the artworks themselves constituted a significant part, see Mark and Horta, *Forgotten Diaspora*, chap. 4; on the ivories, see especially chap. 5.

Portugal since, if European traders did not offer swords, they could not obtain slaves. The import of blade weapons, or *armas brancas*, from Portugal and Amsterdam into Upper Guinea at the end of the sixteenth and the early seventeenth century, and the depiction of this weapons trade on some of the salt cellars, is a central subject of a monograph I recently co-authored with José da Silva Horta. Weapons, both long swords, or *espadas*, and short cavalry swords, or *terçados*, are depicted on numerous salt cellars.

Among the wide range of goods that European and Luso-African merchants traded along the Upper Guinea Coast in the early seventeenth century, cotton textiles were the most important. Linda Newson's seminal analysis of the detailed account books of Manoel Bautista Peres and his associates, João Batista Peres and Antonio Nunes da Costa, underlines the dominant role of textiles. Imported textiles, some of which were produced in Europe and others in India, accounted for one-third of the goods that Manoel Peres imported to the Upper Guinea Coast in 1616.[49] In addition, cloths acquired in Senegambia (and from the Cape Verde Islands) and subsequently traded elsewhere on the coast constituted as much as a quarter of the total number of textiles traded by Peres and his associates.[50]

Finally, cloth served as currency and as a measure of value for all goods. Hence, for example, slaves might be valued in terms of *panos*. Acquired by Portuguese and Luso-African traders either from African long-distance traders (some of the textiles were produced in the interior in the Futa Jallon) or directly from the weavers in exchange for kola nuts (which in turn were obtained in Serra Leoa in southeastern Guiné de Cabo Verde), these cloths were used to purchase ivory. Many of the finest and most expensive cloths were produced on the Petite Côte and in the Cape Verde Islands. Cloth was also readily available in Jalofo, north of the Cape Verde peninsula. Almada writes:

> In all this coastal region, this land of the Jalofos, and as far (as) the Mandingas, fine cotton cloth is available in large quantities, in the form of black and white cloth and many other valuable kinds of cloth.[51]

European traders could save as much as 50 percent on the price by purchasing directly from the weavers, so the availability of cloth further encouraged the development of a coastal trade.[52]

---

[49] Newson, "Bartering for Slaves," 267.

[50] Newson, "Bartering for Slaves," 271.

[51] Almada, *Brief Treatise*, 18.

[52] See Colleen Kriger, "The Importance of Mande Textiles in the African Side of the Atlantic Trade, ca. 1680–1710," *Mande Studies*, 11 (2009): 1–21.

TEXTILES IN IVORY

Ivory was a major trade item; it was acquired by the Portuguese throughout Guiné de Cabo Verde, but especially from the region of Serra Leoa. Frequently, ivory was obtained in direct exchange for cotton cloth, which the Portuguese acquired further north, along Senegal's Petite Côte and from the Cape Verde Islands.[53] They transported the cloth southeast (beyond Cape Vargas) as part of the local coastal trade, which they carried out in small vessels. The Dutch merchant Dierck Ruiters, in the first decade of the seventeenth century, described Luso-African traders who traded for kola in Sierra Leone. They then traveled north to Joal and Portodale on Senegal's Petite Côte, where they exchanged the kola for Cape Verde cloth. As P. E. H. Hair and Colleen Kriger have both noted, Ruiters continued his description by stating, "They also sometimes trade ivory obtained in Serra Leoa for Cape Verde cloths."[54] It should be noted that, within three or four years of Ruiters's visit, most of the merchants who had settled at these two trading centers were Portuguese Jews.

Almada, in his description of coastal societies, refers several times to the use of cloth as currency, particularly for the purchase of slaves. He observes that before they established a fortified settlement at Cacheu (in 1588) the Portuguese "bought slaves cheaply, in exchange for cows and *gibosos*—calves of one year or more—with a few cloths or *sigas*—fixed lengths of *teada* which are accepted as currency among the Blacks in place of cruzados."[55] Elsewhere he reports that the *lançados* living at São Domingos (northwestern Guiné-Bissau) bought slaves in exchange for cotton cloth, iron, and wine.[56] The *lançados* then sold the captives to Europeans who came to São Domingos. Almada's description illustrates what was effectively the direct exchange of slaves for cloth:

> And the lançados sell…at an agreed price, so many cruzados for each slave. But the payment is made, a quintal of cotton for so many cruzados, a cloth for so many, and it is in terms of these values for a cruzado that they fix the agreed price.[57]

---

[53] In the early seventeenth century, as Kriger writes, "Guinea cloth was a major global product with an international pedigree.… It was an African, south Asian, and European commodity.… West Africa was not simply a passive receiver of cloth in the coastal trade with Europe." Colleen E. Kriger, "'Guinea Cloth': Cotton Textiles in West Africa before and during the Atlantic Slave Trade," in *The Spinning World: A Global History of Cotton Textiles, 1200–1850*, ed. Giorgio Riello and Prasannan Parthasarathi (Oxford: Oxford University Press, 2011), 105–126.

[54] Kriger, "The Importance of Mande Textiles," 11, citing P. E. H. Hair, "Sources on Early Sierra Leone (2): Andrade (1582), Ruiters (1623), Carvalho (1632)," *Africana Research Bulletin*, 5.1 (1974): 47–56.

[55] Almada, *Brief Treatise*, 111.

[56] Almada, *Brief Treatise*, 87.

[57] Almada, *Brief Treatise*, 87.

FIGURE 10.3 Ivory salt cellar, Serra Leoa, Sapi/Sape, sixteenth century.
Source: The Metropolitan Museum of Art, Gift of Paul and Ruth W. Tishman, 1991 (1991.435a,b) and ARTSTOR.

Thus, cotton cloth often served as currency for the purchase of slaves. Yet, whereas other crucial trade goods—including ivory itself, as well as a wide variety of blade weapons—figure prominently in the "corpus" of Luso-African sculpture, depictions of Guinea cloth are extremely rare. This is indeed strange, in view of the Sape artists' proclivity to carve images that illustrate the commerce of which the sculpture was itself an important component.

There is one important exception, in the Metropolitan Museum of Art. A salt cellar acquired from the Paul Tishman Collection (1991.435 a,b) incorporates a clear and detailed representation of Guinea Coast textiles (see Figure 10.3). In its form, the piece is quite complex. It warrants a detailed description. Together, the lid and base of the container form a sphere. The lid is divided in quarters by gadrooning, which is characteristic of the salt cellars from Serra Leoa. Consisting of rows of tightly spaced raised dots or tiny spheres aligned within raised thin ridges, gadrooning resembles in miniature the ball-like decorations characteristic of Manueline architecture in Portugal. In addition, an open flower is carved into each of the quadrants. The lid of the Met's salt cellar is topped by a tower-like appendage that takes the form of a fifth flower. Gadrooning extends downward to subdivide the bowl as well as the lid. The bowl sits upon a parasol-shaped hemispherical form that is likewise quartered by gadrooning. This form sits atop an outward-bowed cylinder that rests, in its turn, upon a complex ring with seven protruding triangular knobs. From this ring, four snakes hang down, their heads confronting four dogs that sit on their haunches, heads raised as if in challenge.

Between the dogs are two men and two women, all naked to the waist; the women wear what appear to be cloth wraps or skirts, and the men wear britches, vertically striated to resemble patterned cloth. On the sloping surface of the rounded, conical base, two diamond patterns sit directly above the forepaws of two of the dogs. These squares are approximately the dimension of the torsos of both the dogs and the humans. They are patterned with two concentric lines of tiny balls. In the center of each diamond there is a raised cross.

The lower register, between the alternating dogs and people, is decorated with eight rectangular forms, whose surfaces are embellished by four alternating geometric compositions. It is these eight rectangles, and the two square diamonds above the dogs, that are, in fact, images of Guinea cloths. They represent patterned cotton cloth, likely the "Cape Verde cloth," which played a central role in the commerce carried out along the Upper Guinea Coast in the sixteenth and early seventeenth centuries by Portuguese and Luso-African merchants. Especially noteworthy is the fact that these cloths were often exchanged directly for ivory. These four pairs of geometric designs clearly represent woven cloth. Many of the finest textiles were made at Santiago in the Cape Verde Islands.[58] It is perhaps significant that, by the end of the seventeenth century, one of the centers for the cotton cloth trade was at the English trading station at York Island in Sherbro (Serra Leoa). In the sixteenth and early seventeenth centuries, Sherbro was also a center for the export of the Luso-African ivories.

COMMERCE IN IVORY: THE ARTISTIC REPRESENTATION OF
DIVERSE TRADE GOODS

Sape artists made a point of representing the entire range of goods that were imported and exported by Luso-African and European merchants. Among the most important items whose value was reckoned in terms of cloth were human beings—captives purchased to feed the demand of the Atlantic slave trade.[59]

The men and women depicted on the salt cellars may be divided between a relatively small number who are fully clothed—including, notably, heavily armed cavalrymen and standing soldiers or warriors—and those who are partially or wholly naked. Clothing (and its absence) denotes social status. Around the base of the Tishman salt cellar, the

[58] Kriger, "The Importance of Mande Textiles," 7.
[59] See Almada, Brief Treatise, 87, 111.

Cape Verde cloths alternate with figures naked from the waist up. Their semi-nakedness may indicate captivity. Perhaps they depict captives who would have been acquired in exchange for cotton cloths. The ivory-captives connection is crucial.

If indeed a central concern of the Sape ivory carvers was to depict the wide range of goods that constituted the basis of long-distance commerce in Serra Leoa, one important item is missing: kola nuts. While the earliest Portuguese narrators do not mention kola, their silence was intentional. As George Brooks has observed, they were motivated by the desire to maintain an important commercial secret and thereby to prevent competition in the kola trade from merchants of other European nations. Kola was, nevertheless, a crucial trade item in the coastal commerce. Almada and Donelha, at the end of the sixteenth century, make no effort to disguise the importance of kola, which grew in Serra Leoa, but not in Senegambia further north, and which therefore quickly assumed a central role in the coastal trade that was often controlled by *lançados*.

Among the Muslim populations of Senegambia, where the consumption of alcohol was strongly discouraged on religious grounds, kola was in high demand. Almada, in 1594, observes that the Manding of the Gambia prized kola above other imported goods: "But of all the imported goods the most esteemed is kola, a fruit produced in Serra Leoa... and worth so much in [the Gambia] that they would give anything in exchange for it, foodstuffs, cloth, slaves, or gold."[60] Kola was also traded to the Rio Grande, where the Beafares held it in high esteem.[61]

Responding to this demand, *lançados* and Portuguese from Senegambia acquired kola and carried it north to the Gambia, where it commanded high prices. Again, with reference to the Gambia, Almada adds:

> The chief trade among the Blacks... is the trade in kola, a fruit which grows on a tree; and there are only kola-trees within the territory of Serra Leoa. The kola grows in a bristly container like a chestnut, and is so highly valued among the Blacks that all those in other parts want it and buy it and it is carried as far as to the Moors.... Kola is worth more in the Gambia than in any other river of Guinea.[62]

In his discussion of Serra Leoa, Almada refers to "kola which is the chief commodity of trade from here to River Gambia and to the other rivers of Guinea; it is produced on trees as chestnuts are, in spineless burs."[63] The kola trade was part of the

---

[60] Almada, *Brief Treatise*, 47. For the Muslim populations of the Gambia, most of whom did not drink alcohol, kola was the preferred stimulant and it was a sign of hospitality.

[61] Almada, *Brief Treatise*, 93, 122.

[62] Almada, *Brief Treatise*, 55–56.

[63] Almada, *Brief Treatise*, 19.

coastal commerce and not part of the international trade that, at least officially, went through Santiago in the Cape Verde Islands:

> Many ships sailing out of Santiago Island and out of Rio de São Domingos and Rio Grande made their way to this Serra; those from the island to trade in slaves, wax, ivory and other goods, and those from the rivers to trade in kola and foodstuffs to take back to sell in the other rivers.[64]

Portuguese merchants based on the coast often sent local traders who were in their employ to purchase kola in the Serra. Linda Newson's work is important here. She shows that Manoel Peres's brother, João Batista Peres, while based in Cacheu (between 1616 and 1618), sent trading missions to acquire kola in Serra Leoa.[65] Donelha also mentions kola, toward the beginning of his description of Serra Leoa:

> Kola trees produce kola nuts, like chestnuts, others are much larger; the big ones are called *utos*. The bitter taste…It is a good fruit and the custom is to eat it and to drink water over it. It is a good merchandise, in demand across all of our Guiné, and along the Upper Gambia River 40 kola nuts are worth a cruzado in our money…because if you wish to be paid in *panos*, cotton, wax, or other goods, it is worth a gold cruzado.[66]

The question then arises: Are there no representations of kola nuts on any of the salt cellars? This would seem particularly strange. The nuts grew in Serra Leoa; the artists had to be familiar with them. In fact, several salt cellars do depict kola, but the images are easily mistaken for leaves if one is unfamiliar with the kola tree; even the art historians who have studied salt cellars have not considered this essential item of commerce, as in general they have paid little attention to cross-cultural trade.

A salt cellar in the Allen Memorial Art Museum at Oberlin College is decorated, around the base, by standing figures and crouching dogs that face off against large snakes whose heads hang down from the upper part of the base. The dogs, snakes, and humans are carved in high relief. Behind them, carved in low relief on the surface of the conical base, is a thin horizontal plant stem with what, at first glance, appear to

---

[64] Almada, *Brief Treatise*, 20.

[65] Newson, "Bartering for Slaves," 263.

[66] Donelha, *Descrição da Serra Leoa*, 84–86: "As coleiras dá colas em ourico, como castanhas. As colas são como castanhas, outras muito maiores; as grandes, chamam utos. O sabor amargoso…E boa fruita pera quem a costuma comer e pera beber ágoa sobre ela…. É boa mercadoria, corre por todo nosso Guiné, e polo sertão no rio de Gambea vale corenta colas em cruzado da nossa moeda…porque quer se pague em panos, algodão, cera e outros cousas, vale um cruzado d'oro."

be pairs of oblong leaves with mottled surfaces. But the racquet-like shape and the incised, granular surface patterns suggest that these are, in fact, kola seed pods. (Each pod contains several kola nuts.) The artist was illustrating the world in which he lived. Whether depicting trade goods or political authority, the ivory carvers spoke through the idiom of the familiar. Kola trees and kola pods were familiar to the artist, but not to today's foreign observers. We may assume that the reference would have been equally obscure to the late sixteenth- and seventeenth-century Europeans who acquired these carvings.[67] In a broader sense, art objects that move from one culture to another, or from the territory of one religious affiliation to another, tend to take on new meaning for members of the new culture. A similar process of changing meaning may occur with objects that do not move physically, but whose surrounding culture or religion changes. The result is a sequence of inscribed (and then re-inscribed) culturally specific symbolic meanings.

The clearest representation of kola is to be found on one of the most delicately carved and beautiful of the ivories, in Berlin's Ethnologisches Museum (Figure 10.4). The Berlin salt cellar possesses two particularities. First, the surface of the bowl is embellished by low relief carvings of extraordinary refinement, depicting crocodiles, birds, plants, and geometric patterns imitating woven mats. The plants that are depicted in low relief on the surface of the bowl, curl around the letters *S* and *R* of the Latin motto, like growing tendrils. The second peculiarity of this extraordinary sculpture is highly significant: the bowl is crowned with a strange, flower-like form, consisting of eight rounded oblong shapes radiating from a central point, like the petals of a strange flower. They are undeniably vegetal in appearance. Each has a stubby oblong shape, somewhat like shortened cucumbers. And their surface is uneven, one might say mottled or dappled. This vegetal "crown" represents kola nut pods. Here, prominently figured on the top of the vessel's lid, is the one trade good that was produced exclusively in Serra Leoa. Kola was, in fact, the export item that was in the greatest demand farther north along the Atlantic coast, in Senegambia.

I have argued that the artists expressed a visual logic that focuses on commerce. But in fact theirs was not exclusively a visual semantics. Clearly, the unifying logic was based on intellectual constructs. And the visual manifestation of this logic is complemented by that which is merely implied rather than visually articulated. I have already referred to one manifestation of the merely implicit: the salt cellars

---

[67] Two other salt cellars clearly show kola pods. These vessels are stylistically close to the Allen piece; in fact, in his *catalogue raisonné*, Bassani grouped the three objects together (Bassani and Fagg, *Africa and the Renaissance*, 225). One is in the Museum of Mankind (inv. 1949.A.46177). The other is in the Museo del Ejercito, Alcazar de Toledo. In addition, the base of the Bologna salt cellar is decorated with tendril-like plants that may be intended to represent kola pods. Other ivories may also depict kola. Existing photographic documentation of these pieces is not, however, sufficiently detailed to allow a definitive judgment.

FIGURE 10.4 Ivory salt cellar, Serra Leoa, Sapi/Sape, early sixteenth century.
Source: Ethnologisches Museum, Staatliche Museen zu Berlin, Stiftung Preußischer Kulturbesitz, Inv. No. IIIC 17036 a.b. Photographer: Martin Franken.

are made from (one particular part of) elephants, themselves identified with royalty. To this metonymy one may add the presumed function of the ivories: they served as vessels for holding salt. And salt was itself an important commodity in the coastal trade of Guiné de Cabo Verde. Speaking of the Fulas of the interior of northern Senegal, Almada writes:

> Salt is very valuable in their land, more than any other commodity, and the little that reaches them comes through the Mandingas of the Gambia River— where it is made—and through the Jalofos of Senegal. Only the king and the lords of these lands can afford to buy it … and it is exchanged for gold, slaves, fine cloth, and anything else.[68]

So the utilitarian function of these salt cellars—assuming that the artists were aware of that intended use in European courts—would have added one more element to the visual discourse on commerce.

---

[68] Almada, *Brief Treatise*, 15.

BEYOND ICONOGRAPHY: A VISUAL SEMANTICS

The nexus of interrelated references, both literal and metaphorical, suggests something more profound. Like the visual pun on the theme of elephant in the Vienna salt cellar, these ivories, produced for export, are also thematically focused on commerce, often in a self-referential manner. What I want to suggest here is that we may have insight, through the theme and the pun, into an underlying semantic structure. Hans Belting, in his recent study of perspective and seeing in Islam and the West at the dawn of the early modern period, has provided a pathway for taking cross-cultural iconographic interpretation to a deeper level. In his analysis of the decorative role of calligraphy and abstract ornament in architectural design that evolved first in eleventh-century Baghdad, Belting writes: "ornament—unlike in western art—is not simply decoration, but rather it is a semantic medium like writing and it therefore bears a message, whose deciphering presupposes a [process of] cultural interpretation."[69] The semantic structure that Belting here ascribes to ornament (and to the Qur'anic texts to which the decorative patterns are literally connected) undergirds and unifies the decorative scheme of Islamic architecture in Anatolia and in Baghdad.

Just as Belting elucidates connections among component parts of the decorative structure, so, too, I would suggest, we may take to a deeper level the iconographic interpretation of some densely charged Serra Leoa ivories, by seeking a semantic— or at least a syntactical—structure that connects the entire range of visual images and metaphors.

The argument that I am making here for the existence of an underlying, unifying structure of meaning is quite different from looking for a common theme that brings together and lends meaning to the diverse symbolic or iconographic elements of a work or a body of works. A similar point has been made, I believe, in the context of a discussion of imaginary architecture, by Paulo Pereira. His argument focuses on the synergistic interaction of (painted/depicted) architecture and of text. He adds, also using a linguistic analogy, "Everything appears to constitute a part of an expressive grammar, in which the letters and calligraphy join together with the architecture."[70] Pereira's concept of "expressive grammar" is close to what I am pointing at. I would simply add that Pereira's "expressive grammar" and my "visual semantics" have a

---

[69] Hans Belting, *Florenz und Bagdad, eine westöstliche Geschichte des Blicks* (Munich: C. H. Beck, 2008), 128: "Im Gegenzug ist das Ornament, anders als in der westlichen Kunst, nicht bloss Schmuck, sondern ein semantisches Medium wie die Schrift und also Träger einer Botschaft, deren Entzifferung eine kulturelle Einübung voraussetzt."

[70] Paulo Pereira, "A arquitetura enquanto metáfora: iconografia da arquitetura (séculos XII–XVI)," in *A arquitetura imaginaria: Pintura, escultura, artes decorativas* (Lisbon: Museu Nacional de Arte Antiga, 2012), 93–97, 93.

deeper communicative purpose. That aim, which we might term the discourse of the work, brings us a little closer to the artist's thinking; visual discourse implies the thought by means of which the discourse was articulated.

In the case of these salt cellars, the semantic structure is grounded in conceptions of wealth, power, and social status. Those concepts are here expressed through imagery consistently derived from the local environment and from locally available material culture (or commodities), in a visual syntax that moves us, as outside observers, from the interpretation of discrete symbols to the growing awareness of a consistent, underlying discourse. One key to deciphering this visual syntax is to be found in the animal imagery of bull and elephant, as that imagery is elucidated by detailed sixteenth- and seventeenth-century "proto-ethnographic" description, confirmed where possible by contemporary ethnographic observation. At the same time, the animal imagery, together with references to cotton cloth and kola nuts, to blade weapons, and to human captives, focuses on the specific theme of European-African interaction and commerce.

Crucial to an understanding of what the artists were seeking to express are these multiple and complex references to international trade and to the wide variety of items that were exchanged. In their depictions of weapons, of elephants, of textiles, of kola, and of slaves, the Sape artists created images that represented the commerce of which their art was an integral part.

Visual metaphors and "double entendres" here allude to and comment directly, not only on temporal wealth and power, but also on the religious rituals that, in Guinea Coast society, supported and secured that power. These metaphors refer, as well, to the international trade that lay at the center of cross-cultural contact and communication. The ivories' subsequent peregrinations separated them from the culture and religion that engendered that symbolism, and led both to their desacralization and to the loss of their original socially anchored meaning.

ACKNOWLEDGMENTS

A fellowship—for which I am deeply grateful—at the Research Seminar "Re:Work, Work and the Human Life Cycle in Global Historical Perspective," part of the Humboldt-Universität, Berlin, has enabled me to complete researching and writing this essay. Initial research was carried out while I was a fellow of the Alexander-von-Humboldt-Stiftung, at the Frobenius-Institut, Goethe Universität, Frankfurt-am-Main, in 2006. Unless otherwise noted, all translations are mine.

Contributors

Cátia Antunes is Associate Professor of Early Modern Economic and Social History at Leiden University. She is the author of two monographs on early modern globalization: *Globalisation in the Early Modern Period: The Economic Relationship between Amsterdam and Lisbon, 1640–1705* (Aksant, 2004) and *Lisboa e Amesterdão: Um caso de globalização na história moderna* (Livros do Horizonte, 2009). She also has published several articles on cross-cultural business partnerships and networks in the early modern period. She serves on the editorial board of the *International Journal of Maritime History* (from 2008), the *Tijdschrift voor Zeegeschiedenis* (from 2009), and the *Anais de História de Além Mar* (from 2010). Since 2012, she has been the principal investigator of two large-scale research projects: *Challenging Monopolies, Building Global Empires in the Early Modern Period* (financed by the Dutch National Science Foundation) and *Fighting Monopolies, Defying Empires 1500–1750: A Comparative Overview of Free Agents and Informal Empires in Western Europe and the Ottoman Empire* (financed by the European Research Council).

Guillaume Calafat is a former student and fellow of the École Normale Supérieure, Paris (2003–2008). He is *agrégé* in History (2006) and was Visiting Lecturer of French at the University of California, Los Angeles (2006–2007). A current member of the École Française de Rome (2011–2014), he completed his Ph.D. in History at the University of Paris 1 (Panthéon-Sorbonne) and the University of Pisa in 2013 and is currently preparing a book entitled *Une mer jalousée: Juridictions maritimes, ports francs et régulation du commerce en Méditerranée (1590-1740)*. Member of the editorial board of the journal *Tracés* since 2010, he is the author of several book chapters and journal articles. His most recent contributions include "Ramadam Fatet vs. John Jucker: Trials and Forgery in Egypt, Syria and Tuscany (1739-1740)," *Quaderni Storici* (2013), and "Les interprètes de la diplomatie en Méditerranée: Traiter à Alger (1670–1680)," in *Les Musulmans dans l'histoire de l'Europe*, ed. Jocelyne Dakhlia and Wolfgang Kaiser (Albin Michel, 2013).

Leor Halevi is Associate Professor of History and Professor of Law at Vanderbilt University. A historian of Islam, he explores the interrelationship between religious laws and social practices in various contexts. He is the author of *Muhammad's Grave: Death Rites and the Making of Islamic Society* (Columbia University Press, 2007), a book that won the Ralph Waldo Emerson Award and the Middle East Studies Association's Albert Hourani Award, as well as book prizes given by the Medieval Academy of America and the American Academy of Religion. Halevi is currently at work on a new book that will examine Muslim attitudes toward foreign goods and world trade, focusing on the tension in Islamic law between an economic interest in trade and a religious interest in social exclusivity.

Wolfgang Kaiser is Professor of Early Modern History at the University of Paris 1 (Panthéon-Sorbonne) and *directeur d'études* at the EHESS. He has held fellowships and has taught in Berlin, Aix-en-Provence, Florence, Paderborn, Konstanz, and Paris. His fields of interest are urban history, history of the Mediterranean, the *ars mercatoria*, mobility and control, and cross-cultural trade. His authored and edited books include *Marseille au temps des troubles: Morphologie sociale et luttes de factions 1559–1596* (EHESS, 1992); volume 3 of *Ars mercatoria: Handbücher und Traktate für den Gebrauch des Kaufmanns, 1470–1820*, co-edited with Jochen Hoock and Pierre Jeannin (Schöningh, 2001); *Gens de passage en Méditerranée, de l'antiquité à l'époque moderne: Procédures de contrôle et d'identification*, co-edited with Claudia Moatti (Maisonneuve & Larose, 2007); *Le commerce des captifs: Les intermédiaires dans l'échange et le rachat des prisonniers en Méditerranée, XVe–XVIIIe siècles* (École française de Rome, 2008); *L'Europe en conflits: Les affrontements religieux et la genèse de l'Europe moderne (vers 1500–vers 1650)* (Presses universitaires de Rennes, 2008); *Le monde de l'itinérance en Méditerranée, de l'antiquité à l'époque moderne: Procédures de contrôle et d'identification*, co-edited with Claudia Moatti and Christophe Pébarthe (Ausonius, 2009); volume 2 of *Les musulmans dans l'histoire de l'Europe*, co-edited with Jocelyne Dakhlia (Albin Michel, 2013).

Giuseppe Marcocci earned his Ph.D. in History (2008) from the Scuola Normale Superiore in Pisa (Italy) and is Assistant Professor of Early Modern History at the University of Viterbo (Italy). His publications include essays and articles in international journals, as well as four books: *I custodi dell'ortodossia: Inquisizione e Chiesa* *nel Portogallo del Cinquecento* (Edizioni di storia e letteratura, 2004); *L'invenzione di un impero: Politica e cultura nel mondo portoghese, 1450–1600* (Carocci, 2011); *A consciência de um império: Portugal e o seu mundo, sécs. XV–XVII* (Imprensa da Universidade de Coimbra, 2012); and, with José Pedro Paiva, *História da Inquisição portuguesa, 1536–1821* (A Esfera dos Livros, 2013). He served on the editorial board of the *Dizionario storico dell'Inquisizione* and is foreign correspondent of the *Revue de l'histoire des religions*. His current project concerns the writing of world history in Renaissance Europe.

Roxani Eleni Margariti is Associate Professor of Middle Eastern and South Asian Studies at Emory University. Born and raised in Athens, Greece, she holds a B.A. in Western Asiatic Archaeology from University College London, an M.A. in Nautical Archaeology from Texas A&M University, and a Ph.D. in Near Eastern Studies from Princeton University in 2002. She is the author of *Aden and the Indian Ocean Trade: 150 Years in the Life of a Medieval Arabian Port* (University of North Carolina Press, 2007) and co-editor of *Histories of the Middle East: Studies in Economy, Society, and Law in Honor of A. L. Udovitch* (Brill, 2010). Her current research focuses on pre-modern Indian Ocean polities, on the political, social, and cultural aspects of Indian Ocean merchants' networks before 1500 C.E., and on the social histories of Islamic monuments in Greece.

Peter Mark is Professor of African Art History at Wesleyan University and a member of the graduate faculty in African history at the Universidade de Lisboa. A historian of pre-colonial West Africa, his work has focused on material culture, including the architecture and masking traditions of Senegambia. He is the author of five books, including *The Forgotten Diaspora: Jewish Communities in West Africa and the Making of the Atlantic World* (Cambridge University Press, 2011), written with José da Silva Horta; *'Portuguese' Style and Luso-African Identity: Pre-Colonial Senegambia, Sixteenth-Nineteenth Centuries* (Indiana University Press, 2002); and *The Wild Bull and the Sacred Forest: Form, Meaning, and Change in Senegambian Initiation Masks* (Cambridge University Press, 1992). In 2012–2013, he was Senior Fellow in Berlin at Humboldt University's international seminar: "Rework: Work and the Human Life Cycle in Global Historical Perspective." He has served as invited faculty member at the EHESS in Paris and as an Alexander-von-Humboldt Fellow at Goethe Universität, Frankfurt-am-Main. He is also Senior Researcher at the Centro de História da Universidade de Lisboa, in the research group "Mundos Novos: Expansão Europeia e Conexões Mundiais."

Silvia Marzagalli is Professor of Early Modern European History at the University of Nice-Sophia Antipolis, senior member of the Institut Universitaire de France, and Director of the Centre de la Méditerranée Moderne et Contemporaine in Nice. Her research focuses on maritime trade, merchant networks, shipping, and warfare in the Atlantic and the Mediterranean during the eighteenth century and Napoleon's continental blockade. She coordinated the international project that led to the creation of *Navigocorpus*, the online database on shipping. She is the author of *Les "boulevards de la fraude": Le négoce maritime et le blocus continental, 1806–1813; Bordeaux, Hambourg, Livourne* (Presses universitaires du Septentrion, 1999); with Michel Biard and Pierre Bourdin, of *Révolution, Consulat et Empire* (Belin, 2009); and, more recently, of *Bordeaux et les États-Unis, 1776–1815: Politique et stratégies négociantes dans la genèse d'un réseau commercial* (Droz, 2014). She also co-edited, with John McCusker and Jim Sofka, *Rough Waters: American Involvement with the Mediterranean in the Eighteenth and Nineteenth Centuries* (International Maritime Economic History Association, 2010); and, with Pierre-Yves Beaurepaire, *Atlas de la Révolution française: Circulations des hommes et des idées, 1770–1804* (Autrement, 2010).

Kathryn A. Miller is a fellow at Stanford University's Europe Center and Freeman Spogli Institute for International Studies. Miller has been a recipient of NEH and ACLS fellowships, a three-time grantee of the William J. Fulbright scholarship, and a Russell Sage Foundation research scholar. She received her B.A. from Dartmouth College and her Ph.D. in History from Yale University (1998). Her previous teaching appointments were at Stanford University (1998–2010) and Wesleyan University (2005–2007). Miller's current research is broadly concerned with how religious norms and institutions influence commercial exchanges and forms of cooperation between Christians and Muslims. Previous publications include *Guardians of Islam: Religious Authority and Muslim Communities of Late Medieval Spain* (Columbia University Press, 2008); "Negociando con el Infidel: La actividad mercantil musulmana en la Espana cristiana," in *El Mediterráneo medieval y renacentista: Espacio de mercados y de culturas,* ed. Jaume Aurell i Cardona (Universidad de Navarra, 2002); and "Muslim Minorities and the Obligation to Emigrate to Islamic Territory: Two Fatwas from Fifteenth-Century Granada," *Islamic Law and Society* (2000).

David Harris Sacks is the Richard F. Scholz Professor of History and Humanities at Reed College, where he has taught since 1986. He has been the recipient of fellowships from the Guggenheim Foundation, the Woodrow Wilson International Center for Scholars, the NEH, the ACLS, the Folger Shakespeare Library, and the John Carter Brown Library. Along with publishing a number of articles, essays, review articles, and reviews on aspects of early modern British social, economic, political, and intellectual and cultural history and the history of the Atlantic world, he is the author of *The Widening Gate: Bristol and the Atlantic Economy, 1450–1700* (University of California Press, 1991); editor of an edition of Ralph Robynson's sixteenth-century translation into English of Thomas More's *Utopia* (Palgrave, 1999); and co-editor, with Donald R. Kelley, of *The Historical Imagination in Early Modern Britain: History, Rhetoric, and Fiction, 1500–1700* (Cambridge University Press, 1997). He is presently completing a book on Richard Hakluyt's and Thomas Harriot's conceptions of "discovery" with the working title *The Certain and Full Discovery of the World*. In May 2014, he delivered The Thomas Harriot Lecture in Oriel College, Oxford.

Eric Tagliacozzo is Professor of History at Cornell University, where he teaches primarily Southeast Asian Studies. He is the author of *Secret Trades, Porous Borders: Smuggling and States along a Southeast Asian Frontier, 1865–1915* (Yale University Press, 2005), which won the Harry J. Benda Prize from the Association of Asian Studies in 2007, and *The Longest Journey: Southeast Asians and the Pilgrimage to Mecca* (Oxford University Press, 2013). Tagliacozzo is also the editor or co-editor of *Southeast Asia and the Middle East: Islam, Movement, and the Longue Duree* (Stanford University Press, 2009); *Clio/Anthropos: Exploring the Boundaries between History and Anthropology* (Stanford University Press, 2009); *The Indonesia Reader: History, Culture, Politics* (Duke University Press, 2009); and *Chinese Circulations: Capital, Commodities and Networks in Southeast Asia* (Duke University Press, 2011). He is the Director of the Comparative Muslim Societies Program at Cornell, the Director of the Cornell Modern Indonesia Project, the editor of the journal *Indonesia*, and was recently elected by his peers to serve on the Southeast Asia Council of the Association for Asian Studies for the period 2009–2011.

Francesca Trivellato is the Frederick W. Hilles Professor of History at Yale University. She is the author of *The Familiarity of Strangers: The Sephardic Diaspora, Livorno, and Cross-Cultural Trade in the Early Modern Period* (Yale University Press, 2009) and *Fondamenta dei vetrai: Lavoro, tecnologia e mercato a Venezia tra Sei e Settecento* (Donzelli, 2000). She is also co-editor of the academic journal *Jewish History*.

Index of Names

Subject Index

Lightning Source UK Ltd.
Milton Keynes UK
UKHW012243010322
399418UK00002B/86